Sermons from the Valley

Volume 3

Other books by Father Peter Bowes:

The Way, the Truth and the Life:
The Autobiography of a Christian Master

Steps on the Way

Spiritual Astrology

The Radical Path

The Word Within

Sayings of a Christian Master Teacher

Love is Simple

Pearls of a Fisherman

The Joy of Stretching

Father Peter Bowes

Sermons from the Valley

Volume 3

Sophia Publishing

Woodstock, IL

Sermons from the Valley

Volume 3

First Edition
Published 2017

© 2017 Sophia Publishing
All rights reserved.
Printed in the United States of America

ISBN 978-1-387-29449-7

All citations of *The Gospel as Revealed to Me* and *Notebooks*
by Maria Valtorta provided with permission from:
Centro Editoriale Valtortiano
I 03036 Isola del Liri (Fr) – Italia
Tel. +39 0776 807 032 – Fax +39 07776 809 789
www.mariavaltorta.com   cev@mariavaltorta.com

For information, write to:

Sophia Publishing

509 E. Kimball Ave. Woodstock, IL 60098

Cover Art: Rebecca Gradisek

TABLE OF CONTENTS

One in a Million 1

Let Your Inner Self Come Forth 17

Humility 23

Skills 33

Become Like Me 45

Let Them Go 57

The Corruption of the World 71

Complacency 81

Mary's Gift 91

Are you willing to let go? 103

The Mind of Christ 113

Keeping Faith When Things are Hard 131

God's Judgment 141

Loving Your Challenges 151

Thinking Darkens Light 163

True Motherhood 171

Subtleties 185

Laziness 211

Stop Testing God 221

Being Good 231

A House Divided 243

Letting Go 255

Led by the Spirit	271
Line Up	281
Forgiveness	293
Seven Times	301
Consistency	305
Complacency	319
Sorrow is a Wing	327
Let the Spirit teach you	335
Bridegroom	345
Obedience	353
Perfection	363
God's Seed	371
Get Close	385
Holiness	393
Two Mothers	403
Patience	413
A Great Attitude	427
Dethroned Forehead	435
Sacrifice Isn't Easy	443
Love Your Neighbor	457
Friend To Yourself	467
Jesus Weeps	479
Going Within	491

January 3, 2016
One in a Million

The Gospel as Revealed to Me, Chapter 548. Resurrection of Lazarus

In the Gospel of John, as it has now been read for ages, there is written: "Jesus had not yet come into the village of Bethany" (John 9, 30). To avoid possible objections I wish to point out that, with regard to this sentence and the one of the work which states that I met Martha a few steps away from the fountain in Lazarus' garden, there is no contradiction of events, but only a discrepancy of translation and description. Three quarters of the village of Bethany belonged to Lazarus. Likewise a large part of Jerusalem belonged to him. But let us speak of Bethany. As three quarters of it belonged to Lazarus, one could say: Bethany of Lazarus. So the text would not be wrong even if I had met Martha in the village or at the fountain, as some people wish to say. In actual fact I had not gone into the village, to prevent the people of Bethany, who were all hostile to the members of the Sanhedrin, from rushing towards Me. I had gone round the back of Bethany to reach Lazarus' house, which was at the opposite end with respect to one who entered Bethany coming from En-shemes. So John rightly says that I had not yet entered the village. And equally right is little John who says that I had stopped near the basin (fountain for the Jews) already in Lazarus' garden, but still very far from the house. One should also consider that during the period of mourning and uncleanness (it was not yet the seventh day after Lazarus' death) his sisters did not leave the house. So the meeting took place within the enclosure of their property. Note that little John states that the people of Bethany came into the garden only when I had ordered the stone to be removed. Previously the people of Bethany did not know that I was in Bethany, and only when the news was spread they rushed to Lazarus' house.

I could have intervened in time to prevent Lazarus' death. But I did not want to do that. I knew that his resurrection would be a double-edged weapon, because it would convert the righteous-minded Judaeans and would make the non-righteous-minded ones even more rancorous. The latter, because of this final blow of My power, would sentence Me to death. But I had come for that and it was now time that that should be accomplished. I could have gone at once, but I needed to convince the most stubborn incredulous people by means of a resurrection from advanced rottenness. And also My apostles, destined to spread My Faith in the world, needed a faith supported by miracles of the first magnitude.

There was so much humanity in the apostles. I have already said so. It was not an insurmountable obstacle, on the contrary it was a logical consequence of their condition of men called to be My apostles when they were already grown-up. The mentality, the frame of mind of a person cannot be changed between one day and the next one. And, in My wisdom, I did not want to choose and educate children bringing them up according to My thought to make them My apostles. I could have done that, but I did not want to, lest souls should reproach Me for despising those who are not innocent and should justify themselves with the excuse that I also had made it clear that those whose characters are already formed cannot change. No. Everything can be changed if one is willing. In fact I turned cowardly, quarrelsome, usurious, sensual, incredulous people into martyrs, saints and evangelizers of the world. Only those who did not want, did not change.

I loved and still love little and weak people - you are an example - providing they are willing to love and follow Me, and I turn such "nonentities" into My favorites, My friends, My ministers. I still make use of them, and they are a continuous miracle that I work to lead others to believe in Me, and not to kill the possibility of miracles. How languishing that possibility is at present! Like a lamp lacking oil it is in the throes of death and it dies, killed by the scanty or lacking faith in the God of miracles.

There are two forms of insistence in requesting a miracle. God yields to one with love. He turns His back disdainfully to the other. The former asks, as I taught to ask, without lack of confidence and without tiredness, and does not admit that God may not grant the request, because God is good and who is good grants, because God is powerful and can do everything. That is love and God hears those who love. The latter is the overbearingness of rebels who want God to be their servant and to lower Himself to their wickedness and to give them what they do not give Him: love and obedience. This form is an offense that God punishes by denying His graces.

You complain that I no longer work collective miracles. How could I work them? Where are the communities that believe in Me? Where are the true believers? How many true believers are there in a community? Like surviving flowers in a wood burnt by a fire I can see a believing spirit now and again. Satan has burnt the rest with his doctrines. And he will burn them more and more. I beg you to bear in mind My reply to Thomas, as a supernatural rule for yourselves. It is not possible to be My true disciples if one cannot give human life the importance it deserves: a means to conquer the true Life, not an aim. He who wants to save his life in this world will lose eternal Life. I have told you and I repeat it. What are trials? Passing clouds. Heaven remains and is waiting for you after the trial. I conquered Heaven for you through My heroism. You must imitate Me. Heroism is not laid aside exclusively for those who are to suffer martyrdom. Christian life is perpetual heroism because it is a perpetual struggle against the world, the demon and the flesh. I do not compel you to follow Me. I leave you free. But I do not want you to be hypocrites. Either with Me and like Me, or against Me. You cannot deceive Me. No, I cannot be deceived, and I do not form alliances with the Enemy. If you prefer him to Me, you cannot think that you can have Me as your Friend at the same time. Either him or Me. Make your choice. Martha's grief is different from Mary's because of the different psyche of the two sisters and because of their different behavior. Happy are those who behave in such a way as to have no remorse for grieving one who is now dead and can no longer be comforted for the sorrow caused to him. But how much happier is he who has no remorse for grieving his God, Me, Jesus, and is not afraid of the day he will have to meet Me, on the contrary he pines for it, as for a joy anxiously dreamt of for a whole lifetime and at long last achieved.

I am your Father, Brother and Friend. So why do you offend Me so often? Do you know how long you still have to live? To live in order to make amends? No, you do not know that. So act righteously hour by hour, day by day. Always righteously. You will always make Me happy. And even if sorrow comes to you, because sorrow is sanctification, it is the myrrh that preserves you from the putridity of sensuality, you will always be certain that I love you - and that I love you also in that grief - and you will always have the Peace that comes from My love. You, My little John, know whether I can comfort one also in grief.

In My prayer to the Father there is repeated what I said at the beginning: it was necessary to rouse the opacity of the Judaeans and of the world in general by means of a main miracle. And the resurrection of a man who had been buried four days and had gone down into the tomb after a long, chronic, disgusting well-known disease is not an event that can leave people indifferent or doubtful. If I had cured him while he was alive, or if I had infused the spirit into him as soon as he had breathed his last, the acridity of enemies might have raised doubts on the entity of the miracle. But the stench of the corpse, the putrefaction of the bandages, the long period in the sepulcher left no doubts. And, a miracle in the miracle, I wanted Lazarus to be freed and cleaned in the presence of everybody so that they could see that not only life but also the wholesomeness of the limbs had been restored where previously the ulcerated flesh had spread the germs of death in the blood. When I grant a grace I always give more than what you ask for. I wept before Lazarus' tomb. And many names have been given to My tears. In the meantime you must bear in mind that graces are obtained through grief mixed with unfaltering faith in the Eternal Father. I wept not so much because of the loss of My friend and because of the sorrow of the sisters, as because three thoughts that had always pierced My heart like three sharp nails surfaced then, more lively than ever, like depths stirred up.

The ascertainment of the ruin that Satan had brought to man by seducing him to Evil. A ruin the human punishment of which was sorrow and death. Physical death, the symbol and living metaphor of spiritual death that sin causes to the soul, hurling it into infernal darkness, whereas it was destined, like a queen, to live in the kingdom of Light.

The persuasion that not even this miracle, worked almost as a sublime corollary to three years of evangelization, would convince the Judaic world of the Truth of which I was the Bearer. And that no miracle would in future convert the world to Christ. Oh! How grievous it was to be so close to death for so few!

The mental vision of My imminent death. I was God. But I was also Man. And to be the Redeemer I was to feel the weight of expiation. Therefore the horror of death and of such a death. I was a living healthy being who was saying to himself: "I shall soon be dead, I shall be in a sepulcher like Lazarus. Soon the most dreadful agony will be my companion. I must die." God's kindness spares you the knowledge of the future. But I was not spared it.

Oh! believe Me, you who complain of your destiny. None was more sad than Mine, because I always clearly foresaw everything that was to happen to Me, joined to the poverty, the hardships, the bitterness that accompanied Me from My birth to My death. So, do not complain. And hope in Me. I give you My peace."

We do think that our sorrows are so great and they are merely personal, merely local, confined to our own personal behavior. We don't have the sorrow of the world on our shoulders really. We have the sorrows of our own behavior because we look at the mirror and we see all the ways we separate, and all the ways we haven't been like God, all the ways we've stopped loving, all the things we fear and got selfish with, and we haven't been the hero of our own life yet. We can be, but you have to love, you have to love the hard times and you have to love the good times. You have to love the harsh experiences and the easy ones. You have to be willing to drink the cup that Jesus gives you each day, and sometimes it's tough to drink and sometimes it's easy. Sometimes it's like love and sometimes it's just a reflection of misbehavior. It's hard to see what we have done in the absence of consciousness and the sluggishness of our minds. And if we relied on just the New Testament we wouldn't have the explanations of what he was doing. We even wouldn't have the understanding of why he did, the ways he did and the time he did in the precision of his perfection. You wouldn't have that.

And the churches don't believe in this revelation of Maria Valtorta, so they never get it, so they are stuck with the 2000 year old version. It is okay, just not complete. And it's not full, it's not rich like Jesus' recent gift to us, to Maria. I guess the point is you can have whatever help you want, each individual can have the help he strives for, whatever you want it. You want help overcoming something? They will help you. You want help to understand something, then you get it. People and texts. Text to read, people to help you understand the depths of the teachings. And because that is true you can see that very few people want that, very few people want somebody to help them understand Jesus' teachings, they just think they know. They are arrogant enough to think that if they read a sentence that they understand the sentence. Do you not understand the sentence? I mean a kid is so simple, they say, "What do you mean, Jesus, when you said if my eyes are single? I have two eyes." That is a kid. Even a kid would ask questions simple like that, trying to find out what he meant. And if you ask the ministers what he meant, they don't know, they don't even know what's in the Testament. That is how stupid it is. That is how uneducated they are in the spiritual life. And even some of you who have heard it don't even know, don't even feel what it means to have your eye be single, so your whole body will be full of light. And if somebody wants to know, they have to find out from somebody who knows. They have to be courageous enough to go ask this person because they don't know. Ask another person and they don't even know what's in the Testament. That's an ignorant person who doesn't even read the Testament.

Then you try asking someone who is guessing, and you know that's not it, that it's just a head trip. Then you find somebody with the answer and now you are learning. If you wanted to know, you can find somebody who knows. I know, you have to go through a bunch of people to find it, but you can find it. And this is true for anything you want, anything you would like, any graces, gifts or healing you would like from the Master or from God, you can find them. If you have a mind to pursue, a heart to pursue, you will find the help that you need.

And that's true for every person on the planet. You know you are six people away from every person in the planet. You know someone, who knows someone, who knows someone who knows the president. You know someone, who knows someone who knows Nelson Mandela. Six people away - everybody. So it is not hard to find these people if you have faith, if you have persistence and if you really want to know. That should tell you that people don't want to know, and it also should tell you that those who want to know find those people that do. Jesus says that God will give you whatever you want, whatever you open to as a gift to help you. It is kind of the student sermon that if you ask for help, if you are struggling with something, you get it, and it clears up. It just clears up. And Jesus wants to help people, and if people weren't so numb they would ask more to be helped. That is a grown up who asks God for help. That is what I consider a grown up, one who asks God for help. It's a rebellious child that thinks they can do everything on their own. The satanic whisper is "Yeah you can do that on your own, you shouldn't have to have help, you shouldn't need anybody." That is the satanic whisper in your ear. Why? Because it doesn't want you to be depending on God.

Funny thing about Satan is that Satan wants to destroy you while it flatters you to kill you. The darkness wants to destroy you. They want you destroyed so they flatter you and give you all kinds of stuff that makes you rot, for the ultimate of laughing at you, in your destruction. It is a guffaw laugh of the satanic energy when you fail, because they want you to fail. It wants you to despair, wants you to hate God, just like it does. And Jesus' courage here is that he has to do what his father tells him to do, which is to wait until Lazarus is rotten so he smells, is disgusting, contaminating, and everything else. And he somehow creates this scene where everybody is curious and all the shit headed beings have to come and watch him raise this guy from the dead. Because they were vicious and mean, they want to scope out everything he is doing, wherever he is going, to wait and see him fail in taking care of his friend. And they wanted to see that if there were a miracle, whether it was a lie or some kind of trickery, but they didn't intend to believe because of a miracle like that. The ones that already had convinced feelings had more convinced feelings after he was done. It didn't change too many people at all. A couple people were converted, three or four, maybe ten, by that miracle. The rest were solidified and entrenched in what they already believed. Even in the face of that. I mean just imagine that you know your mom died in the house, she stays four days rotting and smelling, there is no access to coroners and stuff like that, so you are sealing off the room and the air conditioning is on high. You are trying to do everything so it doesn't smell, but it smells terrible. And four days later somebody comes in and reconstitutes her physically, so all the disease is gone, all the rot is gone, the smell is gone and she is dressed and fed. But with your mind you say, "Ah, how could that be?" Well, that is what happened then. Not only were they not supposed to touch anybody who dies because they are unclean, but once they rot, there were a lot of superstitions about others dying from those same things; they didn't know the medical area at the time. So Jesus brings this entire drama together and promises them he is going to do it, and does it, and then he kind of lays into them for their disbelief and that secures right there that he is three and a half months from his death. That called his death right there because he so offended and convinced the Judeans and the sanhedrin that he can do this things but they so don't want him to be the Messiah. They were so convinced that they didn't want him that they kill him. And no one in the world has ever done the things that he did, ever. And even that doesn't penetrate to the brick of their heads. The thing is we are so forgetful and even on our little level. You have a miracle in your day, you call out for God to fix something for you, help you with something. It is fixed, it is cleared out, and by the end of the day you forgot that you asked and you forgot that he helped and you take credit for the whole thing yourself. That is how dense we are. That our gratitude level is so lacking. How can we forget so fast that we asked for help and that he helped us? What is it about human beings that can forget so quickly? You needed help, you asked for help, you got help and then you forgot. Enjoy the help, enjoy the happening, then forget the whole process of how you got the help. You lost your humility right in the end there. In fact, you got amnesia, you lost memory. Is that deep? You didn't intend to become ungrateful, you just forgot that you asked and that you got help. How does that happen so fast? I watch some of you do it in the middle of the day. By the end of the day you forgot that you asked but you got it. So if you are wondering how someone can see a miracle like this and not be changed, look at you. You can get help in the day, Jesus takes care of something, moves the obstacles aside, fixes it, cleans it, opens it up for you and then you forget it by the evening. Because your ego wants to take credit for it, you did it, you did it yourself. That is how fast that happens. Unless you remind yourself that you are nothing before God, you will forget and think that you are something. Humility isn't like something that stays with you, it is something you cultivate, just like love. Love just doesn't come and stay. Now you are wonderful and loving? You have to practice it. You have to continuously do it until you get perfect at it, just like humility, just like purity, just like simplicity, just like receptive mind, like no mind, open to God. No mind at all, just completely open to God. That kind of humble receptivity takes practice. You don't get that just by deciding it. You can decide and it will take years to get to that place through practice. It is not easy to change a pattern. It is not easy to take the death wish out of your life, so that the demons are gone and you really like to be the one with the light, where it is established in you. Just look at how some of your patterns are not established and you will see how much you let those get ripped off, let them be undermined by the darkness, forces of the doubt of the mind.

Until those established patterns are solid and they can't be ruffled, you are not clear yet. Can you be caused to doubt by something outside of you that happens? Then you are still ruffled, able to be ruffled. Think of when you were of the Judeans. There is this Lazarus experience happening and you won't be moved, you don't even like it. That is what they did. It is so stupid. That is how they were so stupid. "I don't like this guy healing this guy. He should be killed. I don't like the fact that he says he is a Messiah and does the miracle, then he turns around and says he is the Messiah again. I don't like that. This is annoying, this is like an argument I cannot win. I am going to kill him." That is what they were doing in their mind. And that is the density of the world right now. They want to kill spirituality, they want to kill devotion to God, they want to kill purity of heart and they want to kill the innocence of human beings.

They want to kill it. They do. Don't think that they don't. What are you doing when you are being mean to a child? You are jading them and causing them to be in a defensive state of panic. You are causing their innocence to go submerge into the depths of where it cannot be expressed or slapped around. You are actually shutting down the beauty of that child by treating them that way. So technically you are saying, "I don't want this goodness showing up in my family, I want to crush it, because it reminds me of my guilt and reminds me what I don't have and I am jealous. I don't like that. I don't like a little kid having a joyful experience. I never had one." That is the whole earth, acting like that right now. They want to kill the innocence again. They want to kill the good and kill anything of the Christ. That is where they are. Watch the behavior of your parents and you can see what they didn't encourage, you can see what they shut down. They don't want that innocent kid to show that they don't have the same purity, the same love, the same fascination with life.

They are jaded and miserable and they don't want anybody in their family to be anything but that. That is the whole Earth now. So your job is to be the rebellious ones. Rebellious in the sense that you will not fall for darkness, you don't go for that lack of purity, you don't go for that lack of innocence. And you won't stand for people trying to kill other people. You won't support it. You won't act on the criticism of other people by criticizing them. You won't add to the negativity, you decide not to do that. And you will be the very few that can do that. Will it take a lot of work to get to that place? Yes, it will. It will take a lot of discipline and you will have to clean out the negative self-reflection that you do. And I am saying it in a positive way because you seem like you enjoy it. You know, "Like I am doing negative self-reflection." If you are putting those words together it looks like you are doing something constructive. Like you are doing some service to mankind - a negative self-reflection. Just change the words of it and it spruces up. I was doing my selfish, separated thing and you called it negative self-reflection. I was hating myself thoroughly, not letting the love of God in, and didn't even ask for guidance. Why don't you guys say the truth? I think it will sting a little bit and you will stop it. You will just stop it.

Sickness, suffering and death came through the satanic energy. Now, to get out of that you will have to suffer the pain of loss of the separation. You will have to love the pain, of the fact that you separated. You separated, you are going to have to love the pain that happens on your way back to connection to God. And a lot of people don't have the courage for that. They don't get very far. A few steps and they stop - three forward, four backwards. That is the world. "If it is hard, I would rather just eat. If it is hard, I would rather just drink." That is where they are at now. The cause you have as rebels is Jesus Christ. And you will be the few that love him. And he said 700 out of the seven billion.

That is not 1%. You math people can tell us. One in a million. That is not good. You know, a million people and there is just one? It means nine people in Chicago and the suburbs too. Wow, just think about that for humanity. What does that mean? Not good. And I know you have kind people at work that have moments of honor and integrity that you run into everyday. But ones who love God and have dedicated their life to God? No, no, no. They don't have anything close to that. They are your average, ok people who have never being thoughtful about God. That is all.

What I would like to know is where the other 700 are? Who are they? Where are they? They are brothers and sisters in Christ. They really are. I don't know where they are, but I can feel them out there, you know? And it is not like a group, it is not like a name, it is not like ten thousand people churches. It is not where they are. There might be one out there, maybe two? I don't know. Real disciples of the Master who have let the Master take them through changes and let them overcome things, help them? How many really allow that? How many don't walk out of their churches and do the same? Same before, same after? They heard a little inspirational music, which is kind of emotional. You feel good with the music, you rock away, and when you are done, same, same. Let's get some beers, fight at home like you always do. What is constitutionally different about that? Nothing. Nothing. Does every desire in you obey the Christ? Is every thought in you blessed by the Christ? Well, let's line those up then. Let's start lining those up. And if it cannot be blessed, dump it. Don't do it again, don't be in those feelings again. It is not right for anyone. If you cannot see your 13 year old daughter saying these things and doing things the way you feel, then don't do it, because they will just mirror you in a heartbeat, energetically. They have been watching you your whole life. Some of you are still mirroring your parents and it is sad because it sucks. Your parents suck. They are good people, blah, blah, blah. You fill in the descriptions, I don't care, but you clearly are following your parents in all ways and you should be following Jesus and Mary.

Otherwise, did you get called? Did they call you on the path where the path is with them, to them, near them? Not that you get to keep your parents on the path. No, you don't. You do not get to keep the old when you are going into the new. Me or them, either way, but you cannot have both. Most of your love of your parents is to need something from them, which I do not call love. I call that guilt or payment plan or manipulation or something. Love isn't binding, love isn't making someone do something, love isn't putting up with my life until they fix something. That is not love. Stalling in my life until they come clean, until they fix it, until they make it good is not life, that is not love. That is not even obedience to God. Come to me all who labor and are heavy laden, I will give you rest. That is what Jesus says. Do you want rest? Don't go to the world, you will never rest. I know you are already convinced, but your cells aren't. The cells of the flesh aren't because they gravitate back down the hill to what they are familiar with. Your head goes, "Yeah, this is not right and the cells go right back down the hill. That is why I am talking about that. If it wasn't so, I wouldn't have to mention it. I would never have a sermon like this. If I see that you guys have already cut loose, all let go of, all forgiven, that you are completely like angels now, then we will talk angels sermon. You would get angels sermon because I could see that you are like angels, and it would be very rare that you would have any proclivity, any leaning or desire for rolling down the freaking hill and getting dirty again. See, you don't want this kind of sermon, change. When I see it, I will give angels sermons, I promise you. I'd like to write one and I will put it aside and I will say that I have it, nobody can read it, it is coming out, right then when it is happening. Angel sermon. God's little angels. And you do, you all have moments of angelical qualities. You do, not very often, you cannot stand it for very long. Until then I am going to encourage you when you are, when you like to be. And I have asked the Master about that. I am saying the same things and he says, "Well, that is what you are going to do." I said, "That is what you want me to do?" and he says, "What else could you do? What do you think I did, over and over, saying the same things to people?" And, what, you get 1500 people out of the whole earth? That is it. And he was perfect, so that is not cool for the track record of the perfect. When you don't do political deals people hate you. They will hate you.

January 10, 2016
Let Your Inner Self Come Forth

From 1944 Notebooks, August 10.

Jesus says:
"You came very close to the truth, but did not reach it perfectly.

Those who are with Me in Paradise and who, for mysterious reasons, have lived through an hour of hell on earth, as you call it, do remember, it's true. But they do not taste its bitterness or see its blackness or receive any more jolts of horror on remembering it. Here everything is light, sweetness, and peace. And nothing can cancel them out, not even the memory of the most atrocious torments undergone. But the memory remains. It no longer hurts, but it survives. It is a source of active charity.

Never again say, my little daughter, never again say, 'If I can be elsewhere, I will not want to remember having lived any more. I won't have even a look any more for this painful earth, where there is so much pain and so much evil.' In reasoning like this, you reason in a human manner. You must not do so. I have placed you outside the little base circle of what is human. I have already placed you in the infinite, joyous freedom of the supernatural. Strip yourself of all residue of the human with holy alacrity and a cheerful will. Be a 'daughter of God' in a complete way.

To be a daughter of God completely means to be one as one is such in Heaven, that is, to possess a love overcoming every obstacle of bitter memory, and, indeed, for bitter memories to be a spur towards greater charity.

Look, daughter. When one is here, in my Paradise, one possesses Love, for Paradise is the eternal possession of God, who is Love. In possessing perfect Love, the spirit experiences a metamorphosis in perfection which overturns even the last residue of human justice. Has a spirit suffered on earth? Precisely because it is aware that one suffers on earth, it has mercy on the earth and devotes itself to active charity out of mercy on the earth.

Has it suffered on earth on account of men? For the earth, in itself, is good. It gives you bread and wool, fruits and fire; it is not an enemy and cruel to you, as man is. But precisely because it knows that on earth it is men that suffer and cause suffering, the deified spirit thus feels a holy will to act in favor of its poor brothers and sisters in exile. All of them poor. Those who suffer and, even more, those who cause suffering, for they obtain for themselves eternal poverty and eternal desolation. My saints, from the beatific bosom of contemplation, do not cease for an instant to work for you that are still wandering in exile, and it is a great joy for them when a smile from Me orders them to come into your midst to assist you and lead you back to Good.

The Paradise of the saints has two faces. One looks towards and delights in God. The other is turned towards their poor brothers and sisters, and this watchful, loving charity will not cease until the last man has finished struggling on earth. The saints ask my Divine Majesty to grant that they may come to you to help you.

Do you see, daughter? Today my martyr Lawrence is looking at the poor earth and poor men with more love than ever, for, immersed as he is in Charity and Wisdom, he sees in that earth and those men one of the two main reasons for his eternal blessedness, and he wants to help them out of gratitude for their having been the reason for his glory. Even if you were in the place of temporary expiation, you would have this active charity for the souls in purgatory do not yet see God, but they already love Him as in Heaven and already have the charitable impulses of the blessed.

Never again say that you want to forget the earth, then. My children never have an egocentric love, but, imitating their Lord, they beam out their rays like suns on the good and the wicked to call them all to the Light. I, your Father, who have so loved the earth, all of whose past and future misdeeds I knew, the misdeeds committed on it by men, and who tore my Word from my breast to send Him to sanctify the earth, have wanted to give you this teaching. My thought knew that among the future misdeeds there would be the deicide. And yet that has not put a check on my love. As it has not checked the loving haste of the Word, or the loving activity of the Paraclete.

Think as a daughter of God, and the blessing of the Father and of the Son and of the Holy Spirit will always be upon you."

No matter what your suffering is, whether it's self-imposed, which is most of yours, or suffering on account of helping somebody else or aiding somebody else in their connection to God or coming close to God, whatever the suffering is - putting up with other people's negativity as you love them, which frees them from their sins - all of that active charity that Jesus is talking about causes some kind of suffering. The suffering of even the compassion of watching somebody suffer by their own hand, by their own mis-thinking, by their own negativity, by their own negative feeling, that's just suffering. Because it's one of those things that people don't have to do, they don't really need that, there's no good that can come from it. They don't have to suffer those things, they're choosing to suffer those things. They want that. And that's a sadness that the ones who serve have to feel, that willful suffering on the part of the people who willfully separate from God.

Anytime you have a negative mood, you're separated from God. Anytime you have a negative feeling, or slowness or sluggishness, you're actually separated from God. You're separating from the love. And that causes anybody around you to suffer. Anyone around feels the pull, the drag on your car. So no matter whether the suffering is self-imposed, or the suffering is given to you by God, you offer that up as part of the work just as Jesus did.

There's a transition in your world, in your life, where you start having less to think about you. There's less to work on, there's less to fret over, there's less to fight with inside yourself, there's less to remember. You're not needing to freshen up the memory so you can freshen up the negative feelings, the negative reactions, you just get tired of it. It's just not interesting anymore. You've done it a thousand times, and every time it's the same, and the feeling in the body is the same, and the tension in your head is the same, and then the doldrums of mind are the same, and you're just tired of it. And you think, "Hey, I'm just going to try and help. I'm going to be a force for good. I'm going to be a presence that can heal people. I can be a blessing when I come into the room instead of a massive neediness coming into a room." Instead of being troubled, looking for a controversy, looking for a disagreement, looking for people to not see me so you can fight with them, you're not doing that anymore, it's boring. You're coming into a room to be a blessing, and the blessing is that you're going to suffer, and through the suffering you're going to get closer to God. You're going to love instead. You're going to act with charity.

You're going to love instead of picking up all the negative feelings. Like who cares? Why would you even care? Yeah sure people have negative feelings, but why are you anticipating each one? Do you read every sentence of a really bad novel? Or do you start skipping when it's really bad? Even you do that. Why don't you start skipping when people are putting out negative energy? Let's skip it. Skip over it. Read ahead, read something else, let it go. Let go of the lousy pages. Let them have the lousy pages and you look ahead to when that chapter ends. Read the next chapter for them in your head. They're stuck on the chapter, but you should be reading in the next chapter, the chapter where they get over that. That's your job, that's your blessing for them. You become the thing that they're gonna wanna want. That's how to serve, right? Simple.

Instead of freaking out, call the police. When they need them real bad, finally their humility comes online. Pride starts to diminish because they're starting to die, so you call them and immediately. That's what happens when you call him. It doesn't mean that God forgets you were being a freak before, but now it's calm. And isn't that the lesson? Not so much that you should feel ashamed for freaking out, but that you should just come back. You just keep coming back so it doesn't happen. Call on God, good things happen. That's the way it works. If you don't know that, you're going to get the density award.

The Son of God is going to act like God. The daughter of God is going to act like God. You're going to become a light of peace and love. Where is reactiveness in that? Where is moodiness in that? Where is doldrums and depression, sadness and forlornness, where is mulling over your problems in that? They can't be in peace, light and love. They can't be there and guess what? The booby prize is that's your real nature. That's who you are inside. So if that's not expressing, you have mirrored yourself with all kinds of crust. You did it. Nobody did it to you. You did it. This isn't your nature.

Avocado, You are a divine being, spirit, clothed in the body. For some of us it's a lighter veil, and some of you are encumbered about by this flesh so much. But it's not supposed to be like that. This flesh is your servant. So why is your flesh your jailer? It should be your servant. It should be that trained dog you say "heel," it heels. You say "sit," it sits. You say "roll over," it rolls over. You say "lie down," it lies down. It goes out to the yard and picks up its own stuff. You bring it back in and it goes to sleep when you want it to. You teach it to do that. To do anything that you want it to do. It shouldn't resist you, it shouldn't fight you, and that's what being a saint is. Somebody who is walking around doing stuff, an act of charity, just like Jesus, just like God.

That's not being super good, you already are, you just don't know it. You're not going to acquire goodness, it's already in you. It's not coming from without looking in, no, it's a living from within and making that outside reflect it, making your outside reflect your inner being. It's not the other way around, clawing and scraping to get inside somewhere. That's a weird thing to think about. That your immensity is going to claw and scrape to get to the inner that's way too immense. The inner's going to come out and express through this hunk of flesh that's such a nemesis.

You want to do it with fierceness? I pronounce to you, you will never do it. It will never happen. You want to do it with a heavy hand? It will never happen. It will only happen with love. Only when you love that flesh of yours into submission will that flesh, and that ego and emotions, and all that head thing you do, submit to the love.

You know how you are, you don't listen to things that don't love you, you rejected that a long time ago. No, this inside is loving you. So let it form you, let it melt away that unhappiness that you seem to enjoy.

January 17, 2016
Humility

The Gospel as Revealed To Me, Chapter 172. The Sermon of the Mount. The Beatitudes (Part Four).

I will therefore substitute another order for the one given to you, when the oath enjoyed great favor to put a restraint on lies and on the easiness of failure to keep a promise. I do not say as the ancients said: "Do not swear falsely, but keep your oath," but I say to you: "Never swear." Neither by Heaven which is the throne of God, nor by the earth which is the stool of His feet, nor for Jerusalem and her Temple which are the City of the Great King and the House of the Lord our God.

Do not swear either by the graves of the deceased or by their souls. Graves are full of the dross of the inferior part of man, which is common also to animals, and with regard to their souls, leave them in their dwellings. Do not cause them to suffer or to be struck with horror, if they are the souls of just people already in the foreknowledge of God. And although they are in such foreknowledge, which is partial knowledge, because they will not possess God in the fullness of His brightness until the moment of Redemption, they can but suffer seeing you sinners. And if they are not just, do not increase their torture by reminding them of their sin through yours. Leave the holy deceased in their peace, and the unholy ones in their pains. Do not deprive the former of anything, do not add anything to the latter. Why appeal to the dead? They cannot speak. The saints because charity prevents them from speaking: they would have to give you the lie too many times. The damned because hell does not open its gates and the damned only open their mouths to curse, and their voices are suffocated by the hatred of Satan and of the demons, because the damned are like demons.

Do not swear by the head of your father or of your mother, or by the head of your wife or of your innocent children. You have no right to do so. Are they perhaps money or merchandise? Are they a signature on a document? They are more and they are less than such things. They are blood and flesh of your own blood, man, but they are also free creatures and you cannot use them as slaves to guarantee your false statements. And they are less than your own signature, because you are intelligent, free and grown up, you are not interdicted, neither are you a child who does not know what he is doing and must be represented by his parents. You are a man gifted with reason and consequently responsible for your actions and you must act by yourself, employing, as a guarantee for your own deeds and words, your own honesty and your own frankness, the reputation that you enjoy with your neighbor, not the honesty, the frankness of your relatives and the reputation they enjoy. Are fathers responsible for their children? Yes, they are, but only as long as they are under age. After, everybody is responsible for himself. Not always just children are born of just parents, nor is it so that a holy woman is married to a holy man. Why then use the justice of a relative as a guarantee? Likewise, holy children may be born of a sinner, and as long as they are innocent, they are holy. Why then appeal to a pure soul for an impure act of yours, such as an oath which you wish to swear falsely?

Do not swear by your own head, your eyes, your tongue, your hands. You have no right to. Everything you have belongs to God. You are only the temporary guardians, the bankers of the moral or material treasures which God granted you. Why then make use of what does not belong to you? Can you add one hair to your head or change its color? And if you cannot do that, why do you use your sight, your word, the freedom of your limbs to corroborate your oath? Do not challenge God. He could take you at your word and dry up your eyes as He can dry up your orchards, or take your children away from you, or crush your houses to remind you that He is the Lord and you His subjects, and that who idolizes himself and thinks he is above God, challenging Him with his falsehood, is cursed.

Let your speech be simply: yes, it is; no, it is not. Nothing else. Any addition is suggested by the Evil one, who later will laugh at you, because you cannot remember everything and you will contradict yourself and you will be jeered at and recognized as a liar.

Be sincere, My children, both in your words and in your prayers. Do not behave like the hypocrites, who, when praying, love to stand in synagogues or in the corners of squares where they may be seen by people and praised as just and pious men, whereas, within their families, they are guilty towards God and towards their neighbor. Do you not consider that that is like a form of perjury? Why do you want to maintain as true what is not true in order to win a reputation which you do not deserve? An hypocritical prayer aims at saying: "I am truly a saint. I swear it in the presence of those who see me and cannot deny they saw me praying." Like a veil laid on existing wickedness, a prayer said for such purposes becomes blasphemy.

Let God proclaim you saints and live in such a way that your whole life may shout on your behalf: "Here is a servant of God." But you must be silent for your own sake. Do not allow your tongue to be urged by pride and thus become an object of scandal in the angels' eyes. It would be better for you to become mute at once if you do not have the power to control pride and tongue, and you proclaim yourselves just and pleasing to God. Leave that poor glory to proud and false people. Leave that fleeting reward to haughty and deceitful people! A poor reward! But that is what they want and they will not have any other, because you cannot have more than one. Either the true reward, the Heavenly one, which is eternal and just, or the sham one, the earthly one, which lasts as long as the life of man, and even less, and which is paid for, after this life, with a truly mortifying punishment, because it is an unjust reward.

It's a human thing to talk about what you want to believe and not what you hope to have and what you would like to be like. But it is really wishful thinking and it's kind of a waste of time. Talk about who you are right now and what you know and what you have and what your relationship is right this minute. Any more is you're conjecturing, and you're hoping, and you're wishing, and you're speculating. You're longing for something you don't have, and you're talking. You're talking. It's wishful thinking. To talk about living a life you're not living is like wishful thinking. Just like bearing false witness, "I'm a servant of God." Well, really? And does everything about you serve? You could say I'm trying to serve God, that would be accurate. That would also be humble. Does everything about you say disciple? Does everything about you say I serve? Does everything about you say I look to Him for how I should behave and how I should act and how I should think? Because otherwise you're in wishful thinking, and then you're blaspheming and you're bearing false witness, you're saying you do one thing but you really don't yet. You're not there yet. So it is more honest to say I am trying to become a disciple or I'm trying to be a disciple, I want to be one, and I want to follow Jesus. Those are accurate, those are true if it's true for you, which it would be in this group. But that I am one? Well clearly not. Because many selfish things happen and many arrogant things happen and many fearful things happen, and you scare yourself half to death half the time and you are selfish a lot, which those things don't actually add up to disciple. So you're going to have to be more accurate, if you are going to follow what Jesus says. To not say more than is true - yes it is or no it is not. It makes you pure in heart to speak like He's asking you to speak. What do you know really? Do you know what you hope for? No you do not yet. Do you know that you have enough faith to trust in the future? Maybe you know that. But you know the thing you have faith in? Not yet, not completely. You have faith in it, but have you experienced it yet, and that's where faith becomes a reality, faith becomes a manifestation in your being. You have faith in forgiveness, are you forgiven? Do you still err? There's the question. "I give you my word I'm not going to err"- Jesus said not to do that. Don't do that. Don't talk shit. That's what He's saying, don't talk shit. Just pray that God help you in each step you're in so that you don't make mistakes, so that you don't err.

But to swear that you won't, or to swear that you will do this and do that? You don't have the understanding of yourself to keep that word, and if you did then you wouldn't say it. You would say by the grace of God I will do this. With God's help I'll be able to do this. If God helps me I will become this. That's true. Those are true things. But to swear by your parents is to swear by something beneath you in most cases, because most of you have advanced past your parents spiritually. And if you have been taken on by Jesus, you have better parents than them already. So you have graduated from those parents to Jesus and Mary as parents, if you have really truly done that. If you have not done that, then you can't say that. This is where you get impeccably honest. If you still have an allegiance to your mommy and daddy, you really have got a whole plate of food that you're eating from that isn't Jesus and Mary. That's just the truth, whether you like it or not. You're still stuck on the four people you're fighting with on who you're going to have an alignment with. Jesus said, you're either with Me or you're against Me. There's no way around that. You're with Me or you're against Me. He didn't leave you any room, he just left you room to decide, that's all. He didn't let you, like, bargain or have competitions - Jesus' love versus your daddy or your mommy's love, he didn't let you do that. He wouldn't allow that. He would just call it - go bury your father, let the dead bury him or leave him, or go home to your daddy. Go home to your mommy. He would tell people to go home, because that's where they're at. They're already stuck in that. They weren't ready to be with Him, because they were really stuck on their wounds and stuck on their energy with their mommy and daddy. This is tough for the world, because the world has blinders on. They don't really see. Are you going to be children of God? Are you going to be children of the losers that hurt you? What are you going to do? You have to be respectful of the fact that they tried to bring you into the world and teach you right. They did bring you into the world, but not through any formal prayer to God for you. It was more or less an accident, and then you came. They did care enough to feed you and clothe you and educate you and give you some things. You can honor them for that. You cannot honor them for the abuse they gave you, you cannot honor them for the disrespect they gave you. You can forgive them. You can just forgive them. And if you want to still fight with them, then you have not forgiven them and you are not with Jesus yet, you are still at home. You are still at home with mommy and daddy.

Don't swear at all He says. Don't make any promises at all. Why? Because you cannot guarantee tomorrow by your prideful word. You cannot guarantee yourself, so don't ever do it, don't ever do it. "In this moment I trust God. In this moment I want to serve God. In this moment I don't have anything else but God." You can say that. You can say, "In this moment I choose trust. I choose love." You can say that. Swearing is pompous. It's pretending you have a strength that isn't really yours. It's God's. Any strength you might have is God's. It's God's not yours. You get it on loan, you get to borrow it, you get to use it, and as soon as you forget where you got it you lose it. As soon as you forget where you got it, you lose it. And your weakness manifests because you stopped relying, you stopped holding Jesus' hand. You let go because you wanted to do it yourself, and then you fall. Every time, no matter how far along you are, that's what happens. Remember it. Remember that. It's going to save you. That alone will save you. But to exaggerate this now: "I swear by strength of my own knowing, I swear by the pride in my own self, I swear by the experience I have, blah, blah, blah, blah, blah." Doesn't it just sound stupid? It just sounds stupid. That's what He's saying, it's stupid, spiritually dense. Because you forgot the basic thing, that all life in you is God. You are on loan to God. You owe everything to God, God can take it all away in a second. To the ungrateful, that's exactly what's going to happen. All of your intelligence that you pride yourself with is on loan to you, it's loaned on your capacity to contain it but so limited by your container that you think it's yours. You actually think it's yours. What did Jesus say to the Pharisees when they're screaming at him to stop John from saying stuff, John the Baptist? "God could raise up these stones to praise Me."

The more humble, the more power that moves through you. The more humble, the more realization of God happens to you. So how do you become humble? You say that you are like a Pharisee? "Oh, I am so humble." That's not going to work. That's just pompous. Yackers, they're mouthing the words of something they do not feel. Do you know that everything that you consider your gifts are God's? You don't own them. Your brilliance, your intelligence, your artistic ability, your maternal energy, your creative abilities. Any of that was a gift to you, loaned to you as long as you use it well. Always honoring God for the gift keeps that gift alive. You stop honoring it, and it starts to wilt and it starts to leave you and disappear. Just like dust in the wind it just blows away. As soon as you start to own it is yours, you lose it because in a way, aren't you swearing by that gift that it's yours? "I swear this gift is mine." You know, really? It's yours? It was given to you maybe and it was yours to use, but did it originate in you? No it did not, at all, none of it did. You see, if this is hard to hear, this shows how prideful you are. If it's easy to hear, then you're getting very close to humility, because you're understanding the truth. The truth is, any gifts we have were given to us. And they're not yours, they're on loan to you. Any skills, abilities, anything in body or mind or feeling were gifts. As long as you know that, they'll magnify. What do they magnify? The Lord. There's nothing else to magnify in creation. God magnifies Himself, because God recreated Himself in a human being. He created Himself in you. You were supposed to be gods, you were supposed to be just like Him so he can see Himself walking around being another Him. That is great joy to Him. And then you soiled it, and you continually soil it by thinking it's you. By thinking it's you.

Don't swear. It'll be simpler. It'll be much simpler. You can't vouchsafe your word - just be true, be true to yourself. Say what is true. You can't guarantee it, because you don't have the capacity or the power to do, so that's what He's saying. Let your whole being be the guarantor of your reality. Let your actions be the demonstration of what you know. Don't speculate. It's going to get you real humble really fast, and you're going to be happy. You will be happy. Because you won't think that a half a step up from where you are is where you'd like to be. That would make you unhappy, wouldn't it? If a half a step up from where you are would make you happy, that means that you're half a step down from happiness, doesn't it? It doesn't mean that anything you would prefer to have, means that you already have something you don't prefer, so that makes you unhappy. And that's a lack of humility to say, "I should have this half a step up from the step I'm on, because I'm unhappy here, but I'm happy if I have this half a step up, so I'm really not satisfied with the life God has given me, not satisfied with not learning it, with not incorporating it into my being, I would like to have that." Lack of humility. Pride. Stop. Get simple. Accept what you have in the moment as a gift to you. And maybe God will expand it, but that's not your business. Your business is to be in the moment accepting what you are given without complaining. Without competing. Without clawing to the next thing and the next thing. And then you'll be content. Then you will be.

January 24, 2016
Skills

The Gospel as Revealed to Me, Chapter 575. Parable of the Torn Cloth.

All the women disciples are busy sewing and mending the damages done in the many months when the apostles were alone. Eliza, who comes close to them with other dry garments, says: "One can see that for three months you have not had an experienced woman with you! There is not one garment in good order, with the exception of that one of the Master, Who on the other hand, has only got two, the one He is wearing and the one washed today."

"He has given them all away. He seemed to be seized with the mania for not possessing anything. He has been wearing linen clothes for many days," says Judas.

"Fortunately Your Mother thought She should bring You some new ones. The one dyed purple is really beautiful. You needed it, Jesus, although You look so handsome dressed in linen. You really look like a lily!" says Mary of Alphaeus.

"A very tall lily, Mary!" says Judas satirically.

"But He is so pure as you are certainly not and neither is John. You are wearing a linen garment as well, but believe me, you do not look like a lily!" replies frankly Mary of Alphaeus.

"My hair is dark and so is my complexion. That is why I am different"

"No. It does not depend on that. The fact is that your candor is on your outward appearance, His is instead within Him and it transpires through His eyes, His smile, His word. That is the situation! Ah! How lovely it is to be with my Jesus." And the good Mary lays her toilworn honest hand of an elderly hard working woman on the knee of Jesus, Who caresses it.

Mary Salome, who is inspecting a tunic, exclaims: "This is worse than a tear! Oh! son! Who closed this hole like that for you?" and scandalized as she is, she shows her companions a kind of... very wrinkled navel, forming a raised ring on the cloth, held together by some very coarse stitches, enough to horrify a woman. The strange repair is the epicenter of a series of puckers that widen out radially on the shoulder of the tunic.

They all laugh. And John is the first - he did the mending - and he explains: "I could not go about with the hole, so... I closed it!"

"I can see that, poor me! I see that! But could you not get Mary of Jacob to mend it for you?"

"She is almost blind, poor woman! And then... the trouble was that it was not a tear! It was a real hole. The garment got stuck to the faggot I was carrying on my shoulder, and when I dropped the faggot from my shoulder, also a piece of the cloth came off. So I just repaired like that!"

"You spoiled it like that, son. I would need..." She inspects the tunic but shakes her head. She says: "I was hoping I could use the hem. But it is no longer there..."

"I took it off at Nob, because it was cut at the fold. But I gave your son the bit I removed..." explains Eliza.

"Yes. But I used it to make cords for my bag..."

"Poor sons! How badly you need us near you!" says the Blessed Virgin mending a garment belonging to whom I do not know.

"And yet some cloth is needed here. Look. The stitches have ended up by tearing the cloth all around, and a great damage has become and irreparable one; unless... I can find something to replace the missing cloth. Then... one will still see it... but it will be passable."

"You have given Me the starting point for a parable..." says Jesus, and Judas at the same time says: "I think I have a piece of cloth of that shade at the bottom of my bag, the scrap of a tunic that was too discolored to be worn; so I gave it to a little man who was so much smaller than I am, that we had to cut almost two palms off it. If you wait, I will go and get it for you. But I should like to hear the parable first."

"May God bless you. Listen to the parable first. In the meantime I will fit the cords on to this tunic of James'. These ones are all worn out."

"Speak, Master. Then I will make Mary Salome happy."
"Yes. I compare the soul to a cloth. When it is infused, it is new, without tears. It has only the original stain, but it has no injuries in its structure, or stains or waste. Then with time and the acquisition of vices, it wears out at times to the extent of tearing, it becomes stained through imprudence, it breaks through disorder. Now, when it is torn one must not mend it clumsily, which would be the cause of many more tears, but it is necessary to mend it patiently and perfectly and for a long time to remove the damage already caused as much as possible. And if the cloth is too badly torn, nay if it has been so rent as to be deprived of a bit of it, one must not be so proud as to pretend to repair the damage by oneself, but one must go to Him, Who is known to be able to make the soul strictly honest once again, as He is allowed to do everything and He can do everything. I am referring to God, My Father, and to the Savior, Who I am. But the pride of man is such that the greater is the ruin of his soul, the more he tries to patch it up with unsuitable means that make the damage more and more serious. You may object that a tear can always be seen. Salome also said so. Yes, one will always see the damage a soul has suffered. But a soul fights its battle, it is therefore obvious that it may be struck. There are so many enemies around it. But no one, seeing a man covered with scars, the signs of as many wounds received in battle to gain victory, can say: "This man is unclean". On the contrary one will say: "This man is a hero. There are the purple marks of his worth." Neither will anyone ever see a soldier avoid being cured, because he is ashamed of a glorious wound, on the contrary he will go to the doctor and say to him with holy

pride: "Here I am, I fought and I won. I did not spare myself, as you can see. Now heal my wounds that I may be ready for more battles and victories." He instead who is suffering from foul diseases, brought about by shameful vices, is ashamed of his sores before relatives and friends, and also before doctors, and at times he is so silly that he conceals them until their stench reveals them. Then it is too late to remedy. The humble are always sincere, and they are also valiant fighters who have not to be ashamed of the wounds received in the struggle. The proud are always false and base, through their pride they end up by dying, as they do not want to go to Him Who can cure, and say to Him: "Father, I have sinned. But, if You want, You can cure me." Many are the souls that because of their pride in not wanting to confess an initial sin end up by dying. Then, also for them, it is too late. They do not consider that divine mercy is more powerful and more extensive than any plague, however powerful and extensive the latter may be, and that it can heal everything. But they, the souls of the proud, when they realize that they have despised all means of salvation, fall into despondency, because they are without God, and when they say: "It is too late, " they condemn themselves to the last death: to damnation. And now, Judas, you may go and get the cloth..."

"I am going. But I did not like Your parable. I did not understand it."

"But if it is so clear! I have understood it, and I am a poor woman!" says Mary Salome.

"And I have not. Once Your parables were more beautiful... Now... bees... cloth... towns changing names... souls that are boats... Such mean things, and so confused, which I do not like any more and I do not understand... But now I will go and get the cloth, because I say that it is in fact needed, but the garment will always be a spoilt one," and Judas stands up and goes away.

Mary lowered Her head more and more over Her work, while Judas was speaking. Johanna instead raised hers, fixing her eyes on the imprudent apostle with indignant authority. Eliza also raised her head, but then she imitated Mary and Nike did the same. Susanna opened her big eyes wide, being astonished, and looked at Jesus and not at the apostle, wondering why He does not react. But no one has spoken or made any gesture. Mary Salome and Mary of Alphaeus, two women with common manners, looked at each other shaking their heads, and as soon as Judas goes away, Salome says: "It's his head that is spoilt!"

"Yes. That is why he understands nothing, and I do not think that even You will be able to mend it. If my son were like that, I would break his head. Yes, as I made it for him that it might be the head of a just man, so I would break it. It is better to have a disfigured face than a disgraced heart!" says Mary of Alphaeus.

"Be indulgent, Mary. You cannot compare your sons, who were brought up in an honest family, in a town like Nazareth, to this man," says Jesus.

"His mother is good. His father was not a wicked man, so I heard," replies Mary of Alphaeus.

"Yes. But his heart was not lacking in pride. That is why he took his son away from his mother too early, and he also helped in developing the moral heritage, that he had given his son, by sending him to Jerusalem. It is painful to say, but the Temple is certainly not the place where hereditary pride may diminish..." says Jesus.

"No place in Jerusalem, even if it is a place of honor, is suitable for diminishing pride or any other fault," says Johanna with a sigh. And she adds: "And not even any other place of honor, whether at Jericho or Caesarea Philippi, at Tiberias or at the other Caesarea..." and she sews quickly bending her face over her work more than is necessary.

"Mary of Lazarus is imperious, but not proud," remarks Nike.

"Now. But previously she was very proud, just the opposite of her relatives, who were never such" replies *Johanna.*

Now of course the apostles are traveling around and are sleeping on the ground, they're walking through the woods, they're walking through mountains and stuff. Their robes are going to get torn and tattered through the experiences of life, as anybody's would, if you didn't have the usual mending scene that you have at home. I think many people have lost that art, of course many women have lost the art of sewing, so don't get proud of yourself that you're the ones who can take care of little boys because I don't like that attitude first of all. Some men know how to sew. It's nonsense, don't do that stuff, and it was pretty thick back then. And it was true that women spent many, many years learning how to do the household things like the sewing and washing, cleaning, designing and things like that. We don't have that these days. I'm not saying we should have that, I'm just saying it's not that way. And they still have their maternal presumption of caring for the men and the men are good at other things.

That's just the physical, practical, side of the thing - but the honest part of the tearing and the mending is that you go to God about the thing that is off. When you tear something, when you make a mistake, when you screw up something, when you fall into a temptation, when you sin - you go to God for the mending. That's what you do. You don't try to mend it yourself and hide it because it looks worse. It'll look worse because your pride says you should fix it yourself. And you fix it yourself and it looks all bruised. You still look bruised. Because you didn't go with a repentant heart to be forgiven - you went with the pride of shame that you didn't want to look bad and you didn't want anybody to find out, so you covered it over. Then you patched it in the best way you could, and its still obvious it hasn't been cleaned up - because without the real forgiveness it's not going to be clean. And without the healing power of the Master or God, you're not going to fix anything. How could you fix that? All you can do is disguise it. Then it made a naval of a huge hole, probably all he could do given his equipment and not a lot of practice with it, because they went fishing, and girls stayed home and did embroidery and they were good at it.

It's one thing to be good at something and know that you can do it - like the women really knew they could mend all these robes, and they fixed them all up in a day or two, because the men were going to all head out again. In some cases they had to make a whole new one because it was so bad. They also cleaned them and got them all ready because they were going to go to Passover pretty soon and wanted them all looking good. It's one thing to know that you have that skill, it's another thing to have an attitude about it or a pomposity about it, or even a criticism that other people don't know how to do it. It's kind of a self-adulating compliment to yourself to say how much you can do and how little the other person can't do. And I consider that, you know, patronizing.

And it's the pride of the women who are saying 'these are my skills,' and they were all doing it – chuckling too and feeling proud of themselves - but they were all still helping. So it's this mix of working, serving and helping, and having an attitude. All at the same time. This is humanity. This is you. This is us. Humanity: having a lot of attitude and a lot of skills and having a lot of opinions about everything. And the way that each of their natures criticized Judas for his ridiculousness is different too. But he's already completely lost - he doesn't even get parables anymore. And he doesn't really want to, he doesn't want to hear them. And everybody else knows how simple this parable is.

You know your soul is something that can be torn or stained and you have to go to the healer, to God, and get it fixed. It's very simple. But Judas is so dark now, he's turned so far, he can't hear anything. There's a part of us, when we're in a bad mood, we can't hear anything, no matter how reasonable it is what somebody is telling us, we just can't get it. It just doesn't go in, because our attitude or negativity at that moment blocks any common sense, or any real sense, or any spiritual sense. You don't want to get it because you're having a bad mood or because you're in a negative state. Well, Judas is in a super-negative state even with Mother Mary there. She just arrived after many months of not seeing Jesus. Everyone should be celebrating, and there's Judas having a stink fit as he normally does.

It's a very important feature to watch in yourself how you undermine a good thing, how you avoid having a pleasant healing or experience. Or you make sure you are extenuating a problem. You know you're focused on a negative thing just like Judas is. There's a part of you that says 'Yeah that's a blessing for them but not for me.' That type of interior thought Judas didn't hesitate to speak out loud. But you do have that inside you, 'Well, they're blessed because they're part of the priest body' or 'Well, they are blessed because the teacher might like them more than me.' You have these ideas. Like 'They've been around longer' - it's just these ideas in your head, even though you may not be as rude as Judas is where you don't outwardly say it, but you inwardly think it.

With the seeds of that pride and ego magnified a little bit, you'll be blurting out stuff, just ridiculous stuff to say. Just magnify that energy a little bit and vocalize it and you'll be acting like Judas. We have all these characters inside of us – you have the John, who just loves Jesus and is simple, and you have the ones who are really boisterous in serving the Master like Thaddeus and James, who were known as the

Sons of Thunder. They're going to do something powerful and rambunctious. Then you have the Andrew, who is laying back to look for someone to be compassionate towards. You know you have various qualities within yourself. You have the Simon Zealot, who has not only lived but he has sinned and been a leper, and is of another race, and has lived and been scared and turned into wisdom. You have that part too. Then you have Mary, and Mary of Alpheus, who just can't stop saying stuff but is usually right – but just can't stop it. Johanna, who is indignant and can't believe it. These different parts of you. She is this stately wealthy woman and she just cannot believe Jesus tolerates this guy. Then there is Peter, who just tries to control himself so he doesn't go over there and hurt Judas. These, these feelings are all inside. Then there is Jesus, who is just loving him and continuously patiently answering him, torturing him with love. Like it's a torture for Judas to be near Jesus now. And Jesus knows it. The simplicity of the parable, even though it was lost on Judas, was mostly for him, but that's how dense people are. Like the one you're given is the one you won't really hear.

It's not like the soldier who goes out and gets scarred in battle but is victorious - that's not a blemish - it might be something that needs healing, but it's not a stain. A stain is a negative thing, an impurity in your motive, a selfishness, a pride and stubbornness in your receptivity towards God. Those are things where you can try to repair them yourself, but then it looks just as bad as before. And then a little worse because you thought you could fix it yourself. That pride is a dangerous thing - that is what took Judas down. That could take you down. Like you could cover and make it look good on your own ideas and make it look kind of okay, or make a patch. But unless you go to God to have Him patch it in the way God does, in the way Jesus does, it's not going to fix. It's just going to look gnarly, it's going to look like you still have it but you've politicized it within yourself.

What I mean by that is that you rationalize it to the point where your pride says 'Well, I do know it's a mistake, but I just don't have the humility to bring it to God. I'm just going to, like, not do it again.' But then there it sits like this navel on your shoulder. How could people not look at that. And the ones who are skilled, like the women, are saying, 'Oh wow what did you do?' 'Oh well, there was a hole and you know I just kind of, you know - stuff'. 'Well that's just terrible,' they say. You ever see someone try to stitch a sock and it just looks like a wart on top of their foot? Well that's what he did. But what did he have? Probably had some fishing line and he just kind of put it on there the best he could just to close it up. A little MacGyver action. That what guys do – they do twine, whatever they can find.

And instead of going to the one who can mend it, which is Jesus who can mend it in the right way, and yes you might still see that you did something to yourself - you gained an experience or you dropped into negativity, and you learn from it and became wiser, but scarred and healed and made whole from it. It's not a permanent blemish unless you fail to go to God with it. If you stamp the thing with pride because only you want to see it, only you want to deal with it, you don't want anyone else to see it - you just stamped yourself with a blemish that is permanent. The soul can't be mended there, because you stained it and you left it stained out of embarrassment and pride. You do have to go to God for everything. You'll have to learn that, in order to be healed.

And it's not a one-time deal - its daily and minutely you go to God with your things. It's a process, not an event. And by this time in Jesus's experience, Judas has turned and has become a disaster. Just a total disaster. And He is not going to stop loving him and He is not going to stop for a little bit more. Until the end He's not going to stop. A Redeemer redeems, a Savior saves. You know they don't get fickle. This isn't like deciding who He likes and who He doesn't like and whether He's going to help him or not - that's not what Jesus does. A true disciple doesn't do that either. That's pride.

And guess what happens in politics. You like who you get something from, or you like who you can use, or you like someone similar to yourself. How is that love exercised? It is exercised in three very minor brackets of your life. You're not loving anyone or everyone or everything, your loving only what pleases you, or what consists with something similar to you. And that's not love. And that you need to get rid of. That kind of love you need to be vigilant not to have. Because I don't call it love. I call it politics. Liking someone you like, liking someone who likes you, liking someone you can get something from, or liking someone who can adulate you. That's politics. Politics. That's gross. That's not what Jesus does. He loves everybody and wants to save everybody and is rejected by most.

That will be your lot. If you're like Him, if you're following Him, that's going to be your lot, your experience. And from my estimating that is my experience. I can love thousands and a few - you know it's not about getting anything back – but a few receive it, that's what I'm trying to say. Jesus wants your love to be clean and pure, so you have to go with your tears and have them repaired. You can't do it. You don't know how - you go to Him. Go to Him for that. You try it yourself, you're going to look funny. He's going to see you and say, 'What happened? Who did this?' Just like the women, they're asking what happened. I can see you didn't have anyone to heal this. That's the same with Jesus, He can see that you tried to do it yourself out of shame or out of pride or fear or ego - that you've tried to heal it yourself and it just looks funny. Don't do that.

January 31, 2016
Become Like Me

The Gospel as Revealed to Me, Chapter 576. Towards Doco, the meeting with the young rich man.

And He has not been long on it when from a caravan coming from I do not know where - a rich caravan that certainly comes from afar, because the women are mounted on camels, closed in swaying palanquins fastened to the humped backs, and the men are riding fiery horses or other camels - a young man departs and, making his camel kneel down, he slides from his saddle and goes towards Jesus. A servant, who has approached him, holds the animal by the reins.

The young man prostrates himself before Jesus, and after his heartfelt greeting, he says to Him: "I am Philip of Canata, the son of true Israelites who have remained such. I was a disciple of Gamaliel until my father's death put me at the head of his business. I have heard You speak more than once. I am aware of Your deeds. I aspire to a better life to have the eternal one that You assure will be possessed by those who create your Kingdom in themselves. So tell me, good Master, what shall I have to do to have eternal life?"

"Why do you call Me good? God alone is good."

"You are the Son of God, as good as Your Father. Oh! tell me what I must do."

"To enter eternal life observe the commandments." "Which, my Lord? The ancient ones or yours?" "The ancient ones already contain Mine, mine do not alter the ancient ones. They are always the same: worship the only true God and respect the laws of cult, do not kill, do not steal, do not commit adultery, do not bring false witness, honor your father and mother, do not injure your neighbor but love him as you love yourself. By doing so you will have eternal life."

"Master, I have observed all those commandments since my childhood."

Jesus casts a loving glance at him and kindly asks: "And do you think they are not yet sufficient?"

"No, Master. The Kingdom of God is a great thing in us and in the other life. God who gives Himself to us is an infinite gift. I feel that what is our duty is very little compared with the all infinite perfect being who gives Himself to us, and I think that we should obtain Him by means of things that are greater than those commanded, in order not to be damned and be agreeable to Him."

"You are right. To be perfect you still lack one thing. If you want to be as perfect as our Father in heaven wants, go, sell everything you have and give it to the poor, and in Heaven you will have a treasure that will make you loved by the father who has given His treasure to the poor of the Earth. Then come and follow Me."

The young man becomes sad and pensive. He then stands up and says: "I will remember your advice..." and he goes away sadly.

Judas smiles ironically and whispers: "I am not the only one who loves money!"

Jesus turns around and looks at him... then He looks at the other eleven faces around Him and says with a sigh: "How difficult it is for a rich man to enter the kingdom of heaven, the gate of which is narrow, and the way is steep, and those who are laden with the bulky weights of riches cannot go along it and enter! To enter up there only the immaterial treasures of virtue are required and one must be able to part with everything that is attachment to the things of the world and to vanity." Jesus is very sad... The apostles look stealthily at one another... Jesus, looking at the caravan of the young rich man move away, says: "I solemnly tell you that it is easier for a camel to pass through the eye of a needle than for a rich man to enter the kingdom of god."

"Who can be saved, then? Poverty often makes one sin, through envy and lack of respect for other people's property, and through lack of confidence in Providence... riches are an obstacle to perfection... so? Who can be saved?"

Jesus looks at them and says: "What is impossible for men, is possible for God, because everything is possible for God. It is sufficient for man to help his Lord with his goodwill. And it is goodwill to take the advice given and strive to achieve freedom from riches. To achieve complete freedom, in order to follow God. Because this is the true freedom of man: to follow the voices that God whispers to his heart, and His commandments, not to be the slave of himself, or of the world, or of respect of public opinion, and consequently not to be the slave of Satan. To make use of the wonderful free will that God gave man to wish Good only and freely, and thus attain the very bright, free and blissful eternal life. Man must not be slave even of his own life, if to gratify it he must resist God. I said to you: "He who loses his life for My sake and to serve God will save it forever."

"Well! We have left everything to follow You, even what was lawful. So what about us? Shall we enter Your kingdom?" asks Peter.

"I tell you solemnly that those who have followed Me thus and those who follow Me - because there is always time to make amends for laziness and sins committed so far, there is always time while man is on the Earth and has days in front of him during which he can redress wrongs done - those will be with Me in My Kingdom. I tell you solemnly that you, who have followed Me in the regeneration, will sit on thrones to judge the tribes of the Earth with the Son of man Who will be sitting on the throne of His glory. And once again I tell you solemnly that there is no one who in My name has left house, fields, father, mother, brothers, wife, sons and sisters to propagate the Gospel and continue My work, who will not receive one hundredfold in this present time and eternal life in the world to come."

"But if we lose everything how can we centuplicate what we have?" asks Judas of Kerioth.

"I repeat: what is impossible for men is possible for God. And God will give one hundredfold of spiritual joy to those who from men of the world became sons of God, that is spiritual men. They will enjoy real happiness, both here and beyond the Earth.

And I also say to you that not all those who seem to be the first, and ought to be the first having received more than everybody, will be such. And not all those who seem to be the last, and even less than the last, as they do not appear to be My disciples or to belong to the chosen People, will be the last. Truly, many who were first will become last, and many who were last, least, will become first..."

It's difficult to imagine your freedom as slavery or your slavery in God as freedom. But what is lined up with Jesus and love and light and grace, that's the slavery you should strive for. Because in that safety you become pure, you become little angels actually. You become goodness personified, light manifested, but only if you take on the process to become beautiful. Because you come coarse and rough, you come egotistical and weird. You come scrapey and scrappy, ready to fight always, determined to augment your position, defensive about every little thing. That's how you come to the Christ. Even if you come with a noble ambition, even if you come with a kind of energetic courage, you come rough and mean. And Jesus encloses you in his love and starts the process of softening you and adding a witness to your weirdness. And you start to not be able to recognize yourself because you look better. And you start to feel smoother and less scratchy, like that speck of dust floating in the waves. And soon you become an opalescent, luminous, reflector of the great light, even having its own luster because you let that work be done on you by the Christ.

You can't do it yourself, you can't just push out a willing goodness out of yourself. You know you can't shove your goodness out, because it will look really stupid and really phony if you try with your ego to be what you think is good. It can't work from the outside in because it will look like a rebel. It will look like you're trying to climb up some other way to get into the kingdom of God without letting the process that divine beings, more intelligent than us, created for us to go through. You can't do it on your own. I'll tell you what, try it, you will never do it. It cannot be done because doing it on your own is a lack of humility. Doing it on your own is pride, and Jesus rejects pride and God flees from the haughty. You do it the way God, the Creator, set it up or it cannot be done. And God would never allow it. God would never allow you to usurp the position of the know it all, doing your thing, getting all good by yourself without that humbleness of knowing that you can't be good unless God allows it, unless God blesses it. Without that humility you become nothing, you'll never amount to anything. How can God use you when you are wild grain? I know, the whole world is stroking people and their egos to 'know what you want,' to 'do what you want to do,' to 'become what you think you are.' It strokes you and suckers you into that, and that's exactly the darkness. A disciple becomes of one mind with the Teacher, not your own mind. A bunch of forty odd weirdo minds? That is not discipleship. Jesus says, it is enough if you become like me, that's enough. And the more they weren't like him, the more he didn't recognize them. He didn't empower them if they wanted to continue to be not like him. He did not give them anything really deep. In their wanting to not be like Jesus they weren't even able to really receive it. They couldn't even hear it, it didn't even get through. Even though he is speaking all the time, it can't get through the webbed cage of your ego, unless you dismantle that ego of yours and submit it to God. And then, by the way, you don't need it after that. You only have the ego to protect you in your fears and your lies of who helps you. Firstly, you help you. That's a lie, you do not help you, you don't even know what to do. Your ego doesn't know what to do, your head doesn't know what to do, you need help. That is the first lie - that you can help yourself - that's a total lie. The more a student has that idea that they can help themselves, the less I let them get close, because they have a wild person in their head that has to submit to the timing qualities of the ocean in order to become that pearl. They don't have to, but if they do submit, they become that pearl. If they don't submit, they will never be that pearl and they will never be empowered. It's simple. And you thought you were doing your own thing, but I am evaluating you. That is my job, to teach you, to instruct you, to take you to a place you cannot go by yourself. If you didn't know that, wake up. If you didn't think there was something to go to, to become, you haven't been listening. At all. If you didn't think there were things you had to leave, you haven't been listening. If you didn't think there were a bunch of things that have to die in you, I can easily point them out to you. But you haven't wanted to know that too much, because what would you be without those things that are meaningless and stupid that you keep being attached to? What would you be without those things? Possibly an emptiness, possibly an openness that God could do something in.

He said that the first parts of the process are much harder because you are enslaved in the love, and the love starts to soften you and work on you, and you get that milky white film around you. You can't actually know what is going on in the early stages, and you can't be all this and that in those stages. That's why it's hard and you're leaving the comfortability of how you used to function, which I don't call comfortability, I call it the prison of how you used to function. You call it freedom, I call it prison. Just like you in your process call total discipleship prison, and I call it freedom. Everything of the world is opposite in the spiritual life, everything. That's why it was hard for people to follow Jesus, because he wasn't saying anything that they could get some kind of tangible, concrete, heavy-handed, material grip on. He wasn't saying he was a King riding into the earth to take over the Romans and oust them from their little plot of sand. He was the king of the world and of heaven, and they couldn't even get that, like you can't get how to be different than all of your problems. You can't even conceive of not having your problems, because they are so familiar to you, they are so much a part of your identity, they are so much a part of your ego structure, and you think that's you. That is the same difficulty in them listening to Jesus, where he's saying 'The Kingdom of God is within you,' and you're saying 'I don't see it,' and He's saying, 'God is within you,' and you're saying, 'I don't feel it, I don't hear it.' Yes, because you're stuck up in the head and jammed up in the ego, no wonder you can't hear it. Anyone can get out of the way to hear God's voice, anyone, anyone. Do you think God would make it so hard to hear Him for somebody who wants to? What kind of concept is that? I know, everyone says that God is within me, but I can't see it and I can't hear it because it's just too hard. Because God is making it so mysterious, God is making it so distant, I can't get to it. Well, you went distant, it's right there. Something you're doing in your head makes you so distant, so get that crud out of your head and stop thinking. Ask for what it is you want and you will get it. It is the same for everybody in every mystic group throughout the history of the world. Anyone who wants to hear God's voice can, but you have to stop thinking. You have to stop thinking in order to do it. I know, I say it all the time, and you say it's just some casual thing that a teacher says. Have you ever tried it, and really listened? You will hear his voice. I'm not kidding, this isn't hard. What's hard is for you to stop being so proud of that shit ticker tape in your head. That's what's hard. You're so attached to that nonsense, gibberish out of your brain. You be still, you calm it down, you shut it up and you listen to the Divine being inside of you and you will hear it. If you have the guts you will do what it says because that will set you free. If you're a coward, you will hear that, and then your ego will say 'Yeah I heard it,' but you won't do anything about it and so you won't change. But if you do what it says and you trust it - and it is God so it will probably take care of you – then you will grow. Anything else is too complicated and God won't bless it by the way. God won't bless your complications. I'm telling you how simple it is. You guys have this problem thing in your head, "I'm going to have problems for so long, it's going to be so long to get over them and then it's going to be kind of uncomfortable to get rid of them and then later I might not have any, and then I'll hear God." Well, how long have you figured that out, how long in each of your minds is that going to take? How long are you going to wait to have the garbage in your head and your own ego willfulness, before you get to that place you can have right now? Right now. Get it out of the way and you can hear His voice and then you can do what He says and it will set you free.

But see, this is the problem with humans, you tell them the royal road and they admire it, they will even write about it, they will even talk to other people about it, and they won't put one foot on the damn thing. Not one foot on that road. But it is such a pie-in-the-sky beautiful thing, and you will talk about it emotionally but never step on that way. That way is the way to freedom and truth and life. You sit back with your head and are quite satisfied with how long you think things take. Arrogance, the arrogance of that ego of yours. Ask me how long things take, I'll tell you the answer. No time at all for one who loves and one who wants, no time at all. How long does it take for you to get over not wanting your problems? It looks like forever. You didn't ask help for Jesus to catapult you into the new life, into the pearl coffer. You're going to do it all yourself. Do it all yourself and that is equal to getting nothing done, going nowhere. Doing it yourself equals going nowhere. I'm being specific with you, because your stubbornness amazes me - stubbornness in staying the same, in having the same problems and wanting them. It's amazing to me when you could be free and feel really good and you prefer not to. I am amazed and I will be patient with you because you like it. But for myself I do not choose that.

I did not choose to stay the same as I was, I would find that embarrassing. I choose God and for God to take me where I can't see and where I have no control. I choose God to form my life in His image, not mine. I choose God to direct my ways, to tell what to think, what to say, what to be, how to spend my time. I am that teacher that you could follow. Are you following? Are you really a student yet of the Teacher? Do you do what I do, be what I am? Do you do that yet or do you do your own thing? Now that just set out the criteria of your discipleship. Are you a disciple or are you a pre-disciple liking the idea of eventually, sometime in the future, becoming one, because you really don't want to do it now? Do you want to follow me then, later, after you indulge your problems and you hone your skills and you get that ego all shiny? Well Jesus doesn't want your ego, God doesn't respect your ego. I'll tell you what God respects and this is going to blow your mind and make you mad too. God respects God, that's it. If He sees that in you, shining out, expressing, He respects that. Nothing else does He respect. Why? Because he is perfect and He loves himself and He wants to love that part of Him in you, if you let it happen. That is the only thing He is going to respect, that's the only thing He is going to love, because He is all infinite goodness and light and He's put that in you. You are sequestering it away, shoving it down and putting a great big mattress on top of it with your ego and your thoughts. He wants you to become recognizable to Him, so you have to let that go, that suffocating mattress of your ego, you have to let it go, so you can become God, like God.

That's the criteria, the only criteria and it's the only one you're going to get for eternity. That's it. You should be able to hear this now. You've been getting clear teachings for many, many years, you should be able to hear this now and maybe, you should be able to do this now. I think with God's help you could do anything, you could do anything. You could look in the mirror and see how much you're willing to do, and how much you've been willing to do. You could see where you are, you could see that discipleship was a dream. You could see it was a goal, but you never fulfilled it, you never became it. It was a great idea, but you weren't one yet. You know why? Because you're holding on, you're just holding on. And you'll have to do much more to show Jesus that you're everything about being an instrument for Him, everything about being a servant of God, not a servant of your ego and just doing your own thing except for holy days, except for classes or except for services. You'll do a little bit of his stuff and the rest of the time you'll do just what you want to do in the way you do it, with the same doldrums, and the same pout and the same anger that you usually do. You guys need to get ready. You're not ready. I'm telling you you're not ready and you're not even close to ready and your faith is not enough for what you're going to be confronted by. I'm saying that with all due respect to you. You do not have enough faith yet for what you're going to need. Everyone is a little different, but generally it's true what I'm saying, I mean generally true for all of you.

Why am I warning you? Because it isn't going to be a test of whether you have a food stock or not, it's going to be a test of whether your faith is strong and your ego and pride are down almost under the sole of your foot. If it's not there, you're going to get in trouble, you're going to be in trouble. I'm just trying to help you. I know things and I've been telling you, but you don't know them yet because your head is so bright, you're so bright, so freaking intelligent, which you claim to be, even though intelligence is God's. All intelligence, no matter where it is, is from God. You do not own that, you do not get a dose of that, you can have as much as you want or as little as you need, depending on your ego. You do not own it. All goodness, all creativity, all intelligence, all power is not yours. Unless you're in that position where you just humbly love that, you're compromised. You are compromised. Humble all that, soon. Or it will be humbled for you. There is great big drama going on and we're going to be caught in a huge wave and I hope you can surf. I hope you can surf. The more ego, the more heavy. The more sensual and dense in your body, the less spiritual, you're just going to be rolled and tumbled and crushed by those waves. You do need to practice getting that shit out of your head. I know you guys are so primitive, you're thinking, 'Well, I had a negative thought about something about food the other day.' I'm not talking about that kind of trivial stuff. I'm talking about the tendency of your head to be able to manage anything, to figure anything out. That's what I'm talking about. That's the ego and the brain taking credit for everything. Jesus can destroy all that in a second with his glance if you wanted him to. If you asked him, "Take these lies out of my head, take this ego thing of pride in myself, take it out of me so that I can know who I am, so I can look in the mirror and find out who I am aside from all that jacked up stuff. Who am I?' Stop thinking and you'll find out, you will find out. Do you want to be a pearl or do you want to be a slave to your ego and your body? That's the choice, that is the choice. He's the eternal judge, He is going to know no matter what kind of lobbying you do or politicking you do, He's going to know without your words what you have chosen. I think you should choose now, when the trees are green, not when they're dry. Choose now. You can't tell Jesus I didn't tell you. I told you, I do my duty, I tell you the truth. I know you don't like it, I don't care, I'm doing my duty.

February 7, 2016
Let Them Go

From 1943 Notebooks, July 10.

Jesus says:
"Listen... Do you know the parable about that father who had two sons: one says, 'Yes, my father,' and then does nothing; the other says, 'No, my father,' and then does what the father asks of him?

I don't want to have you meditate here on the duties of sons and daughters and the beauty of obedience. No. I will only say that this father was perhaps not a model father. Let a proof of this be that the sons did not love him: one lies; the other responds with a refusal which he later overcomes with supernatural effort.

Not all sons and daughters are perfect, but it is also true that not all parents are perfect. The Commandment states, 'Honor your father and your mother,' and whoever violates it sins and will be punished by divine justice. But justice would not be justice if it did not use the same measure towards those not honoring their children. 'To honor' in ancient language means 'to treat a person with reverential respect.' Now, if it is right and proper to honor those who have given us life and have provided for our needs as babies and children, it is no less true that parents must also honor the children that God has granted them to have and that He has entrusted to those creatures who have procreated them so that they will raise them in a holy manner.

Too often fathers and mothers do not consider that they become the depositories and guardians of a prodigy of God the Creator. For every new existence is a prodigy of the Creator. Too often parents do not think that within that flesh begotten of human flesh and blood there is a soul created by God that must be raised for a doctrine of spirit and truth in order to be handed back to God again in worthy fashion.

All children are a talent entrusted by the Lord to a servant of his. But woe to that servant who does not bring children to yield fruit, leaves them idle, showing no interest in them, or, even worse, disintegrates and corrupts them. If God, in a tone of severity, is to require an explanation of those not attending to increasing the value of a talent and inflict a lengthy punishment on those dissipating and killing the soul of a child, God, the master and judge of all that is, by an inexorable verdict will inflict eternal punishment upon parents slaying the most valuable part of children-their soul.

This concerns generalities. Now we shall turn to specifies.

Do you know how you should love your mother in order to be able to go on loving her? With an exclusively spiritual love. The other is useless. She does not see it, does not understand it, and does not feel it. And she tramples upon it, making you bleed in your humanity. I thus tell you: Love her only spiritually. That is, love and work for her poor soul. And I won't say anything more, for you are a daughter, and I don't want you to be lacking in honor towards a mother. I am God and Judge. I could do so. But with you I do not want to do so. Even if a parent is at fault, that parent should be respected because of being a 'parent.'

Love her poor soul. She greatly needs your charity as a daughter. With respect to eternal life, the fathers and mothers who sin against their children need their children's help and their children's forgiveness in order for their punishment to be mitigated.

Reflect a great deal about what I say, without my needing to add anything else. If you pause to consider her as a woman, you cannot honor her. I agree. But consider that she is a soul that is a daughter of God and very, very, very rudimentary. Your charity as a daughter should work to make reparation for her deficiencies - you must enrich her so that she will not present herself as too poor before God the judge.

You have mercy on the infirm and love for little children. But what spiritual childishness is greater than your mother's? And what spiritual infirmity is greater than your mother's? Embrace her dark and dull spirit, then, and lift it up towards the light.

Spiritual love is hard. I know. But it is love with perfection. It is the love I had for so many, while I was a mortal. I knew who would betray me. I knew who would deny me. I knew who would flee in the tremendous hour. Nothing was obscure for me. Well then, I accomplished immeasurable prodigies of spiritual love - for my Flesh and my Blood trembled with repulsion when they felt cowards, deniers, and especially the traitor to be close to them - in order to try to save their spirits.

I saved many that way. Only those completely possessed - I say completely - by the devil were resistant to my lavacre of spiritual love. The others, possessed by one passion alone, were saved before or after my Death. Judas, Annas, and some others were not, for the seven princes of the demons held them in their clutches with seven ropes, and cohorts of demons were in them to carry out the work that made them gems of hell.

Love like this. You will do your duty and show yourself before me as a true disciple. In regard to her, leave the office of Judge to Me. Go in peace, dear soul, and do not sin."

So parents have a mission to stand in for God, and they do an imperfect job. Some do a terrible job, depending on their selfishness, depending on their reactive state, depending on the wounding that they didn't get healed and that they didn't apply for healing, and all of that, and the consciousness that they refused to do. As children, as children of your parents, you are not exempt from judgment in your compassion for them. And it's hard to see your compassion when you're trying to prove something to them. And it's hard for your compassion to come online when you're trying to make them pay or you're afraid of them. You're still angry. And most of you are still embroiled in a knot of argument within yourself about your parents. We've talked about it a hundred times, I know, and as long as that knot's happening, you're still trying to prove yourself right, prove them wrong. You're still trying to get something from them. When Jesus says the solution is one thing only, you have a spiritual love for God, that's it – and to forgive them. Well, if you're still trying to prove that you're good, or get some recognition of something from them, that's not forgiveness, and it's not loving them spiritually. Now, you're still embroiled. How can you hear the voice of God inside you when you're embroiled with this dynamic drama you're having with your parents, or a parent. I think you can measure the level of your stubbornness in accord with your attachment to your parents. The more attached you are, the more stubborn you are. The more you haven't let them go, the more you keep trying to get something from them or teach them a lesson to make them pay, or to prove that you're good, the more stubborn you are. When you've been clearly shown and told thousands of times by me that you should be looking away and be looking to God. So if you want to know if you're stubborn – are you still holding on? Are you still arguing in your head how to get their approval or how to get them to learn their lesson, all that other junk you do in your head?

Jesus is setting it out really clearly that he is the judge of the parents, and he's the judge of the children. You are not, and that's actually none of your business, and he said so. He said it's none of your business. Your job is to love them with a spiritual love, and your job is to forgive them. Your job is to be in obedience to God. That's it. Now, obedience to God is going to make you useful. It's going to make you serve. It's going to make you give of yourself. The very thing you would have wanted a parent to show you how to live is the thing that Jesus and Mary have to teach you. But you didn't really learn it, or they didn't really teach it, or you were too mad to learn it, or whatever it was, that your little ego had problems with. If you're still working on your parents, you're just as rudimentary as they are. Jesus called Maria's mother very, very, very rudimentary. Would you like to be called that? Are you still embroiled with your parents? Then you're very, very, very rudimentary, indeed.

You have to leave that island of littleness to go to the great island of God. You have to leave it, not keep working on it, not keep proving something to it, not fighting with it. You have to leave that little island. I can look around and see that you haven't. You know, I understand it. I understand it and I don't understand it. Maybe Jesus will help me understand it better, how you're so attached to it. Maybe Jesus could give me the appreciation for the attachment that I don't seem to have. It would behove you all to do a little meditation on how many ways you are still attached and still working on the relationship in your head. Like, running it through how the good scenarios could have happened. Running it through how this could fix it. Running through how you'd feel better if *this* was done. Running it through how you could trounce them with your specialness or your argument – just win something, win a few times, instead of always losing to them. You know, you guys have your little axes to grind. Maybe each of you have six axes, I don't know, that you're grinding, on the great wheel of parenting.

Let me give you a sense of emergency, like, if you are starting to have children, and you're still stuck on being a child yourself, how can you fully mature as parent? How can you be a parent? Really, how can you give to that child when you've still got a bunch of homework to do from the first class you went to? How can you be ready to even be showing up for your kid, when you can't stop showing up as a kid? I'm not trying to be fierce with you; I'm trying to help you think. Think it through. For you with younger kids, I'm trying to help that kid have a better life than what you were planning. If you don't finish your homework, how can you go out and play? How can your kid really be with you when you're still stuck on your daddy or your mommy?

They're going to look at you all crumbled up and broken and scared and insecure and angry, and they're going to go, Where is Da-? It's supposed to be daddy, supposed to be mommy, where are they? Well they're busy working on their parents. They don't know how to forgive yet. I'll try to maintain a sense of non-disturbance, so I don't disturb the fight they're having with their parents. I'll try to get innocuous. Tiptoe around the family, so I don't trigger what they already seem to be bothered with. I don't really get them, but I'll just occasionally try to get attention, because they seem to be very busy working on their mommy and their daddy. They don't seem to have time for me, they're just fighting in themselves with their mom and dad's judgments, they don't really have time for me.

I don't know a kid alive that doesn't have that experience. I don't know a kid alive who didn't have a big dose, an injection of that loneliness, because the parent was checked-out in their little fight with mom and dad. I know what you do. I know what you think. You want them to get some love? Then be love! That means, be done with your past. Be done with your grudges and your little 'proving' schemes, proving your worth to your parents, who were blind as bats anyway. How do you prove that you're looking good to somebody who's blind? How can that happen? How can you prove that you really are a shining star when they don't have time for you, to even look in your direction, to even notice who you are? And why wouldn't you get the message pretty quick that you're wasting your time? You got the message that it wasn't happening, and then you got to try-try-try-try-try-try-try-try. And you can't stop trying. And while you're trying, and you have kids, they don't get you, because you're so busy trying to prove to somebody who can't even know you, never wanted to know you, doesn't have the capacity to love you, really, that much, and you're trying like crazy. And I call that stubborn – you're all getting an award, I'm going to get plaques for all of you – I see it in every one of you – You're going to get the stubbornness award for the year. 'I really tried – I can't stop trying – I'm still going to try, and I'm going to ignore everybody around me because I'm trying, trying to get that love, get that recognition that I never got.' So stubborn. Jesus says leave all that, come to the love. You go, that's a great idea, I love the poetry of that. Sounds so poetic. Just won't do it. Actually, my pride will say I'm doing it, but I'm not going to do it. I'm actually going to stay working on the family. Gonna work on the family. Just gonna stay home and work on the family.

I've got news for you. Jesus can't use that. He can't use you when you're divided like that. There's nothing he can do with you when you're like that. You're not amenable to suggestion; you're not prone to inspiration; you can't hear guidance, you can't get out of the way, you can't be quiet enough to let peace happen to you, you can't listen to anything, because you're all preoccupied. And it's sad, because you guys could all be dynamic servants of God. You could let go of the past. You could. I know how to do it, you know, I can dance around you and show you how to do it. But you don't even look at that. You don't even listen. You must think I'm some kind of distortion of creation, that I don't have any of those ties that you have, that I'm not attached in any way to that, that I let go of that forty or more years ago, before you were born I let go of it. Actually, five lifetimes ago I let go of the need for that. And what are you guys doing, hammering away at that cold rock that's never going to budge. Jesus says, come to me, and you say, well, yeah, I'm going to come to you, sure, but I'm going to hammer away at this rock. How stubborn can you be, seriously. Let them go and forgive them. I know, it sounds so easy, sounds so – that was so few words – let them go and forgive them – you guys can say that, repeat after me: let them go and forgive them – and, you know, what happens? Nothing! Nothing happens. Nothing happened. Even if you said it a hundred times. Nothing happened because you didn't do it, and you're not doing it. You guys are glued to your little rock like superglue, and you won't budge.

Here's the sad part for me, I'll just do a little personal, you can't learn from me because you can't do what I do. You can't move like I move, think like I think, respond how I respond, move with the spirit, you can't let life move through you, you can't learn it. You can watch me as an anomaly, as a strange oddity, but you still don't know how it feels, and you don't know how to do it, and you've never done it. I'm the one you should be following, because I do do it, and I know how to do it, and I tell you every day how to do it. Some of you are proud enough to think it's all about skills. It has nothing to do with skills. It has to do with love and getting out of the way, and being willing to be moved by the spirit. That's what it involves. Would that you guys would take the risk and try it. I dance around you constantly, showing you, and you're still blind as a bat, blind as a bat.

Don't you think Jesus wants each of you to do it? Don't you think he thinks you can? Or why would he be telling you that you can, if he doesn't know that you can? It's not about me doing it, but if I'm the only one doing it, then you guys don't exist. You guys don't exist. Jesus was clear in the Brotherhood of Christ. We had about this number of people, forty or so. They were all very happy for me to be doing something. They were super happy for me to be just moving with the spirit and doing all the work, and doing all the teaching and loving and the shining of light and stuff like that, and they were happy to sit on their little rock and not do that. And Jesus called it. It was a little surprising, I didn't ask him to call it, he kind of called it. He said, "Dissolve it," and I dissolved it. They weren't happy. They were mad. Some of them are still mad at me for that. But you know what? It was totally justice. They'd been getting lavished with love and didn't do a damn thing. They didn't change anything. They didn't give of themselves. They didn't really learn it – they heard it but they didn't learn it. They heard it, but they didn't receive it. And Jesus called it – boom. Done. Dissolved it. He said close it up, I closed it up. I didn't dissolve the corporation, I kept it. But I dissolved the board. That was it.

I'm not threatening that, but it looks the same to me. I don't – Jesus isn't going to do that, I think he's going to call the whole earth this time, he's going to call the whole earth. But you guys have an opportunity here to actually kick it in and get rid of your past. Let it go. You're so stuck on it. It's like you can't even conceive of being different than the way the family sees you. You don't go, this is how Jesus sees me, this is what I want to do now. I want to see me as Jesus sees me. I don't care what anybody says. I don't even hear that out of your lips, and I don't hear it out of your actions. I want to see me how Jesus sees me. I want to be just like he says I am. He says go, I go. He says move, I move. He says stop, I stop. He says shut up, I shut up. Can you just do that? I know you can, but would you? Are you going to show your kids what a disciple is? Or are you going to show them what a trying-really-hard-to-get-your-parents-to-love-you is? And while you're doing that, they won't know you, they won't be with you, and you won't be with them, and they will be as lonely as you were. Some of you already had your chance, and your kids are grown, and you did this to them. Okay, that happens. Next time, don't do that. Apologize to God and your kids, and then let it go. Learn from it. Some of you are still arguing that you were actually there with your kids. Really? Do you want to make me laugh? I don't need to know your kid to know you're still stuck on your parents. You're stuck on your parents, your kid gets nothing, a paltry little crumb. That's all they get, because you can't show up for your kid. You're still stuck on your parents. You won't show up. You're still mad, still reactive, still trying really hard to get the recognition your pride deserves. It's all pride anyway.

He gave Maria, who had a terrible mother, her mother beat her, and her mother was terrible to her, just like many of yours, critical and weird, he told her what to do with her: love her only spiritually, and pray for her, and forgive her. How many times have I said that to you? Well at least two, that I know. At least two. And I look around, and I see it, you didn't do it yet, you didn't do it yet, you know? If you were under the great tribunal of the host above, and Jesus and Mary were there, and they'd examined you: Did you let them go? Did you forgive them? You would come up short. You would not be able to say yes. You would not be able to say yes in front of them. So you can't say yes in front of me. When I see that you have, and your heart is clean, and your mind is pure, and you're shining, and you're doing your work, and you're not looking back, I will pronounce you well. I will. I don't want you to be stuck. I don't want you to be holding on. I want you to be free to serve him without any ties to the earth. And pretty soon…You want to wait? You just want to wait? Your ties to the earth will be shaken so bad, it won't be your choice any more. So you won't get the credit for the courage because you won't have any courage, because you didn't do it before the time. When the time comes, it'll shake that tie itself, all by itself, because you were cowards before the time. But if you break that tie now, you'll be useful then. If you don't break the tie, you'll be shaken to the bones because of your stubbornness because you didn't want to hear the voice of one crying in the wilderness, saying, let it all go. Go to God. Repent of your old stuckness. You didn't want to listen. And if you are listening, then do it. Don't take months and months to do this. Don't take weeks to do this. Just do it. Otherwise there will be no credit given to you when God makes you do it. You'll have no credit for that, because there was no courage in that, it was only an emergency that you had to do it. And you get no soul credit for that because there was no guts and no faith. You will get no credit for that, but that tie will be broken. I would rather you do it voluntarily, out of love, out of a spiritual love for your parents, than for Jesus to do it as judge, to call it, and make you do it. You've got your choice. And I've warned you. That's your warning. Do the work, or it will be done to you. Take your pick. A volunteer is a helper. A stubborn one: bulldozers come and move them. Take your pick how you want to do it. I, for myself, do what Jesus says, even at the cost of my life. I do it. I would that you were following me, and you could say that, too. But you can't say it yet, because you're tied to your little parental rock. Even if you think they're dead, blah blah, I know you guys do the literal one me at these moments, because you're head's so thick. "Well, they're dead. Am I really tied to them?" If you really can ask that question, you really need your head examined. After all the teachings, you still ask that question? You need an examination of your head. I've seen people tied for lifetimes to a parent, and they died a long time ago.

If you don't want to hear me, that's fine. Just glaze over. Those people in Taiwan thought they had a lot of time left. Have some of you seen the buildings? In two minutes – boom. Their house, their livelihoods, their jobs, everything

– gone. In two minutes' time. Earthquakes have happened for hundreds of years. But are you ready to say to the Master, Hey, you know, like, I was holding on. I just held on, I'm sorry. I was just holding on, you know? That's all I did, really. I was just holding on.

When I said follow me, did you? Well, I loved the idea. Just loved it. But I really had this other stuff I had to take care of. I had to hold on to these other things.

So, I found myself feeling very sad this morning, and I tried to snap out of it – I think I've snapped out of it, mostly – but I was very sad, because I could see the stubbornness so thick, and the hardness in your hearts, not letting the Master love you, while you're holding on. Actually you have to look away from him to look back at the thing you're holding on to. And that's very sad for me, because you, of all the people in the world, you've had more clear teachings and more repetitive teachings, and more straight-up goods, than anybody on the whole planet. And you should know. You should know. And you just don't. Doesn't even move you, doesn't even move you. Don't show me you're moved, you know, I don't need an outer display of movement, I don't need an outward display of anything. I don't need outward words to know you, to see you. I don't need a description of your process to know what you're going through. Everybody says, but how could that be? Because you have parents you're still attached to, who don't know anything about you, so you're still sure nobody knows anything about you. You're still absolutely sure, stubbornly sure no one can read your mind, no one can read your heart. It's a thirty-second read, for anybody with sight who's let go of their past. It's a thirty-second read. Do you understand? No, you don't. And that's what's sad. You don't know Jesus yet. Jesus goes, sin no more, because he's saying you did, he already saw it, you can't tell him, he doesn't need to know what it is, he said don't sin any more, that means you did it, and now he's telling you to stop. Are you going to go through the details of what your sins are? He already knows what they are. Are you that thick that he can't see? Are you really that thick - that your fine descriptions make any difference at all, in the knowing of you? Any mother who knows anything about love can know anything about that kid just by looking at them, and tuning into them, and feeling. No words are required. I'm sorry that didn't happen for you, but anybody who knows how to do it can do it. Anyone can do that. So then anyone can know what your problem is, just by tuning into you, in a few seconds time. I've been doing it to you for a long time, and I've been telling you that for a long time. I've been telling you that you can do it with each other, without that judgmental little sharp sword that you have. With love, you could do it. So why don't you learn how to do it? Why don't you start doing that, instead of waiting for mommy and daddy to spatula you out of your mud? You know you're never going to get anything from them, and you still wait for them, by the side of the road, in the mud. You muddy up when they come, you actually muddy yourself up when they come by, so you look terrible, so they'll have a little pity for you, a little pathos for you. What is it going to take, I don't really know, my hands are in the air now. There they are, you need to see them, spiritually they were, but now I'll show you.

Jesus looked at the crowds, and they had the same numb look on their faces, the same density, the same stubbornness, I know it. I know you want to be the different ones. Go ahead and do it. Be the different ones that aren't like that.

February 14, 2016
The Corruption of the World

The Gospel as Revealed to Me, Chapter 582. The Eve of the Sabbath before entering Jerusalem.

Jesus, a tall white figure in His linen tunic at the edge of the green-red meadow, lifts up His arms towards the clear sky and raises His very sad face and soul to His Father moaning, "Oh! Father! Will You accuse Me of omitting anything that may save him? You know that I am struggling to prevent his crime for the sake of his soul, not for My life... Father! Oh! Father! I beg You! Hasten the hour of darkness, the hour of the Sacrifice, because it is too cruel for Me to live near the friend who does not want to be redeemed... The greatest grief!" and Jesus sits down on the thick, tall, beautiful clover. He bends His head on His raised knees clasped in His arms and He weeps... Oh! I cannot look at those tears! In distress, in solitude, in the conviction that Heaven will do nothing to comfort Him, and that He must suffer that grief, they are already too similar to those of Gethsemane. And that grieves me too much...

Jesus weeps for a long time in the solitary silent place. Witnesses of His tears the golden-hued bees, the scented clover that waves slowly in a stormy wind, and the clouds that early in the morning were like a thin net in the blue sky and are now thick, dark, piled up threatening more rain.

Jesus stops weeping. He raises His head listening... The noise of wheels and harness-bells comes from the main road. Then the noise of the wheels stops, whilst that of the harness-bells continues.

Jesus says: "Let us go! The women disciples... They are faithful... Father, let it be done as You wish! I offer you the sacrifice of this desire of mine as Savior and friend. It is written! He wanted it. That is true. However, Father, let me continue my work on his behalf until it is all over. And even from this moment I say to You: Father, when I pray for sinners, a victim having no power to take direct action, Father, take my sufferings and force Judas' soul with them. I am aware that I am asking what justice cannot grant. But mercy and love have come from you, and You love what comes from you and is one thing only with you, God one and trine, holy and blessed. I will give myself to my beloved ones as food and drink. So, Father, are my blood and my flesh to become condemnation for one of them? Father, help me! A germ of repentance in that heart!... Father, why are you going away? Are you already moving away from Your word Who is praying? Father, the hour has come. I know. May your blessed will be done! But leave your Son, your Christ, in whom, by your inscrutable decree the certain clairvoyance of the future is diminishing in this hour - and I do not say to you that this is cruelty, but it is your compassion for me - leave me the hope that I may still save him. Oh! Father! I know. I have known since I am. I have known since, not only as word, but as man, I came here to the earth. I have known since I met the man in the Temple... I have always been aware of it... But now... Oh! it seems to me - through your great pity, most holy Father! - it seems to me but a dreadful dream, brought about by his behavior, but not something ineluctable... and that I may still hope, always, because infinite is My suffering and infinite will be the Sacrifice, and may it be of some benefit also for him... Ah! I am raving! It is the man who wants to hope so! The God who is in the man, the God made man cannot delude himself! The mist that for a moment was concealing the abyss from me is dissipating... the abyss already open to swallow the man who preferred darkness to the light... It was your pity that concealed it! It is your pity that shows me it now that you have recomforted me. Yes, Father, also that! Everything! And I will be mercy until the end, because such is my essence."

He is still praying, silently, his arms stretched out crosswise, and his distressed face calms down more and more assuming the appearance of solemn peace. It becomes almost bright with the light of interior joy, although there is no smile on his closed lips. It is the joy of his spirit, in communion with his Father, a joy that leaks out from the veils of the flesh and cancels the marks that grief had impressed and painted on the Master's face, which had become the more emaciated and spiritualized, the more He advanced towards sorrow and sacrifice. In these last mortal days the face of Christ is no longer a face of the earth, and no artist will ever be able to give us that face of man God carved into supernatural beauty by perfect total love and sorrow, even if the Redeemer should show himself to the artist.

It's natural for Jesus to want to continue to hope for Judas until the end. It's natural for him to see the truth of what's happening and also to still pray for him and to ask God to break his heart, open his heart, change him. But he also knows as God, as Christ, that it's not going to happen. And yet his job is to redeem and his job is to sacrifice, serve and to save souls. So it's just constant wanting to love him and wanting to help him.

The earth is one big Judas now. It's just one big Judas, most of the people are now. It's so corrupt. It's just gross, actually. All the movies are satanic - almost every one now - satanic, sensual orgies, pornographic, it's like everybody lost it. They're completely corrupt and they don't have one pang of guilt about it. They went down. Perhaps in the short time that they have available to them they might have some soul that will convert or see the light or ask for help or want to be saved or want to come to Jesus in some way, but it doesn't look like there's very many of them at all. The whole world just mocks at anything real, at anything holy, at anything religious, at anything spiritual - it's a complete mockery. I know that compared to where you were and where I'm talking about might be quite far from those two things, but where the world is compared to Judas? It's like a breath away. A breath away.

God's patience is amazing in his justice and mercy for human beings, but there comes a point where nothing else can happen and no more good can happen. It's like in the nature of a person when the soul has been squashed so thoroughly that the body's ego and the body's desires and opinions and concepts have become so heavy and so tight, the soul just evacuates. It has to leave. That body dies. The soul releases the body from the life-force because the body became so disobedient and so unresponsive to soul that the soul just evacuates and drops that shell - that shell that thought it was in control, that shell that thought it was running the show, that shell that thought it knew itself. And the soul just says, 'You have it. You're going to do that? We're done. That's what death is for most people - the emancipation of a soul that has been so oppressed, so unable to express that it says, 'Okay I'm out of here.' Then the body just completely disintegrates, because that body with its ego and its thinking and emotions, is jacked up thinking it's something. It thinks it has a will of its own, a freedom to do whatever it wants and that's just a couple of afternoons really before the soul goes bye-bye.

Well that's what's happening on the earth on a global scale. That's what happens in an individual when the soul can't express through that body anymore because that body's won't let it, the body's ego won't allow it. Then the soul just goes, it just takes off. It's over.

So I'm amazed at God's patience in allowing such disobedience and such disrespect for anything real on this planet or anything real of God. More and more anything religious is criticized, anything spiritual is erased from everything. It's erased by the willful humans, and then whenever anybody does have a spiritual inclination it's mocked and it's criticized and it's laughed at. Almost in every movie and almost with every conversation with any meaning that happens. So what is Jesus to do with this population that he's completely responsible for? He's the Lord of the planet. He's responsible for our planet and yet what is he going to do when the egos and the bodies are completely disobedient? What is he going to do? He's going to pull it. He's going to pull it. He's going to pull the experiment. It's going to be over. And that will be justice and mercy. Mercy for the ones who still care and justice for the ones who don't, because with this much majority and this much wave of assent and wave of acceptance it will be hard for any of you to stand up against it. You don't have to brace, you don't have to fight, but you have to stay true to the core of the love and the light in you and it's seriously hard. Remember, don't overestimate your strength. Even the apostles who were raised up priests, some Teachers by the time he left, they didn't handle it well. They didn't handle it well. You're not there. You're not where they are. They weakened, they shattered, they faltered and got scared and went into doubt and fear and reacted terribly and they got a little lost. For a good week they were lost. You're not there where they were. You're not strong like that so what is going to happen to you when something so crazy happens like they take Jesus away and you think this is not going to be successful? That's what they thought. They thought he was going to be successful in their limited vision of what the Messiah means, the king or the leadership in an earthly sense, and kick out the Romans. So earthy, so shallow that it frightened them when it didn't go that way and yet his victory is so clear and so powerful. They couldn't get that for a whole week until they saw him again. Then they got it. By that time they had faltered and embarrassed the hell out of themselves. Their pride thought they were so strong and they were clearly not strong and one of them suicided - that's how bad he went. So you're not better than them and you're much less prepared than them. You have much less faith than they do and you have much less evidence of miracles that were right in their face - not in your face that much. You kind of have to hear the story and believe it. They saw it in front of their face every day. They had evidence - you don't. You have to have faith.

Anyway, I accept that the world has grown like a rotting carcass. That's what it has become – a rotting carcass and I'm a little shocked at how far advanced it is in rotting. Even I, who have been telling you that for years, am seeing the rot and the death of the carcass so close, so close. The carcass of the humanity of the earth - it's like a dead carrion. You know why? Because they wanted death, they wanted all the things that produce death. They want all that. They want separation, they want scoffing, they want disobedience, they want indulgence, they want sexual crazy. They want it, and because they want it, they're going to get it, and that's going to cause their death spiritually. That's what they want. It's very sad because they could have had bliss and joy, love and forgiveness and light and healing. They could have had all that and they had opportunities and they were told. Everybody's been told of Jesus in the past 2000 years, everybody on the planet, everybody on every continent has been taught and heard about it and it's on every TV show on Sundays. They could see it every day if they wanted to, on certain talk radio they hear about it all the time, and it hasn't changed a thing. It hasn't changed anything. A few people love him, a few people try to be good and the rest they don't even care.

Now you may be naive and that might be why I'm talking to you because you don't get how serious it is, but I do. It's like they all went to hell and they like it. There's hell on earth. They wanted it – the humans wanted it and that's what they have. Now a little part of you is compassionate towards them because a little bit of a part of you has hell in you because you still enjoy it, you still like it, you still like your problems and you still like your criticisms. You still like your little fears and you still like to scare yourself and you still like to be jealous and compete and you still like to be mad. What difference is that between them and you? A disciple shouldn't be any of those things. Those should never be in a disciple and that makes me get kind of clear with you. Maybe disciple isn't any of those things and calling oneself a disciple can't happen until those things are out. We could do that, but then you guys would quibble and argue in your head because you want to be disciples and yet you want that darkness in you too. I guess you can figure that out – how much of a disciple you are and how much of a world person you are. How much are you with the world perhaps so you don't get so high up above them, perhaps so you don't outgrow them so you can still relate to them, so you can still have friends who are just as corrupt as that part of you that you keep. There are lots of reasons why people don't want to grow too far or too much. You have to examine what it is you want. It wasn't like Jesus sent the flood or the firestorms or tornadoes, it's the humans that are the scourge of the earth right now. They are the scourge of the earth, and as much as you're feeling sorry for yourself, you're feeling angry, you're worried, you're anxious, then you're actually contributing to it. You're actually part of the scourge of the earth. You should be all love, all light, all forgiveness, all faith, all trust, that's what you should be and you can be if you choose it, but you have to want nothing else. What that means is that you have to get rid of everything else. You have to let none of that everything else in. You have to be vigilant. You just can't be wussy because everything will just flow through you depending on the hour of the day. Like, "In the mornings I feel sorry for myself, in the nights I am angry."

Really, you prefer that? You're in charge of that? You want to be in charge of that? Jesus said you could have whatever you want so I'm going to say you want that or it wouldn't be happening. You're not going to fool God and you're not going to fool Jesus. If you mull over a particular emotion, you want that, and that's a decision you're making just like how on a graphic scale the world's making a decision for evil. I mean, complete self-indulgent evil. Like, brazen and entitled, raging evil.

On a subtle level you're choosing to have a mood or you're choosing to stay worried or you're choosing to have a little problem with somebody that's subtle, yes, but it's still negative. What you are choosing and what you have the power to not choose, with just a slight bit of help, you could get it out of your being and never do that again. You could. I've been asking you for years to stop doing it, but I'm telling you these things will get you if you don't get them out of there, they're going to get you. Don't think that Jesus is stupid. He can tell if you still have a whole wedge in there of anger or a wedge of pride or a wedge of attachment to some desire, he can see it. Whether you think he can or not, he's got perfect sight. You come close to him and he's going to say, "What about that?" And you say, "I was holding onto that just in case I need it." "But I told you that you can't serve me with that." "Yeah, but I was holding onto that just in case I need it." And He says, "I understand you were doing that, but how can you serve me when you keep that thing in there? Were you trying to fool me? I can't call you mine if you keep that thing in there. I can't be anywhere near that because it's so different from me, and you're keeping it. You just told me you want to keep that and I'm telling you that you can't be part of me if you keep that thing."

You haven't done the subtle analysis of this like the simple analysis of this. Am I a disciple? What does he want from me? What does he want me to get rid of? And then do it. Do what he says. I could tell you. I have been telling you but I'm just a person. Why don't you get it from him? Take it from him. What does he want you to keep, and what does he want you to get rid of, and proceed quickly to do that. Quickly because you don't know how long you have, and you don't know what little thing you keep, is going to take you down. You do not know. You do not know. None of us know. But you know he had lots of parables about this - the wise virgins who kept their light going, who kept their oil fresh. They didn't know what hour of the night he was coming. Those are the ones he selected. The others, they got lazy and they went to sleep and their oil ran out and then when he came they had to procure oil and they didn't have time. He said, "I don't even know you." He's told you in his parables how he functions, what his criteria is whether you're one of his or not. You already know. Do you just kind of space out and try to forget that?

Anyway, it's really bad out there and I'm not trying to create a mirage for you. It's terrible out there. It's gone completely down, completely down and it's everywhere. When that happens you have to be stronger. Stronger than you are and stronger than you've been. I'm recommending it. That means you have to get tough about what you care about because you aren't yet. You aren't yet. You want to be lackadaisical? You won't make it. You won't make it. Pray for him that he comes soon, and pray for him that he help you because you need it. I'm not trying to be negative about any of this, I'm just saying you need his help. If your pride says you don't, boy, you need to look in the mirror. You need to get your head examined. If your pride says you don't need his help oh God should pity you. God should pity you if you think you don't need his help. And I'm saying as the shepherd of this little flock we're not ready. I'm saying we're not ready. I'm saying you don't have enough faith yet.

I'm saying you haven't kicked out all the garbage yet. You aren't ready. I'm not trying to put you down. I'm saying get ready. Get ready. I know I've been saying it for a while but I'm saying it differently today - same thing a little differently. Get yourself ready. Clean your garment white for the wedding.

February 21, 2016
Complacency

1945-1950 Notebooks, March 30, 1949.

"I taught, 'If your brother has sins against you, go, take him aside, and correct him; if he heeds you, you have won over your brother. If he does not, take witnesses with you so that everything may be confirmed by them. If he does not yield and repent, inform the church; if he then does not yield and listen even to the church, treat him like a gentile or publican.'

This is why for years I have selected witnesses for you. And I now tell you they should get into real action by being present and also speaking on your behalf so that those abusing your patience, courtesy, and respect for the priestly robe will feel uncomfortable with others who are not you...

It is not an offense against charity to be just with the blameworthy and just by exercising justice in every action. Did I perhaps offend charity towards my mother by exercising the heroic justice of doing the whole will of my Father? No, in all truth. On the contrary, by doing this I made her, the Immaculate one, the co-redemptrix. I place this second glorious crown on her head, which she would otherwise not have had. Nor did she refuse to wear it, though it was a crown of boundless pain. Look at us. I was the Son who did not deny his most beloved mother, but set the will of God before her, because that will must hold precedence over other loves, wills, and human rights, even the holiest ones. And look at her: the mother who did not keep her son from doing the will for which he had taken on flesh. Robe your heart in our heroism and act with true charity.

Patience becomes foolishness, as does charity itself, when they are not joined to justice. When I saw that the limit had been reached beyond which patience and charity would turn into complicity and injustice, I, the perfect patient one, separated myself from the blameworthy after severe words. There is no love, no matter how great, that can permit a misdeed by one it loves. Remember this. One must act. One should then pray for the redemption of sinners. But one must act. Always. Because not doing so would mean that one wants to be their accomplices.

And, having dealt with the distant and proximate foundations for our passion and seen the faces, especially the spiritual faces, of our enemies, before immersing ourselves in the real passion, let us pause to contemplate the few friends we have.

Few, and among these few, I had very few among the priests and doctors. But those very few were good. Jairus and Joseph and Nicodemus were among the very few, along with very few others, including the good scribe.

And since I am just, I shall also include among them the great Gamaliel, though it may seem strange to the superficial. His real justice caused him to be absent at my condemnation. A great and serious act at that time and before that assembly. And I remembered him in my heart, tormented by so much hatred, betrayal, and sin in a whole people-my people, taught, miraculously cured, and loved by me - in my followers and, more than followers, my chosen ones, now scattered because the Shepherd had been seized... everyone against me except a few! My people! My Jerusalem! I remembered the gesture by Gamaliel, the greatest rabbi in Israel, a Jew down to the deepest marrow of his bones, encrusted with traditions-indeed, locked in the impregnable jasper of the old doctrine, but still a just man.

He had not been either my friend or my enemy when I was free and strong. He awaited the sign to believe I was the Messiah. But when he saw me unjustly portrayed as an evildoer, though not yet believing I was the Christ, he nonetheless emerged from his reserve to summon the judges, drunken with hatred, back to legality. If he had been able to give a character of justice to his firm belief in the luminous *words of a wise child during a far-off Passover, he would have been on Golgotha with Joseph and Nicodemus. But his belief was too fettered and thus an obstacle to seeing the truth.*

You, too, face some who, because of the rigidity of their faith, create obstacles to seeing the truth for themselves, regarding both you and the work. They are waiting for a sign, as Gamaliel was. Always include them in the ranks of friends, though, even if they do not appear to be such, for excessive justice makes them slow to recognize the truth. And pray that, for them, too, the tremor of a heavenly earthquake will cut through the threefold veil covering the Holy of Holies of their just, closed spirits, which may then see the truth of this work and of yourself, my spokesman, so that our exertion as the one dictating and the one writing may not be futile.

You count yourself blessed if you understand a few things and in fact you gloat a little bit that you get it. You understand, that it makes sense to you. But what have you got, really? You have the pride of your understanding. That you got it, and that is, kind of messy. Is that what you want to settle for? That you understand a few things that other people don't? That you can make sense of the teachings, that the teachings are clear to you, that you get what Jesus was talking about? You understand why he said it, what he's saying and the purpose of what he's saying, and that certainly is more than what most people understand. But you see how complacent it can be in your pride that you get it and thus you're fine? You get it and I want to call you on your complacency.

Hearers of the word, they understand, but doers is another thing. Paul says, "Don't be just hearers of the word but doers of the word." That you become that thing that you're listening to. You become that person who can perceive truth, who doesn't make deals, who doesn't become an accomplice to evil by making some conciliatory agreement which compromises you. That's why he's praising Gamaliel, because he didn't do that, but he's so scoffingly skeptical and so rigidly occluded in his sight that he can't perceive who this man is even though he's hearing the miracles, watching him speak and hearing his truth and seeing how he loves people. It just can't get through the thick wall of Hebrewism of an old crusty Israelite. And we have the same entrenched problems today where people can't get that he's real. They can't get how dynamically powerful and active and in a life Jesus can be. Probably because they don't really believe that they can do it themselves so they think he can't do it in them. And that certainly compromises your devotion and your dedication because then you don't have to try very hard because it probably wouldn't happen to you and we're back to the convenience again.

It's very convenient not to have to change too much because you don't want to startle yourself with having to give in places you didn't plan on. You don't want to startle yourself in ways that actually requires love, in places that's going to take a bit out of you. Whereas before, by sitting near the fence, you could wonder how real it is in support of you not learning how to give. But when you jump in one hundred percent you're going to make it work and you're going to give everything because that's what a real disciple does if he's converted or she's converted. You give everything. You jump in with everything you have. You don't hold back wondering if it's as real as it needs to be for someone like you. You don't manage it so that it's comfortable for you and doesn't, you know, stretch you or jostle your concepts too much, because you don't want your concepts jostling too much because you spent so many years and weeks working on them to keep them that way, to make yourself better than the person next to you.'

In Gamaliel's case he was the most noble of the scribes and Pharisees and the most trained and the most brilliant and the most rigid and the most conforming to the rules, which those guys in their history created. Moses had the Ten Commandments and then they, in their pride, created six hundred and fourteen other ones that they thought bolstered up and perhaps supported the ten and they forgot that they should have gone down to the two and they would have done the ten. If they had just done the two, which Jesus said incorporated the entire ten, which is, "Love God first and love your neighbor as yourself."

So you have to love yourself, you have to love your neighbor. So if you love your neighbor as yourself you can't criticize the neighbor and you can't criticize yourself. Otherwise you're not following the commandments and if you don't put God first and you're first, you're pretty much messed up, really. You're messed up. You're lost because you put yourself first and you don't really honestly want to look at the number of ways you put yourself first. I would like to ask you to do that and I want - I know you're going to get frightened because you get frightened at looking at truthful things - how much everything is about you and how much everything that anybody does is really about you and how much anything anybody asks of you is really about you. It's all you, you, you, everywhere. Selfishness, selfishness everywhere. *'Am I looking good? Are they seeing my faults? Are they taking care of me? Do they really want me? Are they criticizing me?'* Me, me, me, me, me, me, me, selfishness, selfishness everywhere. *'Am I looking good yet? Do people honor me?'* That's a thousand questions all related to selfishness and basically Jesus is talking to Maria and how they share their mission and how the whole - it's a very long passage, it's 80 pages long or something like that - about how she is actually invited into His process of suffering and all the things that she suffered compared to all the things that He suffered and He goes through every one from her birth on and from His birth on and so this is at the late stages of the talk, talking about how they both enter into people who are judging them, criticizing them and much like Gamaliel who has stayed in his justice but he didn't. He didn't defend Jesus because he couldn't see that He was the Messiah. He was so blind he couldn't see. He didn't want Him condemned but he didn't want to advocate for Him. He didn't even want to be His disciple yet because he was waiting, waiting, waiting in his rigidity to understand how real He was. He didn't get it until he was crawling up after the earthquake in repentance but he couldn't see Him then, so he didn't get to see Him again. He had to do it in the spirit because he was blind as a bat as a physical body so now he has to do it in the spirit. That's justice. Jesus is giving him the justice of wisdom.

I would like you to enter into justice and wisdom before it crashes against you. Like, what does that mean? When the truth of God crashes against you, you get to see yourself as before you want to, whether you want to, and the way God sees you. I would rather you see, as a volunteer, how God sees you without it crashing against you because you waited too long and in God's timing. You didn't jump for it, so then God's timing comes upon you to see yourself. But if you did it ahead of time voluntarily there'd be grace because there's a heroic movement in wanting to see. There's a love that supports you in wanting to see what God wants to show you. So you say, "How do you see me?" And you wait and you look and things flash across and the spirit of God shows you things in the mirror of your soul and you look without closing your eyes, running away, thinking your own thoughts, defending yourself, judging, criticizing - you just look and you see and then if you're humble you go, "Okay not cool. What should I do now? I'm sorry, what should I do now?" That humility - you're going to ride on a really beautiful wave into shore.

Everything else is going to jostle you because your pride's trying to stiffen up and your desire nature's trying to hold fast and your ego's trying to keep control and see ahead and know everything before you get to know anything because that's what the ego does - tries to know something before you get to know anything. That's exactly the definition of the ego, 'to know something before you get to know something,' and you can see that that's silly because you can't. You can only guess. The ego can only guess because it can't experience anything. It's a commentator. It's a little ape commentating about your life, that's what the ego is. It's not an experiencer, it's a commentator. You want to hear that in your head all the time, commentary? Commenting about, about, about, not anything you're in but it's about what you could be in or what you were in or what you might be in. That's the ego just yakking away, droning on. When you're in an experience, really - a real one - you don't listen to that because you're in it. You're in one. That's why the Zen monks have to chop wood and carry water - because while you're doing that you can't think about anything else. They want you concentrated to train you out of listening to that garbage. That's why I tell you to serve, to do something, to move your body, to give something to somebody so you don't have time to get all inbreded in your thinking; moldy fungusy in your thinking. Give.

Maria sacrificed her whole life to the dictation of the dictator-person, to Jesus. Can you imagine all day for six years, every day, rain or shine, morning noon or night, whenever Jesus comes to get you - in the middle of the night, any time, you being with Jesus and Him telling you everything - His whole story and you have to manage writing it down, fast? That level of intimacy, none of you are used to. None of you could stand it. You think it's blessed, but when would you have time to worry? When would you have time to go off and be negative, when would you have time to go off and indulge yourself? When would you do prideful, lustful, desirous things, irreverent things that you do? When would you have time for any of that? You're on call every moment of the day for six straight years. 'Now who wouldn't want that?' you say. Your ego says 'Oh, I'd love that.' Uh huh. You can't even stand to feel the presence of God for more than about twenty minutes at a time because if you do that stuff has to die. It's going to croak right in front of you, a lot of the stuff that you cultivate. It will just start croaking and kicking buckets and stuff. And she had enough devotion and love to be with Him on call constantly for six straight years. I mean, He appears to her, He touches her, and He heals her. He heals her heart so she can go on being dictated to. "Yeah, you're having a hard day, I know. Heal." Then He tells her the next scene, "Write this down." "Yeah, but do you see...?" "No, just write this down."

You guys might like it in your fantasy mind and you don't get the presence of Jesus really, how compensating that is for any suffering you might get, because you don't know that yet. But if you did, you would want that experience. You would trust it, you would accept it: that whatever He gives you is good and whatever you go through - however hard - is good for you. And how can you have that experience if you're still reacting to a thousand and one things (and you are, and we've mentioned it)? I've asked you to examine them and you examined a couple big ones and you let those go, and then I examined with you a couple more and you let those go, but you have a whole, you know, bridal suite of reactions that you keep cultivated and you get to access those whenever you want and they keep you from God and they keep the presence of God out. And, unless you're willing to relax into your pain and feel it, you can't bust through it. You can't bust through it. You're still busy trying to teach somebody something. You're going to teach Daddy something, you're going to teach Mommy something, and, as long as you're doing that, you can't feel your feelings and you can't relax in your pain and you can't metamorphose. Done.

February 28, 2016
Mary's Gift

The Gospel as Revealed to Me, Chapter 586. The Sabbath before Entering Jerusalem. The Supper at Bethany.

Mary Magdalene comes back in. She is holding in her hands a thin-necked amphora, ending in a little bill, as pretty as the neck of a bird. The alabaster is of a precious rosy yellow hue, like the complexion of some blondes. The apostles look at her thinking, perhaps, that she is bringing some rare delicacy. But Mary does not go to the center, inside the U of the table, where her sister is. She goes behind the seat-beds and stops between that of Jesus and Lazarus and that of the two Jameses.

She uncorks the alabaster vase and places her hand under the little bill to receive a few drops of a viscous liquid that flows slowly from the open amphora. A strong smell of tuberoses and other essences, a very intense pleasant scent spreads in the hall. But Mary is not satisfied with the little quantity of perfume that flows. She stoops and with a sharp blow she breaks the neck of the amphora against the corner of Jesus' little bed. The thin neck falls on the floor shedding scented drops on the marble pavement. The amphora now has a wide aperture through which plenty unguent flows in thick gushes.

Mary places herself behind Jesus and spreads the thick oil on her Jesus' hair, she sprinkles all His locks with it, she stretches them and then puts them in order with the comb taken from her own hair, tidying them on the adored head. Jesus' fair-red hair shines now like dark gold and is very bright after the unction. The light of the chandelier, lit by the servants, is reflected on Jesus fair hair like a beautiful copper-colored bronze helmet. The scent is exhilarating. Through the nostrils it rises to the head and, spread as it is without restraint, it is so intense that it is almost as exciting as sternutatory powder.

Lazarus, with his head turned round, smiles watching how carefully Mary anoints and arranges Jesus' locks so that His hair may look tidy after the scented massage, while she does not worry about her plaits, which, no longer supported by the wide comb that helps the hairpins to hold them in place, are falling lower and lower on her neck, and are about to loosen completely on her shoulders. Martha also looks at her smiling. The others are talking to one another in low voices with different expressions on their faces.

But Mary is not yet satisfied. There is still plenty ointment in the broken vase, and Jesus' hair, although thick, is already saturated with it. Mary then repeats the loving gesture of an evening of long ago. She kneels down at the foot of the bed, she unties the buckles of Jesus' sandals and takes them off, and dipping the long fingers of her beautiful hand into the vase, she takes as much ointment as she can and spreads it on His bare feet, toe by toe, then on the soles and heels, then up, on the malleoli, which she uncovers by throwing back His linen tunic, and lastly on the insteps, she delays on the metatarsi, which will be pierced by the dreadful nails, she insists until she finds no more balm in the hollow vase. Then she shatters it on the floor and with her hands now free she removes her big hairpins, she quickly loosens her heavy plaits and with that golden, bright, soft, flowing bundle of hair she removes the excess ointment from Jesus' feet that are dripping balm.

Judas, who so far has been silent watching with lewd envious eyes the beautiful woman and the Master Whose head and feet she was anointing, raises his voice, the only voice of open reproach; some of the others, not all of them, had murmured something or had made gestures of surprised but also calm disapproval. But Judas, who has stood up to have a better view of the ointment spread on Jesus' feet, says with ill grace: "What a useless heathen waste! Why do that?

And then we expect the Chiefs of the Sanhedrin not to speak of sin! Those are deeds of a lustful courtesan and they do not become the new life you are leading, woman. They are too strong a recollection of your past!"

The insult is such that everybody is dumbfounded. It is such that everybody stirs, some sit up on the beds, some jump to their feet, and everyone looks at Judas, as if he had suddenly become insane.

Martha flares up. Lazarus springs to his feet striking the table with his fist and says: "In my house...", then he looks at Jesus and controls himself.

"Yes. Are you all looking at me? You have all murmured in your hearts. But now that I echoed your words and I openly said what you thought, you are all ready to say that I am wrong. I will repeat what I said. I do not mean that Mary is the Master's lover. But I say that certain actions do not become Him or her. It is an imprudent action. And an unjust one. Yes. Why such waste? If she wanted to destroy the memories of her past, she could have given that vase and ointment to me. It was at least a pound of pure nard! And of high value. I could have sold it for at least three hundred denarii, as that is the price for nard of that quality. And I could have sold the vase, which was beautiful and precious. I would have given the money to the poor who crowd round us. We never have enough. And those asking for alms tomorrow in Jerusalem will be numberless."

"That is true" say the others assenting. "You could have used a little for the Master and the rest..."

Mary of Magdala seems to be deaf. She continues wiping Jesus' feet with her loose hair that now, at its end, is also heavy with the ointment and darker than on the top of her head. Jesus' feet are smooth and soft in their shade of old ivory, as if they were covered with fresh skin. And Mary puts the sandals on the Christ's feet again, kissing each foot before and after putting the sandal on, deaf to everything that is not her love for Jesus.

Jesus defends her laying His hand on her head bent in the last kiss and saying: "Leave her alone. Why are you annoying and upsetting her? You do not realize what she has done. Mary has accomplished and action that is rightful and good with regard to me. The poor will always be among you. I am about to go away. You will always have them, but you will soon not have me any longer. You will always be able to give alms to the poor. Shortly to Me, to the Son of man among men, it will no longer be possible to give any honor, through the will of men, and because the hour has come. Love is light to her. She feels that I am about to die and she wanted to anticipate the burial anointing for my body. I tell you solemnly that wherever the Good News is proclaimed, this prophetic action of love of hers will be remembered. All over the world. Throughout ages. I wish God would turn every human being into another Mary who does not value things, who entertains no attachment for anything, who does not cherish the least memory of the past, but destroys and treads on everything that is flesh and world, and breaks and spreads herself, as she did with the nard and the alabaster, on her Lord and out of love for Him. Do not weep, Mary. In this hour I repeat to you the words I spoke to Simon the Pharisee and to your sister Martha: "You are forgiven everything, because you have loved completely". You have chosen the better part. And it will not be taken away from you. Go in peace, my kind little sheep found again. Go in peace. The pastures of love shall be your food for ever. Stand up. Kiss also my hands that have absolved and blessed you... How many people these hands of mine have absolved, blessed, cured, assisted! And yet I tell you that the people whom I have assisted are preparing torture for these hands..."

There is deathlike silence in the air sultry with the intense scent. Mary, her loose hair clothing her shoulders and veiling her face, kisses the right hand that Jesus offers her and cannot detach her lips from it...

Martha, deeply moved, approaches her and gathers her loose hair, which she braids caressing her, and then she wipes the tears on her cheeks endeavoring to dry them...No one feels like eating any more... Christ's words make them pensive.

Now, this is the second anointing that Mary Magdalene gave to Jesus and this is even a greater one because it's totally love for him. The first one was a devastation of her past and forgiveness, this is an honoring of him before he dies. There is a part of each of us that loves like this, that knows what is of value and that attends to the reality of the truth of something and is not concerned about what anybody thinks about it or what the world thinks or what anyone comments about it or anybody criticizes it. It's just real. It's just straight up, and even though she knows she's going to get some flack and Judas gives her about as deep a criticism as anyone could give anybody, mean and vicious as he is, she doesn't pay him any mind, doesn't hardly listen to him because she knows he's just a cracker. A little duck quacking in the ditch. She's learned to ignore the comments of men and her attention is on Jesus and her gift is not distracted by anything at all, and Jesus knows the depth of that gift and prophesied for all time that it would always be spoken about her - this gift that she gave anointing Him for his burial. Because he said it was a prophetic gift that she gave because she knows he's going to die and she is pre-anointing him in his body for laying it down.

There is an energy inside of you when you get to this place where you know the good is coming and the good is everything and all the other extraneous things are dropping away, they don't mean anything anymore and you give everything to this most valuable part. That's a couple years' wages for somebody what she used but that doesn't matter to her, not at all. There's a point when you get how important that part of you is, the Christ, the love, the God part of you that everything is abandoned and given away and lost for that one thing of value and Mary's heroism and her courage demonstrate it so everybody could see it. Amazing gift and they're uncomfortable and they're awkward and they don't know what to do about it and some of them are complaining inside of themselves, some of them are criticizing, some of them are, you know, awed and moved by it. And Jesus of course has to explain it to the density of the ego, like what she's doing, and as soon as they get it then they're awed and you know, a couple of them are still upset.

But the true meaning is given by the Christ not by your head and not by your history. Like your remembrance of how things are done doesn't make sense of things. Your memory of your experience of how things are done does not make any sense of things. But when Jesus speaks about what it means, then it makes sense. And that's true for us, sometimes you don't know what you're going through and you don't know why and you don't even know how you'll make it through it. You don't even know what the end product's going to be while you're going through it and only Jesus can tell you what this process is or what this condition you're heading to is but He doesn't really tell you until you're almost all the way through it because he doesn't know if you're going to do it. Why should He explain something to you that you're not even sure you're going to do? But He explains her because her gift is total, and this is what I want you to know. A lot of you want an explanation before you're even a quarter way through your process. You want an explanation. You want to get a preview of something you're not even half-in yet and you only want that to, what? Have a comment about it? Or you want to have like an editorial page describing this process you're not even in the middle of yet? When you're about three quarters of the way through a process, you'll find that

Jesus explains it to you and you get the understanding of it because you're already almost busted through but you do not get that in the first half, ever. You know why? Because He's testing your faith, do you have enough faith to continue?

Do you have enough courage to keep going into the unknown? And the unknown is any development you haven't been at yet. That's the unknown. Any height of spiritual awareness that you haven't touched into is going to take courage to jump into that because it is not known, you do not have experience of it, it's beyond you and the only way to get into it is by faith and by courage. You have to walk in to that experience. Many of you still are mad about that, that you don't get the proper preview and of course your rational mind and your arguments, even to me, are that 'If I understood what you were asking me to do, I would definitely do it.' That's what your argument is, I have heard it a number of times even literally. And I have to tell you, where is humility, obedience and faith required when everything is explained to you before you and your ego decide to do something? What need for faith, and humility, and love and obedience if it makes sense to you to do something? Then your ego can grab onto it and decide it understands it and it can decide it's a great thing to do and you'll never learn faith, humility, love or obedience. Those virtues will not be in your vocabulary, you will not know them. And all the time Jesus is saying, 'Well let's go over to this town,' well they don't know what's going to happen there and there's always something happens on the way but they don't know that and they don't know what it is. Maybe there's a leper, maybe there's a robber, maybe there's a woman, maybe there's a Roman soldier they don't know anything and after a while they stop thinking about it, they stop questioning it, they stop worrying about it and they just follow.

Mary Magdalene learned this a long time before everyone else did because her sin was complete, the forgiveness was complete, her humility was complete, and her love was complete. She had no more questions, no more scrutiny no, more equivocating, and worrying and anxious about the different sides you that have to carry, the different things you have to concern yourself with. She wasn't concerned with any of that because Love had consumed her and eaten up her pride and destroyed the sensualness and the selfishness in her being. It was gone, it was gone. It was gone. She gave everything, and then guess what? She was given everything. That's how it works. She didn't give everything to get everything. She gave everything because she just loved, she wasn't looking for reward, she wasn't looking for recognition, it was too much almost that Jesus said she'd be remembered forever for this. That's too much. She just wanted to love Him and anoint His body for the burial. That's all. Very simple. Amazing act of love and super admirable.

You love with calculation, you love with planning, you love with posturing, you love with manipulation, you love with trying to control. You don't love like this yet, not yet. You can see what reward He gave her for that. You can see His touch of forgiveness. He said she was completely forgiven. You guys are forgiven in pieces and parts and in stages. She was completely forgiven. It doesn't have to be that way for you. You could be forgiven completely if you would be completely repentent, and completely humble and you would be forgiven completely. Same, but you control the process and you eke out your development and you tug-of-war for each thing that Jesus wants you to let go of. It's like a little fight on your hands for that little attitude problem, you fight over that one - you want to keep it because you've felt like it's helped you in the past. All those little itsy bitsy gifts that you give don't even amount to this gift that she gave. You know why? Because you're preserving mostly, you're making sure it didn't jostle you or stretch you or take too much out of you to give that much... yet. Managing it, you know? If the ego has to manage it, it's going to contaminate it. You should be learning this by now as many times as I haven't told you that. Have I told you? Once? Or just this is the first time? That could happen, I'm totally open for you to hear me first, at some point.

What a relief it would be for all of you to stop thinking so much. What a relief to just be like a child that just trusts and Jesus says, "Do this," and you do that. Jesus say, "Go faster," and you go faster. Jesus says, "Quiet your mind," and you do it. Jesus says, "Be still, don't worry," and you don't. Wouldn't that be such a breath of fresh air for Jesus, not to have any resistance in you to do anything He would inspire you to do? That's what He would be hoping from the disciples. That they would be that malleable, open, able to be moved around by His word, by His whim, by His love and that you didn't have to like, assent to it every time and go through a process of discussion and debate about whether you're going to just let Him inspire you or not. You'd just do it, because He says to do it, you just do it. You might want to do that with one of His representatives but that's a little stretch for you because it's too human for you, I know. A little bit too human for you. *I'm just as human as you are...* There's such competition in your minds about people, and you as a big person and other people as just other people. So much contrast in your head.

A transformed person's a transformed person. Why don't you be that? Why don't you be that? He wants that, He wants that for you. He'll do that miracle inside of you if you're open, if you're not fighting' Him every second not to change too much that would shock you. And you have to stop worrying, a super bad habit. You have to stop worrying. You have worry like a disease, like it's one of those coughs that never goes away. You have worry as one of your diseases. When are you going to let that go? When are you going to say, "Jesus I worry a lot. I don't like it, it doesn't seem to be helping, and it just makes me fret and it furrows my brow and lines my face. Could you just take that away from me so I could just be at peace? Just take that worry out of me, I don't know how you're going to get it out. I'd like to stop and I'm going to catch myself when I do but could you help me?" Then you could let him do that for you. It's a huge disease in the world. Some of you get A's in worry and you are very proud of the fact that you can worry about everything and you can think about every possibility. It's like you're proud of it. I have to address them all because you're addressing them all. I'm not worried, I just go, I just look at them and go, "This is this and this is this and..." You have a whole list of them and we have to go through every one of them almost every day. There's some worry that we have to go through because you keep generating them. You keep generating worry and Judas is trying to be so helpful, he's so worried that the poor aren't going to get the money he was stealing from them. So worried.

Mary Magdalene's not worried and that's like a super wealthy thing that she just did. That's a monstrous gift. She doesn't care about the money. She doesn't care about that. It's the best thing ever to give that to the best being ever. Just give it to Him. Would you hold back giving a gift to Jesus? Yes, many of you do and you would, and you piece it out in parts and pieces as you control it and manage it. But that's not what she did--she gave everything. Even losing her looks and her hair was falling all over the place, you know, and that's not cool. She didn't care about that and gracefully she just used that, all those massive locks that are falling down as a towel to soak up and dry off the ointment. It wasn't because she wanted to smell nice. See?

You guys are pretty dense. Pretty darn dense. She just wanted some for herself? No. You have something there you can use, you have hair. That can soak up some stuff, so you use it to dry him.

I want you to stop calculating your growth and managing your process so that Jesus can do a miracle with you of moving you along the way He would like to. Not the way you can manage or you can handle it. The way he would like to. Now that's going to be a rollercoaster ride for many of you. But I would like to see that because I think you're tolerating him rather than letting him do what he does well, which is heal you. You're tolerating him and you're piecemealing it when he could do the whole thing, pretty quickly, if you'd stop doing your thing. Like He can heal somebody just by, "Yes," and it's done. But you - you have to make sure you're so difficult that He has to work on you thousands and thousands of hours just to get a little drop of change in you because of your worried mind.

A receptive mind is a different mind. A worried mind is a vigilant security guard. He doesn't need security guards because God makes everything safe. At least we could do something, you know, distracting for right now, is just to thank God for Mary Magdalene. And if we thank God for her maybe we wouldn't be thinking about ourselves for a couple of seconds. Let's do that.

March 6, 2016
Are you willing to let go?

I'm not going to read you anything so I'll save you that problem. The sadness Jesus feels for the people here is really profound and deep because he can heal everything in them. He could straighten everything out for them, he could fix every problem they have, relieve them of every burden that they are carrying, open their sight, heal their wounds, bring them right back into oneness with their creator and for the most part people don't want that and the few that do eke out these deals of a little change for a little grace and a little change for a little grace and a little grace for a little change because as much as your boldness and your adventuresomeness wants Jesus to heal you of these things that trouble you, you are also really attached to who you think you are so that you keep yourself the way you are and you wouldn't be able to allow, haven't so far, allowed much transformation because it's too disturbing to the psyche to have non-familiar things in your being. Like you have to have it a particular way so you feel comfortable or you feel accustomed to yourself and your ego says, "Well that's how you know yourself because you're this way and this way and you have this trait and this trait and you have this struggle and this struggle." And that's how you know yourself and if you didn't have those you really wouldn't know what to do. You wouldn't know who you were.

The fact is you don't anyway because until you get to that God part inside, the soul and God, you and God, you're a character trying to be a particular way that doesn't have anything to do with who you are and mostly forty seven levels of reacting. God says love and you go, 'how much?' God says "completely" and you say, "Well I did a little, didn't I?" And you always have to get credit from the little that you've done and that can only be asked from a place of not changing very much. You can only ask that, "Have I done any changing at all?" from a place of not changing very much at all and I'm not saying you're being willful about this. I think you just don't know that you are. I just think you're not aware of how willful you are attached to what you're used to and even when you're honest you know that what you're used to isn't making you happy and it isn't that deep and it's not that confident in God. It's not that even trusting in God's love, yet.

Jesus said, "Come to me and I'll give you rest to your souls, come to me ye who labor and are heavy laden and I'll give you rest to your souls." Most of you love that statement but you don't want rest to your souls, you want relief while you get to stay the same. You want to be comforted while you don't have to let go of anything. How much you know yourself is in proportion to how much you've let go. Those are a relationship; correlation. How much you know yourself is how much you're willing to let go of who you think you are. Did you forget that in your family you had to brace? Did you forget that you had to interpret the meanness of the parents as love and twist it in your head? Remember that? Did you forget that the way you were treated, you thought was normal? You had to make it seem normal otherwise you'd have to be scared or super angry. You remember all those years of twisting it and twisting it trying to rationalize it, trying to make it look good, trying to make you feel like it was normal? And now you've lost yourself. You don't even know who you are. You're caked over with all those embarrassing deflections and protections and then somebody says, "Well you've got to let go of all that. Those were all your reactions to meanness and lack of love." But your ego goes, "Well I did well with it." Well sure you did. You defended yourself terribly but was it really love? No, not really. Not even hardly, not even a lot. So then you're going to keep all that? You're going to keep all that style of tension and you're going to keep those ways of bolstering up your ego against the thing that was a lie and you're going to keep that and walk into the spiritual life with that and try to keep it?

Jesus is not fooled by these things. Jesus knows clean when it's clean and he knows love when it's clean and pure and he doesn't know this other reactive soup that you bring him. You bring him the reactive soup, like you love me but I want to keep my reactions, you loved me and I want to keep my self-doubt and I want to keep my insecurities and I want to keep my self-hatred and I want you and I, you, Jesus and me to call this 'disciple'.

He said, "Make the tree good and then the fruit will be good." If the tree is evil, the fruit won't be good. If you try to keep all that stuff just because you spent time on it, just because you spent time defending yourself, or bolstering up your ego, you want to keep all that? It was bolstering up against a lie. The lie was that they loved you and the truth was that they didn't know how so all the work you did trying to convince yourself it was love was a lie. They didn't know how. Can't you just accept that? They did not know how and whatever love was a little, it was very, very little if that. Can't you just accept it and can't you walk off, shake the dust off that experience and just go, that was hard...I must have done that to people? I'm going to walk into real love, I'm not going to pretend that all those things I built up mean anything at all, it was all just my wounds defending themselves. I'm going to let it all go, I'm going to find out who I really am from the one that can see me; from Jesus or Mary." They can see you--they know who you are. They're not distracted by all this nonsense that you do and all these defenses that you've accumulated.

All the ego structures that you choose you seem to keep feeding intravenously. You keep feeding them. They want you as you are and they'll do the work if you're willing. If you're willing they'll clean you up but you will be surprised at the sheer volume of things that you're going to have to let go of that are not you. They are not you as a soul, as a being, as a person. They are not you. They're an accumulated crust of layers and layers of reacting; layers and layers of anger, layers of fear; that's what you've done and that's what we've all gone through and the peel back process is quite tough for you. I can see you holding on for dear life any vestiges of the things that you don't even like, trying to pretend those are you; just holding on and holding on. Do you understand that Jesus can't use those things in you? He can't work through them and he can't bless them because they were wrongly acquired. They were evilly acquired, inflicted some on you, and some by you and some at you. Those things are not useful to Jesus. He can't use them. They're not you and they're not real--they're reactions. They're your fears, your anger, and they're not real. I look around and I see that most of you carry a very large percent of those things that you still think are you. He can't use those. In fact, those do not serve God. They serve your ego and they serve your pride and they serve your fear and they can't be blessed. They cannot be blessed. You can't use them. You cannot serve with those. You can only serve when you don't have them or when you forget them.

You can't help and strain all these God energies through that junk and expect the person to respect it. They're not going to respect it because they can see that it's just like them. It's just like them. They do the same thing-- they try to eke out some kind of gift, love, concern for other people through their vast array of self-protected ego and it's going to come out really funny. You guys know so much now. You know all about the reactions, you know all about the ego, you know all about the resistance in the body, you know all about the spirit actually and you keep, keeping it. These things that prevent the spirit of God from moving within you and you keep them. I know, you're probably thinking that you don't do it willfully but I do think it's willful because you've been informed.

From Jesus' perspective he wants you to come into the love. If you really come into the love, these things I'm talking about will start burning, they'll feel seriously uncomfortable and if you stay in that love and then that fire of his will burn off quickly but that's not what you do, you know. I've seen you. You tough in, so powerful, and then so connected and you feel really good about it and then you run away to try to pre-serve and to re-accumulate the things that you're used to instead of staying in the fire until they're burned, until they're gone, dissolved. Have you ever seen paper burn in the fire? I mean, it turns into like almost nothing, maybe like a cinder of an ash goes away but it turns into nothing, dissolves. That's what happens to your problems when you're near Jesus or Mary.

In a way, it's very hard for me to rationalize how you'd want to keep these problems when you have been shown by some experience and told over and over again how Jesus would take them from you. He would just burn them up, dissolve them, just lift them right out of you, anytime you're ready. Any moment, any second you're ready, he's going to do that and you have a lot of grace to be able to do that and you've been more informed than other people on how that process works and how necessary it is. So, I can conclude that you don't want to do it because you haven't and I can conclude that you do know how because I've told you how and I can conclude that you're not ready to do it yet because you haven't and I guess you're afraid. I guess you're afraid of what you'll turn into if you don't have those things. Like, so dead set on thinking you know who you are that you wouldn't be able to let them go but I know you don't know who you are because who you are doesn't have a problem. I know who you are doesn't have a disconnection or a worry or a fear or an anger or a doubt or a problem. I know that so when I see you trying to convince everyone that you have those things that you're really not. I know you don't know who you are.

So, what are we going to do? How are you going to help me understand you? Why would you do that? How do I get to understand this? I mean I know what you're doing but how are you going to help me help you? Should I just accept it-- that you think you're fine? I should just accept that you're fine even though I can see you're not your soul yet? Should I just accept that? Well my integrity wouldn't allow me to use you. I mean, it just wouldn't because I have standards. At the same time, I could, if that's like a consensus in you that I have to accept you because you have to have your problems then I would accept that. I just wouldn't be able to use you. I can still love you but I wouldn't be able to use you because I know that if I gave you something to do you'd smear your problems all over it and then that wouldn't feel good to me. It wouldn't feel like you're giving a pure gift if you smeared your problems all over the thing you were serving. You see what I mean?

So, I mean, it's a super choice on your part to keep all that stuff or to suffer the unknowing, going into the cloud of unknowing, to find out who you are but you'd have to let go of all the things you think you are to go into that cloud and the cloud is God. In the unknowing is grace. In the knowing you stay out of the cloud, and you stay out of the experience. The more you think you know, the less you're going to find out. This is the path I'm talking about. It's not a path because you know exactly where you're going. No, it's a path because you're being led to something you haven't experienced yet, that's what a path is and you forgot. You forgot your Creator, you really did and we all did. We really did. We got distracted.

Let's say you had a paragraph of words and four of them were Jesus' words and you're going to say the whole paragraph because that's what you do, you say the whole paragraph but every time you hit one of the four words that are his, it lights up and it has a little more juice to it and you're bound and determined to do the whole paragraph of course and he just has to juice those four that are his. That's what you're like right now. That's kind of real, isn't it? Like some things you say are just guided, they're just real, they're connected to soul, they're connected to love but the rest is just smearing your problems around so you can be familiar with them so you can keep them so that it looks like you. He's not going to juice those. He's only going to juice those ones that are like him, those ones that are from him, those ones that have the wisdom of God in them.

I don't know if that helps you or makes you feel worse. Feeling worse is a reaction, ok? Like, you have a problem, go fix it. If you need help, go get the help. Reacting is just wasting time. It's wasting time. Back to what you want, when I see the barrage of words and most of them are just self-serving or self-adulating or self-critical or backing people off because you really have a lot of problems and you don't want them to even bother you or expect anything from you, you know how you use words as a weapon? When I hear that I know that Jesus hasn't inspired any of those words. Those are not the words of truth, that's not the word of God coming through you, that's not the word of love or life. It's not vital coming through you; it's just words of garbage coming through you. You're the manager of that. You're the chooser of that, that's what you want? You want to serve that well? That most of what you say doesn't ennoble mankind, doesn't raise anyone up, doesn't heal anybody, doesn't provide a lighted tunnel through a dark place for somebody, you see but that's what Jesus wants for you. He wants you to be one of those people that inspire, one of those people that speaks the truth, one of those people that can be counted on to always give and always love and always serve and while you have this saddled thing that you're just you with your problems and you can't be changed, you can only be minorly changed and maybe like four percent change over the next quarter because you have an economic problem, you know you have economic goals, four percent change over the next quarter. You know, that's ninety-six percent not changed.

Okay, ninety-two the next quarter after that. Do the math and in a year you'll be at eighty-two or eighty-four. Why? Why? Why are you eking out the gift of your garbage? That's a gift to Jesus, to give your sins as your gift, that's the only gift a human can give, do you understand, in the beginning? You can only give your sins. You don't have much else and as those are given goodness enters you. You have to first give your garbage for you to be filled, all of it, all of it. I know, we get...I typically do, but I haven't seen much sign of it lately but I'll get you into service as soon as there is the majority of you, of yourself, that looks like you want to give. You know before its grace, really, because you don't deserve it yet, you're not there yet but as you start giving you might get there. You might get hooked on it, you might like it so we give it to you a little ahead of time.

That's why some of you with your great critical minds can look at a minister and go, "Well they don't seem like they have it together." Well no, some of them don't but they're getting the grace to be able to do it. You could at least pray for them instead of criticizing them. Pray for them.

So, I don't even know what to do. I'm at a loss, I see what I see, I have to do what I have to do. I have to be obedient. I can only give where there is a vacuum or an opening. I can't squeeze spirituality into a contented reaction. I can't do it, it won't happen, it won't let me. You have to make room. You have to dump everything that you think you know because in my estimation you don't know it and you know, these are the kind of sermons that feel great, I know but you could ask Jesus what's the truth about this instead of listening to me you know, harangue you. You could ask Jesus what's the truth about this. *Am I really holding on to everything that I can scrape together of what I used to know about me or am I willing to let it all go? Jesus, what do you think?* I mean he's up there yakking you know. *I want to know it from you directly. Am I holding on or am I letting go? Have I given you everything? Or, am I preserving myself?* Ask him. See what he says. I may be talking to the wrong crowd. It could happen. I mean some of you might be this huge sainted life happening and I'm missing you. I might be missing you. Check it out.

Ask him what you're capable of versus this snail crossing the sidewalk thing. Ask him what He thinks you're capable of and then line yourself up with it. Line yourself up with it. Are you capable of letting go? Really? I gave you a bunch of things to ask in guidance. We'll see what happens.

March 13, 2016
The Mind of Christ

From Philippians Chapters 1 and 2

Imitating Christ's Humility

If then there is any consolation in Christ Jesus, any comfort of love, any sharing in the Spirit, any compassion and sympathy, make my joy complete; be of the same mind, having the same love, being in full accord and of one mind. Do nothing from selfish ambition or conceit, but in humility regard others as better than yourselves. Let each of you look not to your own interests, but look first to the interests of others. Let this mind be in you which was also in Christ Jesus, who being in the form of God, did not think being equal with God to be robbery, but made himself without reputation taking the form of a servant, being born in human likeness, And being found in human form, he humbled himself and became obedient to the point of death – even death on a cross.
Therefore God also highly exalted him and gave him the name above every name, so that at the name of Jesus every knee should bow, in heaven, on earth and under the earth, And every tongue must confess that the Lord Jesus Christ is in the glory of God the Father.

Shining as Lights in the World

Therefore, my beloved, just as you have always obeyed me, not only in my presence, but much more now in my absence, work out your own salvation with fear and trembling; for it is God who is at work in you, enabling you, both to will and to act for God's good pleasure.

Do all things without murmuring and arguing, so that you may be blameless and innocent, children of God without blemish in the midst of a crooked and perverse generation in which you shine like stars in the worlds. It is by your holding fast to the word of life that I can boast on the day of Christ that I did not turn in vain or labor in vain. But even if my blood has to be shed as a part of your own sacrifice and offering, which is your faith, I am still happy and rejoice with all of you – and in the same way you also must be happy and rejoice with me.

Timothy and Epaphroditus

I hope in the Lord Jesus, to send Timothy to you soon, so that I may be comforted when I know how you are. I have no one like him who will be genuinely concerned for your welfare. All of them are seeking their own interests, not those of Jesus Christ. But Timothy's worth you know, how like a son with a father he has served with me in the work of the Gospel. I hope therefore to send him as soon as I see how things go with me, and I trust in the Lord that I will also come soon.

Still, I think it necessary to send to you Epaphroditus – my brother and co-worker and fellow soldier, your messenger and minister to my need; for he has been longing for all of you and has been distressed because you heard that he was ill. He was indeed so ill that he nearly died. But God had mercy on him and not only on him but on me also, so that I would not have one sorrow after another. I am the more eager to send him, therefore, in order that you may rejoice at seeing him again, and that I may be less anxious. Welcome him then in the Lord with all joy, and honor such people because he came close to death for the work of Christ, risking his life to make up for those services that you could not give me.

Finally, my brothers and sisters, rejoice in the Lord. Breaking with the past to write the same things to you is not troublesome to me, and for you it is a safeguard.

Beware of the dogs, beware of the evil workers, beware of those who mutilate the flesh! For it is we who are the circumcision, who worship in the Spirit of God and boast in Christ Jesus and have no confidence in the flesh – even though I, too, have reason for confidence in the flesh.

If anyone else has reason to be confident in the flesh, I have more; circumcised on the eighth day, a member of the people of Israel, of the tribe of Benjamin, a Hebrew born of Hebrews, as to the law, a Pharisee, as to zeal, a persecutor of the church, as to righteousness under the law, blameless. Yet whatever gains I had, these I have come to regard as loss because of Christ. More than that, I regard everything as dung because of the supreme advantage of knowing Christ Jesus my Lord. For his sake I have suffered the loss of all things, in order that I may gain Christ and be found in him, not having a righteousness of my own that comes from the law, but one that comes through faith in Christ, the righteousness from God based on faith. I want to know Christ and the power of his resurrection and the sharing of his sufferings by becoming like him in his death, if somehow I may attain the resurrection from the dead.

Pressing toward the Goal

Not that I have already obtained this, or have already reached perfection by my own efforts, the perfection that comes from the law, but I want only the perfection that comes through faith in Jesus Christ. Beloved, I do not consider that I have made it my own, but this one thing I do, forgetting what lies behind and straining forward to what lies ahead, I press on toward the goal for the prize of the high calling of God in Christ Jesus. Let those of us who are perfect be of the same mind, and if you think differently about anything, this too God will reveal to you. Only let us continue on the road that has brought us to where we are.

Brothers and sisters, be followers together of me, and observe those who live according to the example you have in us. For many live as enemies of the cross of Christ; I have often told you of them, and now I tell you even with tears. Their end is destruction; their god is the belly; and their glory is in their shame; their minds are set on earthly things. But our conversation is in heaven, and it is from there that we are expecting the Savior, the Lord Jesus Christ. He will change our vile body, that it may be fashioned like his glorious body, by the power that also enables him to subdue all things to himself.

Therefore, my brothers and sisters whom I love and long for, my joy and crown, stand firm in the Lord in this way, my beloved.

You are confronted every day with choices: the choice to attend to the material world, to attend to the cares of life or to attend to the work of God, the service to Christ. I know it is split in your mind because you don't have that sense of heaven and earth yet, where everything you do is a heavenly act. You don't have that. You have divided it up and you have separated it out and you don't invite God into the physical world very well because you think that is your domain. So you do it yourself in those areas.

So here is Paul, listing the perfect thing that he had done, because he was born the first male dedicated to the Lord. He is a Pharisee, he is a Rabbi, and he was perfect under the law. He did everything he was supposed to do. He trained with Gamaliel who was his teacher. He was righteous in every way in an outer way. He considers that nothing. I know he had help considering it nothing. He didn't come on that by himself. Jesus got a hold of him and threw him off the horse and woke him up to something much bigger than what he was planning on doing so that he could count that former life as history, over, completed, finished, and done.

He did under the Law all one could do and still, not a transformed person. He wasn't transformed until grace hit him, until faith started to light up inside of him. Until he had a real experience, he didn't change. He was pompously righteous, he was viciously mean, and he was on his cause. He was persecuting and doing bad things, karmically, but righteous things according to the Jews.

And that is like you. You do your thing, you raise your kids, you go to your jobs, you make your money, you pay your bills, you occasionally wash your car, you do things and you take care of business and that's it, right? That's it. But pressing on to the high mark of the high calling of Christ is a whole different level. That is a whole different level.

What's the high calling of Christ? It is that you become another Christ--that you become a lighted being and that light oozes out of you in lighted thought and loving thoughts. Not sad, worried, moody thoughts--those are not light, those are not love. You press on to something much higher than that--that the Mind of Christ be in you. What does that look like? That is a loving mind. That is a helpful mind. For a minute, I thought John had stolen my sermon, because that is the energy. You could be so wrapped up in yourself or you could help. You could become lined up with the Christ Mind and could start to be of service and start to figure out how God wants to use you. You can't think it through, you have to let it happen. It's interesting what Paul had to say to put a wedge in people's consciousness that Jesus did not think it thievery to have God's Mind. He wasn't stealing it presumptively. It was right that human beings have God's Mind, the Mind of Christ.

Now how do you have that Mind? You think like Christ. How does Christ think? He helps, he prays, he lifts, he unburdens, he feeds, he clothes, he does the things that a servant of God does. He makes things better. Even if it's something small, he sweeps something, even if you help somebody, even if you use your energy compassionately, you are entering into the Mind of Christ.

It's a pretty special evaluation to look and see what they would write about you if you died today. What would they write about you? "Well I worried a lot and I improved a little," is that what they would write? "I haven't served yet much but I am thinking about it." Is that what they would write? I am actually thinking about serving now, I am leaning in the direction of giving of myself that really hasn't occurred to me," and that's what they write on your stone. How about, "you burned yourself on the fire altar in service and you gave everything that you could. You didn't have a great effect but you that's what you did. You burned yourself in flame for God." Now you can't think about the results because it depends on who you're with and where you're at and whether the people respond to you or not. That doesn't really matter. The thing is what your heart is doing.

Some of you are looking ahead to the time when you could really be influential, meanwhile you're not. The time when you could really kick it in, but meanwhile, you haven't, where you could really let go, but up to now, not so. Or you really wouldn't be self-concerned anymore but that hasn't happened. Or you wouldn't preserve anything because you have to have time for your moods. But that hasn't happened yet. Now Paul has been serving relentlessly across Asia, Asia Minor and all that, for years when he is talking like this. He has probably been imprisoned four times, he has been shipwrecked a couple of times, he's been beaten and stoned 6 times and he's a veteran. He is a veteran disciple. He is just good at it. Nothing stops him and Jesus doesn't let anybody kill him yet. No matter what they try to do, he doesn't get killed because he's given his life over. He has given himself completely so Jesus has use for him, in this massive ministry that he does. He spreads the gospel to the gentiles, more than anyone else ever did. It is just because he has not thought it robbery to have the Christ Mind. Because God's zeal filled him and he let it. He let it move. Actually the apostles weren't nearly as successful in spreading the gospel as he was. It is sad but it's the truth. He called himself an apostle by adoption because he didn't meet Jesus, he heard about him and he was met by Jesus after Jesus left. Jesus rounded him up, you could say, he rounded him up, put a bridle on him and a saddle and said you are the work horse and I'm going to use you. And he said, "Fine, my life sucked up until now."

You know, when something beautiful happens, you see that everything else pales and you are willing to let it go. You just are. And that may not have happened to you yet. Things haven't paled for you yet for you to let go to find them just not meaningful anymore. So, he knows the body is just not that important but the spirit is. He has already been almost killed, like 5 or 6 times. He knows that that is just trivial. So, what should we take away from this reading about Paul? That some people are really good at what they do and they are very convinced about Jesus and there is not a doubt in their mind and not one thing that they do is selfish anymore. It's just not. That is out to lunch, it's gone. Now, that would be cool for you, all of you, to get to the place where not one thing that you do is selfish anymore. That whatever joys you have, you are being obedient, that whatever goodness you are going through it's because God is asking you to do that. Whatever you are taking care of with yourself is because you are under obedience. If you have to buy a new dress or a new outfit, you go do that. If you have to go rest, you go rest because you are being told to do it. You are not thinking it through selfishly, you are just obedient and you are trusting. You are trusting that

God will take care of you. So you are under orders that would be really good.

Most of you have places where you will serve and the rest of the bulk of the time is pretty much your own thing, doing your own thing. The question for you, how can Christ use me? That is what you should be asking. Every moment ask, "How can Christ use me, now?" You can even ask, "How can Christ use this mood I am in?" "How can Christ use this doubt I am going through?" And fix it. Fix it so you can become like Him, you can have His Mind. Let this Mind be in you that was also in Christ Jesus. Do you really need your own private little mind? It hasn't done any good, hardly, it hasn't really helped.

March 20, 2016

The Gospel as Revealed to Me, Chapter 470. A lesson on marriage to a mother-in-law who is discontent with her daughter-in-law.

Jesus smiles a quiet pitiful smile for the jealous old woman. But, being as kind as ever, He does not reproach her. He feels pity for the suffering mother and tries to cure her. He lays His hand on her shoulder as if He wanted to guide her, because she is blinded by tears, perhaps to make her feel, through His contact, so much love that she may be comforted and cured, and He says to her:

"Mother, and is it not right that it is so? Your husband did so with you, and his mother did not lose him, as you say and think, but she felt that he belonged less to her because your husband divided his love between his mother and you. And your husband's father, in his turn, stopped belonging completely to his mother, to love the mother of his children. And so on from generation to generation, going back in time to Eve: the first mother who saw her children divide with their wives the love which they previously had exclusively for their parents. But does Genesis not say: "This at last is bone from my bones and flesh from my flesh... This is why a man will leave his father and mother and will join himself to his wife and they will become one body."

You may object: "It was the word of a man." Yes, but of what man? He was in the state of innocence and grace. He thus reflected without any shadow the wisdom which had created him and he was aware of its truth. Through grace and his innocence he possessed also the other gifts of God in full measure. As his senses were subdued to his reason, his mind was not obscured by the fumes of concupiscence. And because science was proportionate to his state, he spoke words of truth. So he was a prophet. Because you know that prophet means a person who speaks in the name of another person. And as true prophets always speak of matters concerning the spirit and the future, even if relating apparently to the present time and the body - because in the sins of the flesh and in the facts of the present time are the seeds of future punishments, or facts of the future have roots in ancient events: for instance the coming of the Savior originates from Adam's sin, and the punishments of Israel, foretold by the prophets, were brought about by the behavior of Israel - so He who urges their lips to speak things of the spirit can but be the eternal spirit who sees everything in an eternal present. And the eternal spirit speaks through saints, because he cannot dwell in sinners. Adam was a saint, because justice was complete in him and every virtue was present in him, because God had instilled the fullness of His gifts into His creature. Man has to work hard now, to attain justice and possess virtues, because the incentives of evil are in him. But such incentives were not in Adam, on the contrary grace made him little inferior to God his creator. So his lips spoke words of grace. And this is a truthful word: "A man will leave his father and mother for a woman and he will join himself to his wife and they will become one body". And it is so absolutely true, that the most good Lord in order to comfort mothers and fathers included the fourth Commandment in the Law: "Honor your father and your mother". A commandment that does not end with the marriage of man, but lasts beyond marriage. Previously good people instinctively honored their relatives also after they left them to set up a new family. Since Moses it is an obligation of Law. And the purpose of it is to mitigate the grief of parents who were too often forgotten by their children after they got married. But the Law has not cancelled the prophetic words of Adam: "Man will leave his father and mother for his wife." They were just words and they are still valid. They reflected the thought of God. And the thought of God is immutable because it is perfect. So, mother, you must accept without selfishness the love of your son for his wife. And you will be holy as well. On the other hand, every sacrifice is compensated on the Earth. Is it not pleasant for you to kiss your grandchildren, the children of your son? And will the evening of your life not be peaceful and your last sleep placid with the delicate love of a daughter near you, to take the place of those daughters who are no longer in your house?..."

It's kind of seriously dismaying to the Apostles that the morning before, there was so much celebration and honoring and praising for Jesus for all the good things he did. There were thousands of things that he did. Thousands of healings and amazing teachings that they never heard before from any Rabbi and it was worthy of every praise and the praise was honest. The praise was real, and healings and massive changes of a person's life by contact with him and as it usually is with people, they have a very short memory and their good feelings are so short lived. They have good feelings the one day and a bad mood the next. That's pretty much most people and for them to stay consistent day to day in the praise or stay consistent in the gratitude day to day--it's really not the human lot to be able to be that consistent. They're really fickle and such is this for these people who were personally affected by him or personally healed by him or taught by him or changed by his words and if they heard his words, they were moved by it. Most people who heard him were moved by it and changed by it—the ones who weren't were out to trap him in something that they were comparing to the Rabbi or something.

Jesus, he's not fooled by the praise of all. He is not even remotely moved by it in some ways because he knows what he's headed for and he knows this is like the eruption of emotion before the true feelings come out, which is to kill him and to get rid of him because he's trouble. He's going to take down all of the routines, all the rules and regulations of the temple that were simply hypocrisy and meanness and corruption, like he says.

For him to persist or for them to allow him to persist, their whole structure of what they think is righteous is going to crash. They don't understand that it's going to crash anyway, but to get rid of him, they get to keep their traditions. To get rid of him, they get to keep their little programs and systems in place. They get to keep the mercantile people outside the temple, getting the money, and their feeding frenzy to give to the priests and the Rabbis because they get kickbacks. Everybody gets kickbacks on all those deals for pigeons and lambs. There's all the tips and stuff that the Rabbis get. It's all corruption so that they can buy their garments, they can deck out their houses. Jesus knows that and they know that and they don't want that structure destroyed. Too many deals, too many traditions, too many set in their ways, too many things jostled by Jesus who just is not going to tolerate or support any of those deals or any of that structure because it is against God. It's against love.

As those structures get created, they set up positions of lowly and highly, privileged and unprivileged. Those are against God. They're against love and compassion and thus, they are corrupt. The more you do that, the worse it gets to the point where they reject their own Messiah that they have been waiting for for two thousand years. When you look at your life, you have these moments of exalted feelings of love for God and praise for the beauty of the healings that happen and the graces that come down upon you and then the next minute you're in a bad mood. You are sniping at somebody in your head about something that they should have taken care of, or should have done, or should have been thoughtful of you and you're the same kind of fickleness as these people were. In a way, you are your humanity, you're one of humanity and Jesus' tears are real and copious and in his mercy, which is refused, then the punishment comes because that's the nature of God. God's mercy can take you out of the mud and turn you into an angel, but your refusal makes the punishment come where you have to pay for your sins. That's what happened to the Jews and that's forever. They get to pay forever, as long as they want to stay pridefully Jewish, they're going to pay forever.

As soon as they can humble themselves and accept the Christ, then they will be forgiven, but that would take quite a blow to the big ego there, to their pride. What are the chances? Very little that that will happen. They're super entrenched in their pride, even to this day. They're still waiting for the Messiah, which means that they denied that he came, they even lied about it, that he didn't really come, that's what they say. This is the thing about sin. If you are entrenched in sin and you love sin and you do sin and you go back to sin, God's mercy can't be with you, only the punishment can. That is what you pay. You end up paying for that and there's Jesus pronouncing the verdict upon the city, the one city that should have been the one to be able to understand him. It was the main city that rejected him, so the curse of God is upon it. It would be good (just as a small interior personal practice) to remember what you're jubilant about, to remember what your happy about and remember what you praise and remember what your grateful for, that you hold that day to day, that you don't let it slip and slide, and that would show your consistency and that would show a certain kind of courage and a certain kind of stability in your discipleship that you wouldn't just fall off you know, one thing to the next thing day to day. It would show gratitude and reverence for the Christ, who actually blessed you in many ways with many graces and you would not forget that. You wouldn't be able to forget. But when you forget, the Law's activated and the justice of

God comes upon you. And then when you remember the graces, the Law's loosened and softened and grace comes in and helps you with things that you might have had to pay severely for because that's what the love does--it forgives and it softens and it loosens things and it smoothes things over and lifts you up out of things. But when you forget, then you're back in the Law getting slapped around by your own consciousness.

As soon as you forget about God, you're doing it on your own, so now you're under the law again. Then justice is part of the law, it is. You can't get around that. You can have what you want and then you pay. You know how that is--you can indulge a moment and then suffer. You've done that thousands of times--you indulge yourself a couple of times then you suffer for days because you enlisted the Law and the Law has justice and God in it. Do something selfish, you're going to pay. You didn't think of that when you're selfish, but you should think of that when you're selfish, you'll pay, because you're not under trust anymore or grace or faith or submission to God or surrender to his will, you're doing your own thing. So why wouldn't you pay for that? It's like the Jews are going to pay and they've been paying for 2000 years and they are still going to pay, because the justice of God was unleashed by their lack of gratitude for the Messiah being sent to them and then the gentiles got the gift. They're the ones that received the gift because their heart could feel it. Their heart could open and be grateful for it.

The ones who were humble enough to know that they didn't own the Messiah, were the ones who received the Messiah and the ones who were pompous enough to think that they could own it and tell it what to do, lost it completely. They lost it. We forget that humility is the fulcrum that takes you out of your humanity into your divinity. We forget that. You want to stay human? Don't use humility, because it will keep you from being human. You'll become divine. You want to stay human? Don't do humility, because the power of God flows into a humble person and divinizes you, sanctifies you and you're more than you were and you're more than that hunk of flesh in seconds. I don't think I have ever been happy about Palm Sunday, ever, not because I don't like the celebration. It's just that I always saw it as phony and false and I still do. Because the celebration should stick, and when a celebration doesn't' stick, it isn't deep and it isn't real and it doesn't last. When gratitude is whether the sun is shining or not, that is not a deep gratitude. That's not real gratitude. That's not all the way through the cells. That's just fickle because the sun's out that particular day.

When the masses get together in a mob, they are stupider than they are individually, as individuals. When you get a mob in a celebration, half of them don't know what they are celebrating, but they are all doing it together because it's frenzy, it's a frenzy. But is it personal? We don't know what the frenzy is about. Mobs are stupider than individuals, they are denser and they are more malleable and more easily influenced because it's a mob. That's why it's not that trustworthy. But Jesus' real feelings are there as just weeping. That's what you need to take away from the scene that he is weeping over the opportunity lost by a vast portion of people. That same weeping is for parts of you that just are gnarly and they do their own thing and they like it their way and they think they're right and they think that they prefer it. Jesus is weeping over those parts in you. Think of it that way--I think it's better. Those parts that think you know that are attached to what you think you want, like have a really strong opinion about things, he's weeping over that. Because those are the parts where redemption hasn't entered yet, because humility hasn't happened yet, because you know you're humble when you realize that you're getting help. When you think you're doing it yourself, you're never humble.

When you think you can figure it out own there's no humility there. But when you're humble and you really need the help and you know you're getting it, and then the grace comes in. That's when the grace hits you. That's when gratitude starts to flower in your being, because something bigger than you is happening and helping you. That praise is real and there were people who were justly needing to praise him for all the gifts that they were given and some were faithful. But in the mob scene, everybody goes crazy. Everybody goes crazy. He warned the apostles that it would turn into a frenzy and they would panic and run--his own apostles--and they did run. Even *they* couldn't stay stable in the middle of the crazy frenzy of the mobs. They couldn't keep it together and they had been with him every day, 24/7 for three years. They couldn't keep it together, and you are strong? You're the strong ones compared to them? They weren't strong when the test came. You haven't even been slightly tested in comparison. That's where humility should kick in. If they couldn't do it, how could you? So that should goad you into getting much closer and cutting out all of your negative slump things that you go through. That you just don't go there anymore, just to get strong, just to become somewhat strong. They were shocked that he was weeping. Even that was shocking after so much celebration. Why is he weeping? They couldn't understand it. It's hard to understand weeping when the sight is clear.

Sometimes you make decisions that are for your comfort. That makes me very sad because in your comfort, you have just chosen weakness. That is liable to take you away from Jesus and that makes me sad. In the moment, you're not worried about it. In the moment, you don't think it's a problem, but I do. I do. Because the ramifications of those kinds of decisions--if you amp up the test a little bit, will take you out and how can you predict when a test won't be amped up for you? How can you predict when a temptation will hit you hard versus easy? You can't. So when you make those kind of decisions that you want, a kind of a pleasant journey into selfishness, I am sad for you, because you are not practicing being strong. You definitely aren't. So if a test gets stronger, you will not make it and he's weeping over that too. He is weeping over all the disciples that he made and all the healings that he did, which are going to show absolutely no gratitude in the next 3 days. You don't think that's sad? You should think that's sad.

April 3, 2016
Keeping Faith When Things are Hard

The Gospel as Revealed to Me, Chapter 616. The morning of the Resurrection. Mary's prayer.

"Abraham, the road is farther down. Why are you climbing up, going the long way round, on this impracticable path?" says one of Engedi, warning the old head of the synagogue.

"Because I have to show something to the Master and ask Him to do one thing more, to be added to the great gifts He has already granted us. But if you are tired, go home, or wait for me here. I will go by myself" replies the old man, who plods on panting, along the difficult steep path.

"Oh! no! We will come with you. But it grieves us to see you tire so. You are breathless..."

"Oh! it is not the path!... It is something else! It is a sword piercing my heart... and it is hope swelling it. Come, my children, and you will see how much grief there was in the heart of the man who relieved all your sorrows! How much... not despair, certainly not, but... he who always told you to hope in the Lord Who can do everything, realized he could not possibly expect to have joy any more... I taught you to believe in the Messiah... Do you remember when I used to speak of Him without any fear, when I could do so without harming Him? And you would say to me: "What about Herod's slaughter?" Yes. It was a sore thorn in my heart! But I clung to hope with my whole being... I used to say: "If God sent His star to three men, who were not even from Israel, to invite them to worship the Child Messiah, and He led them by it to the poor house unknown to the rabbis of Israel, to the princes of priests and scribes, if in a dream He informed them not to go back to Herod, in order to save the Child, is it possible that, even with greater power, He did not inform His *father and Mother to flee taking the hope of God and of man to a safe place?" And my faith in His safety grew stronger and was attacked in vain by human doubt and the words of other people And when... and when the deepest grief for a father seized me when I had to take a living being to the sepulcher and say to him: "Remain here as long as your life lasts... and consider that if the desire for your mother's caresses or any other reason should urge you towards the town, I would have to curse you and be the first to strike you and relegate you where not even my most desolate love could relieve you," when I had to do that... I had to cling even more to my faith in God, the Savior of His Savior, and say to myself and to my son... to my leprous son... see?... leprous... : "Let us bow our heads to the will of the Lord and believe in His Messiah! I Abraham... you Isaac, immolated by disease, not by fire, let us offer our sorrow to have a miracle And every month, at each new moon, when I came here secretly, laden with foodstuffs... clothes... love... which I had to leave far from my son... because I had to come back to you... my children... to my blind wife, to my feeble-minded wife, whom dreadful grief had made blind and dull... and I had to come back to my childless home... without the peace of reciprocal conscious love... and to my synagogue to speak to you of God of His wonders... of the beautiful things He spread in the universe and I could see with my eyes the corroded sight of my son... whom I could not even defend when I heard people speak ill of him, saying that he was an ungrateful son, or a criminal who had run away from home... and every month, when making this pilgrimage to the sepulcher of my living son, as I was saying, I used to repeat to him, to encourage him: "The Messiah is on the earth. He will come. He will cure you Last year at Passover, when I was looking for You in Jerusalem, during the short time that I was away from my blind wife, I was told: "He really exists. He was here yesterday. He cured also some lepers. He is going round the whole of Palestine curing, comforting, teaching". Oh! I came back so quickly that I looked like a young man going to a wedding! I did not even stop at Engedi, but I came here and I called my son, my boy, my dying seed, and I said to him: "He will come!". Lord... You have done all sorts of good to our town. You are going away, but there are no sick people left... You have blessed even our trees and animals... And will You not... You have already cured my wife... but will You not have mercy on the fruit of her womb?... A son to a mother! Give back a son to his mother, You, the perfect Son of the Mother of all graces! In the name of Your Mother have mercy on me, on us!....."*

Everybody is weeping with the old man who has spoken with such powerful and heart-rending feelings...

And Jesus clasps him in His arms, while he is sobbing, and He says to him: "Do not weep any more! Let us go to your Elisha. Your faith, justice and hope deserve that and much more. Do not weep, father! Do not let us delay any longer from freeing a man from such horror."

"The moon is setting. The road is a difficult one. Could we not wait until dawn?" say some people.

"No. There are many resinous plants here around us. Pick some branches, light them and let us go" orders Jesus.

They climb up a narrow troublesome path; it looks like the dried bed of alluvial water. The reddish smoky torches crackle spreading a strong smell of resins through the air.

A cave with a narrow opening, almost hidden by thick bushes which have grown near the edges of a spring, appears beyond a narrow tableland split in the middle by a crevice into which flows the water of the spring.

"Elisha has been there, for years... awaiting death or the grace of God..." says the old man in a low voice, pointing at the cavern.

"Call your son. Console him. Tell him not to be afraid, to have faith."

And Abraham shouts in a loud voice: "Elisha! Elisha! Son!" and he repeats his cry, trembling with fear because there is no reply.

"Is he perhaps dead?" some ask.

"No. Dead, just now, no! At the end of his torture! With no joy, no! Oh! my boy!" moans the father... "Do not weep. Call him again."

"Elisha! Elisha! Why are you not answering your..."

"Father! Father! Why have you come at this unusual time? Is mother perhaps dead, and you have come to..." the voice, which was previously far, has come nearer, and a specter moves the branches concealing the entrance; a horrible specter, a half-naked corroded skeleton... who seeing so many people with torches and sticks, imagines I wonder what, and withdraws shouting: "Father, why have you betrayed me? I have never left this place... Why have you brought people to stone me?!" The voice moves away and only the undulating branches are left to remind people of the apparition.

"Comfort him! Tell him that the Savior is here!" urges Jesus.

But the old man has no strength left... He weeps desolately...

Jesus then speaks: "Son of Abraham and of the Father in Heaven, listen. What your just father prophesied, is now being accomplished. The Savior is here and your friends of Engedi are with Him and the disciples of the Messiah have come to rejoice at your resurrection. Come and be not afraid! Come as far as the crevice, and I will come, too, and I will touch you, and you will be cleansed. Do not be afraid, come to the Lord Who loves you!"

The branches are shifted once again and the frightened leper looks out. He looks at Jesus, a white figure walking on the grass of the tableland and stopping at the edge of the crevice... He looks at the others... and especially at his father who appears to be fascinated and follows Jesus with his arms stretched out and his eyes staring at the face of his leprous son. He is reassured and comes forward. He walks with a limp, because of the sores on his feet... he stretches out his *arms with their corroded hands... He comes before Jesus... He looks at Him... And Jesus holds out His beautiful hands, He raises His eyes to Heaven, He gathers, He seems to be gathering within Himself all the light of the infinite stars, shedding its pure brightness on the impure, putrid, corroded flesh that looks even more dreadful in the red light of the burning branches, which people are waving to give more light.*

Jesus leans over the crevice, with the tips of His fingers He touches the tips of the leprous fingers and says: "I want it!" with such a beautiful smile that it cannot be described. He repeats: "I want it!" twice more. He prays and commands with that word...

He takes one step back opening His arms crosswise and says: "And when you have been cleansed preach the Lord, because you belong to Him. Remember that God loved you so that you might be a good Israelite and a good son. Get married and bring your children up for the Lord. Your very bitter bitterness has been cancelled. Bless the Lord and be happy!"

He then turns round and says: "You with torches, come forward and see what the Lord can do for those who deserve it."

He lowers His arms, as open and covered by the mantle they prevented people from seeing the leper, and He moves aside.

The first cry is from the old man kneeling behind Jesus: "Son! Son! You are as handsome as when you were twenty years old. And just as healthy! Handsome, oh! You are more handsome now!... Oh! A board, a branch, something, that I may come to you!" and he is on the point of rushing forward.

But Jesus holds him back: "No! Joy must not make you infringe the Law. He is to be purified first. Look at him! Kiss him with your eyes and with your heart, but be strong now as you have been for so many years. And be happy..."

In fact this is a complete miracle. It not only cured, but it restored what had been destroyed by disease, and the man, about forty years old, is as whole as if he had not suffered from any disease; he is only very thin, which gives him an ascetic fineness, which is not common but supernatural. He waves his hands, kneels down and blesses... he does not know what to do to tell Jesus that he thanks Him. At last he sees some flowers among the grass, he picks them, kisses them and throws them beyond the crevice at the Savior's feet.

"Let us go! You people of Engedi, stay here with your head of the synagogue. We will go on towards Masada."

"But you don't know... You cannot see..."

"I know the way. I know everything! Both the ways of the Earth and those of hearts, along which God and the Enemy of God pass, and I see those who accept the latter or the Former. Remain here with My peace! In any case it will soon be daybreak and with the burning branches we shall have light till dawn. Abraham, come here, that I may kiss you goodbye. May the Lord always be with you, as He has been so far, and with your family and your kind town."

"Will you not come back to us again, Lord? To see my happy home?"

"No. My road is about to come to its end. But you will be in Heaven with Me, and your dear ones will be with you. Love me and bring the little ones up in the faith of the Christ... Goodbye to everybody. Peace and blessings to all those who are here and to their families. Peace to you, Elisha. Be perfect out of gratitude to the Lord. My apostles, come with Me..."

As you have had experience in your own life of suffering the law of karma, suffering the effects of your own bad actions coming back to you, you should be able to understand this man who became a leper out of his own sins and visibly stained to the point where he had to be rejected from society and live in a cave alone while he's rotting and putrefying. We have all had experiences of falling short or making a big mistake or losing something that we could have kept had our hearts been in the right place or had our faith been stronger or whatever.

Even this man whose wife was blind and was cured and then he had a son, his only son then he became diseased, he lost everything, I mean he lost everything and he is a rabbi and he is a faithful one and he believes in Jesus and he is true. His is not perfect but he is certainly suffering, and that is an example for us of how to handle when bad things happen when karma comes back on us how to handle things with faith. And the reward is great and he said to the man, he said to Elisha that your "faith deserves it." In other words, in your consistency you didn't scream at God, you didn't hate God for your sins coming back on you. And because of that he blessed them and went out of his way so he blessed the whole family. They had to suffer for 20 years and they had to suffer maybe the whole life up until that point. And some of you have carried your blemishes and your sins for many, many years and some of you are faithful even in carrying the pain of that and its hard. But if you trust and you have faith and you ask for help, when the time is right, you will get healed, you will get blessed.

When you rail against God for the condition you are in, when you are mad at situations and people because of the situation that you are suffering that you created, the grace can't come. You can't deserve that kind of healing unless your heart is in the right place, unless your love is active and your faith is strong. Now some of what you carry is because you created it and it is justice coming back to lay on you and to bear upon you and some of it you just haven't let it go. So you are carrying burdens that you don't really have to carry. And the way to find out is let them all go and if one sticks to you, that's the one you have to carry. You know if one stays with you, you have to carry that until it works itself out or till the karma is paid or till God decides to lift it, you have to carry. All the others can be let go of because your consciousness feels like you need them to beat yourself up which God does not want you to do that. God simply wants you to be with God and suffer things gracefully if you have to and to bear your burdens with faith, with trust, if that's what is necessary without any, you know, attitude. Why shouldn't things be hard? I know there is this theory on the planet that nothing should be hard. Well you put out negative energy, it's going to come back, it's going to be hard. How could it not be hard? I would get rid of that theory that things shouldn't be hard. With grace and with love and with faith, things get easy, but when there isn't any of that, it is supposed to be hard. Wouldn't you think that a wise divinity would make sure that anything out of accord with itself would become hard! Don't parents who are conscious and watching make it very hard for the child when they don't conform to the family pattern and it is right that they should because you're forming that kid in society and the first society is the three of you. How are they going to confirm to the big society if they don't confirm to you? So you train and you drill and you repeat and you repeat and until they get it.

There is this theory on the planet that things shouldn't be hard. I want you to disrupt that. Anything that you have ever learned and is worth learning took a lot of effort. If it's music, an instrument, a science, you studied, you drilled, you worked, you stretched, you spent hours at it, sewing, whatever, you know, techy work, hours focused on that in order to get good at it. Medicine, a lot of people in medicine here. You had to drill, you had to study, you had to work hard, you had to repeat, you had to like just breathe it in. It wasn't easy! Why is any good thing easy? It is not. It is hard. A relationship, how do you get a relationship? You're just supposed to just like know each other? No, you work at that. Two people-- you don't spend any time together, you don't ever spend time finding out about each other or talk to each other? That's not a relationship. That won't be one because you didn't put any work in. You didn't put any time in. Anything worthwhile is going to take effort. You've had that but you forget these things. Like I know the theory that everybody has in the world and you guys have had it too that things shouldn't be hard. How many of you have felt that way, that things shouldn't be hard? Four. Ok, all of you. That's right and you still have that as a prejudice. That if it is hard, it must be wrong. The ones who have embraced the hardness of trial and the hardness of learning, their movement of life doesn't look like an effort at all because they have already gone over that hump that things are hard. So what? So you learn it and then you get good at it. Anyone who is excellent at anything when you watch them do it, it looks easy, it looks like butter, the tennis players, the sailors, the medicine people, the carvers, the arts, it looks like they are doing nothing beautifully and they went hours and hours and hours, days and days and months and years to get that good at what they do to make it look so easy.

That's what it's going to take. The joy of them being able to do it is so wonderful but they will never tell you that it wasn't hard. None of them would say "oh that was easy practicing for seven hours a day, that was just fun not having any friends and not going out to recess, just fun," no they would never say that. The athletes who every time they are not in school they are running or swimming, you know that's not fun, it's work but they get excellent at it. And this man was there when Herod killed those babies this guy, this rabbi, he was around. So he has been faithful for 33 years and been clipped bunches of times. His wife blinded, son lepered and had to let him go. He has been clipped and bruised and his faith did not shake. He stayed faithful to the Messiah. His love stayed, his heart stayed ok.

I mean he was sad I guess for all of the pain but he didn't lose his faith. I mean that's pretty hard right? To have you own son go to a cave because he has leprosy and once a month you give him food and clothing, supplies and you are not supposed to be caught seeing him. You can't touch him and you can't be near him and then a wife who is blind, and then he's got to go to the synagogue and preach the joy and the love of God and the faith in the Messiah. His getting clipped boom boom hard. Some of you have not been clipped that hard and you complain all the time. He didn't complain so this is the gift that Jesus brings him. Heals his wife, heals the son and blesses him with a personal relationship and that's what happens when the attitude's right and when you're not complaining that something is hard. So don't do that.

April 10, 2016
God's Judgment

The Gospel as Revealed to Me, Chapter 190. Arrival in the plains of Esdraelon at the sunset of Friday.

The sun is setting in a red sky when Jesus comes in view of Johanan's fields.
"Let us quicken our pace, My friends, before the sun sets. And you, Peter, go with your brother to inform our friends, Doras' men."
"I will go indeed, also to see whether the son has really gone away." Peter stresses the word "son". And he goes away.
In the meantime Jesus proceeds at a slower pace, looking around to see whether any of Johanan's men are about. But He can only see the fertile fields, in which the ears of grain are already well formed.
At last, a face, wet with perspiration, appears among the vineleaves and an exclamation is heard: "Oh! Blessed Lord!" and the peasant runs out of the vineyard and prostrates himself at Jesus' feet. "Peace to you, Isaiah!"
"Oh! You remember also my name?"
"It is written in My heart. Stand up. Where are your companions?"
"Over there. In the apple-orchards. But I will tell them at once. You will be our guest, will You not? The master is not here and we can welcome You. In any case... what with the fear, what with the joy... it is better. Just imagine, he gave us a lamb this year and will allow us to go to the Temple! He has given us only six days... but we will run all the way... We will be in Jerusalem, too... Imagine!... And thanks to You." The man is in his seventh heaven of delight because he has been treated as a man and as an Israelite.
"I have done nothing, as far as I know..." says Jesus smiling.

"Eh! no! You have done a great deal. Doras, and the fields of Doras, and these ones here, which are instead so beautiful this year... Johanan was informed of your visit, and he is not a fool. He is afraid and... and he is afraid."

"Of what?"

"He is afraid that what happened to Doras may happen to him. Both with regard to his life and to his property. Have You seen Doras' fields?"

"I have come from Nain..."

"In that case You have not seen them. They are a complete ruin. (The man whispers that in a low but clear voice, like someone imparting a secret concerning something dreadful.) They are all ruined! There is no hay, no fodder, no fruit. Vines and orchards withered... Dead... everything is dead... like Sodom and Gomorrah... Come, I will show You."

"It is not necessary. I am going to see those peasants..."

"But they are no longer here! Did You not know? Doras, the son of Doras, has scattered them or dismissed them, and the ones he sent to the other country places which belong to him, must not speak of You, or they will be lashed... Not to speak of You! That will be difficult! Also Johanan said so to us."

"What did he say?"

"He said: "I am not so foolish as Doras and I will not say to you: 'I do not want you to speak of the Nazarene'. It would be useless, because you would do it just the same and I do not want to lose you by lashing you to death like untameable animals. On the contrary I say to you: 'Be good as the Nazarene certainly teaches you and tell Him that I treat you well'. I do not want to be cursed, too". Of course, he can see what these fields are like after You blessed them, and what the ones You cursed are like. Oh! Here are the ones who ploughed the field for me..." and the man runs to meet Peter and Andrew.

But Peter greets him briefly and proceeds on his way and begins to shout: "Oh! Master! There is no one left! They are all *new faces. And everything is laid waste! He could very well do without any peasants here. It is worse than the Salt Sea!..."*

"I know. Isaiah told Me."

"But come and see! What a sight..."

Jesus pleases him after saying to Isaiah: "I will stay with you. Tell your companions. But do not go to any trouble. I have enough food. All we need is a barn to sleep in and your love. I will come back soon."

The sight of Doras' fields is really distressing. Fields and meadows are dry and barren, vineyards are withered, the foliage and fruit of trees are completely destroyed by millions of insects of all kinds. Also the garden-orchard near the house looks like a desolate dying wood. The peasants wander to and fro uprooting weeds, crushing caterpillars, snails, earthworms and the like, shaking branches under which they place basins full of water to drown little butterflies, aphides and other parasites which cover the leaves and eat away the plant until it dies. They endeavor to find a sign of life in the vine-shoots, which break like dry wood as soon as they are touched and sometimes fall off the main branch, as if the roots had been cut by a saw. The contrast with Johanan's fields, vineyards and orchards is most striking and the ruin of the cursed fields seems more impressive when compared to the fruitfulness of the others.

"The hand of the God of Sinai is a heavy one" *whispers Simon the Zealot.*

Jesus makes a gesture as if to say: "How right you are!" *but He does not say anything. He only asks:* "How did it happen?"

A peasant replies between his teeth: "Moles, locusts, worms... but go away! The steward is faithful to Doras... Don't cause us trouble..."

]Jesus sighs and goes away.

Another peasant, who is bent under an apple-tree earthing it up, in the hope he may save it, says: "We will *reach You tomorrow... when the steward goes to Jezreel for the prayer... we will come to Micah's house."*

Jesus makes the gesture of blessing and goes away.

When He goes back to the cross-road, all the peasants of Johanan are there and joyful and happy they surround their Messiah and take Him to their poor dwellings.

"Did You see, over there?"

"Yes, I did. Doras' peasants are coming tomorrow."

"Of course, when the hyenas go to pray... We do that every Sabbath... and we speak of You, we tell what we heard from Jonah, from Isaac, who often comes to see us, and what we learned from You in Tishri. We speak as best we can. Because it is impossible not to speak of You. And the more we suffer, the more we are forbidden, the more we speak of You. Those poor people... they drink the essence of life every Sabbath... But how many there are in this plain who are in need of knowing, of knowing You at least, and yet they cannot come here..."

"I will see to them as well. And may you be blessed for what you do."

The sun is setting while Jesus enters a kitchen blackened by smoke. The Sabbath rest begins.

Jesus' sigh is probably the main characteristic of this whole feature story. And he sees the fields he hears about it, he hears that the peasants have no work anymore because there is nothing to do because there is are no plants, no trees, nothing. He just sighs in the reference that God punishes people. And it's just a sigh because it is true and that's the inevitable justice of God that people have this huge indictment that that would be unfair for God to judge the world or for the justice of God to come upon a particular family or a particular person.

Yet God created them and they were created with an admonition to be good and instruction to be like God because they were created in His image, and that there would be some kind of result if you don't. Because people are still reacting to their parents' uncharitable ways, they projected onto God that God is also going to be unfair to them. And so the judgment is already in by most people that if anything bad happens, God unfairly treated people. You know the saying in the question is always, 'Why did God let this happen?' Oh why not? That's my question. Why not? If the justice of God is completely in God's department because He created the world, then it is Justice and it is fair that certain things would die. Certain things would atrophy. Certain things would be declared unfruitful and no more bother the ground. And that happens for us. There are certain things that do not work and the more you persist in them not working, eventually they are going to get called. They will get called like you keep trying to do this, you keep trying to do hatred work, you keep trying to have your grudge be acceptable or you keep trying to have your resentment blessed or you keep having your tension accepted by people or your insecurity, you want your insecurity accepted by everybody. And the justice of God is going that's a sin, that's actually a sin, all those things are sins. They are not conditions and states you just have to suffer. They are things you are creating. And those are sins and so there is going to be justice upon you. You're going to put it out and it's going to come back.

Doris was incredibly mean and he beat his servants. He killed a couple, he killed a mother and father and their kids were orphaned and he sent them away and wouldn't feed them and Jesus took them in. And that was like 6 or 8 months ago and he let God's judgment come upon this guy's whole world. And it turned into this. Everything dried out everything was eaten away. Everything was destroyed I mean everything. And then the neighboring land not. That is a very stark message. It's like when you see and I remember as a kid in Indiana the tornado came down the street and it did 3 houses on this side, jumped across, skipped this one hit a house over here and crossed the street and continued on the other side. It missed this one house and it got this one on this other side. The precision of it was crazy. It was uncanny that that tornado would come down and miss two houses and hit 5 all on the same street. And I did wonder as a kid "What must be going on in those houses that God had to destroy them?" I mean, destroyed. Like, gone. I mean I can't understand it as a kid. You cannot understand who is doing what to whom or who needs to wake up or who needs a big shock or who needs to get startled or who needs to die because that is big picture, you know even today your adult mind can't really get it. Like this big picture of why people are taken, why people are judged or how they judged.

There's just this energy in most people's psyche that it's a bad thing and it shouldn't be happening and that God is actually quite fickle and wrathful and mean and angry. And that's been going on for thousands of years--this kind of judgment against God by the little puny people who were created by Him. We are small, so we are little, so we are puny compared to the magnificence, the Majesty of God. We are just a drop in the bucket, a drop in the ocean. And it is humbling to know that there is that judgment that comes. For most of you, you are not humble about it, you are worried about it and would be very upset about it. But if you lived your life each day with the knowing that you can, with the respect for your life and other people that you could and the acceptance and faith in your life that you have been admonished to have. Then every day you could be judged and it could be the end and you will be fine. Each day you would die and it would be over and you would be fine with it. Because there wouldn't be anything you were missing. There wouldn't be anything you did not take care of, there wouldn't be anything that you had failed to express that you needed to because you know, the books are balanced, the books are balanced. And then that trust, that humble trust in God that if you get to stay or if you get to be taken hey it's okay. You are still in God. You are still loved as a soul. You are still within God's consciousness in or out of your so important flesh body. It is a different perspective isn't it that the Judgment is actually a beneficent, benevolent thing. Benevolence means good love. God is essentially benevolent. Good love--that is what it means. What a lesson to all the other farmers in the neighborhood as well. You know you better treat people right, you better be generous with orphans and sick people. You better not be mean to your people and beat them cause this could happen and it is a crude lesson. We should be more sophisticated than that but we are probably not. There are mean things that we do that are just as bad as what Doris was doing.

Like in the student sermon, you're mean to yourself that is just as bad as if you are mean to somebody else. And Jesus knows all about it. He is the one that ordered it. He is one with God. He ordered that upon him but he is acting like God did it because really that's what happened. God would bless the prayer of course if Jesus made it. But his benign acceptance of these things as normal are showing the apostles that this is what happens when people are way out of line. Yeah they can be out of line for a long time to the point of killing those parents and orphaning those kids and treating people for many, many years terribly. He got away with that for years being like the worst guy in the neighborhood, right? The worst guy in that little town. Everybody knew it and they talked about it, he was mean and he kept doing it, he kept doing it and then he runs into Jesus and then the judgment comes upon him. It's the end of it and that's the way the Earth is right now. The people in the Earth are very mean to each other, and people are killing each other, really organizing mass killings and organizing mass conspiracies to rip people from their freedom.

How long will that go on? As long as God allows it because when God says that is it it is over. Because this is God's world this is not the little humans' world were a couple of presidents, or a dictator's world or races of humans' world, this is God's world and you know, it will be justice when the scales are balanced. It will be justice. And it will be horrible but just like it was horrible for Doris' family and his crops and everything. He lost his wealth completely, he lost everything but I don't think anybody felt bad for him. No one felt bad for him. They don't want that to happen to them. Johanna did not want that to happen to him so he has established fairness among the ranks and fairness among the slaves so that he does not treat anybody in a way that would get Jesus up in arms like that again. He is fearful. He is fearful, that is the most crude form of righteous behavior is when you're scared. So you do right because you're scared. You don't do right because you love, you do right because you are frightened and that is the old way. That's the old way. That's what all the rules and laws of the Jews were for, is to scare people into being good because they didn't have it within themselves just naturally so they had to be regimented to be good.

Well you have the right to be whatever. And there is no lash upon you, there is nobody whipping you, you are not enslaved you can do what you want, you're free. Except you have this thing called conscience and you have this thing called the Judgment of God awaiting you and that is what you do in your retrospections at night, quickly without any big deal is scan the day to see if there is anything you could have not done and anything you could have done better. It's a quick thing, it's not this long sit-down torture yourself to death with a half hour trying to stay awake. It's a quick thing where you just go, "Is there anything that I do not want to do again? Is there anything I think I better to do better?" That is your retrospection for the day. It's very simple because that's the thing that's going to keep up your connection strong with the one who made you. That will keep you strong. And if you just make those little revisions every day, a little more of the good, a little less of the weirdness, you won't be worried about God's judgment anymore because you will be doing it every day--a little dose each day. You already know it. You already know what the judgment is because you practiced. That is pretty simple.

Then you don't have to be Doris getting a huge whack of surprise. For billions it's going to be a huge whack of surprise on the planet but for you I hope it's not. I hope you have cleaned up to the degree that you can, that you are pretty clear with your love for God and you don't have too many huge problems and big warts that you have to deal with. They are done, you just finished them. Then the judgment will be like a little small wave on the beach, you know and it goes over you and it's done. Everybody else it might kill them, it might drown them. But for you? That's what you do on the ocean, like a little thing. Alright that's it.

April 17, 2016
Loving Your Challenges

1943 Notebooks, December 22, 1943.

Jesus says:
"To recognize the benefits which are received is, even among men, an obligation and a sign of a gracious heart. You judge the ungrateful severely. And rightly so.

But, how should God judge, then? When you succeed by God's assistance and see your enterprises prosper, why don't you find a word for Him who has given you that joy? Why do you say, 'I have done this? Why, swollen with pride, do you exclaim, 'The Lord necessarily had to listen to me because I am deserving of his help'? No. If the Father were to give you what you deserve, He would have to pulverize you.

But He, in relation to you, who are hard in mind and heart, rebellious and depraved, sacrilegious and lying, does not fail to keep his sworn promise to be your Father. And a Father, even if indignant at the behavior of his son, is never less of a father, if he is a holy, just man. God is most holy and most just. Well then, God does not annihilate you as you deserve, but calls you back to Himself with a reproachful voice in which love is always fused.

He calls you once, twice, a hundred times. With his flashing of power He reminds you that, even if you create other gods for yourselves, He is the only God and his words are always the same ones written on the stone of Horeb.

You, to whom it seems more comfortable to serve a mute, impotent idol (mute and impotent in holy works), scorn God's voice and command because you deem them burdensome and constricting. But what fate is more burdensome or what dominion is more constricting than the one you impose on yourselves, made by the will of men, who are quite different from God, away from whom they have turned their faces and hearts, and who can give you only what they give you: pain and death?!

Now I say to you, 'Pray.' Among you there is still a minority capable of heeding Me, of praying and suffering for the world. To these I say, 'Pray'.

It is time to divert the severity of the torment which has begun with prayer and immolation. Pain and faith make you acceptable to the Lord, your God. Speak, then, in favor of all. Take God with the noose of love. He, whom no force binds, is like a little bird caught in a net when a soul encircles Him with love. He surrenders and blesses. Remind God of his benefits, not because He needs to be reminded of them by you, but to show that you remember them. While the world blasphemes and kills, sing hosannas to the Lord and love. Love is more powerful than strength and defeats even hell. Love overcomes everything, O my beloved ones.

Love will bend God, who has grown rigid in the face of the lack of love of a whole world, and will obtain from Him the only miracle which can save you. Love will open the hearts of men and give them spiritual sight to see their inner horror, which is becoming a collective horror Love will lead man back onto the ways of God. When you love, you will no longer do evil, the great evil done knowingly, as you now do.

It is not burdensome to follow God. He asks you for nothing but love and obedience and respect for his Majesty, superior to all earthly authorities. In a spiritual circumcision, amputate from your hearts that which is a ring of sin impeding them from beating in the honest rhythm of Good and growing in holy Charity.

It is up to you to choose between my blessing and my curse. I respect your will. I set forth to you only the fruits of the former and the latter My blessing will give you bread and peace, serenity in your days and prosperity in your interests. My curse will leave you your wars and massacres and itself give you drought or inclement weather, pestilences and *famine, for God's punishment cannot give you things to fill your two base loves-belly and purse-with.*

Choose. And don't say that I don't love you because I do not impose good. Too many among you pray to Satan so that he will work his prodigies for them. You would destroy Good if I imposed it on you.

It is first necessary for you that worship the Beast not to be a people, but for those who remember God to be a people. Evil will then be offset by God and neutralized by it; And not only this, but the good you do will attract Heavenly Good in an ever-increasing measure, for God asks for nothing except to pour Himself out upon you in love, and you would experience the era of peace promised to good men at my birth."

Good Morning. The qualities of God are infinite and it would be good to remind ourselves of some of those qualities very often because those are the qualities that not only do we admire them but we would like to strive to become them. The only way to become them is to have the blessing of the one who knows them, the blessing of the one who carries those gifts. He can dispense them to you, if you are open and willing and you make room for them. Making room for them is not as easy as you think. It is not just acquiring something to put it on top of the already filled space. No, you have to empty out to get some of those qualities and gifts from God. You have to empty out. You have to make a space for them. You have to clear out resentments and grudges and opinions and concepts. You have to clear out attitudes that have been sitting there comfortable. How can God pour into a full container, a blessing? If you are full of your worries or full of your commentary about life, how can God pour a blessing into that space? It is not empty, it's not a vacuum, it's not an open space, a request to be filled, and it is just going to slough off.

And Jesus is reminding us, once again, that love and goodness and all the gifts that we admire in ourselves and others are from God. That is something we forget often. You can see in your development that you have worked on certain qualities that have increased. You have become more cheerful, maybe light hearted, less heavy, less burdened by your sufferings and your problems than you used to be. So you have seen progress in yourself. You have seen that struggles aren't as hard in certain areas and there are other struggles coming to light that you didn't even know you had. That is like growth and you'll have to work with those as well. You will have to overcome those. There are always an infinite number of things we can do to become more perfect. As you let go of one gnarly little habit, that frees your energy up and increases the love and power, the goodness in you and that shows up another thing that has to be let go of. It is not going to end. Because perfection is always perfecting and the progress continues and the infinite possibility is always ahead of you. Even if you become all light and all love, there is still more. There's still much, much more. When we've become one with Jesus and he has become one with God, there are more luminous perfections. He will point them out to you because he is the mediator for those he is mediating between you and God, you and His Father, you and something bigger than Him. Remember he is a created being, God is not a created being, God was before time, before anything. Infinite. So the best we can do, because we didn't generate ourselves, is to emulate all the qualities of the being that created us. And Love is the most important one. So, are you loving towards your challenges? That is what I want you to work on now. I want you to love your challenges. I want you to have great love for them, for their transformative power over you. I want you to love the things that are obstacles to you. And love the things that are trying and difficult. As you do that, you will probably see yourself getting more patient. You'll see yourself getting less reactive, and you'll see yourself overcoming. This is part of the reason why you don't see yourself breakthrough to the other side of a victory is because you react and you mope and you get depressed and you actually sit down when you actually should bust through. You sit down when you should bust through. Now you can't do it with your ego because you will fail, you will fall on your face. But you can bust through with Jesus helping you. Jesus, help me to bust through this pattern to change it to overcome this situation, to overcome my tendencies.

I want to remind you of a couple things Jesus said and he said a few times, "We, God and I, respect the will of man." They respect human beings choice, which means, they can't interfere. If your choice is to make it hard, they can't make it easy. If your choice is to take a lot of time, they can't make it go quickly when you want it to take a lot of time. They respect the freedom for a human being to choose how they would like it to be. If you think a problem takes forever to overcome, they can't interfere with that because you haven't asked them to interfere with that. You haven't asked them to, make my problem go quicker. Because, you have said, I want my problem to go on forever because I want to struggle with this a lot. They have to respect it. They have to leave you in that, honor you, for deciding that way. It is a very respectful and loving position, to let somebody choose what they want and learn from it. They would certainly help you change that if you ever wanted to change it but they have to let you be in the situation you want to be in.

Now you could learn that in terms of fellow adults. Now with kids, there is a way not to accept that because you have to move them along and that is your job. But with fellow adults, you have to accept the decisions that they make. You don't have to be silent, you could say, 'It seems like you want that to take a long time.'" Or 'It seems like you want to hold onto that because you don't want to let it go.' You can say the truthful thing and still respect them in the decision they are making.   Like, 'I want to be miserable.' Now won't everyone around you go, that is really silly, but OK. If you want to be miserable, that is your business. I hope you learn from that and actually I am going to secretly pray that you get tired of it. But I am not going to tell you that. And I am not going to force you to get over it because you seem to get over it when you're ready. I guess. You love misery it seems like and I'm not going to interfere, but I hope that God helps you see how silly that is. That is how you pray for people. You still respect their choice and let it be if that is what they want but you apply God's help if they want it, if they can accept it. Now what this does, it doesn't do a lot for your ego who likes to shove things around and see that they got shoved. That is what the ego is; it likes to shove things around and see that they got shoved and take credit for it. There is not much fruit in that. Being patient with a soul who hasn't come on line or who doesn't want to change anything or wants to change so little it's almost imperceptible. You know, there is no food for the ego when you can't budge them and they won't budge. What does the ego say? 'Oh I did that.' No it didn't do anything; there was nothing the ego could do. Because even God won't force a soul.

Now, there are events like death, which change things and if people wait long enough, that could happen before they change anything. Death could happen. Then there are other big events like there is world karma, like cyclic events and world events that have been ordered from the beginning. And they are going to come, whether people are ready for them or not. And that will move things along or move things out of body or move people out of body or souls out of body if necessary. Those are a little more cyclic and a little more cosmic. And remember God puts up with a lot until he says, 'No, we have to change this.' You have that in terms of laws in the country where the country decides it is no longer OK to drink and drive, it's no longer okay to sexually abuse children or you are going to jail. You know, before the 80's, they didn't have those laws, if they had them, they didn't enforce them, it didn't come into the consciousness but then the laws of the country are going to say, 'Okay, no more of this, we are not going to have this anymore.' And then it becomes a decree and everyone has to go along with it and everyone gets evaluated by this new law. And that is when the whole mind of the country or the whole mind of the people decide and say, "That's it, we can't do this anymore. We can't have this." And that is a step for the people to go, "We have to live at a higher level so this lower level has to be called unlawful." Then there are penalties for that and jail time and court cases or whatever.

That's changed and evolved over time, over the last 5,000 years, it's refined and refined and refined. Now we have a super complicated legal systems in most countries with everything related to everything else. And people defining what that can't mean and what that does mean, what that will not mean and you pay a lot of money for people to determine what means what. It is called blurring, the blurring profession. Create a law and someone comes in and blurs it and charges a lot of money for that. There are professions that do that. That is their job. With this thing about respecting the will of a person, you know, it's not really blurry, like, what do you want? Well, what you have so far is what you want. That is so simple and yet you don't really think of it very often. I really catch you being too complicated to get how simple that is. Like the experience you have is the thing you have wanted and you're having it. And you say to me (and I know there is an argument going to start now), 'Well, I don't want this.' And I say, 'Well that is not true, because you have this experience happening to you now, within you, you are participating, it's happening in house, in your body and in your mind happening and you had to create that.' 'Well I don't want it.' And my answer to you is very simple, if it's still happening, you still want it more than you don't want it. You haven't tipped over the scales to not wanting it enough to say, Ok that's it, I'm going to do something about this and this is going to change. This is why; it's so beautiful to respect a person in the choice they are making. I know we are so projective onto parents; any authority figure gets your projection from your parent image in your head that they should fix you somehow, that they should do something to you to make you change. That is the projection. All of a sudden you stop being an adult and started being a kid again and then you are looking at your mommy and daddy, whoever that authority figure is and they are supposed to fix you. Well, that is a violation of your free will as an adult. And it really is a crazy thing to ask someone else to do something when you are sitting on the thing yourself.

When you could pray and go, 'I need help, I don't want to be this way anymore, please, Jesus and Mary, help me to dump this feeling out of my being and cleanse it out of my cells and get it out of my mind and take it out of my habit structure so I never do it again and I'm done.' When I see that, I know you are going to change. And I almost can't prevent it because it's so clean. But when I hear, 'Well, why didn't you help me with this?' I hear only this (translation), 'I don't want to change and if you were a big enough parent, you would make me change.' God set it up that that is not fair. That is disrespect to a soul's choice. So any real being who is lighted and conscious and one with God would never violate your will because Jesus and Mary don't violate your will because God respects your will. And I know this is going to flip you out because you don't really get it or you wouldn't project on authority that they should fix you when you won't choose what you will. If you really knew this, I would see no more expecting authority figures to make you change or you're going to brace against them trying to make you change. I would see none of that anymore, because you would just choose what you want, when you want it. You might be inspired by something we say, and you want to do that so then you would do it. But you start declaring it and you make prayers for it and you ask for help for it, it would start happening. It would just happen. Nobody would stop you. But that passive position of, 'Well, if you bring the silver spatula up and you take me up a level, I would do it. I would definitely rise up, I would then if you did that with me, I would be rising up as you lift me up.' How many of you really thought that? You know what I mean? Don't admit it. Thank you, one, two, three people. How about the slow people want to admit it? How about the really sluggish ones, the Taurus's, any of the Taurus's want to admit it? Alright, let's go. That is interesting; it is not really an adult position to say 'I'm waiting for you to give me a reason to change. I'm waiting for you to help me change because I don't know if I can do it myself.' That is not the point, that you can't do it yourself, it's that you won't unless someone gives you a reason to do it. Which means you are totally passive, you are not thinking whether you should or not. You are thinking whether somebody is important enough for you to make a change for. What does that translate to? They have all the power and you have none. And that is against what God teaches which is, a human being gets to choose what they want. And they have chosen and are choosing and they are in the experience they want right now and no one is stopping them.

Now you could decide hey, I don't want to do that anymore. I want to be alive and happy and conscious and awake. I want to be useful, I want to be an instrument and I want to be a servant of God, I want to be a real disciple with a consciousness of a disciple and I want to be awake. Now, how am I going to do that? Well then somebody is going to come along and say well, you can't think this way anymore and you can't act this way anymore if that is your prayer. Now, that is helpful to you even though annoying. Because who wants someone saying what you can and cannot do anymore? Nobody likes that. You don't even like doing that with yourself. And yet you have to, if you are going to change anything. You have to stop something and start something else, if you are going to change anything. You have to stop being sad and start being happy. That's a change. You stop moping in your sadness and your anger and you want to start giving. That's a change. You'd have to want to do that. Nobody can make you. I know I cajole, I encourage, I tempt you, I poke at you to try to do that. Don't even think for a minute that I think I have the power to make you do anything. I do not. That is why I have a sense of humor about it. That is why if I pressure you I back it off immediately, because I want to see what you are going to do with your own will about something you care about.

I am not going to take credit for your change. I am going to take credit for bothering you, yes. But I am not going to take credit for your change; you are going to take the credit because it's something you want. So my ego is not invested in you changing, I don't want your ego invested in anybody else changing. I don't even want your ego invested, period, in anything. I want you to know what you want and I want you to understand that God respects your will and wants to support that. As Jesus was describing, you can go the evil way or the good way, depending and that is going to matter a lot. It's really going to matter a lot. And some of you sitting sluggish, not choosing, that's the lukewarm masses.

They are not choosing anything because they are waiting. They are waiting for the big parental spatula to come on the scene. I know if you are really honest, half of you are doing that, waiting for the spatula to come along. I know that hurts your pride and everything but it's embarrassing for you to be doing that. From my point of view, for you to be still doing that after what you know and after what Jesus is willing to help you with for you to be still doing that, is embarrassing. That's my cajoling factor, in terms of respecting your will.

See, I just cajoled you, I nudged you, and I insulted you a little bit. You know how stubborn you are, that doesn't even phase you, you say, 'That's what he does.' I know how you handle it, you say, 'He's just jostling me, I can be myself.' And that's what you do, you start being yourself again, which is sluggishly waiting for the spatula instead of choosing what you want to be and asking for help for that. If you are miserable, do you love that? Do you like to wear that like a wet blanket? Do you love that? Why do you do it then? Do you think you are getting any mileage out of it? Do you think anybody is actually concerned about your wet blanket? Do you think anybody alive and cheerful would give you the time of day for your wet blanket? You have got to be kidding me. You have got to be kidding me. And anybody who listens to that crap about your wet blanket isn't showing you any compassion at all. It's contributing to that sin of holding onto that because you know better. You can give that to Jesus and it will be gone but if you are holding onto it that is your first main sin, holding on. Anyway, I think you will all figure it out because I respect your will.

May 1, 2016
Thinking Darkens Light

From 1943 Notebooks, October 15, 1943.

Jesus says:
"The Church has applied to Mary, my blessed Mother, the praises which the spouse in the Song expresses for his beloved. And, in truth, no other creatures in the world have so much of a right to receive those praises for themselves, if we also set aside, and above all, the sensuality which celebrates physical beauty, great in Mary as well, for her exclusion from original sin had made Mary a perfect creature, like the first two created by the Father. And the first two, the sublime work of the Creator, had the physical beauty of the body created by the Father, in addition to the incorporeal beauty of the innocent soul.

Physical ugliness came to man as one of the many consequences of sin. Sin did not wound only the spirit. It brought that wound to the flesh as well. From the spirit, which had lost Grace, came instincts against nature, the fruit of which has been the monstrosities of the race. If man had not known sin, he would not have known certain stimuli and would not have made degraded and accursed alliances which later, over the ages, have been a burden with the impress of ugliness upon the first, original beauty.

And even when man did not go so far as to debase himself with certain sins, wickedness, taken to the point of delinquency, marked stigmata upon the faces of the evil and their descendants, stigmata which you are still studying today to repress delinquency.

But you scientists who study them ought to begin to remove the first stigmata of delinquency from your hearts: the one that makes you rebels against God, his Law, and his Faith. It is necessary to care for the spirit, not repress the sins of flesh and blood. If man, by caring for himself first of all, were then to be concerned about the spiritual education of his brothers and sisters, recognizing this spirit

Which is the motor of your acts and not denying it with words and more with the works of a whole life, delinquency would diminish to the point of becoming the sporadic manifestation by some of the poor mentally disturbed.

Physical ugliness is a sign of one's own or of a remote union with Evil to such a point that, in the time of Moses- when for a whole set of reasons, which I explained to you one day, it was necessary to use a severity and absolutism which I later modified With my doctrine of love-the deformed were excluded from the divine services. It was not to teach men to be lacking in charity towards the unfortunate that this law had been given by Justice. But it was to put a check on men's animality, with the fear and terror that their sins against nature would generate deformed people excluded from divine service, the supreme aspiration of the children of Israel.

Afterwards I, Eternal Wisdom, came, incarnated for you, and I modified the Law in the fire of my Charity and in the light of my Intelligence.

Centuries and centuries had passed since the time of Moses, and, in spite of all the laws, man had fornicated with Evil, with Lust pushed towards monstrous aberrations, with Ferocity also taken to the point of masterworks of criminality. Upon the children of the children of these millions of sinners the stigmata of the distant sins of their forefathers were imprinted, while, under the sheath of unlovely flesh rendered deformed by physical defects and horrendous illnesses, there beat a heart more worthy of God than that of so many hearts of physically beautiful beings.

And then I, the fruit of Love and the bearer of love among men, to teach you love, taught you to love the unfortunate; I called to myself the lame, the blind, the lepers, and the mad, and I healed them when appropriate; I always loved them with a special love and taught you to love them that way.

This also reflected a reason of lofty justice. Could I, who had come to redeem the deformities of the spirit and to love your deformed spirits to the point of holocaust, to give them back the beauty worthy of entering heaven, fail to love the physically deformed, whose deformity was a cross which by itself redeemed the spirit that was able to carry it?

No. The Savior loved them and loves them-the unfortunates of the earth. And if He cannot work the miracle upon all of them of making their members, destined to perish, perfect-He cannot for reasons it is useless to explain to men-He can give his divine assurance of the possession of Heaven to all those mortified by an infirmity if they are able to suffer their trial of martyrdom without doubting the goodness of the Eternal One and without rebelling against their destiny by turning it into an accusation against God.

Let them love me because of pain, too. I will reward them for their love, and the forsaken of the earth will become the triumphant in Heaven.

My Mother, the Blameless One, the All-Beautiful, the One Desired by God, the One Destined to be my Mother, possessed the harmonious integrity of her members, in which the fashioning thumb of God, who had created her in his perfect likeness, was evident.

The work of the artist has labored for so many centuries to represent Mary. But how can perfection be represented? Perfection issues from the inside to the outside. And even if you can create a perfect form with the brush and the chisel, you cannot introduce into it that light of the soul which is something spiritual and which is an ineffable divine touch appended to a flesh which is holy, a touch that you see shining from within upon your brothers and sisters and that makes you exclaim, 'What a saintly face!'

How can you represent Mary? The All-Holy One of the Lord! Every time she appeared and you then toiled to reproduce her appearance, those blessed with the vision of her exclaimed, 'This work is lovely, but it is not Mary. She is beautiful in a different way, with a beauty which you cannot reproduce and which is indescribable.'

Could you reproduce Mary-you, to whom, as comfort in the trial which was imminent, I granted the vision of my Mother and Yours-could you, even if you were an outstanding painter or sculptor? No. You stated that even your skilful words as an educated woman capable of writing are poor and insufficient to describe Mary. You said She is 'light,' to express that which is most beautiful arid indescribable in the world and compare it to my and our Mother.

It is the spirit of Mary, which emerges from the veils of her immaculate flesh, that you cannot describe, O children of hers and brothers and sisters of mine. Sanctify yourselves so as to see Mary. Even if, just to imagine, you were see only her in Paradise, you would be blessed. For Paradise means a place where the vision of God is enjoyed, and whoever sees Mary is already seeing God. She is the stainless mirror of the Divinity.

You see, then, that the praises of the Song are exactly appropriate for Mary, who, with her pure soul in love, wounded the heart of God, who is her King, but who contents her in her loving desires for you, as if she were his Queen.

I would like you to strive to love Mary, within the limits of your strength, just as you must love God with your whole self to love means to imitate, out of a spirit of love, the one who is loved. And I have made this into a sweet command: 'People will know that you love me when they see that you do the works that I do'. Now I give you the same command regarding my Mother: 'They will see that you love her when you imitate her.'

Oh, if the world were to strive to imitate Mary! Evil, in all its different manifestations, which extend from the ruin of souls to the ruin of families, and from the ruin of families to the ruin of nations and of the entire globe, would fall in defeat forever, for Mary keeps Evil under her virginal heel and if Mary were your Queen and you were truly her children, subjects, and imitators, Evil could no longer harm you.

Be Mary's. You will automatically be God's. For she is the enclosed Garden where God remains, the holy Garden where God blooms. For She is the Fount from which there flows the Living Water that ascends to Heaven and gives you the means to ascend to Heaven: Me, the Christ, Redeemer of the world and Savior of man."

Some of you are growing more beautiful daily and it's not because you're doing things at the salon or the spa. That has nothing to do with it, actually. Maybe that's a maintenance feature that you find necessary. When you're not thinking about yourself and you're thinking about others, a glow comes over your face and your complexion changes and the cells that used to be tense or otherwise disturbed are smoothed out and shine. It's a very simple thing. It's a spiritual thing.

It's not in any cultivation of the flesh that you find holiness--it's in the forgetting about the flesh and cultivating love that you start looking beautiful. If you think about love then you have to think about how you can care and you have to think about what people might need and you have to stop thinking about you. You have to start thinking about the movement of energy called love that will move through you from God to this person who has God in them. You'll start thinking appropriately instead of thinking about yourself. As soon as you start thinking about yourself, ugliness starts to follow you. As soon as you have your problems, you start getting less beautiful. It's the spirit that makes it beautiful, not your attention to your physical form.

Mary didn't concern herself with her body at all, but she cared for it like it was God's because God had chosen her. Just like God has chosen you. And you can care for your body the way that God would want you to because God chose you. It's a choiceful thing on the part of the human to be chosen by God because actually God and Jesus want everyone with them. You don't have to go very far or very long or very deep to feel that he longs for you to come. Even in the state that you're in, even with all your prideful reactions, even with your stubborn holdings-on to things you are upset about. As soon as he wants you to come he starts dissolving those. What do they want you there for? Why do they want you there with them God and Jesus? Why do they want you with them? Ever wonder? Because they created you and they know what you are capable of and they know who you really are. One of them. You're a God in the making. And so they want you undistorted coming home to be with them.

Sin distorts, and reactions to pain distort and misconceptions distort and enjoying having a problem distorts you and makes you not look yourself. The sins that he's talking about that makes people deformed goes down the family line. There might be a whole family line of tradition of lust or sensuality or taking advantage of people or using people. Over the line, a soul would be drawn into that genetic line because they would have had a longing to do that too and so they would go in and have stained flesh or distorted looking flesh because the whole family line has been doing that for generations. You would only be drawn into that if you had that kind of energy. Then you'd be born ugly or something like that. That doesn't mean it can't be changed. Anything can be healed with effort and longing and faith and drawing close to the Christ. Everyone who became really close to the Christ with great faith was healed. Their deformities, imbalances, distortions, twisted bodies, no sight, if they had a hemorrhage disease that bled all the time, it was healed. Why? Because they went out of the old way into Jesus' way. That's simple. He promised it. "Come to me and I will give you rest." Lay all of your burdens at my feet and I will dissolve them in front of you in fire. I'm paraphrasing.

Also when you over-cultivate the body, you think it's yours and you can't glorify God. You're thinking it's you and it wasn't a gift. It's a little 3 dimensional space where God places himself and asks you to honor it. But when you get outer-focused on the body, you're going to get ugly because you are off balance. You're out of connection.

You forgot how you were created and why you were created. If you devote your actions to love and Jesus and Mary, everyone will start feeling good around you and your appearance will change. We've always said that about the illumination that when you take it on. But some of you took on the light and you forgot about it because it's old hat for you because you lacked humility in not actually working with it or you still lack humility in not working with it. But if you would work with it and soak it up and let it shine through you more, you would turn into light and love. You would turn into how you were created and not how you thought. Thinking damages and darkens light. Thinking darkens light. If that's the only thing I get through to you today I think I'm done. Thinking darkens light. Lust is thinking, "I don't have all the things I need but I need to desire it from somebody else or something else." So that's a distortion of thinking. That's thinking in malice, an indictment that God did not give you everything that you need so you must crave. So that darkens light because that's thinking. It's thinking that you're not ok, enough, or not what you need. Thinking darkens light.

May 8, 2016
True Motherhood

The Gospel as Revealed to Me, Chapter 642. The Blessed Virgin Takes up Her Abode at Gethsemane with John Who Foretells Her Assumption.

Mary is still in the house of the Supper room. All alone in Her usual room, she is sewing some very fine linen cloths, like long narrow table-cloths. Now and again She raises Her head to look at the garden and ascertain thus the time of the day by the position of the sunshine on its walls. And if she hears a noise in the house or in the street, she listens carefully. She seems to be waiting for someone.

Some time goes by so. Then there is a knock at the door of the house, followed by the rustling of sandals of someone who rushes to open it. Voices of men resound in the corridor and they become louder and louder and closer and closer.

Mary listens... Then She exclaims: "Are they here?! What on earth has happened?!" While she is still uttering these words, somebody knocks at the door of Her room. "Come in, brothers in Jesus, My Lord" replies Mary.

Lazarus and Joseph of Arimathea enter, and greeting Her with deep veneration they say: "Blessed are You among all mothers! The servants of Your Son and our Lord greet You", and they prostrate themselves to kiss the hem of Her dress.

"The Lord be always with you. For what reason, and while the ferment of the persecutors of the Christ and of His followers has not yet ceased, have you come to Me?"

"First of all, to see You. Because seeing You is still seeing Him, and thus we feel less distressed because of His departure from the Earth. And then to propose to You what we have resolved to do, after a meeting in my house of the more loving and faithful servants of Jesus, Your Son and our Lord" Lazarus replies to Her.

"Tell Me. It will be your love that speaks to Me, and with My love I will listen to you."

Joseph of Arimathea now begins to speak and says: "Woman, You know and You have said so, that the ferment, and what is even worse, still last against all those who have been close to Your Son and God's, either through relationship, or faith, or friendship. And we are aware that You do not intend to leave these places, where You have seen the perfect manifestation of the divine and human nature of your Son, His total mortification, and His total glorification, through His Passion and Death as true Man, through His glorious Resurrection and Ascension, as true God. And we also know that you do not want to leave the apostles all alone, as you wish to be a Mother and guide to them in their first trials, You, the See of Divine Wisdom, You, the Spouse of the Spirit Revealer of the Eternal Truths, You, eternally beloved Daughter of the Father Who from eternity chose You as Mother of His Only-Begotten Son, you, the Mother of this Word of the Father, Who certainly taught You His infinite and most perfect Wisdom and Doctrine, even before He was in You, as a creature that was forming, or He was with You as a Son Who grows in age and wisdom to such an extent as to become the Master of masters. John told us the day after the first astonishing sermon and apostolic manifestation, which took place ten days after the Ascension of Jesus to Heaven. You, in turn, know, as You saw it at Gethsemane on the day of the Ascension of Your Son to His Father and as You were told by Peter, John and other apostles, that Lazarus and I, immediately after the Death and Resurrection, began to build a wall around my kitchen garden near Golgotha and at Gethsemane on the Mount of Olives, so that those places, sanctified by the Divine Martyr's Blood, that dropped, alas!, warmed by fever at Gethsemane, and frozen and clotted in my garden, may not be profaned by Jesus' enemies. The work has now been completed, and both Lazarus and I, and his sisters with him and the apostles, who would suffer too much *not having You here any longer, say to You: "Take up Your abode in the house of Jonah and Mary, the keepers of Gethsemane".*"

"And Jonah and Mary? That house is a small one, and I love solitude. I have always loved it. And I love it even more now, because I need it to get lost in God, in My Jesus, so that I may not die of anguish, not having Him here any longer. It is not fair that human eyes should be laid on the mysteries of God, because He is God now more than ever. I Woman, Jesus Man. But our Humanity was, and is, different from every other one, both because of our immunity from sin, also from the original one, and because of our relationship with God One and Trine. We are unique in these things among all creatures past, present and future. Now man, even the best and most prudent one, is naturally and inevitably curious, particularly if he is near an extraordinary manifestation. And only Jesus and I, as long as He was on the Earth, know what sufferings... yes, also shame, uneasiness, torture is experienced when human curiosity pries into, watches, spies upon our secrets with God. It is the same as if they placed us naked in the middle of a square. Think of My past, how I have always sought secrecy, silence, how I have always concealed, under the appearance of the common life of a poor woman, the mysteries of God in Me. Recall how, in order not to reveal them even to My spouse Joseph, I almost made of him, a just man, an unjust one. Only the angelic intervention avoided that danger. Think of the life so humble, hidden, common, led by Jesus for thirty-three years, how easily He would withdraw and become isolated when He was the Master. He had to work miracles and teach, because that was His mission. But, He told Me Himself, He suffered - one of the many reasons for the severity and sadness that flashed in His large powerful eyes - He suffered, I was saying, because of the exaltation of the crowds, because of the more of less good curiosity with which they watched every action of His. How many times did He order His disciples and those He had cured miraculously, saying: "Do not mention what you have seen. Do not mention what I have done for you"!... Now I should not like human eyes to inquire into the mysteries of God in Me, mysteries that have not ceased with the return to Heaven of Jesus, My Son and My God, no, on the contrary they last, and I should say that they increase, thanks to His goodness, and to keep Me alive, until the hour comes, for which I have longed so much, of joining Him forever. I would like only John with Me. Because he is prudent, respectful, loving with me like another Jesus. But Jonah and Mary will know..."

Lazarus interrupts her: "It has already been done, o Blessed Mother! We have already seen to it. Mark, Jonah's son, is among the disciples. Mary, his mother and Jonah, his father, are already at Bethany."

"But the olive-grove? It needs to be taken care of!" Mary replies to him.

"Only when it is time to prune, to plough and pick the olives. So, only a few days each year and which will be even fewer, because in those periods I will send my servants from Bethany with Mark. You, Mother, if you want to make us happy, my sisters and me, will come to Bethany in those days, to the Zealot's solitary house. We shall be close to one another, but our eyes will not be indiscreet with regard to your meetings with God."

"But the oil-mill?..."

"It has already been transferred to Bethany. Gethsemane, completely enclosed, the property even more reserved of Lazarus of Theophilus, is awaiting You, Mary. And I assure you that the enemies of Jesus, out of fear of Rome, will not dare to violate its peace and yours."

"Oh! since it is so!" exclaims Mary. And she presses her hands against her heart, and looks at them, with a countenance that is almost ecstatic, so blissful it is, with an angelic smile on her lips and tears of joy on her fair eyelashes. She continues: "John and I! Alone! We two all alone! I shall seem to be once again at Nazareth with My Son! Alone! In peace! In that peace! Where My Jesus gave forth so many words and so much spirit of peace! Where, it is true, He suffered so much that He sweated blood and received the supreme moral sorrow of the infamous kiss and the first..." A sob and a very painful recollection interrupt her words and upset her Face that, for a few moments, has once more the sorrowful expression it had on the days of the Passion and Death of Her Son. She then collects herself and says: "There, where He went back to the infinite peace of Paradise! I will soon send Mary of Alphaeus instructions to look after my little house in Nazareth, which is so dear to me, because the mystery was accomplished there and my spouse, so pure and holy, died there, and Jesus grew up in it. So dear! But never as much as these places where He instituted the Rite of rites, and He became Bread, Blood, Life for men, and He suffered and redeemed, and He founded His Church and, with His last blessing, He made all the things of Creation good and holy. I will remain. Yes. I will remain here. I will go to Gethsemane. And from there, walking along the outside of the walls, I shall be able to go to Golgotha, and to your kitchen garden, Joseph, where I wept so much, and I shall be able to come to your house, Lazarus, where I have always had so much love, in My Son first, and then for Myself." "But I should like..."

"What, Blessed Mother?" they both ask her.

"I should like to come back here as well. Because together with the apostles, we had decided, providing Lazarus allows us...» «Everything you want, Mother. Everything I have, is yours. Previously I used to say so to Jesus. Now I say it to you. And if you accept my gift, it is always I who receive a grace."

"Son, let me call you so, I should like you to allow us to make of this house, that is of the supper room, a place for meetings and for the brotherly agape."

"It is just. In this place Your Son instituted the new eternal Rite, He founded His new Church, elevating His apostles and disciples to a new Pontificate and Priesthood. It is just that that room should become the first temple of the new religion: the seed that tomorrow will be a tree, and then a huge forest, the embryo that tomorrow will be a complete vital organism, and that will grow more and more in height, depth and width, spreading all over the Earth. Which table and altar are holier than the ones on which He broke the Bread and laid the Chalice of the new Rite, that will last as long as the Earth?"

"That is true, Lazarus. And, see? For it I am sewing clean tablecloths. Because I believe, as no one will believe with equal strength, that the Bread and Wine are He, in His Flesh and in His Blood; Most holy and innocent Flesh, Redeeming Blood, given in Food and Drink of Life to men. May the Father, the Son and the Holy Spirit bless you, o good wise men, who have always been compassionate to the Son and to His Mother."

"So it is decided. Take this. It is the key that opens the various gates of the enclosure of Gethsemane. And this is the key of the house. And be happy, as much as God grants you to be and as much as our poor love would like you to be."

Now that Lazarus has finished speaking, Joseph of Arimathea in turn says: "And this is the key of the enclosure of my kitchen garden."

"But you... you are quite entitled to go in!"

"I have another one, Mary. The market-gardener is a just man, and so is his son. You will find only them and me there. And we will be prudent and respectful."

"May God bless you again" repeats Mary.

"Thanks to you, Mother. Our love and the peace of God to You, always." They prostrate themselves after this last greeting, they kiss the hem of her dress once again and they go away.

They have just gone out of the house, when another moderate knock is heard at the door of the room in which Mary is.

"Come in" says Mary.

John does not make her repeat it twice. He goes in and closes the door, somewhat worried. He asks: "What did Joseph and Lazarus want? Is there any danger?"

"No, son. There is only the satisfaction of a wish of mine. A wish of mine and of other people. You know how Peter and James of Alphaeus, the former the Pontiff, the latter the head of the church of Jerusalem, are desolate at the thought of losing Me, as they are afraid they will not know what to do without Me. James in particular. Not even the special apparition of My Son to him, and his election by the will of Jesus, comfort and fortify him. But also the others!... Lazarus is now satisfying this general wish and makes us the masters of Gethsemane. You and I. All alone there. Here are the keys. And this is the key of Joseph's kitchen garden... We shall be able to go to the Sepulchre, to Bethany, without going through the town... And to go to Golgotha... And come here every time there is the brotherly agape. Lazarus and Joseph are granting us everything."

"They are really two just men. Lazarus received a lot from Jesus. That is true. But, even before receiving, He always gave everything to Jesus. Are you happy, Mother?"

"Yes, John. So much! I will live, as long as God wants, helping Peter and James and all of you, and I will help the first Christians in every way. If the Judeans, the Pharisees and the priests are not wild animals also towards me, as they were for My Son, I shall be able to breathe my last where He ascended to His Father."

"You will ascend as well, Mother."

"No. I am not Jesus. I was born in a human way."

"But without stain of origin. I am a poor ignorant fisherman. With regard to doctrines and scriptures I know only what the Master taught me. But I am like a boy, because I am pure. And so, perhaps I know more than the Rabbis of Israel, because, He said so, God hides things from the wise and reveals them to the little and pure ones. And that is why I think, or better, I feel that you will have the destiny that Eve

would have had, if she had not sinned. And even more, because you have not been the spouse of an Adam-man, but of God, to give the Earth the new Adam faithful to Grace. The Creator, when He created our first Parents, did not destine them to die, that is to the corruption of the most perfect body created by Him, and made the most noble among all the bodies created, because it is endowed with a spiritual soul and with the gratuitous gifts of God, whereby they could be called "adoptive sons of God", but what He wanted for them was only a passage from the earthly Paradise to the celestial one. Now You have never had any stain of sin on Your soul. Not even the great common sin, the heritage of Adam to all human beings, affected You, because God preserved You from it by a singular unique privilege, as from ever, You had been destined to become the Ark of the Word. And the Ark, even the one that, alas!, contains nothing but cold, arid, dead things, because, really, the people of God do not put them into practice as they should, is and must always be most pure. The Ark is, yes. But among those who approach it, Pontiff and Priests, who is really as pure as You are? No one. That is why I feel that you, the second Eve, and Eve faithful to Grace, are not destined to death."

"My Son, the second Adam, Grace itself, always obedient to His Father, to me, in a perfect manner, died. And of what death!"

"He had come to be the Redeemer, Mother. He left His Father, Heaven, He took Flesh upon Himself, in order to redeem men, through His Sacrifice, give Grace back to them, and then elevate them once again to the rank of adoptive sons of God, heirs to Heaven. He had to die. And His Most Holy Humanity died. And you died in your heart seeing His cruel torture and His Death. You have already suffered everything to be the redeemer with Him. I am a poor foolish boy, but I feel that you, the true Ark of the true living God, will not be, you cannot be subject to corruption. As the cloud of fire protected and guided the Ark of Moses towards the Promised

Land, so the Fire of God will attract you to its Centre. As the branch of Aaron did not wither, did not perish, on the contrary, although detached from the tree, it put forth buds, leaves and yielded fruit and lived in the Tabernacle, so You, chosen by God among all the women who lived and will live on the Earth, will not die like a plant that withers, but You will live forever, with Your whole Self, in the Tabernacle of Heaven. As the waters of the Jordan opened to let the Ark, its bearers and all the people pass in the days of Joshua, so the barriers that the sin of Adam placed between Heaven and Earth will open for you, and from this world you will pass to the eternal Heaven. I am sure of that. Because God is just. And the decree issued by God for those who have neither hereditary nor voluntary sin on their souls applies to you."

"Has Jesus revealed that to you?"

"No, Mother. The Spirit Paraclete tells me, He who the Master informed us would reveal future things and all truth to us. The Comforter is already telling me in my spirit, to make less bitter for me the thought of losing You, blessed Mother, Whom I love and venerate as much and even more than my own mother, because of what You have suffered, because you are good and holy, inferior only to Your Most Holy Son among all present and future Saints. The greatest Saint." And John, deeply moved, prostrates himself venerating her.

The love that they had for Mary – Lazarus and Joseph – they gave her everything. They gave her everything that she needed to be in the position that she was in, to be safe from the world, to be able to walk around without being seen, to be in her secrecy and her silence, to be in her devotion. They honored that. They built a wall around the entire garden in Gethsemane, and they gave her the supper room and everything. This is what happens when you love. You give everything. And it's an example, for you. Lazarus didn't hold anything back, Mary and Martha didn't hold anything back, Joseph of Arimathea didn't hold anything back. And John devotes his whole life to her while she's on the planet. I mean, he was appointed so by Jesus, but he would have anyway, because she would have needed someone as a buffer, someone pure as a buffer between the world and her consciousness. You could apply to her for your gifts, and for love, and for compassion. You could apply to her for how to hold the mystery of your communions with God, because she's the example of one who respects it totally and displays it hardly at all to anyone, except if they were pure.

That same kind of secrecy is held by those who are really having an experience of God. If you're not having much of an experience of God, and you're not very secretive about anything, because you don't know what's valuable and what isn't valuable, and you haven't learned that yet because something's not that much different than something else. But when you're having an experience of God, it's so different than everything else you're going through, that it rises up as the highest thing, the deepest thing, and the most powerful thing in your life, and it changes you – about what you value, about what's the most valuable. It's not so much about what people think. It's not so much about getting somebody to like you or not like you or getting somebody to go along with your ego. It's about that you value this one beautiful thing. And everything else doesn't matter; people's opinions about you don't matter. In fact, she doesn't care to be with people, she's going to stay with just the support of the Priests and the disciples and that's it, and hardly any interaction with the world, who, she's very convinced, hates God.

She's not afraid of them; there's just nothing there for them. They're not receptive. She knows that. I wish you could know that about the world. If you knew that, I don't think you'd be so interested in it. I don't think you'd be so happy to find out how they feel about you. Mary would not have been interested in how anybody feels about Her, whatsoever. She was already in love with the Being who loved her and was conscious. So she's not interested in anybody's opinion. Even if they had beautiful things to say. She wouldn't have been interested in it because she has the fulfillment in her that most people look outside for.

She's the example of how to grow something within, until it becomes so full and so real that everything else becomes false. Everything else becomes shallow and superficial. She's not just wispy, fake, and shallow, in the sense of, she just wants to be private. Because people can do that with their ego and just go, "I don't want to be around people, I don't want to be jostled, I don't want to be influenced by the world." And you can do that for all the wrong reasons, because of your, you know, prideful sensitivity. No – She knows the world hates God. She knows there's nothing in the world that loved Jesus. Only the few that he chose and the few that followed him love Jesus. If you get that, you're at a different level. You're at a different level. You're not wondering why people like you or don't like you. You're surprised if they do, and you're wondering if it's real. And you're wondering how deep it is. Because most people don't know how to love, and they don't know how to respect pure, loving, God-like things. They don't.

So your audience should be Jesus and Mary, God, and fellow brother and sister disciples. That should be your audience. Those are the ones you should be mostly concerned about. You can love all the people, because occasionally, out of the vast mass hordes of selfish ones, somebody might rise up, and they need to see somebody who's shining. So you need to be open to that, although I know that's rare now. That's rare for anybody from the world to be moving towards heaven. There's too much against them now. There's too much – you know – the big snowball is rolling downhill. That's how it is for most people; they're rolling down, they're going away, they're heading out, they're giving up. That's what the world's doing right now. But don't be too closed off to the possibility that somebody's looking, because there are people that are looking. It's one in a thousand, though. It really is, right now, one in a thousand...one in ten thousand is probably more accurate.

But Mary's example to you is to hold to what is real and hold to what is valuable, and not be concerned or curious about anything else, not interested in anything else. She didn't go read the paper, she didn't go to do coffee to see how the world was doing every morning, just to keep up on current events and stuff. There was no interest in that whatsoever. And she was around for fifteen more years after Jesus died - ascended. Because what interest in the world would have gained her anything? What could she have learned by that? She knew it all, felt it all, and experienced it all, and had the Oneness within herself; she didn't need any of that. That's true for you, on the deepest level. You don't need anything else. But you haven't allowed yourself to rise up and sink into that, the Self-containment, being contained by the Self.

We celebrate mothers today, and most mothers are, you know, embarrassing. That's the best we can say. Embarrassing. They love in the puniest way, in the most selfish way possible, and so proud of it. And when you put Mary next to that, it's like a twelve-year-old having a kid, that's how embarrassing it is, that's how developed they are compared to Mother Mary. She's not mad at them, and she doesn't disdain that, but it's clearly so different when one is not selfish at all, not egotistical, and one is devoted to God, versus one who has all that other crap going on, all that other impurity going on. And I'm going to remind you that that's a choice, that is not a condition that you have to suffer, that is a choice that you're making. That's all it is, it's a choice you're making. Everything you're experiencing is a choice, or it wouldn't be happening.

Mary chose to walk along the edges of the garden, to walk along the walls, to not be seen, to go to Bethany, to go to Golgotha, to go to where her Son was crucified, to go to the places where He suffered and to be not seen. "Cause the only thing that mattered to her was Him, and God. And the nascent church, to support them in their insecurities and in their worries and in their newness, their inexperience in evangelizing and bringing people to the Master. She's been with the Master from the beginning. She was with God before she was with the Master. Understand? She was the first. There's no separation. It's not like she's missing any steps. She didn't skip any beats. Always faithful. Always one with God. Always strong against stupidity. Always strong against temptation. Never faltering in her faith. That's what a woman can do; that's the strength of a woman, if she's convinced of something. That's who we honor today, but that's not how the world does it. They honor, you know, the bio-people, biological people. When I think of Mother, I think of her. I think of all these other practitioners of motherhood as an experiment, trying to get it right, or trying to do better, or trying to raise it up somehow, in the most positive read of it.

Honor the goodness that you can. Do not honor the selfishness. Don't ever honor the selfishness, if you want your integrity to stay intact. Never honor the selfishness of another person. You can even honor the potential, I suppose, that's kind of a gift. But don't honor the selfishness of another person. Ever. Do you want your selfishness to be honored? "You were so proud. I want to honor that. You were so scary and so fearful and so dominating, and I just want to honor that about you." Do you see how it sounds stupid? Don't honor the lack of integrity in another person.

Honor the goodness that is, maybe, dormant, honor the goodness that may be dormant, honor the beauty of the possibility of a deep love that could, any day, happen if the person chose to. Honor that. That makes sense. The rest is you're making a deal with darkness – don't even do it. Because you know what? You're apologizing for your own lack of perfection.

Jesus didn't say, "At every turn, apologize for your lack of perfection." No, He said, "Be perfect. Be good. Be Light. Be Love." That's what He said. So falling short of that, don't pat yourself on the back for any falling-short of that, ever. And, I know, you can be kind to people who are announcing their adulation to a biological mother, that's all right, but don't be fooled by it. Don't be fooled by it. Were they so much higher, that you could look up to it? No, they were trying, maybe...maybe...maybe. You want to look to Mary? You can't get that close to God without being strong and courageous and powerful and intense and decisive. You cannot get close to God without being decisive. And isn't that exactly what the feminine challenge is – to be decisive? To decide not to dip into the darkness? To decide not to get negative? To decide to be positive? To look to the good in everybody? That's a decision, and that's what Mother Mary always did. Always looked to God. Always looked to the God in people. Always saw the difference between how much of God was expressing and how much wasn't expressing. Not to be negative/evaluating/critical, no. Just to see. Just to see it, and to support the good, to support that growing up in them, getting stronger in them. That's your job, that's a mother's job, to make the young ones strong. That's the mother's job.

May 15, 2016
Subtleties

The Gospel as Revealed to Me, Chapter 467. The parable of the distribution of water.

"Listen to this parable.

A wealthy man had many subordinates in numerous places of his state, but not every place was rich in water and fertile soil. Several places suffered from lack of water, and people suffered even more because if the ground was cultivated with trees which could withstand the drought, people suffered very much from the shortage of water. The rich owner instead had, close to the house in which he lived, a lake rich in water which gushed from underground springs.

One day he decided to make a tour of his estate and he saw that some places, those closest to the lake, were rich in water, whereas others, which were remote, had none, except the small quantity which God sent as rain. And he also noticed that those who had plenty of water were not kind to their brothers who were deprived of it, and begrudged them even with a pail of water with the excuse that they were afraid of being without. The lord meditated on the situation. And he decided thus: "I will divert the waters of my lake towards those who are closer to it and I will order them not to refuse water any longer to my distant servants who are suffering because of the parched land."

And he undertook the work at once and had canals dug to take the good water of the lake to the nearest parts of his property, where he dug large cisterns so that abundant water should gather there increasing the supplies already existing, and from each part he had smaller canals built to feed other more remote cisterns. He then summoned the people living in those places and said to them: Remember that I have not done all this work to give you superfluous quantities of water, but I did it to assist, with your help, those who lack also what is necessary. Be, therefore as merciful as I have been" and he dismissed them.

Some time passed and the rich owner wished to visit all his possessions once again. He saw that the nearest ones had become more beautiful and abounded not only in useful plants but also in ornamental ones, in vats, swimming-pools, fountains placed everywhere around the houses.

"You have turned these houses into abodes of rich people" remarked the lord. "I do not have so much superfluous beauty myself," and he asked them: "Do the others come? Have you given them plenty water? Are the smaller canals fed?"

"Yes. They have been given as much as they asked. And they are over particular, they are never pleased, they are neither prudent nor moderate, they come and ask at any time, as if we were their servants and we have to defend ourselves to protect what belongs to us. They were no longer satisfied with the small canals and cisterns. They come as far as the large ones."

"Is that why you have enclosed these places and placed these wild dogs in each of them?"

"Yes, that is the reason, sir. They used to come in without any consideration and expected to take everything away and they spoiled..."

"But have you really given water to them? Do you realize that I did all this for them and I used you as an intermediate link between the lake and their parched land? I do not understand... I had as much water diverted from the lake as to satisfy everybody without any waste."

"And yet you must believe us: we never denied them water." The lord set out towards his remote possessions. The tall trees fit for arid ground were green and leafy. "They have spoken the truth" said the lord seeing them rustling in the distance. But when he approached them and walked under them he saw the parched soil, the almost withered grass on which emaciated sheep grazed with difficulty, the sandy vegetable gardens near houses and then the first farmers: sickly, with feverish eyes, downhearted... they looked at him and lowered their heads withdrawing as if they were frightened.

He was surprised at their behavior and he called them. They approached him trembling. What are you afraid of? Am I no longer your good master who has taken care of you and with provident work has relieved you of the shortage of water? Why are your faces so sickly looking? Why is this land so arid? And the sheep so lean? And why do you seem to be frightened of me? Speak without fear. Tell your master what is afflicting you."

One man spoke on behalf of everybody. Lord, we have been badly disappointed and deeply grieved. You promised to help us and we have lost also what we had previously and we have given up every hope in you". "How? Why? Did I not let water come abundantly to the nearest people with instructions that the abundance was for you?"

"Is that what you said? Really?"

"Most certainly. The level of the ground prevented me from bringing the water here directly. But with goodwill you could have gone to the little canals of the cisterns with goatskins and donkeys and taken as much as you wanted. Did you not have enough donkeys and goatskins? And was I not there to give you some?"

"There you are! I told you! I said: 'It is not possible that the lord has given instructions to deny us water. I wish we had gone for it!'"

"We were afraid. They told us that the water was a reward for them and that we were to be punished." And they informed the good master that the tenant farmers of the privileged possessions has told them that the landlord, in order to punish the servants of the arid fields because they were not producing more, had given instructions to measure not only the water of the cisterns but also that of the old wells, so that while previously they had two hundred baths of water a day for themselves and the land, and they had to carry it with much fatigue for a long distance, now they did not even have fifty and to have enough for men and animals they had to go to the brooks at the borders of the fortunate places, where water overflowed from gardens and baths and take that muddy water, and they were dying. They were dying of diseases and thirst and vegetables and sheep were also perishing...

"Oh! that is too much! And I must stop it. Take your goods and chattels and your animals and follow me. You will fatigue a little, worn out as you are, but then you will have peace. I shall proceed slowly to allow you to follow me, in spite of your weakness. I am a good master, a good father to you and I see to my children." And he sets out slowly followed by the sad crowd of servants and animals who, however, were already rejoicing in the solace of their good master's love.

They arrived at the possessions very rich in water. When they were at the borders, the master took some of the strongest men and said to them: "Go and ask for some water in my name." "And if they set the dogs on us?" "I shall be behind you. Be not afraid. Go and say that I sent you and tell them not to close their hearts to justice, because the water belongs to God and all men are brothers. Tell them to open the canals at once."

They went and the landlord followed them. They stopped at a gate and the master hid himself behind the enclosure wall. They called and the tenant farmers went to the gate.

"What do you want?"

"Have mercy on us. We are dying. The landlord has sent us with instructions to take the water which he brought here for us. He says that God gave the water to him, he gave it to you for us because we are brothers and that you are to open the canals at once."

"Ha! Ha!" laughed the cruel people. "These ragged people are our brothers? You are dying? So much the better. We will take over your places, and we will take water there. We will *certainly take it there in that case! And we will make the soil fertile. Water for you? You are stupid! The water is ours."*

"Have mercy. We are dying. Open the canals. It's the master's order."

The wicked tenants consulted with one another and then they said: "Wait a moment" and they went away. They then came back and opened the gate. But they had dogs with them and heavy clubs... The poor people were afraid. "Come in, come in... Are you not coming in now that we have opened the gate? And then you will say that we were not generous..." One of the men went in imprudently and a shower of blows rained on him while the unleashed dogs rushed upon the others.

The landlord appeared from behind the wall. "What are you doing, you cruel people? Now I know you and your animals and I will strike you" and he shot arrows at the dogs and he went in. He was severe and angry. "Is that how you carry out my orders? Is that why I gave you this wealth? Call all your people. I want to speak to you. And you" he said to the parched servants "come in with your women and children with your sheep and donkeys, with your doves and all your animals, and drink and refresh yourselves, and pick this juicy fruit and you, little innocent children, play among the flowers. Enjoy yourselves. There is justice in the heart of your good master and there will be justice for everybody."

And while the thirsty people ran to the cisterns, dived into the swimming-pools, and the cattle went to the vats and they were all full of joy, the others came from all directions looking frightened.

The landlord climbed on to the edge of a cistern and said: "I had all this work done and I made you trustees of my order and of this treasure, because I had chosen you as my ministers.

But you failed in the test. You appeared to be good. You should have been good, because welfare makes people good, grateful to their benefactor and I had always assisted you by giving you the tenancy of this well-watered land. Such wealth and choice has made you hardhearted, more arid than the land which you have made completely arid and more sick than these people parched with thirst. Because water can cure them, whereas you, with your selfishness, have parched your spirits which are not likely to recover, and the water of charity will flow back into you with great difficulty. I will now punish you. Go into their lands and suffer what they suffered."

"Mercy, lord! Have mercy on us! Do you want us to perish? Are you less compassionate towards us men than we are towards animals?"

"And who are these? Are they not men, your brothers? What mercy did you have on them? They were asking for water and you gave them blows with clubs and treated. them sarcastically. They were asking for what was mine and which I had given, and you refused them saying that it was 'yours'. Whose water is it? Even I will not say that the water of the lake is mine although the lake is mine. Water belongs to God. Which of you has created one single drop of dew? Go!... And to you, to you who have suffered, I say: be kind. Do to them what you would have liked done to you. Open the canals which they closed and let the water flow towards them, as soon as possible. I make you my dispensers to these guilty brothers to whom I leave means and time to redeem themselves. And the Most High entrusts you with the wealth of His water. More than I do so that you may be providential for those who have none. If you can do this with love and justice, being satisfied with what is necessary, giving what is superfluous to the poor, being honest, not calling yours what is a gift given to you, a deposit more than a gift, great will be your peace and God's love and mine will always be with you."

That is the end of the parable and everybody can understand it. I only say to you that rich people are only the depositaries of the wealth granted to them by God with instructions to distribute it to those who suffer. Consider the honor which God grants you by calling you to be partners in *the work of providence in favor of poor and sick people, of widows and orphans. God could ram money, garments, food on poor people. But in that case He would deprive rich people of great merits: those of charity towards their brothers. Not all rich people can be learned, but they can all be good. Not all rich people can take care of sick people, bury the dead, visit invalids and prisoners. But all rich people, and even those who are not poor, can give a piece of bread, a drop of water, cast-off garments, and they can welcome to their fire places those who are shivering, and can give hospitality to those who are homeless, and are exposed to rain and dog-days. He is poor who lacks what is necessary to live. The others are not poor, they have scanty means, but they are still rich as compared with those who die of starvation, privations and cold.*

I am going away. I can no longer assist the poor people of this area. And my heart suffers thinking that they are losing a friend... Well I who am speaking to you, and you know who I am, I ask you to be the providence of the poor who are being left without their merciful Friend. Give them alms and love them in My name and in memory of Me... be My continuators. Relieve My depressed heart with this promise: that you will always see Me in the poor and that you will receive them as the most true representatives of Christ who is poor, who wanted to be poor out of love for the most unhappy people on Earth, and to expiate, through His own indigence and ardent love, the unfair prodigality and selfishness of men.

For those of the temple, those Pharisees and scribes who knew the Testament, they knew the scriptures by heart, and everybody learned by heart. Very few people read or were literate. It was passed down, so it was memorized by the time you were a small child, you memorized everything, and you knew the scriptures inside and out. And there's Jesus saying, 'Look at the scriptures, you see Me act that way. Look at my actions and you see it's in the scriptures. You should be able to tell. You're not stupid. You should be able to tell that I am the manifestation of the scriptures.' But they could not hear that. They could not hear that. And you know, darkness prevents people from seeing. It prevents people from knowing something about themselves.

It's a shock to most of you when I call a certain attitude a sin, or I call a certain behavior, a certain thinking style a sin, or darkness. I call it darkness. In the beginning of hearing that, it was a shock, because it's so customary and normal for you to think that way. For somebody to call it darkness or evil or sin, it was startling. And the same thing for Jesus, and He comes as pure Light and pure truth coming in and saying exactly what is and what is not, what is of God and what is not of God. The people are startled. It's a startling thing. In the beginning when your eyes are dull, you can't tell the difference between a sin and just an attitude or just an idiosyncrasy or just a stylistic difference, one person to the other.

Then as you grow, somebody says, well that particular thought is mean, and you're startled by that. You didn't realize it was mean. In fact, just calling it mean now makes it a problem for you. And later when we say a particular attitude of irritation is a sin, or a particular kind of anticipation is a sin, or a particular kind of curiosity about what's going on with somebody else, if it wasn't for you to be able to help them. Just being curious about what's going on with them, without any love on your part, is a sin because you're meddling in knowing something about the other to compare them with you. And so, that is like an impurity in your system, to need to compare that because it's only your ego that needs to evaluate that. See how they're doing compared to how you're doing. That's not to be helpful. You're not desiring to pray for them so that they raise up, maybe even raise up way past you. That's alright, you know, because that's a prayer. That's a gift. That's love. But just to ferret out what's going on with the other person so you don't look bad, that's darkness. That's evil. Or that you don't look any worse than they do because you are trying to decipher where they are.

And those are the subtleties of the ones that live with God. Everything starts to purify. Everything that used to be just common place and unexamined is now up for scrutiny. And Jesus is trying to take you somewhere, is trying to take you somewhere into Light, into more heaven, into more grace, into more truth. And if you're a disciple, you'll want to go. And you should be enthusiastic about that even though there's quite a heavy wind trying to blow that old stuff off of you as you turn more and more into Light. That heavy wind is like a hurricane sometimes, blowing stuff that's attached to you, but it is not you, but it wants to blow it away from you.

In the time left, Jesus said, in the time you have left, you can grow into this perfection. And you need to. I don't know if you're strong enough to be able to handle all the self doubts and all of the world press against truth, and the world encouragement against reality, real reality. I don't know if you have the strength. And I'm not trying to put you down. I'm just saying, He's even saying, in the time left, you need to get even closer to the truth, and you need to get more light shined on you, and from within you, out to your world. And you need to be more energetic in allegiance to the truth. Because in these times, more and more people are fading away. And they're fading away in mind. It's like well, it's not that important. That's the first stage of fading away. Why is it such a big deal? That's another point of fading away. And I don't know why they're making such a big deal out of this thing. That's another thing. It starts to undermine your faith, and you're starting now to think a bit like the world.

The world says, "I don't know what this God thing is." I think we're having a one world order. I think it's going to be one economy. We'll all be taken care of, we'll be cashless and we'll be chipped. And this is going to be good, and it's just going to be better for everybody. And everybody will have everybody's information. And the evil people will be removed. And that's good. And this is the superficiality of the brain. That's people being super superficial because the more control people have on other people, the less freedom to choose they have. Now that sounds good, because to scared people it sounds protective. Weak and scared people like that kind of structure because it gives them a false sense of security. But the very structure that they are complacently accepting is the very structure that keeps them from becoming Divine beings. It'll keep them just hammered down into the mass, hammered up from below, hammered down from above. So excellence will not be allowed. Different thinking won't be allowed. Creativity will have to be circumcised. And it will have to be confined to what is acceptable by the powers that won't be threatened by it. So that's going to all get hammered. Self-expression, creativity, intuition, no, no, no, no. That won't be allowed when you have the masses getting taught how to behave that conforms to the darkness. And I know, you've heard it all, but you're not tuned to the subtleties of these suggestions. The suggestion is, what's the big deal? That suggestion alone means it's just a matter of opinion. 'I don't know why you're getting so bent out of shape. I don't know why you're taking this so seriously. I don't know why you're actually trying to be good here. Nobody really appreciates it.' This is the world mind. This is the darkness. This is the satanic energy telling you your efforts don't matter, telling you that you can't really amount to anything really because everything is all programmed against you. But He said, the one who endures to the end will be saved. And He talked about this time period where are you are going to be severely tried. And you think the trial is going to be like Gladiators and prison or something, lions in the lion den, or something like that. You're still in that drama scene with Cecil B. Demille. You're still out there. You don't really get it that it's the malaise of the dullness coming over you that is the marching of the armies of the darkness. That's the malaise that is going to take most people down. But the ones that are faithful, the ones that endure to the end, the ones that stay steady in that storm, they are going to be with Jesus. He said it. He promised, not a hair of your head will be hurt. You will be tried and tested and persecuted. But you will not be hurt if you stay faithful to Him.

I think you can take that as comfort, but I also think you need to get yourself together like in your weaknesses. If your desires are just raging, you need to control them. If your habit of being emotional is just wild, wind that back in, get control over it. If you're judgments of other people are just outrageous in your head and you can't stop them, you need to shut your brain up and learn how to shut it up. And do something very creative and positive to keep that brain from doing that shit in your head. Because that's called discipline. Do anything except be negative. Do anything hard and long and as long as it takes until that negative stuff stops. Do whatever it takes to have the negative thing stop inside you. That's called self-discipline. If you don't demonstrate that, Jesus is saying, 'Well you are weak, your muscles are weak, your dedication is weak, your determination to be with Me is weak. How can I rely on you? You can't even discipline yourself.' And nobody's checking up on you, except if you have interchanges with your brothers and sisters and your negative stuff starts spouting out, they need to say something to you. They need to say, What are you doing? This is weird what you're doing. It feels bad what you're doing. Stop it. That's what they should say. They don't need to go into the particulars, because nobody needs to get into your particulars. Who cares? If it feels bad, it just feels bad. You just say it feels bad. I don't like it. You don't need to know why. You don't need to explain it. You just say that feels bad. You can back away. Just say I'm out of this. I'm not going to do this. This feels bad. That's all you need to say.

That should be enough of a cue to the rest of your brothers and sisters that you better examine yourself and what you're doing. Because if they have to say it, it means you didn't discipline yourself. Maybe you weren't aware. Maybe you weren't aware what you were doing, putting out negative energy. But somebody should say, hey you're putting out negative energy. And you don't have to say, Oh, how was I... woah, stop! And you stop right there. If it feels negative, then it probably is. Then just stop. It doesn't matter what you're saying. It doesn't matter why you're saying it. Just freaking stop it. Because you're putting out garbage. Stop doing that. Save Jesus and Mary a lot of work by not fouling the air around you with negative fears and worries and conscious dipping into the darkness. It'll help Them a lot. Because then they'll be able to count on you because you're not going to dip. Are you going to dip? Yeah, you're going to dip. So they can't count on you. Are you not going to dip? Oh, I can count on you. You know how, dipping. Let's just call it dipping so you don't have to judge yourself. Well I dipped a little bit. Yeah, you did. Okay well when you were dipping, Jesus can't count on you. Because you dipped. You went unconscious. You lost your focus. You lost your purpose which is to give, to serve, to shine light, to love people. You lost your purpose when you did that. That's called dipping. When you do that, who can count on you? Everybody can dip. Anybody has the skills to dip. You know, like don't pat yourself on the back for that. But try not to do that anymore. Cut it out. So that Jesus when he looks at you goes you're not that dipper. You're not dippers. You're steady. I can count on you. That's what it should be.

These guys He's talking to, these Pharisees, the temple idiots, He can't even talk like that to them. He has to tell them that they can't see, that they're not able to hear. They can't see, they can't hear, they don't know. And they can't even see the obvious, which is He's actually demonstrating the fulfillment of the prophecies. Every one of them, hundreds of them. And they're too dense to see it. How do you talk to people like that? You tell them they're blind and you walk away. Pretty much that's all you can do. You're just a blind person. We could say it differently in our language, you're an idiot. And a fool, and I'm walking away. There's no talking to you. You're like a brick wall. But for disciples, we talk a little differently. We talk a little differently about receptive people. We say, You know that goodness that you are inside, way in there, that you're sometimes avoiding? Why don't you express that? That's how we talk to disciples. We don't force them. We don't make them. We don't push them around. We say, You know that goodness that you're suspecting that you are? Why don't you express that? Why don't you go ahead and express that now? And how about consistently? How about consistently? And some of you go, aw that's going to be hard! Do you know it's harder to be negative than it is to be good? Did you know that it takes more energy and it takes more stress to be negative then to be good? Same with the smiles. It takes less muscles in the cheeks than to frown. It takes more work, more work, to frown and to look sad and miserable than it does to smile. I wonder why that is. Is that a trick God put on us? To make it a little less work to be happy than to be miserable? I think it is. You know God is super smart. Okay, you're going to be miserable. Okay it's going to be a little more work, all right. That's God from a huge perspective. You want stress? Okay, that's fine. It's going to be harder. Go for it. This is the wisdom of God. It's confounding to the brain. But it's way bigger. It's like game over. With God, it's always game over. Slam dunk. You know, it's over. And you're thinking you're winning. It's not like that. You win when you go along with obedience and love and service. That's when you win. That's when you win and everybody wins. Everybody around you wins. And God wins. God will always win, but you'll be participating instead of fighting it. I want to leave you with a thought: you don't really know what to do, but Jesus does. And you don't really know how to be happy but Jesus does and you don't really know how to work less and work smarter but Jesus does. So maybe we could learn that. Maybe we could learn how to do that.

May 22, 2016

The Gospel as Revealed to Me, Chapter 472. The treacherous request of an opinion about an event that occurred in Gisela.

"Listen. A man who had been away from home for a long time on business, learned, when he came back, that during his absence his wife had been unfaithful to him, to the extent of giving birth to a child, who could not be of her husband, as he had been away for fourteen months. The man killed his wife secretly. But he was denounced by a man who had been informed by the maid-servant and was killed, according to the law of Israel. The lover, who according to the Law should be stoned, has taken shelter at Kedesh and he will certainly try to go to other places. The illegitimate child, whom the husband wanted to kill as well, was not handed to him by the woman who suckled him and she went to Kedesh to excite the pity of the true father and convince him to take care of his son, because her husband is opposed to keeping the illegitimate child in his house. But the man rejected her and his son stating that the latter would be a hindrance to him in his flights. What is Your opinion on the matter?"

"I do not think that it can be judged any more. All judgement, whether right or wrong, has already been given.

"Which judgement, according to You, is just and which is unjust. There is disagreement among us concerning the punishment of the murderer.»

Jesus stares at them, one after the other. He then says: "I will speak. But first answer My questions, whatever their weight may be. And be sincere. Did the man who murdered his wife belong to this town?"

"No. He settled here when he married the woman who is from here."

"Did the adulterer come from here?"
"Yes, he did."

"How did the man find out that his wife had been unfaithful to him? Was their sin known in public?"

"Not really, and we do not know how the man was able to find out. The woman had been away for months saying that, as she did not want to be all alone, she was going to Ptolemais to stay with some relatives, and she came back saying that she had brought with her the little son of a relative of hers who had died."

"When she was in Giscala was her behavior impudent?"

"No. In fact we were all surprised to hear that Marcus had an affair with her."

"My relative is not a sinner. He is accused but he is innocent » says one of the three men who had never spoken so far.

"Was he a relative of yours? Who are you?" asks Jesus.

"The first of the Elders of Giscala. That is why I wanted the life of the murderer, because he not only killed, but he killed an innocent » and he looks sullenly at the third man, who is about forty years old and who replies: « The Law says that the murderer is to be killed."

"You wanted the lives of the woman and of the adulterer."

"That is the Law."

"Had there been no other reason, no one would have spoken."

The dispute becomes animated and the two antagonists almost forget about Jesus. But the one who was the first to speak, the oldest man, imposes silence saying impartially: "It is not possible to deny that a homicide has been committed, neither can one deny that there has been a fault. The woman confessed it to her husband. But let the Master speak."

"I say: how did the husband find out? You have not answered My question."

The man defending the woman says: "Because someone spoke as soon as the husband came back."

"In that case I say that his soul was not pure," says Jesus lowering His eyelids to veil His eyes so that they may not accuse.

But the forty year old man who wanted the death of the woman and of the adulterer exclaims: "I did not hunger for her."

"Ah! it is clear now! It was you who spoke! I suspected that, but now you have betrayed yourself! Assassin!"

"And you are an accomplice of the adulterer. If you had not warned him, he would not have escaped us. But he is your relative! That is how justice is done in Israel! That is why you are defending also the memory of the woman: to defend your relative. If she were the only one involved, you would not worry about her."

"And what about you, who hurled the man against the woman to take vengeance for her refusals?"

"And what about you, the only witness against the man, and you paid a maid-servant in that house to be helped by her? One witness only is not a valid one. That's the Law." A terrible uproar!

Jesus and the old man try to calm the two men who represent two opposed interests and trends and who reveal an incurable hatred of two families. They succeed with some difficulty and Jesus now speaks calmly and solemnly, after defending Himself from the accusation of one of the two opponents, who said: "You Who protect prostitutes..."

"I not only say that consummated adultery is a crime against God and one's neighbor, but I say: also he who craves lustfully for the wife of another man commits adultery in his heart and commits a sin. It would be dreadful if every man who has craved for the wife of another man should be put to death! Lapidators would need to have stones in their hands all the time. But if the sin often remains unpunished on the Earth, it will be expiated in the next life, because the Most High said: "You shall not commit adultery and you shall not covet your neighbor's wife," and God's word is to be obeyed.

But I also say: "Woe betide him who is the cause of scandal and him who informs against his neighbor." In this case everybody is guilty. The husband: was it really necessary for him to leave his wife for such a long time? Did he always treat her with the love that conquers the heart of a companion? Did he examine himself to ascertain whether the woman had not been offended by him before he was offended by her? The law of retaliation says: "An eye for an eye, a tooth for a tooth." But if it says so to exact amends, are these to be given by one only? I am not defending the adulteress. But I say: "How many times could she have accused her husband of that sin?"

The people whisper: "It is true! It is true!" and also the old man from Giscala and Gamaliel's disciple agree.

Jesus goes on: " I say: why did he, who caused such a tragedy out of revenge, not fear God? Would he have liked all that to happen in his family? I say: the man who ran away and who after enjoying himself and causing ruin now disowns also the innocent child, does he think that by fleeing he will escape the eternal Avenger? That is what I say. I also say: the Law exacted the lapidation of adulterers and the killing of murderers. But the day will come when the Law, necessary to control the violence and lust of men not fortified by the Grace of the Lord, will be modified, and if the commandments: 'You shall not kill and you shall not commit adultery' remain, the sanctions against such sins will be referred to a higher justice than that of hatred and blood. A justice, compared with which, the surviving ever false undeserving justice of human judges, all of whom are adulterers, and perhaps several times adulterers, if not even killers, will be less than nothing. I am speaking of the justice of God Who will ask men also the reason for lustful desires which are the causes of revenge, delations, murders, and above all will ask them why they deny guilty people time to redeem themselves and why they compel innocent people to bear the burden of other people's faults. They are all guilty in this case. Everybody. Also the judges urged by opposing reasons of personal revenge. One only is innocent. And My pity is for him. I cannot go back. But which of you will be charitable to the baby and to Me Who am suffering for him?" Jesus looks at the crowd with eyes expressing sad prayer.

It goes on.

You can see the confusion in judging, you can see the confusion in the self-righteousness and demanding recompense for something that you think is wrong that somebody else does. But you're often just justifying your own selfishness when you're asking for somebody to pay for something. And that's what he's talking about...he's talking about everybody would have to be stoned if the Judgment of God was going to come up on them...about were they lustful? And were they insensitive? And were they mean? And did they care? And were they concerned with the baby? Were they concerned with the woman? Did they provoke each other to adultery by their meanness? There are a hundred questions that they really can't answer. They didn't want to answer those questions. But this is the kind of thing that someone with spiritual sight would have to see. You'd have to see all the motives behind these decisions that people make and this harshness that they create in themselves in looking at their neighbor. Like, why are they harsh? Why are they scared for behavior in a neighbor? Is it because they do that too? And they don't want to be judged for it? That's why they're harsh with that neighbor? Are they distracting off of their own sense of guilt by accusing another person? These are the things that were coming up in the conversation with Jesus, and this is the problem with the selfish motivation that you're not cleaned, you're not pure. It's not like what is the decision of God here, it's no, what do I get out of this by seeing it in my direction to back people off from judging me. It's complicated. It was even hard to follow wasn't it? It's complicated, who's talking, what are they saying and everybody has a little bit of truth and so it's hard to figure out who's saying what. And that's what it is with disputes among two of you.

You each have a point, you each have a perspective that given that that's the only perspective, you are right. But you're not the only perspective and so you're not completely right because you need the other perspective to be fully just and merciful in your judgment. And that's not how you present, you don't present everybody's side. That's not how an individual presents. They present my side, the side that makes sense. My side. And then everybody should just, oh yes we will bow down to your side because it makes so much sense and yet there are other perspectives besides your own and there are other people with eyes as well and ears as well around that see things from a different vantage point than you do, and may be seeing some things that you don't see at all and may be you see some things that they don't see. Okay, so there's room for understanding? There is room for compassion? There's room for love?

And these two men are arguing over this situation, wanting a murder, wanting the stoning, wanting the payment, wanting the judgment against these people. You know they have a different perspective and they all are using the law to justify the righteousness of their decision. And you do that too, you justify the heaviness of your hand and the heaviness of your mind based on something you read or something you heard or something that was done before, some history that's been accomplished, or the law, the law of the land, you know that there's a bunch of justices that you pack your case with while your heavy-handed in your bias or mean in your approach like non loving, that's the problem, and that's what Jesus is, he said you're all wrong, you're all off. You all should be stoned. There wouldn't be enough stones to carry around to deal with all the people's misjudgments.

And so what is the best thing to do in that situation? Well people have to lighten up. That's the only thing you can do. You have to kind of...okay people get weird...you have to get philosophical just like Jesus was. They're not enough stones to lapidate you all, so let's just get compassionate on people's situations that people screw up, and people have strange ideas, and people do things that they're never going to get away with them, because God is just. Even if they get away with it in this life, they won't get away with it in the next life.

And so he's really telling you to relax. He's telling you to relax your opinions, he's telling you to relax your judgments, your heavy-handedness, your harshness, your meanness, and your righteousness, he's telling you to relax. And if you trust in God you're not going to be so heavy-handed on your neighbor. I mean look in the mirror and then you'll stop all heavy-handedness if you even reflect on the mistakes you made this morning, you'll probably just get lighter. You know when you had an idea, and somebody didn't have that idea and you were scraping against it and a little gnarly and you got a little irritated but you didn't say anything because you're so good in not saying anything but it bristled through your skin you know, that kind of gnarlyness. If you just look at yourself you've got plenty to look at you don't need to look at your neighbor that much for their imperfections. And I believe we're all, in this community, I think we're scared of being honest with each other... I'll reference that later, but I believe that's the truth. We're still protecting ourselves quite a bit and only a guilty conscience protects themselves. I mean figure out another reason why.

If you're completely transparent, you're just fine, you know you're fine, and you're acting fine...like you don't hold back anything and you don't really hide anything...and you're not protecting anything.... there's nothing to protect. But when you know their is selfishness afoot or there's harsh judgments or there's desire nature things that are happening or those little anger management problems that you're having within yourself privately, you know that you're going to protect yourself with other people. And you're going to get the most touchy person is the most at fault within themselves. And they're not doing anything to anybody else, but the most touchy person has the guiltiest conscience. And it doesn't really matter what you're guilty about, nobody needs to know, we're not going to peer into your, you know, cloudy privacy to try to find out what your little smirk is, your little smudge is, who cares? But the fact that you have it means you're protecting a cloudy space because a clear person doesn't protect anything, they don't have to, but a cloudy person protects their cloudiness and I'm suggesting that people shouldn't be interested in your cloudiness. If you're going to be cloudy nobody should be interested in you. Because you're kind of full of it. But if you knew you're full of it because you're cloudy, maybe you'd work on yourself and you wouldn't be touchy with other people because you would know that you're living in a cloud. All by yourself.

And isn't that what Jesus is doing with these two guys and this little crowd? He's like mirror mirror on the wall who's the ugliest of them all and they're all ugly. They're all full of it and every time he puts the mirror up, and he puts a mirror and he puts a mirror and they see themselves, they see themselves, and pretty soon they're out of gas trying to accuse, they're out of gas running their little justifications for having these people murdered. And that's serious, you're going to murder somebody, you're going to take somebody off planet because of a rule and a law and a judgment because you're just mad and it's inconvenient to have that person around because maybe they make you feel guilty or it's inconvenient to have that person around because they're interfering with your lust for that woman. So Jesus is just messing everybody up. And causing them to reflect back on themselves...are you righteous? Are you clean? Are you free from sin? Are you free from these things that you're accusing other people of? The touchy ones are protecting. The guilty ones are accusing. And is this not what you do?

The ones that have a clean conscience that have gone to Jesus and say these are my faults, these are my sins, these are the things I would like help with, these are the mistakes I have made, they don't protect themselves because they've done their work, they've done the responsible thing of taking it to the Master and having it healed. Or at least getting some start with the healing. The rest are trying to look good because they don't feel good.

So this is the level of honesty that I would like our community to begin to rise in to. We're not there, we're not even close. We're not even close, and I'm not criticizing, I'm just saying this is the work we have to do. This is the work we have to do to get to this level of honesty. I can enumerate many of the specifics of these details, maybe I'll do that later, we can get into it on what I'm observing and what I see and how this could be applied but I'm not going to do it here...or maybe you can tell me because I think you know. Except I'm probably going to help you, I'd like it to go faster than that, you know when I want to expedite things I'm not going to wait for you to come up with beautiful ideas, because that's not expeditious. You guys aren't the great expediters of change, not yet. I mean, you know, you can write it on a little post-It note 'I'm not the great expediter of change.' I think it's honest and we can turn that into 'I am one of the expediters of change' when you become one. Then that's a new note for you, put that right on the mirror...'I am an expediter of change, I have graduated' that could be nice, that would be great you can be, but you'd have to be less cloudy and more honest and you'd have to be more loving. You have to be.

The word adulterate means to make impure. Make impure. And so when you adulterate a law, or adulterate an idea, you twist it into something that's sort of personal and selfish, you have made it impure. Like if you take a teaching that people need to be God-like and you hammer on people because they're not God-like you have adulterated that teaching. Because how can you be god-like and be heavy-handed? You adulterate the teaching. How can you be loving and also scared to death of making a mistake at the same time? That's an adulteration of the teaching of love.

Love is a relaxing thing that becomes yourself and scared of making mistakes is exactly opposite that. You're waiting for some demon to pop out of you, you're scared to death it may happen through your words or your thoughts so that's the difference in love, there's no love in that, we're scared that some badness is going to show. Very different, that's an adulteration of the teaching. You were the light of the world but I guess not, because something could pop out. You're not the light of the world if you have a bunch of crap inside. Has the light moved the crap out and you've given it to God in communion you know, then you don't have that crap anymore. Are you the darkness of the world? Okay, well then you're consistent. That's consistency because then you're scared and worried and judging of other people because you're the darkness of the world. That makes sense, that's not adulterated. But if you're trying to be the light of the world and you're scared to death of making a mistake then you have adulterated the teaching. You're not love and light when you're scared to death of making a mistake. Or when you're judging everybody... well, what if they're making a mistake?

So this is a level of honesty that I'm going to ask you to rise into for your own health and safety. Health and safety class, home economics, this is good, let's get into it....and then the details I can deal with later.

May 29, 2016
Laziness

1943 Notebooks, October 18, 1943

Jesus says:
"The secret of the soul that does not want to lose its Love-God-must be-I have already spoken to you thereof-to remain ever fixed upon God with the faculties of its soul.

Whatever you do, manage to keep your spirits fixed upon Me. In this way you will sanctify every action of yours, making it pleasing to God and supernaturally useful for you. Everything is prayer for the one who is able to remain in God, for union is nothing but love, and love transforms even the humblest actions of human life into acts of adoration agreeable to the Lord.

I tell you in truth that, between those remaining many hours in church to repeat words from which their souls are absent and those remaining in their homes, in their offices, in their businesses, and at their jobs, loving Me and their neighbor for my sake, remaining united to Me, the latter pray and are blessed by Me, while the former do nothing but perform a hypocritical practice which I condemn and disdain.

When the soul has been able to reach this loving knowledge of succeeding in remaining fixed in Me with its faculties, it produces continual acts of love. Even in material sleep it loves Me, for the flesh falls asleep and awakens with my Name and the thought of Me present, and while the body rests, the soul goes on loving.

Oh, the holy marriage of the soul with its God! A spiritual tie which the human eye does not see, but, if it could see it, it would see a circle of fire surrounding God and the creature, and as God's rejoicing increases, the creature's glory increases, a holy circle which in Heaven will be a nimbus on your glorified brows.

The soul, obstructed as it is in the flesh, sometimes undergoes the weariness of the flesh as a recoil. The temptations of Satan, more or less serious faults-I am not speaking about mortal sin, which violently separates the soul from its God, but about the slighter sins which, no matter how slight, result in spiritual fatigue-disappointments, sorrows, and life events, along with other causes, provoke weariness in the souls of those who are less formed in the life of the spirit.

But you must react to it. It is like one of those physical languors which precede the consumption of the flesh. Woe if it is not combated at the outset! But woe three times over if the languors of the spirit are not combated which lead to spiritual somnolence and, slowly, to the death of the soul.

God does not love the lazy. He does not love those who prefer their comforts to the good Lord. God punishes those who grow lukewarm. He withdraws.

Your good God calls you to awaken, asks you to receive Him, shows Himself to be concerned in having sought you out, and requests your hearts to take refuge therein. Why, don't you realize that the most beautiful tabernacle for your Lord is your heart? The good Lord tries everything to bring you out of spiritual slumber and spiritual laziness. He sometimes even tries to force open the mystical gates of the heart and seeks to enter. He then withdraws because He resorts to violence only rarely. He always leaves you free, even if leaving you free is painful for Him because He sees that you use freedom badly.

Sometimes-indeed, almost always-the soul notices the coming of its God, feels his attempt at entering, and, since the soul remembers it has been created by God, it feels itself starting with sweetness.

You oppress the soul; you do not follow it in its desires, but it is averse to dying in you. It is the last to die; it dies after the mind has died and the heart has died of pride and lust; it dies only when you kill it by taking away from it Light, Love, and Life-that is, God. But until it has died, it starts with joy and beats with love when God approaches it. Woe to those who do not want to second these movements of the soul. They are like patients who, by continual acts of imprudence and disobedience to the doctor, aggravate their illness more and more until making it fatal.

When your souls dissolve with sweetness because they feel God beyond their gates, second your souls' motion. Leave all concern for the flesh; set this proud flesh of yours on its knees; recognize the rights of the queen enclosed in you, of the queen who wants to follow her King; and adore the benignity of the King, who has come to you to love your souls, which you kept imprisoned, who has come to love you and give you the pledge of salvation for this flesh of yours as well, which you are so concerned about, but for which you are unable to do anything really useful.

God wants your flesh, too, to shine with light and supernatural, eternal beauty at the final resurrection. To shine for the holy works done in earthly life, for the works done while following the impulses of the soul moved by God.

"If you knew what a great grace every coming of God-Love is! If you understood, you would say in every instant, 'Come, Lord Jesus! Come to guide my soul! Be my King and my Master' If you knew, You would mark every encounter, every coming, among the fortunate days of your life as men. And in truth no event is so glad as the one when I enter with my love into your hearts to save and lead you, beyond life, to true, eternal, and blessed Life.

When by your carelessness you have let your Master pass by, afflicted over your spiritual inertia; when remorse, the cry of conscience which is never completely silent, even in the most depraved, awakens your souls, which you have dazed in lukewarmness and material concern, be prompt in applying a remedy. Seek God at once.

Consider that without God one wanders over ways of death until perishing forever. Consider, too, that God is merciful and has a charitable heart for you. He immediately hears your cry, which calls Him, and even if for your punishment He remains hidden for some time, He is not far away. You do not see Him, but He is already close to you with his heart as a Father who forgives the wayward son and longs to clasp him to his heart.

Seek God at once. Get by the guards patrolling: the traps the Enemy spaces out along the way to keep a soul from escaping from him to take refuge in God. Go ahead and let Satan, envious and cruel, strip you out of vengeance.

It is better for you to enter eternal life stripped of humanity, but rich in spiritual wealth alone, than accompanied to the threshold of God by affections, honors, and earthly joys, to be cast out because you have already had everything and do not deserve anything else, having preferred to have this 'everything', which falls and drags you along in falling, to the only thing necessary to have: the coin to enter eternal Life, accumulated with labors, efforts, spiritual patience, holy petioles gleaned hour by hour by obeying my Law out of love for Me, mystical pearls obtained with pain suffered out of love, eternal rubies created by your wanting to be my children-over against the voices of carnal nature, the acts of mockery and revenge of the world, and the seductions and wrath of Satan-wanted by overcoming oneself and the enemies of oneself, whether men or demons, wanted by crushing the flesh, provided the spirit wanting to follow God's Will is made to triumph, wanted to the point of sweating living blood, as I did in the face of the strongest temptation, the strongest fear, and the strongest divine Will which man could possibly endure.

If you knew what a 'no' of yours is, when spoken to the forces of the flesh, of the affections, of wealth, and of honors in order to be faithful to the One who loves you! If you knew what it is to be ready to let even dear things be taken away from oneself so as to be God's entirely!

Certain forms of despoliation, endured with resignation, if not with rejoicing-for one can rejoice even over health immolated for God's purposes, but one cannot rejoice over a tomb closing upon a father, a mother, a spouse, a son, a brother (I was Man among men, too, and remember what it is not to hear a beloved voice any longer,

not to see a house animated by a relative, and to behold the dwelling of a friend devoid of his presence)-certain forms of despoliation endured with resignation have the value of a martyrdom, Maria; remember this. They have this value, as does the martyrdom of a life offered for the coming of my Kingdom into hearts, of the fevers and illnesses endured so that the fevers of souls and the illnesses of spirits will ebb.

And both forms of martyrdom will receive the reward for martyrdom: the purple stole of those who have come to Me by way of a great tribulation, a procession of fire which will follow the Lamb together with the white procession of the virgins, the latter at my right, the former at my left, for these heroes of the spirit are truly the children of my Heart, rent by a martyrdom of love, as the others are those born of Mary who most resemble the Mother and the Son of the Mother; they are the ones who lived in the role of men with the sentiments of angels: beyond flesh and blood.

With every means of yours, with holy boldness, seek the Lord. Seek Him to make amends for former laziness. And once He has been found, never separate yourselves from Him.

In Him is the Good that does not die. In Him is Life and Truth. If you remain in Him, you shall not perish. If you live in Him, you shall not die, you shall not know errors. Like a boat safely entering the port because its pilot knew how to steer it, you, guided by Christ, shall enter the port of Peace. I, who do not lie, tell you so.

Never deny Me, children whom I love. Be faithful to Me, and I will give you glory."

I know there's such tendency to think you have to do something, and that's a misconception on your part. How do you stop being lazy if you don't do something? One of the first lazinesses is not asking God for help. That's lazy because when God or Jesus helps you, everything goes well. Things dissolve in front of you, obstacles are removed, obstructions are cleared away and problems are lifted sort of magically just because you asked for help and that's the grace of the Master. And that's the way to do it if you really want to move along and if you want to do it yourself you know you're really going to struggle, you're going to take credit, your ego is going to get involved, you're going to weigh every sacrifice whether it inconveniences you, you are going to weigh every assault on your ego whether you can stand it or not, you're going to fight, basically. Every inch of progress that Jesus wants you to make to get closer to God you're going to argument it. They want you with him which means they want you in perfection which means they want you to be good, they want you to be cleaned up, they want your selfishness gone, they want you in a completely receptive, illuminated and regenerating state.

That's what happens when you get close to them and they know you're going to have to leave some things in order to get close to them. They know that because you can't have it both ways. You can't have your carnality, your flesh attachments, you can't have your relative's attachments and your major attachments. You can't have that and be close to God because there has to be one God and that's the most worshipful one and every other worshipping is idols and false and you secretly worship a lot of idols. I know because I can see them and I know you are not great sinners so you have that going for you. You know, in the relative stage of life, you're not bad people, you're not great sinners. You know you have very particular selfishnesses that don't seem that big a deal to the world and from the world's point of view they might be miniscule. They might not even notice them, but from Jesus' point of view they're taints on your polish, metal that has not been polished up yet. Little sins he calls them, sins of the flesh, sins of commission and omission, not mortal, you know like serious things against the Mosaic law, but the laziness is letting those hang around I guess. I guess that's lazy just letting them hang around because they're not as bad as some. You know you're not as bad some people, even that thought alone is kind of lazy. Does that help you to think that you're not as bad as some; do you get like a lift out of that? It must be because you think it, you actually do think it, you evaluate, you compare and contrast and then you say, well I'm not as bad as that person, so it seems like you like this kind of thinking. And that's the only thinking that lets you settle in and let the haunches down because any other thought, like, "how close am I to God? How close does God want me to be?" would be super motivating.

Does God want me closer? Well, God says that he loves me and God wants me with him and Jesus said he wants us with him and okay, what' stopping us? What would stop me from running into his arms or coming right into that embrace? What would stop me, you know what's holding me back? That's what they want. Don't even think that they don't want that, they said they wanted it. They really do want that. They want you where they are, okay? So why isn't that happening? They are actually going to help you do it. Their grace is going to magic carpet ride you right into their presence, just for the asking. You don't even have to become anything. You just have to ask them to take you close and they will. And I know Jesus takes great pains in describing this in 1000 ways and it's like four pages of how God and he love you, basically and I know you couldn't even hear it. You say okay, okay you just said something like that, like the last paragraph was almost like that, and the last one before was like that and the last one was slightly nuanced, they're all the same and it's a lot of words and I get it, but why is he still talking?

Why do you think he feels like he has to keep talking? Because he knows you don't get that He is the most brilliant Being that has ever walked in this Solar System. He knows we don't get it so he keeps trying and he keeps explaining and he keeps describing and he elaborates that and then he elaborates his elaborations. You know, no Virgo could keep up with the content of this ever and yet it's like you tune it out. I can feel you tuning it out because he said something like that in the last paragraph. Why do you think he is assaulting you with his love if he doesn't want to melt your heart and wake you up and draw you in? That's what he's doing. I don't know if you feel it but I'm amazed that he keeps saying what he keeps saying in so many different ways and so elaborate, so brilliant, so real and there's nothing truer.

Everything He says is the truest thing you'll ever hear ever in any incarnation. And we're like you know national density week he must feel that density in the humans or he wouldn't be trying so thoroughly, so completely thorough in his love and his descriptions of love. Why don't we just give into it? Why don't we just give into it just finally? He wants us with him, he wants to love us. Why don't we just let him and why are we doing it ourselves anyway? He didn't say, "Go out and do for yourself and then I will come along and stamp you with approval." He didn't say that. He didn't say, "stop what you're doing, be perfect and then later you can decide whether you like me." He didn't say that either. He said, 'I want you with me now in whatever state of brokenness or partiality or unworked or unfinished product that you are.' Why? Because he knows how to do the rest. He can do the rest if you're submitting yourself to him, if you are open and receptive, and if your pride isn't so big you have to do it yourself, he is going to help you. Maybe that's what the laziness he's talking about is that we don't let him do it. That feels lazy to me that we don't have the guts to actually let him help us. Is that what it is? Or are you so ashamed of yourself that you can't even let him get close to you because you'll find out who is the dense one? As if God can't see you and Jesus can't know you whether you're distant or close, know exactly where you are and exactly what your problem is and exactly the remedy to heal it. Do we have to dumb them down in order to ask them to help us? How about just know they know everything perfectly forwards, backwards, past, present and future about you and your job is to just to do what they say, let them come, call them in, be with them, that's your job they'll do the rest. I even say it to you come around, you come around and guess what happens, I work on you, energy works on you, life force works on you, you don't know what's going on that's not your job. Your job is to let it work on you.

Your job is not to figure out what's next, your job is to let the grace and the love work on you. So then let's get practical, just ask for that and show up for it, like open up for it. That's what he wants and I know you couldn't hear half of what I just read to you. I don't know what you do with your heads when words are happening. You know, it's like some kind of brain fog goes over you and it's like oh God he's talking about probably like love again. I think that's what's happening. Something is going on in your head and it's almost like lethargy. There's Jesus talking and then oh God you know, and you're starting to faint. I know you're not going to remember half of what he says. There's no way but some of you don't even pay attention when he says it the first time let alone try and remember something. You're going to have to feel it, otherwise it won't retain, it cannot retain.

So I think the laziness is not wanting to feel. That's the laziness - not wanting to feel the pain, not wanting to feel the separation, and not wanting to feel the love-- those are the lazinesses that we're talking about. You're going to have to feel all three. You can't just say, oh I like that one. No, you're going to have to feel all three of them - the separation, the pain and the love, otherwise you're not going to be recognized by him as you're mine. Remember he said that a bunch of times in different ways said that the judgment comes and you tell me you gave give a glass of water to some dude, you know, dutifully and maybe really stiffly. He is going to say, I never knew you because if you did it to the least of his people you did it to me, he said a bunch of times. You know, it's pretty simple.

June 12, 2016
Stop Testing God

Poem of the Man God v3 ch. 377. Jesus Speaks at Bethany.

Jesus is now in the middle of a crowd of children looking at Him ecstatically; so many little faces looking up at Him, so many innocent eyes, so many little smiling mouths...
The veiled ladies take advantage of the confusion to go round at the rear of the crowd and come behind Jesus, as if they were urged by curiosity to do so.
The Pharisees and scribes come back with two sick people who seem to be suffering from severe pain. One particularly is moaning in his little litter, and is completely covered with a mantle. The other one, apparently, is not so seriously ill, but is certainly very ill, because he is reduced to a skeleton and is panting.
"Here are our friends. Cure them. They are really ill. Particularly that one!" and they point to the moaning one.
Jesus lowers His eyes and looks at the sick people, He then looks up at the Jews. He darts a dreadful look at His enemies. Standing behind the group of innocent children, who do not reach up to His groin, He seems to be rising from a wreath of purity, to be the Avenger, as if from that purity He were drawing the strength to be so. He opens His arms and shouts: "Liars! That man is not ill! I tell you! Uncover him! Or he will be really dead in a moment, for attempting to deceive God."
The man jumps out of his litter shouting: "No, no! Don't strike me! Here, you cursed ones, take your money!" and he throws a purse at the feet of the Pharisees and takes to his heels...
The crowds howl, laugh, boo, applaud...
The other sick man says: "And what about me, Lord? They forced me out of my bed and they have been using

violence on me since this morning... But I did not know that I was in the hands Of Your enemies..."

"Be cured, poor son, and may you be blessed!" and He imposes His hands on him, after making His way through the children.

The man lifts for a moment the blanket covering his body and he looks at I do not know what... He then stands up. He is nude from his thighs downwards. And he shouts and shouts until he becomes hoarse: "My foot! My foot! But who are You, Who can give back what was lost?" and he throws himself at Jesus' feet. He then stands up, jumps precariously on his little litter shouting: "My disease was eating away my bones. The doctor had torn off my toes; he had cauterized my flesh and had cut me up to the bone of my knee. Look! Look at the scars. But I was going to die just the same. And now... It is all cured! My foot has been restored... It is no longer painful! I feel well... strong... My chest is free... My heart is sound! Oh! Mother! I am coming to share my joy with you!"

He begins to run away. But gratitude stops him. He goes back to Jesus and he kisses His blessed feet repeatedly, until Jesus, caressing his head, says to him: "Go! Go to your mother and be good." He then looks at His enemies, who have been held up to ridicule and says: "And now? What should I do to you? What should I do, people, after this ordeal?"

The crowds shout: "Let the offenders of God be stoned! Death to them! No more snares for the Holy One! May you be cursed!" and they begin picking up lumps of earth, branches, little stones, ready to throw them.

Jesus stops them. "That is the word of the crowds. That is their answer. Mine is different. I say: Go away! I will not soil My hands striking you. The Most High will take care of you. He is my defense against the wicked."

The culprits, instead of being silent, do not hesitate to offend the Master, and although they are afraid of the people, they shout foaming with anger: "We are Judeans and we are powerful! We order You to go away. We forbid You to teach.

We banish You. Go away! Enough of You. The power is in our hands and we are making use of it; and we will use it more and more, persecuting You, cursed usurper..."

The thing I want to focus on is the words of the crowds after they hear the Pharisees testing him again. They are trying to trick him and catch him in some lie--with their own lie. The lie that they sent a person that doesn't really need to be cured. They are also forcing another man. Not out of grace would they ask the Master. They want to force him to heal somebody. He does because the man is receptive. The thing I want to focus on are the words from the crowd: "No more enemies for the Lord. No more trickery for the Lord." That's what I want to look at today.

A lot of us have what I'll call a scoffing disposition, a skeptical demeanor, an aptitude to question and make God prove God's self to us in order for us to be faithful. In order for us to follow God, we kind of have to make God prove himself to us. And I guess that's because we are super special. And we're more special than God because we want to make God prove he is the Creator and God is the love of the universe. And even the crowds, they speak the words 'No more tests, no more curses for the Lord.' And that would really be something if we could get to that place, where we're not demanding some sign that if it's worth it for us to follow God. That if God really loves us a lot and blesses us in a great way and gives us a couple things we really want, then we'll be faithful. Then we'll do what God wants us to do. It's the same Pharisee trick, all of the time that's coming from our own insides. Not too deep, I should say. But some part of our being that demands that God acquiesce to please us and then we'll be faithful. It's a great test and this is the thing. That one of the commandments is that we don't test the Lord our God. You don't test his love. You don't test his grace. You don't test his faithfulness. You don't test his dominion. You don't scoff at God, demanding

God please you. This is what the Pharisees do. And this is what made the Pharisees demons.

Even the compassion of the crowd is 'Leave the guy alone. Let the Lord do the work he came to do.' And that we have not let inside of ourselves as much as we need to. Let the Lord do with me what the Lord wants to do with me. And that might make me look at something, make me confront something, make me let go of something, make me relinquish my hold on control, make me open myself to other people, make me reveal my feelings to other people without being suspicious. Let God's work be done in me, not let me demand that God prove Himself so that I can be safe because that's prideful mockery. That's obstinate pride that you tell God that you're special and that if God finds you special, maybe you'll do a little bit for God. And that's the oldest trick in the book. Jesus didn't fall for it with these people. In fact, he threatened them with death if they do that again. That's pretty heavy.

That's one the three main temptations that Jesus had to undergo. The satanic energy knew that Jesus was the blessed Messiah. He knew that the prophecy was that the angels of God would, if he fell from a high place, they would catch him by his feet so his feet wouldn't be broken by the fall. They would take care of the fall. And so he's asking Jesus, 'throw yourself down and worship me and I'll give you all the dominions of the world, because I own the world.' That's what he's saying because he does seem to own the world and own people's hearts. And he's going to give all of that to Jesus if Jesus would worship him. And that's testing. The answer was, "Thou shall not test the Lord thy God." That's the answer to these kinds of thinking: if I get blessed in a certain way, then I'll be good. And if I get the things I want, then I'll open up to people. And if I get the things I want in the way I want them, then I won't be so nasty to people.

These are the kind of deals people make. And Jesus, he already passed this test. Apparently, nobody else has because we still make these deals. And it would be really wonderful, to stop testing Jesus. He is the Lord. He is the perfect one. He is the one love, the one light in creation that is completely reliable, completely perfect. And we still make these demands on him. If he gives me this, then I'll give a little bit of myself. And if he takes care of this problem that I have, then I'm going to be faithful. And if he cares for me in such and such a way, then I'll feel a little bit special and stop being moody. You have these deals that you make. And those are completely of the darkness. They're all of the darkness. They have nothing to do with God. Nothing. God says, "I created you. I am the Creator." There is no question. You little creatures can question me as the Creator if you want to but that leads you away from my heart. God is the soul actor in this creation. Do you understand? I know you don't understand, or you wouldn't be doing these things. Of course you don't understand. I mean, you're very intelligent. You understand my words: God is the only actor in creation. You can repeat that to me many times but you have no idea what I just said. And you have no idea what it means. Like what is acting in and through you should be God, not your ego, not your emotions. God. That, I would say, that you think God is important. Then I think your love for God is honorable and then you won't be testing the Master and testing God and cursing the Lord and setting up traps for him to see if he's good enough for your largess to worship him, I should say large ego, to be able to follow him.

In every situation, there is this temptation to make you bigger than God and God your little servant. And Jesus is not happy with that, you see. He threatened this guy's life because he was an imposter but then he revealed who set him up and paid him. And then for those guys, that threat stands for them. They would be killed if they kept doing that. That's the thing. If you test God, you have actually cut yourself off from the light. You killed yourself. You've actually killed yourself or are killing yourself. Maybe it's in stages, in phases, but it's certainly starting to happen because you're the one who is going to decide whether God is important. You're the one that is going to decide if God's energy, acting in a particular part of your life, is important. I'll translate it a bit further for you: you're going to decide whether God should guide your life in the areas where you would rather guide it yourself. Even the crowds said, when they saw how ridiculous the Pharisees were being, 'Can we just stop testing him? He's the Lord!' They got it and that's just the mass mind. That's just the masses. They're not the enlightened. Some were disciples in that crowd but these were just the regulars of human beings were saying 'Can we just stop testing God and deciding whether God is ok for us?' It's really incredible. It's like the plants going 'I don't know if I really like the Earth, really. I don't know if the Earth is a safe place to be, really.' That's what it's like. That's the same level from a different viewpoint. 'I don't know if it's safe to be here. Maybe we shouldn't be here on Earth as plants.' You see how ludicrous, how silly that is? It's ridiculous. The Earth is providing for these plants and the whole cycle and the big picture. Each little plant doesn't have the big picture. They just have their little picture. 'I grow green and then I flower. Then I plant seeds. That's what happens to me. I seed, I flower, I grow green. Then I make stems, maybe I make stems. Maybe I make bark. I don't know. I'm going to get bigger. That's what I do.' That's all they know. Not very complicated for the plant. And they are not questioning their existence.

You know, you were created. Drill it in. You were created. You didn't create yourself. So therefore, you have a prototype inside of you of the being that created you that wants to express through you. In other words, the God part of you wants to express through this apparatus. And there's the apparatus making contingencies and bargaining and fretting and fighting and setting up rules and setting up conditions about whether or not it will allow what the divine energy wants to do through you, and setting up tests for God. The meditation that you should be doing is: 'God inside of me, how do you want to express through this? This flesh, at this point, as dense as my flesh is, as dense as my feelings are, how do you want to express through this at this time? Not, 'what's my perfect expression? I won't do anything until then.' That's just another mockery of God. 'How do you want me to express myself now? What do you want me to do? I have no idea.' That would be very humble and super honest. 'I don't know anything.' That's super honest.

The crowds got sick of the Pharisees because of all of the lies. Jesus called them liars straight up. I could do that with you. I could say, 'You want to serve God. You say you do. You're liars.' I'm not heavy about it right now. I'm just light. Jesus said you're a liar if you are keeping your emotions so important. Then you're a liar. When you're bargaining with God to make you special, and you're not going to give anything or love anybody until you're special, then you're a liar. Don't you see? It's the same, you see? These teachings are the same. Those applied to any parts of us that are crowds, Pharisees, sick people, or just people in general. These teachings apply to all of us, and many different parts of us. Don't you have the crowds in there that say, 'that's not fair?' You have the crowds inside of you. And then you have the disciples that can't believe anyone is saying anything about it. And then you have the humble that get healed and they just want to worship. And then you have the liars. You have them all. Aren't you tired of all the parts? Can't you just be one thing to somebody? One thing, son or daughter of God that's learning how to master life, who's learning how to be and learning how to love and getting all that rudeness out of you, all of the crudeness rudeness out of you. Just let it go. There's no need. God doesn't want you to have it. God does not want you to struggle with it.

A struggle is an attachment and a struggle is a violation in your obedience to God. An attachment is pride and violating your obedience to God. Attached to what? What could you possibly be attached to that would be beautiful and loving? God. Jesus. Mary. Those are the attachments I'd like to see and no attachments to anything else. In other words, attachment to truth, attachment to love, attachment to light. Those are the things that are not going to get you into trouble. And you will not be prey to the darkness if you are attached to that. But you are prey to the darkness with your moodiness, your touchiness, your feeling sorry for yourself, your separations, your judgments of other people, your criticism of yourself or others, and any other crap you can think of which we can numerate that would get you away from God.

My theory in this sermon is why can't we not test God? Why can't we just stop testing God? God's fine. You're not saying God is fine, Jesus is fine. The teachings are fine. The truth is fine. Everything is pristinely beautiful. Are you there with that? Are you pristinely beautiful? Are you tuned with the truth? Are you part of the love? Are you the shining light? See what I mean? If that's not happening, you have fallen away from that truth, from that standard of disciple. You let yourself fall. Why did you let yourself do that? Jesus says, "Come back. Just come back." Stop testing God. Stop fighting, stop thinking. Just stop thinking, and you'll be back. Does a plant need to think? No, it just needs to grow stuff. Absorb water, absorb sunshine. It's in its nature to do this. Photosynthesis. It doesn't really have to think photosynthesis. It doesn't have to think 'absorption of water.' It doesn't have to think, 'ok root system.' It doesn't have to think. It's just a part of its nature. It's relaxed. Plants aren't straining. You can't see them straining. But humans, they have a right to be weird. The plants and animals don't have a right to be weird. They have to be what they have to be. They can't do weird. Only humans can do weird, because they have thoughts. That's why they can be weird. Ok, try to relax through all of this and stop testing God.

June 19, 2016
Being Good

The Gospel as Revealed to Me, Chapter 518. In Jerusalem. The meeting with the healed blind man. The speech that reveals the good shepherd Jesus.

"The time of the new Law has come. Everything is renewed and a new world, a new people, a new kingdom are rising. Now the people of the past do not know all this. They know their times. They are like blind people taken to a new town where the regal house of the Father is, but they do not know its location. I have come to lead them there and take them into it and that they may see. But I am the Door through which one enters the paternal house, in the Kingdom of God, in the Light, in the Way, in the Truth, in the Life. And I am also the One Who has come to gather the flock left without a guide and lead it to one only sheep-fold: the Father's. I know the door of the fold because I am door and shepherd. And I go in and come out as and when I like. And I go in freely, and by the door, because I am the true shepherd.

When a man comes to give the sheep of God other instructions or tries to mislead them taking them to other abodes and other ways, he is not the good Shepherd, but an idol shepherd. Likewise, he who does not go in by the door of the fold, but tries to enter in a different way, jumping over the enclosure, is not the shepherd, but a thief and an assassin, who goes in to kill and steal, so that the stolen lambs with their wailing voices may not draw the attention of the watchmen and of the shepherd. False shepherds are trying to insinuate themselves also among the sheep of the flock of Israel to lead them astray from the pastures, far from the true shepherd. And they go in ready to tear them from the flock even by means of violence, and if necessary, they are also willing to kill them and strike them in many ways, so that they may not speak informing the shepherd of the tricks of the false shepherds or they may cry to God to protect them from their enemies and the enemies of the shepherd.

I am the good shepherd and My sheep know Me, and those who have been for ever the watchmen of the true fold know Me. They have known Me and My Name and they mentioned it to make it known to Israel, and they described Me and prepared My ways, and when My voice was heard, the last of them opened the door to Me saying to the flock awaiting the true Shepherd, the flock gathered round his crook: 'Now! Here is the One Who I said would follow me. One Who precedes me because He was before me and I did not know Him. But for Him, that you may be ready to receive Him, I have come to baptize with water, that He may be revealed to Israel.' And the good sheep heard My voice and when I called them by their names they came to Me and I took them with Me, as a good shepherd does when he is known to the sheep that recognize his voice and follow him wherever he goes. And when he has let them all out, he walks in front of them and they follow him because they love the voice of the shepherd. But they do not follow a stranger, on the contrary they run away from him, because they do not know him and they are afraid of him. I also walk ahead of My sheep to point out the road to them and be the first to face dangers and show them to the flock, that I want to lead to safety in My Kingdom."

"Is Israel no longer the kingdom of God?"

"Israel is the place from which the people of God must rise to the true Jerusalem and to the Kingdom of God."

And what about the promised Messiah? That Messiah that You say You are, is He not to make Israel triumphant, glorious, the master of the world, subjecting to His scepter all the peoples and revenging Himself, oh! revenging Himself cruelly on all those who subjugated it since it was a people? So, nothing of all that is true? Are you denying the prophets? Are You saying that our rabbis are stupid? You..."

"The Kingdom of the Messiah is not of this world. It is the Kingdom of God, based on Love. It is nothing else. And the Messiah is not the king of peoples and armies, but the king of spirits.

The Messiah will come from the chosen people, from the royal stock, and above all from God, Who generated Him and sent Him. The foundation of the Kingdom of God, the promulgation of the Law of love, the announcement of the Good News mentioned by the prophet began from the people of Israel. But the Messiah will be the King of the world, the King of kings, and His Kingdom will have no limit or boundary, neither in time nor in space. Open your eyes and accept the truth."

Just the fact that someone is trying to get into the sheep fold is probably a good thing you could think. But in any way and at all costs? To jump the fence or find some other way to get in besides the door and greeting the person who opens the door and acknowledging the door opener? That has its own integrity and humility. But if somebody wants to get into the sheep fold, why do they want to get in without using the door and without going through the person who opens the door? That would be some kind of egotistical thing, selfishness, fear; maybe they are desirous to have something they don't want to pay for. In other words they don't want to acknowledge the one who opens it for them. They don't have the humility or gratitude for somebody opening the door for them and because of the seeds of that kind of thinking, he says they are coming to kill and steal. Because that's where that kind of thinking goes when there isn't humility and there isn't integrity and there isn't love that is honorable or responsible. There are other deals that are probably getting made that He would call stealing and killing. Somebody that comes into the sheep fold in some other way besides the way He set out have other motivations, and those other motivations are killing and stealing. He didn't just show you how it degrades and how it progresses to thieving and killing. He just said that's what it is. And that's what real honesty does with you in yourself when you start to see a certain selfish pride in something or a certain inclination to do something the way you would like to do something. There's that pride in there. There's a little edge - maybe a little animosity or insecurity to be overridden so you'd have to do it yourself without help and without asking for help.

So the seeds of the problem are in it and that's why you can't get in. If you get in you get found out and get thrown out because that's what happens with truth and reality. You are either with God because you understand that God is everything or you're trying to be with God because of other reasons - other machinations in there, other motivations that aren't simply pure.

Jesus is the good shepherd and he loves his sheep and the sheep hear his voice and know him and follow him. If he leads the way because there's danger, then after he leads them all through they go all in and he goes ahead and leads them again. That's the nature of the pasture of God. There's so much more perfecting to grow into and to become and more God to become. But people want to join things that seem to be popular. They don't want to necessarily do the changes that are necessary to be in that situation. Some of you have certain imperfections that you allow and are accustomed to. Certain idiosyncrasies that you don't think are a problem because they don't seem to be worse than anyone else's and you keep them around while they don't actually let you be perfect. They are not good because it's usually you against the other person or you better or not jerked around by the other person. You making sure you're distinct from the other person. And those are all ego things that are contaminations in your psyche and they are old ways. Not God's ways, not goodness. They are just ridiculous basically. When you keep those around for the simple reason that other people have much worse you're not allowing this goodness to teach you how to be good. You are not allowing perfection. I think people deliberately avoid perfection. Your whole theory is that it's impossible to be perfect and your mantra is nobody's perfect. And that's a very good justification to not even try, isn't it? Why bother? Nobody's perfect.

Well God is perfect and Jesus and Mary are perfect and any really good saint is perfect. How do you figure that? And he told us to be so everyone else is disobedient, aren't they? Everyone else is disobedient if they are not perfect because He said we should be. So what prevents you from being perfect? Attitudes, opinions, concepts, fears, pride, longings, worries, all those. So those aren't goodness are they? Goodness will become perfect and goodness is the start of perfection. So just be good and that's just a decision. You know what goodness is: happy disposition, no sulking or pouting, grudging, no resentment, no fears, no pride. Willingness, service, caring, enthusiastic, happy. All goodness. You can do that and you do that in moments during the day. You have some spirit-filled, lighthearted interchanges. You have some openness to ideas and the spirit moving. In moments. That's when goodness started. Goodness was starting to manifest right there, and then what did you do? I don't know. What did you want to do? You probably didn't want that goodness for too long because it was uncomfortable, wasn't it? It's going to shake the foundations of the ego and break your pride. It's going to break it. It's a choice to be good and it's a simple choice. Stop thinking negatively and I would venture to say stop thinking at all. That's so simple.

So just do what's in front of you and do what will help and you'll be one of the sheep enjoying the shepherd guiding you into goodness. He's the good shepherd. He's not the shepherd of pain, you're the masters of pain because that's what you dish out and that's what you get back. He's the shepherd of goodness. On the way to goodness will there be pain? Yes. Will you suffer on the way to goodness? Probably. Always? No. Sometimes yes. Occasionally you will suffer on the way to goodness but that's no excuse for you to be mad about that. You descended out of goodness by your own choice and by your assent into goodness there's going to be a little bit of suffering. If you took a month off school in high school and you go back to school because you thought better of leaving school well you've got a month of catch up just to get to exam time. That's the same that has happened here on the planet. People went away out of class, they weren't even learning. They didn't even care. And all of a sudden their heart feels like they want to care again and they get back and someone tells them they have a lot of learning to do and a lot of catch-up and a lot of letting go to do. Well life is suffering is all you teach. No, I teach you to get back to goodness and on the way to goodness the pain of you having chosen not goodness is what's bothering you. That's what's bothering you and that's when your little courage thing falters like a little itsy bird. You sure had the courage to go away from goodness, why don't you have the courage to go back into goodness?

You have to follow the Master, the good shepherd if you're going to become good, if you're going to become obedient, docile, malleable sheep in the nature of God. They provide the clothing of the world. They clothe the world with warmth. They do other things. They feed the world as well. But you can figure it out if you don't have too many ideas. Knock on the door and let the shepherd open the door to the pasture for you. And what's that pasture? It's into the Kingdom of God. Where is that in you? Farther than you think. Why? Because you can't get there by thinking. You can only get there by love and purity. Why would you want to go there? You're going to lose all of your idiosyncrasies. That's not worth it. How are you going to be able to be all that if you went in there? How would you be able to be more special than another person in there? Well you wouldn't be. Would you be totally loved? Yes. Would you be loved more than another person? No. So that's where the head can't figure this out. How can God love 7 billion people and that's only on this itsy bitsy planet all at once? And completely? When there are billions of planets with people on them. Billions. All these little schoolhouses across the galaxy and the solar system all across the universe, little schoolhouses like this one with billions of people on them that God is actually giving them everything that they need whenever they can open and whenever they can stand it. Whenever they ask. This is a perfection you don't understand. We could start to be perfect by becoming good. We're not going to be that perfect like God to be able to carry the worlds and respond to every prayer in the Universe and fulfill everything at the instant that they do it. This is way beyond us because God is huge and we are little. God is old. We're not old.

So what does Jesus want? He wants you with him. What does that involve? He's going to take you somewhere. Do you need to know where? It's none of your business. That's how you should think about it. Don't you just want to be where he is? The sheep do. They don't think 'Hey, I wonder where he's taking us' they don't even think like that. They don't think 'He's taking us too far I know it.' They don't think like that, like you humans do. 'We've walked for hours!' They don't think like that. Real sheep don't think like that. They are just happy to be with him. They listen for the bell from the sheep ringer and they follow it. They follow the lead sheep because he has a bell around his neck or a collar whichever. You find Jesus talking like this throughout the Poem (of the Man God) - 8000 pages or more talking like this all the time. He's talking about how he's the one and how he's going to take you into love and into goodness and into perfection. Because you did go away or you at least have to have the humility to admit that you did decide not to be perfect because you decided not to be good. At least have that humility.

If you think about it this way, this decision to be good, that's the decision that will get you right into perfection. You're going to be good, responsible, you're going to care. You're going to be open to other people, share yourself, move your energy, give your effort and you're not going to do anything else. Then you're going to head into goodness. What does that mean? You're at the first stages of perfection and there are a billion stages but you'll be at the first stage. And that's what Jesus ordered you to. To be perfect. And he ordered you to be good. Anything else, any selfishness, you're on your own. You're applying the law to your demise. In the density of this world there's no thought that perfection could happen. In the density of your brains each one of you has this density. You don't think it's possible. In fact thank God it isn't so you can keep your desire nature. That's how you think. Thank God I don't have to be perfect yet because I can still do what I want. In the secret cells of your constitution you actually feel this way and if it wasn't so I wouldn't tell you. You'll have to rebel against the tendency of the flesh to be the great teacher. Like your little flesh body is your great teacher. It is not. Your flesh body knows nothing. And if you believe that you're not perfect and you can't be, you're kind of an idiot because someone of divine nature says "be perfect" and then you come along with your undivine nature and say 'I can't be.' See the idiot part of that? Either Jesus is an idiot or you are. Well idiots don't say perfect things like Jesus teaches. He's not the idiot, let's just establish that fact. So anybody who doesn't believe what he says thinking 'I can't be perfect' is an idiot. Now what they could say is, 'I don't have the courage and I don't have the intestinal fortitude and I don't have the guts to be perfect because I love my selfishness and I love taking advantage of situations and other people and I'm not ready to be good right now.' That's what they could say if they were honest. You're not going to get around this one because certainly I'm not going to let you and we're going to keep talking about it until you do it. In that sense you could stay non-perfect as long as you prefer but I'm not going to stop talking about it.

Goodness is the way to be perfect. Perfection is like per and fact. Per means coming through and fact means making it a manifestation. So perfection means having something of divine nature starting to come through. That's what goodness is. That is an instantaneous choice with your power that you make any instant of the day and I would just like you to keep it up so you don't go 'Oh that was so tiring being good early this morning at 10. I need to just coast now and rest because that took so much out of me to give some goodness for a change.' So perfect means to make a fact of goodness. Now you know how this is from your own experience. When you start to meditate it's hard to concentrate and you want to sleep. But as you practice it starts to happen. It's the same with goodness and perfection. It starts to happen where you're starting to think the best of things. You stop balking and hiding and you start to show up. The goodness is starting to happen. Maybe it will become habitual and exciting and addicting. I'm sure Jesus wants it to be your one addiction, goodness. The only good addiction is to goodness. Now anyone can do this because we've seen little children take care of somebody when they see the person needs something, they have compassion. We see goodness everywhere. But where do we not see it? All the time. That's the problem with humans. They are so inconsistent and selfish they can't keep anything up for more than a few minutes.

Well goodness is a giver not a rester and a taker. Goodness is a giver. Just decide. Do you think the sun in the sky just says 'I don't know if I can keep this up?' And that is a powerhouse of giving that we all would die without. Can you give like that? That is a minor sun in the great Lords of the system. That's a minor Lord in the Universe compared to God. That's like a baby sun. Some suns are 20,000 times that in brightness, intensity, and power. What's that dude doing? You have no conception of giving because you can't even appreciate consistency of that love for just this system. But you are like that as a baby, it's just you can't believe it. You can't believe that you can be good. Can you see that kind of mentality? Death sentence. Please get that thickness out of your head and just decide that it is. Make sure that the feedback from other people call it good and not some kind of selfishness because you definitely have to clean that up. The point is, with a group like this you have known goodness and you have done it. Fits and starts I admit and you should have the humility to know that. It's fits and starts goodness and it has worked when you did it which means you can do it. Why isn't that all the time? I explained it already why.

Jesus was all the time. His disciples were all the time. They became that - all the time goodness. Goodness gracious that's what they were. Some of you have fits and starts goodness, I see them. It's not a great light I admit but there are moments. I'm not super impressed by it but I'm impressed that it's happening at all, but I'm not super impressed with your consistency. I don't think consistency is a word you can describe yourself as yet. I mean I'm not going to say that you can because I don't think you can. But goodness you could actually keep it up for the whole day. Let's work for that high goal of good for an entire day. I know right now we're working on an hour, maybe 10 minutes of goodness until we get kind of irritable or get sad or something stupid. Or we have to bite someone's head off after an hour because we've been good. Something like that. But what about a whole day? I know it's an ambition right now for us as a community for us to be good for a whole day. Even so I'm probably going to want to stretch that. I'm going to predict that. If we get a whole day of goodness a month I'm going to want a week and would I ever be satisfied? That's the question, wouldn't it be? Probably not. Is Jesus ever satisfied in encouraging us to be good? No he's not. Is he irritated? No. Is he mad at you? No. He just can't believe it. But yeah, he wants you to be good. Like always. Forever and ever for the rest of your existence. He really does. He knows you can. He was a person just like you and if anyone can you can. That's the law. If anybody can, then you can. So then you can. You're going to have to start.

So when you get that little crusty feeling inside, you're going to have to break that or have somebody nudge you or bump you or something like that. Stop it! What the hell are you doing? You have a brother or a sister going, 'You're doing that again.' Do you know when you do that "enh" thing? Kind of sense it? It has a look on it. A look on the face, you know? Anybody who's good can see it. So you guys want to see more? Get good. You'll see it everywhere but you can't judge it because that's not good. You just have to see it. You just say, 'Wow, you're doing that thing. I hate you because you're doing that thing?' That's not good. You see the difference? That's not good. To be irritable if people aren't good enough is not good. You see what I mean? I'll help you with the details. You can't really, don't start with any details. I have simple things that I call real details and you have other things that I do not value.

Goodness - just decide it. Say to Jesus, "I want to be good. Can you help me?" And he will.

June 26, 2016
A House Divided

The Gospel as Revealed to Me, *Chapter 269. The Dispute with the scribes and pharisees in Capernaum. The Arrival of the Mother and brothers.*

Jesus descends the two little steps of the threshold and comes forward. He stops erect, severe and calm in front of the group of scribes and Pharisees and staring at them with keen eyes He says to them:
"Also on the earth we see that a kingdom divided into opposed parties becomes weak internally and can be easily attacked and laid waste by nearby countries that make it their slave. Also on the earth we see that a town divided into conflicting parts does not flourish and the same applies to a family, the members of which are divided by mutual hatred. It falls to pieces and becomes a useless nibble, which is of no use to anybody, and the laughing stock of fellow citizens. Harmony is shrewdness besides being necessary. Because it keeps people independent, strong and loving. Patriots, citizens, relatives ought to ponder on that when for the caprice of an individual advantage they are tempted to have separations or commit abuses, which are always dangerous because they are alternative in parties and they destroy love. And such shrewdness is practised by those who are the masters of the world. Consider Rome in its undeniable power, so painful to us. Rome rules the world. But they are united by one mind and one will: "to rule". Even amongst them there must be differences, aversions, rebellions. But they lie at the bottom. On the surface they are one block, without cracks or perturbations. They all want the same thing and they are successful because of that. And they will be successful as long as they want the same thing.

Consider that example of human cohesive shrewdness and say: if the children of this world are like that, what will

Satan be like? The Romans are demons, as far as we are concerned. But their heathen satanism is nothing compared to the perfect satanism of Satan and his demons. In their eternal kingdom, without time, without end, with no limits to cunning and wickedness, where they rejoice in being detrimental to God and men, and to be harmful is their very life and their only cruel painful enjoyment, they have attained with cursed perfection the fusion of their spirits in one will: "to be harmful". Now if, as you state, to insinuate doubt about My power, Satan is the one who helps Me because I am a minor Beelzebub, does it not follow that Satan is divided against himself and his demons, if he drives them out of the people possessed by him? And if he is at variance with his followers, can his kingdom last? No, it is not so. Satan is very shrewd and does not damage himself in the hearts of men. The aim of his life is "to steal - to damage - to lie - to offend - to upset." To steal the souls of God and the peace of men. To damage the children of the Father grieving Him. To lie in order to mislead. To offend in order to rejoice. To upset because he is disorder and cannot change. He is eternal in his being and in his methods.

But answer this question: if I drive out demons in the name of Beelzebub, in whose name do your sons drive them out? Are you willing to admit that they are Beelzebub as well? If you say that, they will consider you slanderers. And if their holiness is such that they will not react to your accusation, you will condemn yourselves confessing that you think that you have many demons in Israel, and God will judge you in the name of the children of Israel accused by you of being demons. Therefore whoever may pass judgment, in actual fact they will be your judges, where judgment is not suborned by human pressure.

If, instead, as it is true, I expel demons through the Spirit of God, that would be evidence that the Kingdom of God and the King of that Kingdom have come to you. Which King has such power that no adverse force can resist Him. Thus I bind *and compel the usurpers of the children of My Kingdom to depart from the place they have occupied and give Me back the prey so that I may take possession of it. Is that not what is done by one who wants to enter a house inhabited by a powerful man, to take his property, rightly or wrongly acquired? It is. He enters and ties him, and then he can plunder the house. I tie the dark angel who has taken what is Mine, and I take away from him the good property he has stolen of Me. And I am the only one who can do it, because I alone am the Strong One, the Father of the future century, the Prince of Peace."*

"Clarify for us what You mean by saying: "Father of the future century". Do You think that You will live until the new century and, still more foolishly, do You think that You, a poor man, will create time? Time belongs to God" asks a scribe.

"And are you, a scribe, asking Me? Do you not know that there will be a century that will have a beginning but no end, and that it will be Mine? I shall triumph in it gathering round Me its children and they will live forever like the century that I shall have created and I am already creating it, giving the spirit its true value above the flesh, the world, and above the infernal angels whom I expel because I can do everything. That is why I say that those who are not with Me are against Me, and those who do not gather with Me, scatter. Because I am He Who I am. And he who does not believe that, which was already prophesied, sins against the Holy Spirit, whose word was announced by the prophets, and it is neither false nor wrong, and must be believed without resistance.

And I tell you: men will be forgiven everything, all their sins and their blasphemy. Because God knows that man is not only spirit, but also flesh and his flesh, when tempted, is subject to sudden weakness. But blasphemy against the Spirit will not be forgiven. He who has spoken against the Son of man will still be forgiven, because the weight of the flesh enveloping My Person and the man who speaks against Me, can still mislead. But he who has spoken against the Holy Spirit will not be forgiven, either in this or in future life, because the Truth is what it is: clear, holy, undeniable and manifested to the spirit in such a way that it cannot mislead. Only those err who deliberately want to err. To deny the Truth spoken by the Holy Spirit is to deny the Word of God and the Love given by that word for the sake of men. And the sin against Love is not forgiven.

Every tree bears its fruit. You bear yours, but your fruit is not good. If you give a good tree to have it planted in the orchard, it will give good fruit; but if you give a bad tree, the fruit it will yield will be bad and everybody will say: "This is not a good tree". Because a tree is known by its fruit. And how can you think that you are able to speak well, since you are bad? Because a mouth speaks of what fills its heart. Because it is out of the superabundance of what is within us, that we act and speak. A good man takes good things out of his good treasure; a wicked man takes wicked things out of his evil one and he speaks and behaves according to what is within him."

If you ask Jesus to clear you of negative feelings, negative desires, and negative inclinations, He will do that. And then your house will be clean. But some of you don't want that. Some of you want to have both. You want to have the good things and you want to keep the bad things together and then you're not going to be able to stand it. In other words, your house won't stand. It won't last. You won't be able to be consistent because you have two warring parties in your being. One is the selfish old thing, you know, the past stuff: your old memories and hurts and legacies of your past – and then you have these new inspirations to be good and to be loving. Then they're going to war with each other and you won't be able to stand it and you won't be able to stand on one side or the other. You won't be able to be consistent because you're getting torn in two places by two things.

Two very powerful things: your traditions (which are mostly negative) and these inspirations to be spiritual (which are all positive).

So, at the same time, you can't take your negative feelings and get mad at your negative feelings and try to get rid of them by your negative feelings. In other words, you can be mad at the thing you want to get rid of because that's like Satan casting out Satan. That doesn't work. You can't be horrendously offended by the thing that offends you and hope that leaves. That's not how things are done. That's not how things are changed. You don't aggress against the thing you don't like because that's the same energy. Satan casting out Satan is an impossibility. Negative energy casting out negative energy? Impossible. They're the same thing. Fear casting out fear? Not going to work. Pride? Too proud to be prideful and you're going to get rid of pride real pridefully, right? How's that going to work? So you can't get all huffy when you try to get rid of something. Decisions aren't really angsty. They're like, real worried. You want to get rid of worry so you worry that you're going to make a real worried decision to get rid of worry. You see, that's the problem and the whole spiritual life hinges on this teaching.

Love casts out fear. Obedience casts out disobedience. Faithfulness casts out worry. You know? Humility casts out pride. It's not, you know, a more humble person, you know, is what's needed. Or a more prideful person to get rid of the pride. Stronger, angry person to get rid of the minor angers? That's not how it works. In other words, when your house is divided and you have all this stuff jammed into one person, you won't be able to stand very long on one side of the fence or the other. You're going to flip back and forth inconsistently.

I know there's a lot more in Jesus' words than what I'm going to focus on. I'm not going to focus on the rest of it. You hopefully will learn something from the rest of it.

If you make deals that you would like to be somewhat more spiritual and you also want to hold onto whatever you've accumulated so far, you are a house divided and you won't be able to stand that very long. You'll have to lie to keep that up and you'll have to become miserable and try to hide it. If I hold onto my past and try to bring in the kingdom of God, I have got a huge conflict on my hands. Thus, the real path is difficult because it is a conflict: The new with the old. They're in opposition to one another and yeah, we do gradually, we don't focus that strongly on the harshness of the change and yet, if you lull out to keep both, you're going to be miserable. You're going to be miserable. That's just the way it is. Try to hold on to what you've got while you let go to what you will become? You're going to be in pain. You're going to be miserable. And some of you are. You do know this feeling. And maybe it's a little less miserable than you used to experience but it's still miserable.

Why does the ego have to keep so much stuff to pretend that it's got something? I see all the egos as empty and meaningless and stupid. And then I see your divinity as the most beautiful thing and there's a fight on your hands between those two. You won't stand. Jesus said, 'A house divided won't stand.' You'll have to choose.

He's going to make you choose whether you want to. You want to do it gracefully? You can do it on your own. You want to wait? He's going to force you. And I'm not sure you have the strength to be forced. Nobody likes to be forced but, you know, He's going to call it. He's going to call the judgment in and you're going to be forced to choose. Why don't you do it on your own? He'll give you more credit if you do it on your own than if you choose Him because He forces you.

If I force you to love me versus go to hell, and you do love me, what credit do you get? A little. Right? That's what the judgment's going to do for some people. There's going to be the laggards who are the last minute people who go, 'Well, I didn't know. I didn't know. I wasn't sure. I wasn't sure. Okay, I will,' because they're being forced and forced by time and forced by karma and forced by history because history's going to force all of us unless you choose on your own, by yourself, with your own heart. That person is going to have a little bit deeper relationship with Jesus than the other people who choose by pressure, by circumstance, you know? Reluctantly holding on and then giving in.

You know, if you had a kid and this thirteen year old kid, and you're asking him to work in the yard and he won't and he won't and you have to kind of brow beat him and now you have to encourage him and now you have to bribe him practically to have him help you in the yard and then finally he does. What's the difference between that thirteen year old and the other who just goes, 'Would you go clean up the yard?' and he just goes out and does it?

Now one gives you joy and the other was work. You had to work to get him to do that and it was sad because you had to encourage and then you had to give something and then you had to help him try and then, you know, you had to encourage him, practically drag him along. It's a lot of work with that kind of a disciple when you have to drag them along and they just don't want to do it themselves on their own. They get credit for doing it. You know they do, if you dragged them along, but not the same credit as the pure one who gets it who just does it because they just get it because they want that.

I'm telling you, it's not so black and white is it anymore? Where you have the volunteers and then you have the reluctant, they will give in and do it. And then you have the resisters who finally will give in and do it. You know, there are various kinds of people we have, all because you kept the old with the new. All because you are a house divided. You're still trying to long for those old desires that made you sick and made you unhealthy and made you sad. You're still holding on to those and then you have these, you know, heroic moments where you're holding on to the view that Jesus gives you about how you could be in the Kingdom of God: How you could be pure, how you could be perfect, how you could be love, how you could be good, and you like that and it's very stimulating. It's like, you know there's moments of that possibility because you've had some experience of that. And then you have this huge, lead ball holding you back with a chain on your second vertebrae. You drag that chain along towards the Kingdom of God.

Did you ever think of turning around and cutting it off? I mean, that's easy. Just turn around with bolt cutters and cut it off – completely. Walk away. Don't look back. There are stories of people who were told to do that. Lot did it. He walked away from his town and all his job and stuff and just walked away and didn't look back. That's the end of it. It's over. He let it go. These are people, like, 4000 years ago, 3000 years ago did this. What's our problem? Why don't we walk away and not look back?

The heart is what makes you contaminated because you have divided desires in there. Have one desire and you become pure. You have many desires and you become impure. Now how did you get impure? You had many desires and the whole environment had many desires and all your models and examples had many desires and you learned that so you became impure because everybody around you is impure and you followed along. When you were a baby you just learned impurity and that's what you did. You thought, 'That's what society does. This is what civilization does. It's what people do. It's what my parents do. That's all we have to do, just be impure.' But Jesus is saying something else, 'Out of the abundance of the heart, the mouth speaks,' and out of the heart comes all this manner of nonsense. Those are the contaminants, inside your own heart, not outside – not other people, not food, not toxins. You are the toxin, coming from your heart. That's what defiles you. Nothing else does.

He said, 'Listen well. Not what goes into the mouth defiles you but what comes out.' And then He said, just to give you, like, a break, 'He who has ears to hear, let him hear.' In other words, you don't have to hear this. You can go with the Pharisees and have your 624 rules about food and stuff and pretend that you're pure by all these practices. In other words, He's saying that all of these practices are stupid. Completely stupid. And these are the hypocrites that are accusing Jesus of casting out devils by the prince of devils. The same kind of people who have all those kind of considerations and rules are the same ones who are accusing the most perfect one of being contaminated.

Now all these things are going on inside of you. Every part, every character is going on inside of you. There's the Christ, the Self, in you saying, 'Come. We'll be good together. I want to love you. Would you let me love you?' And you're going, 'That sounds good.' And the Pharisees go, 'I don't know if you can break through all of this encasement that I'm in,' because He keeps talking about it generously, that the flesh is weak and He mentioned it a few times in this reading – how the flesh is kind of the hard thing that easily falls. And you have that experience many times. The flesh just kind of gets you and the desires of the body and the emotions, they just overwhelm you. You let them happen and it happens. He has compassion for that. He said to the Apostles, 'The

Spirit is willing,' you know, 'but the flesh is weak.' It is weak so you guys have to be more vigilant, and you have to be stronger, and you have to practice keeping your word to yourself – more than you ever did.

Why? If you want to be of God, you do. If you want to be like everybody else, you're doing better than them. I appeal to your pride now. You're doing better than the world. Go ahead and relax now. That appeals to your pride.

Are you doing as well as a person who's completely obedient to God? Mmm mmm. Mmm mmm. Not even close. And I'm not doing this to be critical. I'm doing this to show you the difference. To show you the difference. And, just to be philosophical – and I don't mind doing that occasionally – if you're happy, I'm happy. In other words, if you're happy where you are, I'm happy where you are. If you've given it all you've got and you've gone the full mile, and you're pretty satisfied, then I'm satisfied.

Am I lying? No, I can actually decide that where you are is all you want. I can decide that if you help me decide that. I can decide that. Where you are, as far as you've gotten, is all you really want and that's as far as you want to be. I can decide that with you, in support of you, but I wonder if we have a whole divided thing going on that I'm going to have to like, accept. We are not talking about me accepting that for me. We're talking about me accepting that for you. I'm not a house divided and I do not accept that ever within me, because I was asked not to.

So I'm not even almost asking you, I'm asking you what you want and I think it's for you to examine, 'What do you want?' You want a divided house? I mean, you can have that. I know it's miserable and I know, ultimately, you'll feel a little bit steadied by the fact that you can accept that, and then sad. You'll start to feel sad. I won't be as sad as you.

It gets down to what you want. It really gets down to what you want. So figure out what you want.

July 3, 2017
Letting Go

The Gospel as Revealed to Me, Chapter 276. The avid man and the parable of the rich.

"Listen," says Jesus. "It is true that the alterations of the spirit are reflected on one's face. It is as if the demon appeared on the surface of his possession. Only few people who are demons, either in deeds or appearance, do not disclose what they are. And those few are perfect in evil and perfectly possessed. The countenance of a just man, instead, is always beautiful, even if his face is materially disfigured, because of a supernatural beauty, which from the interior exudes exteriorly. And it is not just a saying, but a real fact, that we notice a bodily freshness as well in those who are free from vices. The soul within us envelops our whole being. The stench of a corrupt soul affects also the body, whereas the scent of a pure soul preserves it. A corrupt soul drives the flesh to obscene sins, which age and disfigure the body. A pure soul incites the body to a pure life, which grants a fresh complexion and imparts majesty.

Endeavour to keep your youth spiritually pure, or to revive it, if you have already lost it, and beware of greed, both for sensual pleasures and for power. The life of man does not depend on the abundance of his wealth, neither in present life and much less in the next one, eternal life. It depends instead on his way of living, as well as his happiness, both on the earth and in Heaven. Because a vicious man is never really happy. On the contrary, a virtuous man is always happy with a celestial joy, even if he is poor and alone. Not even death upsets him. Because he has no sins or remorse making him fear to meet God, neither does he regret what he leaves on the earth. He knows that his treasure is in Heaven and like a man who goes to take the inheritance due to him, a holy inheritance, he goes happily and solicitously towards death, which opens to him the gate of the Kingdom where is his treasure.

Store up your treasure at once. Begin in your youth, you young people; work incessantly, you older people, who are closer to death because of your age. But since the date of death is unknown, and a child often dies before a venerable old man, do not postpone the work of storing up your treasure of virtues and good deeds for the next life, lest death should reach you before you have placed a treasure of merits in Heaven. Many people say: "Oh! I am young and strong! I will enjoy myself for the time being on the earth, and I will turn later." A big mistake!

Listen to this parable. A rich man's estate had yielded a good harvest. A really miraculous harvest. He looks happily at so much abundance piling up in his fields and threshing-floors and which is to be stored in provisional sheds and even in the rooms of his house, since his barns cannot hold it all, and says: "I have worked like a slave but I have not been disappointed by my fields. I have worked as much as for ten harvests, and I am going to rest just as long. What shall I do to put away all this crop? I do not want to sell it otherwise I would be compelled to work to have a new crop next year. This is what I will do: I will knock down my granaries and build larger ones, capable of holding all my crops and my goods. And then I will say to my soul: 'Oh, my soul! You have aside goods for many years. Rest, therefore, eat, drink and have a good time.' The man, like many more people, mistook his soul for his body and mixed the sacred and the profane, because in actual fact a soul does not rejoice in revelries and idleness, but languishes. And the man, like many, after the first good harvest in the fields of virtue, stopped, as he thought he had done everything.

But do you not know that once you have laid your hand on the plough you must persevere for one, ten, one hundred years, as long as your life lasts, because to stop is a crime against oneself, as one denies oneself a greater glory, and it is a regression, because generally he who stops not only does not proceed further, but turns back? The treasure of Heaven must increase year by year to be good. Because if Mercy is benign to those also who had few years to store it up, it will not be an accomplice of lazy people who in a long life do little. It is a treasure increasing continuously. Otherwise it is no longer a fruit-bearing treasure, but an unfruitful one, which is detrimental to the readily available peace of Heaven.

God said to the foolish man: "Fool! You mistake body and wealth of the earth for what is spirit and you turn the grace of God into evil. This very night the demand will be made for your soul, and it will be taken away and your body will lie lifeless. And this hoard of yours, whose will it be then? Will you take it with you? No. You will come to My presence despoiled of earthly crops and spiritual works and you will be poor in the next life. It would have been better if you had used your crops for works of mercy on behalf of your neighbor and yourself. Because if you had been merciful towards others, you would have been merciful to your own soul. And instead of fostering idle thoughts, you could have plied a trade which would have given an honest profit for your body and great merit for your soul until I called you". And the man died that night and was severely judged. I tell you solemnly that that happens to those who store up treasure for themselves but do not grow rich in the eyes of God.

Go now and avail yourselves of the doctrine explained to you. Peace be with you."

The lesson is clear, I think, for all of you. You don't know how long you have to enjoy yourself, you don't know how long you have to work or serve or grow or learn, you don't know, nobody knows. God knows. But more than that I want to talk about a condition of usefulness and I want to talk about a condition of acceptance and it's similar to the meditation where you are having to confront how much you think you can be and how much you can change.

In some ways you don't know how much you can change because you haven't tried it and you don't know what to change into often because you don't have a concept of what it is that you can change into. So you are kind of stuck a little bit like a galley slave area where you know that there are strokes and there is the beating of the drum, each stroke you have to go forward and you have to go backwards and you just keep it up until they say rest and you put the oars down and that's the limitation of your life. It's like you work, you play, you sleep, you eat and you move along, you know, and it's kind of very limited. It's designed to satisfy your concept of what's possible and the reason I am saying it that way is because your concept of what's possible, that's your slave ship. That's the thing that keeps you tied to the oars and stuck to the mast and you know sitting in your seat. You have a small idea of what's possible for you.

But Jesus has a huge idea of what's possible, and it's not anything you can do. It only can be done to you if you stop thinking what can be done to you. He can only do something to you if you stop having an idea of what can be done to you. He can only make you something if you stop having an idea of what he can make you into. Now I am getting right to the core of the definition of letting go. Letting go is not knowing what the hell is going on and being very happy about it, because if you are mad about it, you are not letting go. Because if you are mad about it, you have an idea of how it should go or at least you think you have an idea and you are trying to get away from getting upset about it. If you are upset about it, you have an idea about how you think things should go. But how is God going to turn you into a lighted vessel and a glorious manifestation of the God head in full love and light if you have a lot of ideas. You are not going to do it. You are not going to personally do any of this. That's not for you to do.

It's the Divine one that causes this magical transformation in you if your lump is given to him and he kneads you and works you and changes you, and you are not capable of doing that. None of the humans are capable of doing that. And there is a lot of effort placed in holding fast to a little bit of consciousness and then patting yourself on the back for a little bit of uplift in consciousness. When you didn't do any of that yourself and as you pat yourself on the back for what small progresses you have made, I am not trying to insult you but you should be insulted for that kind of thinking. You stop your growth, because you lock on to a concept that you are little bit better than you used to be or you are little lighter than you used be heavy you used to be kind of oppressed and now you are a little freer in your thinking. You used to be slovenly now you are lively or whatever your little minute gradations of evaluation of where you are you think you are. It was not for you to evaluate from the get go, from the beginning of your existence. It was not for you to limit what gifts of God, God's trying to move through you and that's the very thing that Satan actually advises you to evaluate, how far you would like to be and how far you have come and to pat yourself on the back and to drum up the ego to the point where you can figure out where you are heading and where you have been and none of that is real and none of that is true. You can't figure it out and the more you try it figure it out, the more you stop your growth and what is the growth anyway, it's not your job and it's not your opinion, it's not your regime. It's God's thing to get you to a place where you are not in God's way anymore, when God's trying to move spirit through you, you are not in the way and God's trying to move consciousness in you, you are not having ideas.

We talk about letting go and you know the definition but you don't know the experience. Letting go of where you think you should be, how far you have come how far you need to go or where God wants to take you, that's just like drop off point where Jesus wants to take you, you don't have any concept of that but you don't want to know because then you can't control it. You don't want to know where he is going to take you because then you can't control it. I have news for you - where you are is kind of stuck. It's where you have accepted to be, which is not what he wants. He wants you where He is, not where you think you are okay. He wants you where He is. He has the ability to take you as long as you don't tie your rope off to yourself to every tree that you come by to stop your growth to moor yourself to your past which you are so proud of. I am not proud of your past, I think your past sucks. I think your past should be deleted from your memory so that you can move into real life. I am always an advocate for letting go of all attachments, I have always said that, there is never a time where I have not said that. Why do I say that? Because I can see you are so attached to your memories, to your minute picture of what is possible for you. I have no such concept of what is limiting for you.

I have sadness for you holding on to your limitations. I am trying to let those go so I don't have to look at you and say it's sad what you are doing to yourself because I have to love you and I don't have to, I just do and I am not going to be contributing to your limitations. I do know that you must enjoy where you are so proud of arriving, you must enjoy it or you would tell Jesus take me out of this hell. Bring me out of this prison, get rid of my concepts so I can open to your Light and your love, wake me up so I can be happy, that's what you would be doing. No, you are kind of content to be in your rut that you are used to so that you can say to yourself, I know myself pretty well and I am sure you don't know yourself at all, I am sure you don't know yourself at all. Because anybody who truly knows themselves would never tolerate that, they would never go there, they would never settle in to who they think they are because they are a work in progress, they are a light in the making, they are a God, a Christ in the forming, they would never settle in. They wouldn't be mad at themselves but they would never settle, they would never get comfy in anything at all and if you are getting comfortable, you have just stopped temporarily, during the day, you stopped. The only way to get to this place I am talking about is to first accept I do not know anything and the next one is that I am really happy about it and the third one is I am going to let Jesus guide this and I don't know where I am going. I don't know what I am going to turn into and you know what, I am happy about that, that's how to break all this crap in your concepts. Most of you are just congealing a stiffness around a concept of who you think you are so that you cannot be jostled and do not have to be shaken out of your complacency. And don't think I am not looking at it, don't think I have not studied it. Don't think I don't know you, for one minute, don't think that. I am not criticizing, I am amazed that you would settle for these limiting things and you even imagine it's you. I am amazed, after all the things that I say, and all the jabs into your stiffness and all the pokes into your complacency, that you haven't got a fire under your butt at this time in your life. But I have not been successful, I know that. I goad, nothing happens, I motivate, no movement, I roll the stone, it stops. That's how it is, that's how Jesus did it with all this people. He rolled them like a stone, moved them lovingly with his foot and they just roll to a stop.

The next time He comes He has to do it again. Why, because they are stuck in the concepts of who they think they are and they don't want it to budge, they won't budge. They just don't want it to budge, they will not be moved. You know why? Because their ego has gone well this is me, this is probably all I can accept. This is probably all that can happen for someone like me and you know that's all so self-serving because you never have to give, do you? You never have to change and you never have to take the great adventure of going into the unknown and being led where you can't see and shown what you have never known and to become what you have never done yet in your lifetimes. So you are not a great adventurer, not yet. Adventurers go where no one has gone before, they go into an unknown experience, they haven't experienced yet, that's an adventurer. Ones who like to get settled in what they already know are by definition not adventurers. See the problem. What am I going to do with this motley lot, what am I going to do? I mean I know what to do but I am not sure how to get you out of your slave ship rowing position. I don't like that galley slave thing, I have done it, I don't know if you remember but I did it, I did not like it. We worked hard, that's all we did. We worked until the arms fell off and the heart broke and they died and they just throw it overboard. Years and years of that and that was life. That's what I think you guys are doing with your lives. You are on the galley slip. That's what we do, and do the same thing, the same way, with the same mind and the same temperament, the same emotions the same feeling because that's who we think we are. I mean are you a slave. Are you faithful to the galley or are you faithful to God? People aren't happy on the galley ship and I can see many of you are not happy, I know you try to be cheerful but many of you are not happy. I am not kidding. I am not going to lie to you. I see that you are not happy. If you are lying to you, you are going to tell me you are happy and I can see that you are not and are we going to have an argument about it or are you going to be somebody saying, "Okay, alright. I am not happy. Alright now, how do we get happy?" See? We would have to do that first before we have a goal to get happy.

If there is no honesty then it's just my opinion. I am ragging on you, nagging you, while you pretend to be happy and I am noticing that seems like you are not and then you want to argue, and we are going to argue about whether you are happy or not. And I am going to win because I am going to stop talking to you, not because you have convinced me but because you win, you win, you win. You can have what you want.

You are not going to change my idea about it when I can clearly see it. I don't know if you have tried that before, trying to change my attitude, my opinion about things. It's not really one of those things that works with the rock. It just doesn't work, you have tried it before. No, nope, I can be gracious with you, I can thank you for your opinion and I can honor you for having such a strong one you know but does it phase me at all and does it change anything that I see? Not at all, not at all. I am not here to be malleable, I am here to set the pace, I am here to set the standard, I am here to pioneer and cut through the forest where you can't see. I am the way shower and you follow as reluctantly or as egotistically as you prefer and I have to come back and get you every other week. I have to come back and say, 'Okay remember that God loves you?' and you say, 'Yeah, I was miserable and I forgot, and remember that God was going to take all your sins? No I wanted to keep them. I was going to try to work them out on my own. Remember? These are the densities that I am facing. Well, I thought I was released and then I took it back, I just grabbed it back when I went to my car. Well that's nice we are getting like an F minus in effectiveness here. I know the grade the world gives me its F minus and I know what grade the Master goes, he says 'they did that to me.' So then I get an A, even though it's very unsatisfying. But you guys have to give me an F minus because that is true, that's as effective as I am. I have to have a sense of humor about this or I am just going to cry, because it's the stuff that you guys value so much and they are such lies and you value it so much and it's so bad for you and you want it so much that you won't let it go and it's amazing. There is a certain math problem in there that I can't figure out. You are holding onto something that doesn't help you and you are holding onto something that doesn't make you free, and doesn't make you feel good. I just say 'That's like buying a house that depreciated before you bought it.' Between the time that you signed the papers and the time that you close the house, it dropped fifty thousand dollars but you know that ahead of time so you buy it anyway. That's what it feels like to me. It's an economic attachment. I am going to buy into a concept that diminishes my self-esteem and my dignity and cuts me off from God and takes me away from love hmm same thing, just different example. First of all, you can't do it yourself so if you think you are going to try then you will always fail. And if you don't submit your anatomy and let it go, and give it to Jesus and let him do something with it that you won't know what he is doing, it won't happen. And if you are so valuing that anatomy of yours that you are going to keep it intact that it is, you can't give it up to God and God can't do anything with you because you are holding. I want to see you all happy and I want to see you all lighted up and letting go and really in the true meaning of what that means.

You have no idea what letting go means and I don't think you have ever meditated on what letting go means because you don't know anything about it yet and we say it all the time and because the words seem so simple, you think you know what it means. How about dying to the old self? Now we will meditate because that sounds awesome but letting go we won't meditate because we know what that means.

Letting God turn you inside out, shape you down and shake all that garbage out of you until you are barely just what he wants you to be-- that's letting go. We don't want to know what that is because what did we spend all that time building up our ego for if we were going to be shaken up and shaken out, and dump all that stuff out. Why would we do something like that? Why would we submit to that when we worked so hard to build up such a big fat ego?

He said unless you do that you will have no part with me. Unless you give all, lay it down, come and follow me, you will have no part with me and some of you are riding two horses and I think that's a groinal split for some of you. You want to ride two horses like the world and your power and your ego and your missions and pride and you ride the humble disciple horse, you want to glue them together. Well they have a different mind, at some point there are going to split in the road and some other things are going to split. You know when the hard times come the tough they go with god and the un-tough go with the world and I venture to say you are not strong enough when that choice hits even to know which one you are going to take. Only a few of you are strong enough now to know which choice you are going to make. Just because you are here doesn't mean that you have been tested. It means you are pretty sure, it means you are fairly dedicated, it doesn't mean you have been tested yet and I am not sure how you would handle that and most of you, your Achilles heel is right what you know it is, I don't need to mention them. Each person has one, your Achilles heel is sometimes your kids or sometimes your mind or sometimes your sensuality or sometimes your career or something. It's like whatever your Achilles heel is, don't you think Satan is going to use that against you and you haven't been tested like that yet, you have not been tested about that or if you have, you are losing. A transformation should make you happy and your face should look younger and life should start moving again. Just like He said, the pure have a resonance and an enveloped happiness coming into their flesh a youthfulness, some of you are working on your age for some reason which seems like it's a sadness and unhappiness, stuckness, opinions and concepts. That makes you sour, unhappy, old and slow. That's not what life does to a person. That's not what blessings do to a person-- it just doesn't happen that way. Yeah, you are going to get grey hairs over time but that doesn't mean you have to be unlively. It doesn't mean you have to go like to first gear, never get in the passing lane, slow everybody up on the highway of life, right?

Anyway, it's all concepts, all concepts, painful, and Jesus watches them and you are so attached to them, wanting them. He has to go give me that and you go, 'Noooo! I don't know if I will be myself without them.' That's what you say inside, that's what you say. 'I don't know if I would be myself without them.' He said give them all to me, and you say, 'I won't. I am getting around to it, I know it.' What are we going to do? I can feel them dripping off you but they are not going away, they are just oozing. You know how oozing is different than falling off? You get that, feel that, I hope so, because oozing is like it's generated from within, it's got its own generation plant in there, and just keeps spewing, versus falling away. Then the person is coming alive, flowering, because they are letting go, they are letting go, letting it go. So if you find yourself a little lethargic or a little stuck it's because you have latched on pretty heavy to a bunch of concepts that are death producing. Death producing. That's why things are sluggish and don't move because you locked onto something that's killing you. There is no other reason. It's not cosmic, it's not Jesus is incapable of doing something to you. He is incapable of violating your will just as I am. I can't say, 'Oh, let's just magically grow,' when your whole body says, 'I don't think I know what that means, I don't know if I want that.' I can't do anything with that. We can't do anything with that because you haven't submitted your anatomy to the Master, to say 'Do with me whatever you want. I have no idea who I am.' I don't hear that from you, I hear, 'no way.'

When you have little spats with each other oh boy are you coming from that place of, 'I know who I am' and you are doing something against this thing who knows who he is or she is. You know who you are. That's a joke. You would be happy and actually when you are happy you don't have to go I know who I am. Happy people don't say stuff like that, they don't have to preserve anything, they don't have to brace against you or fight with you or push you around, because they are happy, they don't need that. They don't need you to recognize to be there because they are tranquil. They are tranquil in themselves. See what I mean? So all these things that you do, you get a little territory and you growl over it, it's just, that's not really you, that's not you, that's like what? That's how you should determine it. Somebody does that and you say, 'What?' When anybody does that in our community I think it's appropriate to go, what? That's appropriate. Don't say any words, don't say any more, doesn't need any more description than what. What's going on? What's happening? What are you doing? That's enough. Don't say any more. No more criticisms. Just say, 'What?' I think it's fine. I think it's a beautiful thing to say. It's a profound thing. What? I think it's eloquent. What? And you can do that with a lot of love and smiles and say, 'What?' Sort of smile about it. You have to try, you have to practice. I have to practice smiling. What? See what I mean? No. Alright, well it's a good try anyway. Talk to Jesus about it. You can try it, okay? That's where we are at-- trying a little light on that thing you know and darkness closes it back up after I have done that. It's okay, it's my life. It is my life. It's my life. It's fine.

What do you think he did? Taught like this all the time and he had to walk out of town while they went back to the same old ways with a two percent shift in their consciousness. A two percent shift in their consciousness every time he talked to them. I know. I was there. It's like a two percent shift in their consciousness, that's progress, it is. You have to be positive about these things, a two percent shift in your consciousness is night and day right now and if you do that you know every week you are getting there, you will be getting there. Why does it have to be so hard that you have to submit, you know, such a huge mountain of resistance, to just let go two percent, each time you are talked to? I am not complaining, I am asking you why you are holding off? Why? Why is it so important to hold on to things that don't even make you happy? You tell me that and I would probably get better at what I do if you answer that for me. You tell me or I will just forget asking you. The reason I ask rhetorical questions, that nobody ever answers that's just fun for me as well just so you know it's fun too.

Anyway, there is God inside smiling and going are going to get over this. Are you going to get over this human thing, this pretending to know thing? Are you ever going to get over that? Because that's God talking to you inside you, ever going to get over this pretending you know stuff. Can't you let me tell you, you have to pretend to know? Can I tell you, believe me that's where God is at, looking at you going you think you know, you have no idea. I created you, know what the hell is your problem. You guys are babies in letting go. I pronounce you babies in letting go, I pronounce it so, it is so. You are neophytes in the letting go department and I would like to challenge you to let go like a kindergartner at least. Just that would be a healthy transition. The kindergartener letting go versus I don't know if I even want to that's like baby, you know. But somebody who is helpful has to let go of a lot more than that. They can't even be empowered to help anybody, I mean I am telling you the truth, you like all those structure and systems because you had the military guy telling what those were. I am not like that. I think you need to grow into it. It's an art form not a structural ordeal.

The problem with those little structures is people get to them, they sit down and drop into the lower one. The problem with my lack of structure is when you are really there oh are you there, you don't even know what that is. Thank God you can't call it anything because you are really there. That's the problem with my area. You are going, there is no stripes on your arm, you are not the pre Sergeant and then post Sergeant and then the after Sergeant, then Sergeant major, you are not getting all that crap in your head, whatever that means, the DIT, the deacon, the new deacon, the old deacon, the dead deacon then the priest whatever you have in your head, garbage. Just garbage. It's about love. How much do you love? Do you love a little to a certain kind of shiny place? You can call it whatever you want. I call it loving to a certain shiny place. Why do I do that? Because you guys want to latch on to something and call it a bench and then sit your fanny down on it-- that's why. When you sit your fanny down on that bench, you just stopped. So you want benchmarks? I don't.

July 10, 2016
Led by the Spirit

The Poem of the Man-God volume 3 chapter 363. At the Temple. The "Our Father" and a Parable on True Sons.

Jesus says:
"I solemnly tell you that those who seem to be illegitimate are instead true sons, and those who are true sons become illegitimate. Listen to this parable.

Once there was a man who had to absent himself from home for a long time because of some business engagements, when his sons were still very young. From the place where he was, he used to write letters to the older sons to keep them in due respect for their father, who was far away, and to remind them of his teaching. The last son, who was born after the father had left, was still at nurse with a woman who lived far from there, in the country of the man's wife, who was not of his race. The wife died when the son was still a baby and away from home. His brothers said: "Let us leave him where he is, with our mother's relatives. Perhaps our father will forget about him and we will gain by it, as there will be one less to divide the property with, when our father dies." And they did so. The child was thus brought up by his mother's relatives, he was unaware of his father's teaching, he did not even know that he had a father and brothers and, what is worse, he bitterly considered: "They have all disowned me as if I were illegitimate," and he even thought that he was, as he was so deeply hurt at being rejected by his father.

It so happened that when he grew up and found a situation because, embittered as he was by the above considerations, he had conceived a strong aversion also for the family of his mother, whom he deemed guilty of adultery - he went to the town where his father was. And without knowing who he was, he approached him and had the opportunity to hear him speak. His father was a wise man. As he did not receive any satisfaction from his remote sons - who by now behaved as it pleased them and were on conventional terms with their remote father, purely to remind him that they were "his" sons and therefore he should bear that in mind in his will - the old man devoted himself to giving good advice to the young people he approached in the land where he was. The young son was attracted by such righteousness, which was so fatherly for many young men and he not only approached him but he availed himself of every word of the old man, thus soothing his embittered spirit. The man was taken ill and had to decide to go back to his fatherland. And the young man said to him: "Sir, you are the only person who has spoken to me with justice, elevating my spirit. Allow me to follow you as your servant. I do not want to relapse into my previous evil state." "Come with me. You will take the place of a son, of whom I have never been able to get news." And they went back to the paternal house together.

Neither the father, nor the brothers, nor the young man himself realized that the Lord had once again gathered together those of the same blood under one roof. But the father had to shed many tears because of the sons known to him, because he found that they had forgotten his teaching, had become greedy and hard-hearted, without faith in God, but with many idolatries in their hearts: pride, avarice and lust were their gods and they would not listen to anything which was not human profit. The stranger, instead, approached the Lord more and more, and he became just, kind, loving and obedient. His brothers hated him, because their father loved him, although he was a stranger. But he forgave them and loved them, because he had understood that peace is to be found in love.

One day the father, who was disgusted with the behavior of his sons, said: "You have taken no interest in your mother's relatives, and not even in your brother. You remind me of the behavior of Jacob's sons towards their brother Joseph. I want to go to that country to find out about him. I may find him and be comforted by him." And he took leave both of the sons known to him and of the young stranger, whom he gave a sum of money that he might go back to the place from which he had come and start a little business there.

When he arrived in the country of his dead wife, her relatives told him that the forsaken son had changed his original name Moses into Manasseh, because by his birth he had really made his father forget that he was a just man, as he had abandoned his child.

"Do not do me wrong! I was told that all traces of the boy had been lost, and I did not even hope to find any of you. But tell me. What is he like? Has he grown into a strong man? Is he like his mother who died in giving birth to him? Is he kind? Does he love me?"

"He is strong, indeed, and he is as handsome as his mother was beautiful, but his eyes are dark. And on his side he has the same birthmark as his mother. And he has a slight lisp, like you. He was grown up when he left here, exacerbated by his fate, as he doubted his mother's modesty and he bore you ill-will. He would have been kind if he had had no ill-will in his soul. He went across mountains and rivers as far as Trapetius to... "

"Did you say Trapetius? In Synopy? Tell me! I was there and I met a young man with a slight lisp, he was alone and sad, and he was so kind although he appeared to be rather harsh. Was it him? Tell me!"

"Perhaps it was. Look for him. On his right hand side he has a dark birthmark in relief, as your wife had."

The man departed at once, hoping to find the stranger in his house. But he had left to go back to the colony of Synopy. And the man followed him... He found him. He made him go to his house to examine his side. He identified him. He fell on his knees praising God Who had restored his son to him, a son who was much better than the others who were becoming more and more brutish, whereas this one had become more *and more holy during the months which had intervened. And he said to his good son: "You will have the share of your brothers because, without being loved by anyone, you have become more just than they are."*

Was it not fair? It was. I solemnly tell you that those are true sons of God who, although rejected by the world, despised, hated, insulted, forsaken as if they were illegitimate children, considered a disgrace and calamity, know how to surpass the sons who grew up at home but rebelled against its laws. The fact that one comes from Israel does not entitle one to enter Heaven, neither is that destiny guaranteed by the fact that one is a Pharisee, a scribe or a doctor. It is necessary to have good will and follow the Doctrine of love generously, becoming new in it and children of God in spirit and truth through it.

You, who are listening to Me, must bear in mind that many who feel safe in Israel will be supplanted by those whom they consider publicans, prostitutes, Gentiles, pagans and galley-slaves. The Kingdom of Heaven belongs to those who can put new vigor and faith into their lives by accepting Truth and Love."

You have all endured, it might be the right word, endured the change from the old order to the new order, for the last three years. You have put up with the dissolving of form, the dissolving of structure, that had been growing more and more calcified in your minds and in your hearts, and you were thinking in terms of outer positions where you could comfortably sit as places of spirituality instead of thinking of spirituality as the kindness of your love and the generosity of your willingness. And gradually we have been dissolving that over time and you are left a little bit adrift now to wonder where you really are and that's by design and by the Master's and the Mother's decision to have true spiritual beings in their body and not corpses with titles. And many of you haven't really resolved the corpse scene but you know there is no juice there and there is no benefit to it. At least you know that and that's a dissolution of form, it's required for the spirit to move. The more congealed you are in your concepts of where you are and who you are, the less spirit moves.

When spirit moves it takes you places you didn't plan, and it guides you into things that you didn't know you had the capacity and you didn't know you had the skills or the capabilities or even the talent or even the personality for a particular thing, you didn't even know. But when you let the spirit move, it stretches you into marvel of marvel what God wants, not what you want. What God thinks you are capable of not what you think you are capable of. And we are still having labor pains, in this delivery and we are still having nostalgia, for the comfortable laziness of the past. To live in the spirit means you have to be led, moved on the wings of love and it has nothing to do with your head.

It's cool in the story how the spirit just moves the father and the lost, adoptive son and moves them together and then verifies the truth by the mark on the side. Meanwhile the ones that are stuck in the mud and stuck satisfied in their inheritance and demanding of the father that they give them when he dies he passes his wealth onto them when they really don't respect him at all, kind of hate him. We still have that condition inside of you. You still have that condition of expectation of your parents which is like hate for the father in this scene. You still have attitude and opinion. You are not humble, not loving, and not obedient towards the truth of what the ancestry teaches. But you have humbleness and faithfulness to your old ways. And they were rejected in this scene in this parable. Those prideful conceptions of who you are cannot enter or stay in the kingdom of God because they are not you. They never could be you, they never will be you, and in the future they cannot be you.

One of the problems that I see in our community although you are all committed to be here and you have all been somewhat faithful in your consistency (I am not criticizing that part) I am just calling attention to one part--the part where you are holding on to your concept of you. It's certainly painful for Jesus and Mary to watch because they know who you are but you don't. So you are holding on to a concept of who you think you are which you don't know. You don't even know who that is and they have the picture of who you are and what is possible for you and you are not moving quickly towards their concept. You are not led, moved and willing to go into the unknown, like you don't know yourself but they know you. They know who you can be, you don't. They know what's possible for you, you don't, but you eke out. It's like your pride is saying well I have got some things together. As long as you are on that side of the equation, where you are calculating how much you have together, you can never be on the other side of the equation where you are led by the spirit into you know not what, into becoming you know not who you are going to be. It's like you are stuck in the possessiveness of what you think you know and no movement of spirit can move there because you are satisfied in it or at least you are fearful around it, hugging it. It's like you have spent three years, reluctantly letting go of a bunch of concepts and still trying to hold on and maintain some semblance of who think you are.

When you are led by the spirit, you are not supposed to know anything. You are not supposed to have yourself set, like you think you know who you are. Clearly many of you don't know who you are because you are clearly struggling with the same things that are blocking you from a long time ago. If you are a soul and you are a God being and a spirit mostly, and you are wearing this prisoner who has very set ways, then you are a restriction. The spirit is restricted by your prisoner which is your body and your emotions and your ego. You are imprisoned. When you are not imprisoned you are being led with love and grace and energy to everything that you are doing. When that energy and love and grace isn't happening you are constricting it and pinning it down and holding it tight. Holding it tight to what. To what you used to think. Not what you will think, nobody holds things tight to the thing that they will think, they only hold things tight to the thing they already thought which means that you are stuck in the past concept of who you are and that includes your past reactions to the people you demanded so much from and you are still doing it.

Now, I have been discussing with myself, because I am a good conversationalist, I don't know if you guys are with me, but I am with myself, I have been discussing with myself, how long it takes to forgive. Just a philosophical question, like how long it takes to just forgive. And for some of you it's going to be maybe two thirds of your life or maybe ten years or maybe like six months and a year, or whatever, and I am marveling at that, because I don't think that's really true. As I was discussing with myself, I was thinking that forgiveness is something that you just do it, like you just freaking completely do it. So if I totally forgive you, I am not waiting for you to make another mistake. Because in order to do that, to anticipate you making another failure or making another error, I would have to hold back some scrutiny and be suspicious that you actually had changed or I had actually released you. I would have to be holding back a little bit anticipating you not handling the thing I am forgiving you for, not changing in the thing I am forgiving you for. And so many justifications to not forgive because you might make an error again, you might be mean again, you might not come through again, so shouldn't I hold a little bit of my forgiveness for that eventuality that you would probably be imperfect, that's one side of the forgiveness problem. The other side of the forgiveness problem is I haven't got what I need from you yet so I cannot release you.

Nobody even asked God if I should hold this person to account until they satisfy me before I forgive them. "Jesus would you like me to hold this person liable and also responsible and accountable as long as we both shall live until I can forgive them?" You can see that that's not forgiveness. You can see that that's what you are doing. You can see that if you still have resentments or animosities or trembling fear or insecurity around your parents that you have technically not forgiven them. And I see it everywhere and I am wondering why you need to have that kind of stuck old energy in your psyche and in your relating rather than be free as the spirits, free as the wind in the loving embrace of your Creator and Jesus and Mary. I don't get it. I don't know why it's taking so long and why your concept is so long term in this forgiveness piece. Like without grabbing on to that thing that you are clutching, and that demand that you are making that judgment that you are having, you would be uncomfortable. And I don't have the answer for why you do that. Because I don't think forgiveness is anything but instantaneous. Otherwise I can't call it forgiveness. You decided, it's done, it's finished. And if you aren't doing that then you have not forgiven, and you can do this 30, 60, 25, 80, 7 on me if you like I don't care but I am talking about the thoroughness of it. You want to piece it out in four parts okay that's your style. You want to lengthen this out for 15 year program, the people have to die first and then you might forgive them, oh that's so big of you, you gave such, you gave so much love in forgiving them, what a great thing you did waiting 15 years to forgive them till after they die. How much love you had to just give it over and let go of your resentments and your fears and your hurts, how big your heart was that you gave so much.

I am hammering on your concepts because they are in your way; they are in your way not in my way. I have done the thing I am asking you to do. It's no big deal. I am in peace and love but I want to see you that way. I think you will feel better, that's my goal, for you, to feel better. That's my service to you to unchain your heart and to free you from your puny humanity. That's my job. I want you to have the courage to forgive completely and stop holding and I want you to have the courage to be honest about all the lies you are telling yourself about how much you have done. I can see it in your energy field whether you have let go or not. I can see it in your talk whether you are still loyal, I can see it in your body whether you are still your mommy or your daddy's boy or girl and that shouldn't be the case anymore. That should never be the case for a grown up and for a spiritual adult. That's unheard of in my world, that's just unheard of. Did Jesus pay for you? Then He adopted you. Were you an orphan before that adoption? Yes, and some of you still are even though you claim that your devotion to him is so deep. Well if he adopted you, then He is your parent now and you have no other parents. If that's not happening, then you are holding. You are just holding and I have to wonder and I would like you to wonder why? Why? I want you to find out why. I know why. But I want you to find out why. Doesn't do me any good to know everything. It does you some good to find out some things, it will do you some good to really question and go into meditation. Why am I still holding it? Have I really forgiven everybody? Why am I still moody? Why am I still so touchy? Why am I still so selfish if I have forgiven everybody? These are questions you should be asking in guidance. Let God give you sentences-- not just a yes or a no. So cheap for you, because you didn't want to pay much attention to Him so you turned his answer into a yes or a no. How cheap you are in your relationship with God. He can talk to you. He created all the words of all languages. He has written all the books of Truth of ever anywhere. He could probably speak to you in sentences, if you would shut up long enough. If you would stop straining it through your past opinions you would hear it clearly. I don't speak to shame you, I speak to edify you. Look it up. Shame I mean. So this whole long enduring process of forgiving I don't understand it. Maybe you can tell me why it takes so long and how you can eke out you know 1000th percent of forgiveness over the next twelve years. How do you do that? How clever that is. How thick the head when you do it. How do you do that and call that honest. Do you really need problems? Is that the point that I am missing here, that you really need problems, you have to have them and you are lonely without them. Is that what we are looking at? Is that what I need to understand about you is that what you need to tell me, is that what I need to learn about you is that you have to have problems and it's just my theory that you don't?

What does Jesus want? He wanted disciples to be like Him. Do you think He wanted them to keep their problems? Do you think He wanted them every day or every week to be wondering why they left home and wondering how their parents are and always thinking about the past? You think He wanted that? You think that was cool for Him to have all the apostles going, "God I haven't been home in a while. Where is my responsibility to my dad and mom?" Some people did actually ask Him that and He said from this point on you have no responsibility to anybody but God and to me. Earthshaking. And it's true, if you are listening to God that's who you respond to and God will take care of your kids if you have any. If you have listened to Him He would have taken care of them lot better than you, if you had listened to Him. So where do we stand? I don't know. You tell me where you stand with this whole thing and if you are reflecting a little bit I think you will be able to find out where you stand.

July 17, 2016
Line Up

PMG v.3 ch.368. The Thursday before Passover. Instructions to the Apostles.

"And if I came to reproach you?"
"It does not matter! At least - you two agree, don't you? We shall at least know what is to be done!" Alphaeus' two sons nod assent.
"Well, I do promise you. However, believe Me, the Paraclete will make Himself understood by your souls. But I will come and say to you: 'James, do this and that. Simon Peter, it is not right for you to do that. Judas, fortify yourself to be ready for this or that.'"
"Oh! very good. I feel better now. And come often, mind You! Because I shall be like a poor lost child, who does nothing but weep and... do the wrong thing..." And Peter almost begins to weep now...
Judas Thaddeus asks: "Could You not do so for everybody, even now? I mean, for those who are doubtful, guilty, abjurers. Perhaps a miracle..."
"No, brother. A miracle does a lot of good, particularly that kind of miracle, when it is granted at the right time and in the right place, to people who are not mischievously guilty. When, instead, it is granted to people mischievously guilty, it increases their guilt, because it increases their pride. They mistake the gift of God for weakness of God, as if God implored such proud people to allow Him to love them. They consider the gift of God the result of their great merits. They say: "God humbles Himself before me, because I am holy." Then the ruin is complete. The ruin of Mark of Josiah, for instance, and of other people with him... Woe to those who take that Satanic road. The gift of God changes in them into poison of Satan. To be blessed with unusual gifts is the greatest and safest test of the degree of elevation and holy

will in man. Very often man becomes humanly exhilarated with them, and from spiritual he becomes entirely human, he then descends lower and becomes a demon."

"Why does God grant them then? It would be better if He did not!"

"Simon of Jonah, when your mother wanted you to learn to walk, did she keep you in swaddling- clothes and in her arms all the time?"

"No. She put me on the floor with my legs free."

"Did you ever fall?"

"Innumerable times! Also because I was very... Well, since I was a child, I wanted to do things by myself and I maintained that I did everything well."

"But you no longer fall now!"

"Of course not! Now I know that it is dangerous to climb on the back of a chair, that it is wrong to make use of rain-pipes to descend from the roof to the ground and that it would be foolish to try to fly from the fig-tree into the house, just like a bird. But when a child, I did not know. And if I did not get killed it is a real mystery. But little by little I learned to make the right use of my legs and also of my brains."

"So God did a good thing in giving you legs and brains, and your mother also did a good thing in letting you learn at your own expense?"

"Most certainly!"

"And God does likewise with souls. He gives them gifts, and like a good mother He warns and teaches them. But then everybody must consider by himself how to use them."

"And if one is a blockhead?"

"God does not give gifts to blockheads. He loves them, because they are unhappy, but He does not give them what they could not appreciate."

"But supposing He did give them, and they used them wrongly?"

"God would treat them for what they are: disabled people, and consequently not responsible. He would not judge them."

"And if one is intelligent when one receives them, and later becomes silly or mad?"

"If the change is due to disease, one is not guilty of not using the gift."

"But... one of us, for instance? Mark of Josiah... or... somebody else, then?"

"Oh! In that case it would be better for him not to be born! But that is how the good are separated from the wicked... A painful but just operation."

"Which is the interesting subject of your conversation? Does it not concern us?" ask the other apostles who, thanks to the width of the street, have been able to join Jesus.

"We were speaking of many things. Jesus told me a parable on the leprosy of houses. I will repeat it to you later" replies Peter.

"What superstition, however! Really worthy of those days. Walls are not affected by leprosy. Foolish ancient people applied animal characteristics to clothes and walls. Absurd theories which make us ridiculous" remarks the Iscariot displaying his learning.

"Not quite as you say, Judas. Under an apparent fiction, suited to the mentality of those days, they achieved an important scope, which corresponded to holy foresight. Just like many other precepts of old Israel. Precepts safeguarding the health of the people. It is the duty of legislators to keep people healthy, it honors and serves God because people are creatures of God. Therefore they are not to be neglected, as we do not neglect animals and plants. It is true that the houses that are called leprous, do not have the physical disease of leprosy. But they have position and construction faults, which make them unhealthy and are revealed by stains called "leprosy of the walls". In the long run they are not only unhealthy for man, but they become dangerous because they can easily fall. Thus the Law prescribes what is right and orders the houses to be abandoned and restored and even to be pulled down, if after being repaired, they still show signs of the disease."

"Oh! What harm can a little dampness do? It can be dried with braziers."

"Then the dampness will not show exteriorly and the deception is greater. The dampness will grow in depth and corrode, and one fine day the house collapses burying those who are in it. Judas, Judas! It is better to be exceedingly watchful than imprudent."

"I am not a house."

"You are the house of your soul. Do not let evil filter into your house and crush it to pieces... Watch over the safety of your soul. You must all be watchful."

"I will watch, Master. But tell me the truth, have my mother's words made a deep impression on You? She is ill. She imagines things. I must have her treated. Cure her for me, Master."

"I will comfort her. But you are the only one who can cure her, relieving her anxiety."

I don't really want you to be worrying about your imperfections, or your leprous house, I want you to be thinking about God and I think that's super appropriate because the more you think about your problems, the bigger they get and the more you think about your problems, the more comparisons you make between the times you felt good and the times you felt bad. Then your pride gets in there and says you felt good some of the time and you get all complicated when you do that. Either you are beating yourself up in insecurity or you are feeling great because you are feeling a little bit better than you used to. But in every way that's not healthy for you. It's better to be thinking of God and thinking of God's love for you, and how you can be close and how you can be so peaceful, so joyful and so light filled that you just emanate that. If you can focus on that, you won't have time for fear and pride, it won't be on your agenda. You won't neglect the good things in your nature. Jesus of course is talking to Peter about him practicing and learning to do things well, and making all those mistakes that his mother let him make. It is how we learn, you know. We try praying for the things we want and we end up getting them, and then we decide that they are not all of the things that we wanted and then we make better prayers that are more precise, more clear. They are simple and they are more exactly what we want verses before when it's just random stuff we can get and that's how we practice. It's the same thing when you help other people. You help other people with the motivation to feel better about yourself often. So you help them with things that you think would be good if you had received that help which basically is very superstitious. Does everybody need what you needed? You don't know that but that's what you do in the beginning when you are trying to help, you give them the thing that you would have wanted. Then you find it's like flying from the rafters over to the house or the tree to the house and you fall, because you are hoping that that person needs the very thing that you need and they don't. They need what they need which isn't what you need.

That's how you practice, you learn and the mother watches, you fall and get up and try again, do it a different way, maybe get a ladder instead of flying. In the same way you might want to actually ask the person what it is they need and not presume that you know, and that's getting more artful and taking care of people. Then when you are super artful you ask inside what they need because they may not know how to describe it or they may not even know what they need, but God does. So you ask God and you give them that and they may look at it like it's a foreign thing you just gave them, but it is what God wanted to give them. Maybe it takes them three days to accept it, maybe it takes them a week to get that that was actually a gift from God through you. They don't get it. They are not going to get it right away, some people. And you get better. Better at listening, better and better at serving and that alone takes the leprosy out of your life. What is this leprosy? It's a mildewed condition of rot. It's consuming itself, it's like working on its own corruption, it's like a mold or fungus in wood and it starts to soften it and moisten it and rot it and the strength of the wood is missing. The walls are holding on to a non-strength board and they start to sag. And then you don't see it for a long time, then it goes. It's the same when you hold on to a concept that isn't established in God. It's a weakness, and you keep bolstering it up or you keep trying to ignore the lack of foundation that it has, and its weakening, weakening because it has no real support from God.

Many of you have experienced the loss of a habit because it wasn't held up by any truth. In other words if it wasn't supported by truth, the habit you kept doing you kept wanting to. You kept supporting it with your ideas or at least acceptance, you kept doing it and it had no foundation at all and just simply collapsed. That habit doesn't feed you anymore, it doesn't make you better, it doesn't enliven you, it doesn't make you happy. A lot of your habits are like this but you do them anyway because you haven't learned yet, just like a kid. They keep trying to pick up a toy and the toy is heavy and they fall, it's kind of like what happens with you. You keep grabbing something that's not good for you and you fall, and how many times can you do that before you learn it? I don't know, twenty, a hundred, two, depends on how reflective you are in your soul and in your mind, how fast you learn this. And how long you want to be on the planet. Like the house, the house was for Judas' soul. He said, your body, your emotions and your mind are the house for your soul. How are you doing with that? How lined up with your soul are those things? Are your feelings lined up with your soul, do they do the same thing, want the same thing? Is your head lined up with your soul so you have the same ideas and the same longings, the same striving and the same desires? When they are not lined up, there is rot in the system, something is weakening and you can't tell. You can always tell because there is a fight, there is a fight between your soul and your desire nature, or the fight between your ego and your soul. You know there is conflict there or there is tension there, so you know that something is not lined up, that's how you'll know.

Wouldn't it be great if they were just lined up, like what you want, what your head wants, what your emotions want and your body wants is what the soul wants? That's a person who has no more fight. They have become victorious, they have won, they have lined everything up in one thing and that's a thing that you choose. It's not something that's an accident, it's not something magical, it's something you choose - you choose that, you choose to submit your emotions to God and have them change because of God's way. You submit your mind so that your thoughts are not just doing whatever, they start to think God's thought. Gods thoughts and your souls thought that's what you are thinking, and then the body, the body is an instrument of what, random access, wild desire? No, an instrument for the soul, so that house is not rotten, so the house is lined up perfect. This is something that the person wants. Now your soul is bigger than your body, your soul is stronger and will last immortally so these three things will not last. If you make these three non-lasting things line up with the soul, you will be at peace and you will be happy. It doesn't mean the world will be impressed, it will not. It doesn't mean there will be peace on the Earth, there will not be peace on the Earth, but it means you will be lined up and you will not be struggling and you will not be leprous in any way. That takes a little work, you have to love. You have to love the head, mind, so that it submits to God's will. You don't fight with it because you will never win. You have to love your body so that the body obeys the soul. Because the soul is bigger and knows better. And you have to line the feelings up so it's what God feels and what your soul feels. How do you do that? You pray. You ask for help. And if you can't hear anything, act like Jesus, act like Mary. You might have to meditate on them to find out what they are like, because that's a pinnacle of what a human being can be. That's your goal and if it isn't your goal then you don't understand yet, you don't even understand goals yet. That is the pinnacle possibility of perfection a human could have. And it starts with love. Meaning that if you love lining up with God, that will start happening to you. If you love submitting your mind so that you have God's mind, that will start happening to you.

Many of you are still fighting in these things rather than using love to change it. If you love your house, you tear out a section and throw it away and you put a new section in. If you love your house you don't just get nasty and critical and mean to the house. You shore it up, you support it, you can take a section out, you put a section in. If you watch these construction guys taking off a porch they rip it out, they put temporary posts there to hold up the overhang. They rip the rotten porch out in a day, support it and then the next day they start framing it and two or three days later, there is a whole new front porch. That's what you do when you love your house. You don't just criticize it every day, you just make the effort to go fix it, just like you would fix a thought or you would fix a feeling or you would fix some habit in the body. You go at it positively, not as a fight, not as an aggression against this thing that you think is so strong in you. If you think it's so strong in you, you haven't decided to let it go yet. And Jesus is very compassionate and He is talking about practice. He is saying that the first efforts are just ridiculously awkward and he understands it, that's what kids are, that's the way you guys are. The first efforts are awkward and you have to practice and practice and practice and finally you know you are doing it, it's happening. That's how it works. If you love yourself well enough and if you let the love penetrate into you well enough, you will do all of this in a positive way. There will be no need for negativity or criticism in any of your progress. That's for people who are not sure they want to change. That's why they get irritable, that's why they get negative, that's why they get angry at themselves because they are not sure they want to, they are not sure they can and they don't make a dent. They aren't sure they want to make the effort yet so they can get kind of nasty about it. But somebody who is going to fix their house, and you and the neighbors watch, the thing is changed that week, it's changed. You didn't see the neighbors getting really mad, you didn't see him going out and saying they hate this house because of the way the porch looks. They don't do that. They just see that there is a cost, there is definitely a cost and there is definitely a hiring of some people, then there is a whole big production, there is a big mess, usually and then all of a sudden, it's done. That's somebody who has decided to change it.

There is a cost when you change something you know. You can't resist the fact that it's a lousy porch, you can't resist that anymore because you have just decided you don't want one anymore. You see it's the same when you change a habit or change a pattern or change a negative attribute in yourself. It will stay there as long as you want it to but as soon as you don't, you hire the right contractors, which are Jesus and Mary, and they come in and they remove it and you have to learn to live without it. You have to learn to accept the new condition of not having that, which for some of you is quite difficult. I can see that you really do like the old ways even though you know it's right to pray for the new way, so then you have this fits and starts change thing. You want to change, you don't want to change, you like the old way you like the new way, then you are right in the middle. That's when the contractors take many many days off in the middle of their project after they start the project. They barely take it out and the porch looks like that for a month because that person hasn't decided that they really want that change. Some of you are like that. You have had the porch taken off for like a year and just held up on stilts because you can't decide to have a new porch yet. Anyway what is the porch? It's the place where you receive people, isn't it? People can't even use the porch because its being remodeled. It's the same with a rotten house. Nobody can use it while the construction is going on and that's what's happening.

How can you serve when there is construction? How can you serve when you are not sure what you are going to hold onto and what you are going to let go of? And I hope you get the sense of how much freedom you have to take as long as you want on things, to hold onto things as long as you would like, and to let go of things as fast as you want to and to have as much grace as you could possibly accept if you asked for it. This is the way, this is the whole planet and everybody. How much freedom you have. But there is the soul saying, 'Are you going to inhibit me, do you want to inhibit me? I would like to express here.' And the ego says, 'Within conditions I will let you express because I have my way too. I have to have some of myself here, I have to know it's me, you know. Nobody would even notice me, my parents didn't notice me so I really want to make sure I am noticed because if I just be a soul, I don't know who I am going to be so I've got to get some notice here, I have to get some satisfaction in my ego so that I can hold onto stuff.' Love is the answer. You have to start loving yourself enough to be happy and to have a completely well system, completely well. Then if somebody approaches you, you don't have to tell them your problems because you don't have any. You don't have to project your problem on their energy field and then be suspicious of them or maybe scared of them that they might have something that could hurt you, because if you are healed nobody can hurt you. If you are full of love and light nobody can touch you, but you are definitely feeling not there yet. You are very touchy so obviously you are still scared which means you are not full of love and light yet. I am just showing you where you are so you can know what the work is, and if you need a part of your house repaired please do it, just decide to do it and get it repaired.

July 24, 2016
Forgiveness

Poem of the Man God Volume 4 Chapter 421. The Repentant Sinner Is always To Be Forgiven.

Jesus, Who is about ten meters ahead of them, turns round, a white shadow in the night, and He says: "There is no limit to love and forgiveness. There is none. Neither in God nor in the true children of God. As long as there is life, there is no limit. The only obstacle to the descent of forgiveness and love is the impenitent resistance of the sinner. But if he repents, he is always to be forgiven, even if he sinned not once, twice or three times a day, but much more frequently. You also sin and you want to be forgiven by God and you go to Him saying: "I have sinned! Forgive me". And forgiveness is pleasant to you and it is pleasant to God to forgive. And you are not gods. Consequently the offence given to you by people like yourselves is less grave than that given to God, Who is not like anybody else. Do you not think so? And yet God forgives. Do likewise yourselves. Be careful! Watch that your intolerance does not become detrimental to you by causing God to be intolerant towards you. I have already told you, but I will repeat it once again. Be merciful in order to have mercy. No one is so sinless as to be inexorable towards a sinner. Look at your own burdens before considering those weighing on the hearts of other people. Remove yours from your souls and then turn to those of other people to show them not the severity that condemns, but the love that teaches and helps to be freed from evil. In order to be able to say - and not be silenced by a sinner - in order to be able to say: "You have sinned against God and against your neighbor" it is necessary not to have sinned or at least to have made amends for the sin. In order to be able to say to those who are dejected because they have sinned: "Have faith that God forgives those who repent" - as servants of God Who forgives repentant souls - you must show so much mercy in forgiving. Then you will be able to say: "See, repentant sinner? I forgive your sins seven and seven times, because I am a servant of Him Who forgives countless times those who repent of their sins as many times. Consider then how the Perfect One forgives, if I know how to forgive, simply because I serve Him. Have faith!". You must be able to say so, and say so with your deeds, not just with words. You must say so forgiving. So if your brother sins, admonish him kindly, and if he repents, forgive him. And if at the end of the day he has sinned seven times and says to you seven times: "I repent", forgive him seven times. Have you understood? Will you promise Me that you will do that? While he is away, do you promise Me to be indulgent to him and to help Me to cure him making the sacrifice of controlling yourselves when he does anything wrong? Do you not want to help Me to save him? He is your brother in spirit as he comes from one sole Father, by race as he comes from one sole people, by mission as he is an apostle like you. So you ought to love him three times. If in your family you had a brother who grieved your father and exposed himself to censure, would you not try to correct him so that your father suffered no longer and no one spoke ill of your family? So? Is your family not a greater and holier one as its Father is God and I am the First-born? Why, then, do you not want to console the Father and Me and help us to improve the poor brother who, believe Me, is not happy to be so?..."

I think it's easy for us to see people's mistakes because we're so attentive to our own and we're so scared of our own and we're so self-conscious about our own and, secretly, we want other people to make mistakes so our mistakes don't seem as bad to us. And, with all that attention on mistakes, is it any wonder that we have no real ability to forgive ourselves or other people for their mistakes without making them big by paying attention to them. It is no small revelation that we make lots of mistakes. It's not really illuminating. It's not interesting that you fall, that you fail, that you forget things, you know, to do things, that you don't follow through on things. There's lots of mistakes that can be made – countless – and, every day, there's probably many. And all you have to do is ask for forgiveness.

You don't have to bemoan the fact that you're making mistakes because that assumes that you shouldn't be making mistakes and that you're ashamed of yourself for making mistakes and then you're going to do all that sulking, pouting, shameful stuff, you know, to avoid the love - you avoid the forgiveness I guess. Is that why you do it when you could just go and get forgiven, like, right away? Not later after you've mulled it over, dragged yourself under the wheels of a few cars. You could just go get the forgiveness immediately, without waiting. Without doing all of that ego stuff: How bad you are, you know. How right you were in the middle of your wrongness. You know how you do that? How you weren't totally wrong, just partially wrong? The other person was wronger than you and they really need to cop because I don't want to look at myself right now. All to keep your problem. But Jesus says, 'Give me your problems. I'll take 'em.' And go to the forgiveness, get it done, and then you're clean.

But what if you are clean and what if you are forgiven? What if you're fresh? Wouldn't you have something to do? You'd have something to do I think. I don't know what that would be, but you'd have something to do. Maybe you'd have enough energy to go and have another problem. Maybe you'd have enough energy to help somebody with theirs. Maybe you'd have enough energy to stay without problems, to keep that balance.

It's complicated because you can see that your brother or your sister fails in things and makes mistakes and sins during the day and you can also see that they're getting blessed in these kind of amazing ways. And then your head gets in there and starts to evaluate, 'Well, why are they getting a blessing if they're making mistakes? And, I make mistakes too and I'm not getting the same blessings they're getting.' And all of a sudden you're jammed up real bad inside yourself because you're trying to figure out something that's too perfect for you. Like, God's evaluation of human beings is too big, too wide for you. Like, why does God keep forgiving us? Why is God's love that permanent that God keeps wanting us to get better and keeps giving us a chance and keeps cleaning the slate for us - cleaning our diaper? Why? Because He loves us.

But we don't do that with our brother and sister. We tally up and keep track of spreadsheets of the things that they could've done better and spreadsheets of the things that they screwed up with and we need to caution up around a person who makes a couple of mistakes so that we don't have to trust them. In other words, we don't have to love them. We don't have to give to them, forgive them, think well of them, pray for them because they're scoring up pretty good on the negative side. And all that stuff is wrong. That's wrong thinking. And Jesus is warning us not to do that.

How are we going to help Him love people and forgive people, if we have that kind of mind? How are we going to invite people into His embrace if we have a scathing view of them on the way to Jesus? A critical view of them, on their way to Jesus. We should be making it so benevolent that they could go to Him and be loved and forgiven and that He'll remember their sins no more. That's what we should be representing. Not, 'Oh, you did badly, I've done badly, so neither of us are in competition for the best person in the world.' That kind of mind is sick. It's really just sick, and I want you to know that it's sick. That's an illness in you if you have to compare like that. The illness is that you're not looking at the love and going into the love, you're thinking about how everyone's stalling on going into the love just like you are. That's just such a sick mind.

Go to the love, get forgiven, and then enthuse everyone else about that. That's what you should be doing. Get everybody very enthusiastic about how God wants to forgive them, because God forgave you. And do that every day until you don't think about anything else. And, if you've got stuff to be forgiven, would you have the intestinal fortitude to admit it and go to Jesus and have it forgiven? If you're bracing, you've probably got something that needs forgiving. And, if you're stuck on something and you're worried about something, you probably have something that needs to be forgiven. Just release, go there, and do it. Stop holding. Stop fighting the fact there's something to be released.

Do you think that you're going to fool God by holding on to something and spinning it with your editorials? God doesn't see the truth in the thing you're struggling with? Even if, let's say, you're struggling and you don't even know what it is. You go, 'This could be a big problem Jesus - I don't even know - but it's a struggle and, if it is a sin, I'm giving it to you. Please forgive me for it. Show me what I'm doing so I can see it.' Don't figure it out on your own. Let Him show it to you.

The Path makes everything painful and then makes it easier but you have to go through the pain first – the pain of seeing how nasty you've been. The pain of seeing how stubborn you've been in holding your sins.

I wonder if a spiritual community is just a community of people who are in competition for who holds it the longest

– who holds onto their problems the longest. I have a different view of community. I have a different view of spiritual community like, dynamic souls who are helping other people. I have that view. That's like a dream. That's a dream I have. Not the, 'holding onto my stuff so it doesn't look bad and also holding onto my stuff a little bit less than you do.' Where is the forgiveness if you're nursing your wounds or struggling against the truth of something inside yourself? Where can the forgiveness move when you don't give it all to Him? Where can a problem fester if you give it away? Where is this altar where problems are kept and worshipped? Get that out of your house. If you have sins, you let them go. If you have resentments and fears, you let it go. If you have what you call problems, which are just illusions, you give them up to God so that you don't have them anymore. And that's not a pipe dream. That's an instantaneous, present moment reality, you can have. And if one little bubble of problem, you think - the mirage of a problem - bubbles up in your little swamp, you give it to Him immediately. You spend no time on it at all. Otherwise you are being selfish. You're just being selfish because you're going, 'I have this little thing. It's all for me. This little problem takes me out of the game. Don't give me the ball. I'm out of the game right now working on an illusion. I'm working on an illusion of my separation with my Divinity. I'm working on an illusion of pretending I'm not loved by God right now. Please leave me alone. Stay away. I've got an illusory problem I want you to know about and you back off.' That's what it really is.

If Jesus said He would take them, then what's the lag time between you noticing you have one and Him taking them? That lag time is selfishness. That's all it is. You call it whatever you like, make up stuff. That's what it is. Any lag time between the noticing of a problem and releasing it is selfishness because He said He'd take it from you. And He wasn't kidding. He takes it, absolves it, and destroys it, and it's gone. So you holding it is tremendous selfishness and tremendous stubbornness. And I don't know why you like to feel bad. I don't know why you like to feel bad. I can guess because I understand human stupidity, but I don't know why you enjoy that so much.

That's not what Jesus wants for you. That's not what He paid the price for. That's not what He can relieve you of in an instant, if you'd just ask Him.

So, why don't you ask yourself why you have to carry that stuff and why you have to mull over your problems and nurse them and juice them and inject them with juice? Why do you do that? I want you to find out why you do that. Because, in fact, you do. It's not a question if you do it. You, in fact, do it. What do you get out of that and what's the big finger to God that you're doing in that moment? What is that for? Get into it. Like, really do some work on it, so you understand yourself better. Because Jesus is going, 'Oh my God. You guys are capable and, because of your problems, not able.'

He's got to be wondering why you like them. He's got to be wondering that, because I am wondering that. Maybe it's the concept that everything has to be drudgingly slow and so you're just making up work for yourself or something. I don't know what that is. It's a sack cloth and ashes addiction? What is it? What are we doing from the Piscean Age? What are we doing? Paying it all off yourself? Well Jesus did that for you. You don't have to do that. You just have to give it up. Is that what it is? We're still in the Piscean sludge? The age of activity is you go get cleaned up and you get busy. That's the Aquarian Age. You get cleaned up and you get busy. This is a two thousand year period we're going to be in. Clean it up, get busy. Not faith that you can suffer for the rest of your life.

I think the suffering that you're doing to yourself is not fun compared to the suffering of taking on people's and helping people. That's fun. It's hard and it's persecutions and everything else but the one you do to yourself is grotesque. I think it's the appropriate word.

Find out why you do it and find out what you're getting out of it because I would like you to know and I would like you to really have a little talk with this part of you. Have a little 'Come to Jesus' meeting with yourself on this. Okay.

August 7, 2016
Seven Times

PMG v.3 Ch. 421.

The Repentant Sinner Is always To Be Forgiven

"There is no limit to love and forgiveness. There is none. Neither in God nor in the true children of God. As long as there is life, there is no limit. The only obstacle to the descent of forgiveness and love is the impenitent resistance of the sinner. But if he repents, he is always to be forgiven, even if he sinned not once, twice or three times a day, but much more frequently. You also sin and you want to be forgiven by God and you go to Him saying: "I have sinned! Forgive me." And forgiveness is pleasant to you and it is pleasant to God to forgive. And you are not gods. Consequently the offense given to you by people like yourselves is less grave than that given to God, who is not like anybody else. Do you not think so? And yet God forgives. Do likewise yourselves. Be careful! Watch that your intolerance does not become detrimental to you by causing God to be intolerant towards you. I have already told you, but I will repeat it once again. Be merciful in order to have mercy. No one is so sinless as to be inexorable towards a sinner. Look at your own burdens before considering those weighing on the hearts of other people. Remove yours from your souls and then turn to those of other people to show them not the severity that condemns, but the love that teaches and helps to be freed from evil. In order to be able to say - and not be silenced by a sinner - in order to be able to say: "You have sinned against God and against your neighbor" it is necessary not to have sinned or at least to have made amends for the sin. In order to be able to say to those who are dejected because they have sinned: "Have faith that God forgives those who repent" - as servants of God who forgives repentant souls - you must show so much mercy in

forgiving. Then you will be able to say: "See, repentant sinner? I forgive your sins seven and seven times, because I am a servant of Him Who forgives countless times those who repent of their sins as many times. Consider then how the Perfect One forgives, if I know how to forgive, simply because I serve Him. Have faith!" You must be able to say so, and say so with your deeds, not just with words. You must say so forgiving. So if your brother sins, admonish him kindly, and if he repents, forgive him. And if at the end of the day he has sinned seven times and says to you seven times: "I repent," forgive him seven times. Have you understood? Will you promise Me that you will do that? While he is away, do you promise Me to be indulgent to him and to help Me to cure him making the sacrifice of controlling yourselves when he does anything wrong? Do you not want to help Me to save him? He is your brother in spirit as he comes from one sole Father, by race as he comes from one sole people, by mission as he is an apostle like you. So you ought to love him three times. If in your family you had a brother who grieved your father and exposed himself to censure, would you not try to correct him so that your father suffered no longer and no one spoke ill of your family? So? Is your family not a greater and holier one as its Father is God and I am the First-born? Why, then, do you not want to console the Father and Me and help us to improve the poor brother who, believe Me, is not happy to be so?..."

Jesus talked about forgiveness many times, so obviously we have a problem with forgiveness, we have a problem doing it because we have trouble imagining that we could be forgiven for the things that we do. We even have trouble discovering what we do, admitting what we do and feeling the pain of what we do. We have trouble even seeing it so we can't even imagine somebody else actually fully seeing it and asking for forgiveness because we haven't done that either. There's so much incredulity when it comes to someone getting cleaned up or someone being freed up or someone being forgiven or changing or someone completely letting go of an old habit that they don't want anymore, it's done. To them it's done, to all the people that know them they can't believe it. They can't believe that anybody can change like that because they are holding onto so many things that they haven't changed themselves, so they have the same feeling about the others as they do to themselves. They are the scoffers and the skeptics who can't believe that transformation can happen because they haven't let it happen in them and yet Jesus said, "If you ask me I will help you and if you repent your sins I will forgive you." And who seems to be the last one that doesn't believe that? The one that can't forgive himself or herself. I know you have a secret fantasy that if you are forgiven you probably won't stop doing it or if you know that it's not good to do you probably don't believe that you can say no and never do it again because you don't know what your word means anymore. Maybe you did when you were a child, but you don't know now. Your word doesn't mean that much - you say no and you know you're not going to follow it or you say yes and you know you're not going to follow it. You have had a lot of evidence of that, your word meaning nothing. But a true disciple of Jesus, their word means everything. They say it happens, they forgive it and it's done. They repent, it's serious and it's done, it's sincere, it's finished.

So what is it in you that believes that it can't be taken or even if you go through the motions of being sorry and asking for forgiveness that it isn't gone? What is it in you that needs it not to be gone, that lets it linger in there and lets it accumulate again and then revive itself, be the same as it was before when you decided you didn't want it? What is it in you that likes it, keeps it? And the compassion of Jesus knows this, so if he says somebody comes to you seven times or twenty times or a hundred times asking for forgiveness for the same thing in the same day you forgive them. Now what are you teaching them by doing that? You're teaching them how God treats you when you sincerely want to change or you sincerely let go of something, God forgives you. God's not harsh like you are, God just forgives you because ultimately God wants you to feel his love. Are you going to feel his love if he's harsh with you? No you wouldn't. God wants you to love him and wants his love to be in you and wants you cleaned up and wants you changed into something that he made you, not this aberration that you have created for yourself by your reactions. Love does not that, love keeps drawing you in and cleaning you up and forgiving you and changing you and helping you. That's how I want you to be with your brothers and sisters and that's what Jesus is asking us - be the same way that God is with all the people you are involved with, so they can feel his love through you. Not your intolerance, not your skeptical mind that can't believe that anyone can change because you don't believe you can change, that supportive, loving compassion that knows anybody can change if they want to and they ask for help. Anybody can change. God can forgive anything if you let it go, if you ask him. God's love wants you in his love and wants you cleaned up, forgiven so you can be in his love. He wants you reconciled to his family so you are part of the family again, not a little wayward son or daughter doing your own thing. Somebody who is in the graces of the Father. That means cleaning up, that means coming clean, that means saying the truth and that means owning your stuff, repenting and saying honestly where you went off so you can be brought back into that oneness which is what God wants. God didn't create you as the best part of himself to reject you, he created you to be one with him. The only rejections that have been made are yours in your head. In your head. How hard is that?

August 14, 2016
Consistency

The Gospel as Revealed to Me, *Chapter 486. At the Temple for the feast of the Tabernacles. Sermon on the nature of the Kingdom.*

A great murmur runs through the crowd. Gamaliel, who is all alone on his carpet, raises his head again and casts a sharp glance at Jesus.
"So, when will the Kingdom of God come? You have not replied..." *urges again the previous Pharisee.*
"When the Christ will be on the throne which Israel is preparing for Him, higher than any other throne, higher than this Temple."
"But where is it being prepared, as no preparation is evident? Is it possible that Rome will allow Israel to rise again? Have the eagles become so blind that they cannot see what is being prepared?"
"The Kingdom of God does not come with pomp. Only the eye of God can see it being formed, because the eye of God reads inside men. So do not go looking for this Kingdom, where it is being prepared. And do not believe those who say: "They are plotting in Batanaea, they are conspiring in the caves in the desert of Engedi, and on the shores of the sea." The Kingdom of God is in you, within you, in your spirits which receive the law that came from heaven, as the law of the true Fatherland, the law, which, when practiced, makes one the citizen of the Kingdom. That is why John came before Me to prepare the ways to the hearts of men so that My Doctrine could enter them. The ways have been prepared through penance, through love the Kingdom will rise and the slavery of sin, which interdicts the Kingdom of Heaven to men, will fall."
"This man is really great! And you say that He is an artisan?" *says in a loud voice a man who was listening*

attentively. And others, apparently Judaeans judging by their garments, probably instigated by Jesus' enemies, gaze at one another dumbfounded and then approach their instigators asking: "What have you insinuated to us? Who can say that this man is leading the people astray?" And others ask: "We are wondering and would like you to tell us this: if it is true that none of you has taught Him, how can He be so wise? Where did He learn so much wisdom if He never studied with a master?" And they address Jesus asking: "Tell us. Where did You find Your doctrine?"

Jesus looks up full of inspiration and says:

"I solemnly tell you that this doctrine is not mine, but it is of Him who sent Me among you. I solemnly tell you that no teacher taught Me it, neither did I find it in any living book or parchment or stone monument. I solemnly tell you that I prepared for this hour listening to the living being speak to My spirit. The hour has now come for Me to give the people of God the Word which has come from Heaven. And I do so, and will do so to the last, and after I have breathed My last, the stones, which heard Me and did not soften, will experience a fear of God greater than that which Moses felt on Sinai, and in such fear, with the voice of truth, blessing or cursing, the words of My rejected doctrine will be engraved on stones. And those words will never be deleted. The sign will remain: light for those who will receive it, at least then, with love; absolute darkness for those who not even then will understand that it is the Will of God that sent Me to establish His Kingdom. At the beginning of Creation it was said: "Let there be light." And there was light in the chaos. At the beginning of My life it was said: "Peace to men of good will." A good will is the one which does the will of God and does not oppose it. Now he who does the will of God and does not oppose it, feels that he cannot fight against Me because he feels that My doctrine comes from God and not from Myself. Do I perhaps seek My own glory? Do I perhaps say that I am the Author of the Law of grace and of the era of forgiveness?

No. I do not take the glory which is not Mine, but I give glory to the Glory of God, the Maker of all good things. My glory is to do what the Father wants Me to do, because that gives glory to Him. He who speaks on His behalf in order to be praised, seeks his own glory. But He Who can receive glory from men, even without seeking it, for what He does or says, but rejects it saying: "It is not My glory, created by Me, but it proceeds from the glory of the Father as I proceed from Him," is in the truth and there is no injustice in Him, as He gives each person what belongs to them without keeping for Himself what is not His own. I am, because He wanted Me."

Jesus stops for a moment. He scans the crowd prying into consciences. He reads in them and weighs them. He resumes speaking: "You are silent. Half of you admire Me, the other half are wondering how they can make Me be silent. Whose are the ten Commandments? Whence do they come? Who gave them to you?"

"Moses!" shouts the crowd.

"No. The most High. Moses, His servant, brought them to you. But they come from God. You have the formula, but you do not have the faith, and you say in your hearts: "We did not see God. Neither we nor the Hebrews at the foot of Sinai." Oh! not even the thunderbolts which set the mountain on fire while God shone thundering in the presence of Moses, are sufficient to make you believe that God was present. Not even thunderbolts and earthquakes serve to make you believe that God is among you to write the eternal pact of salvation and of condemnation. You will see a fresh dreadful epiphany very soon within these walls. And the holy secret places will come out of darkness because the kingdom of the light begins and the holy of holies will be extolled in the presence of the world and will no longer be concealed under the triple veil. And you will not believe yet. What is therefore needed to make you believe? That the thunderbolts of Justice may strike your bodies? But Justice will be appeased then and flashes of love will descend. And yet, not even they will write the Truth in

your hearts, in all your hearts, neither will they give rise to Repentance and then to Love..."

Gamaliel's strained eyes are now gazing at Jesus...

"But you know that Moses was a man among men and the chroniclers of his days left you a description of him. And yet, although you know who he was, from Whom and how he received the Law, do you comply with it? No, none of you observe it."

The crowds howl protesting.

So God has a plan, and it's going to happen whether people like it or not. The only result will be half will form on one side and half will form on the other side. Half will not be able to hear the truth or be mad about the situation and half will hear the truth and their hearts will be opened and they'll love God more. That's the promise. It's not a cautionary promise; it's not a tentative choiceful thing. It's a declaration of dependence and independence. The ones who love evil, they'll be depending on the devil and the ones who love God will be dependent on God. One will be in the love, the other will be in hate. One will be healed and made one with God and the other will be with their darkness and their suffering and the suffering they self-imposed. That's the declaration, that's not conjecture or speculation it's just a promise. And we have had all these thousands of years, many lifetimes to prepare ourselves for the choice and the choice is not waffle, tentative, uncertain, it's like, "I will be in the love, I will be in the light. I will be part of the peace. I will be an instrument for God. I will be learning to be more and more like God" - that's one choice. The other choice is "I don't like this. I don't like God. I don't like the whole plan. I don't really like not having my own way and I want to indulge myself and I want to be an individual and be wild and I want to take what I can get and rip people off if I can before they rip me off. I want to just be selfish." That's the other side.

Everybody's had a long term chance to get this figured out and I can see some of you haven't totally decided yet. Your head decided 'yes this is what I want' but your body didn't really decide that yet in some cases. Your emotions too so you have these warring factions inside your being and it would be nice to have a talk with them and get them all on one page and get them all to decide one thing. And a decision isn't a decision until there's action following it. If there's some kind of plan that carries out how you're going to maintain that behavior and what kind of fences and structures you set up for yourself, you do behave the way you would like to behave. If that follow through isn't really there then you don't really have much of a conviction yet. You have ideas but no conviction and no follow through. The follow through is really important because there are many people with beautiful strivings and wonderful sentiments and a lot of emotional sappiness for God and for Jesus. The churches are filled with them.

Today's one of those sappy days when people get sappy and emotional, musical about Jesus and there's no follow through after the service and into the week which would mean they're going to hold themselves to the standard of light, forgiveness, no negative emotions, all of that. They have to keep themselves in line all week. Otherwise they're just lip serving this whole disciple thing or lip serving their love for Jesus or their dedication to follow him, but they can follow him for a few hours, that's it. In some cases they have 3 hour services. Those are tediously long and in some of the Russian orthodox churches they stand for 3 hours motioning and gesturing, signing the cross all the way down to the ground and plagiaristic kinds of formulas that have no meaning, except that you probably think you're holy if you run your hand all the way down to touch the ground or I don't know, put your lips on a relic. I don't know what they're doing but there are all kinds of formulas that they follow that make them think that they're holier than the rest of the people. But they have this problem all the other churches do. They walk out of there and they become just a pedestrian who's yelling at the kids, screaming at the dog or running into things because they can't concentrate, or breaking things because they can't keep their mind on what they're doing - problems that everybody has. How do you follow through all week with the faith, the love, the respect for God, the respect for brothers and sisters that you were so dedicated to in the moments of the service? At least you had a longing appeal in your heart to become that, to rise up into that. So it's the decisional process of making sure your body, your ego, your emotions, your mind, all your dedication of that week and stay up at that level. I know it's a stay up at that level thing because it's a fall otherwise. But as soon as you do this for a number of weeks you have a new pattern where it feels so normal to be there that there's not much tendency to fall if you can keep the pattern, if you can keep your consistency during the week. But then there's that selfishness thing that comes in that we want what we want, we want a little break, we want to get nasty, or we want to get negative or we want to yell or we want to jab somebody or we want to have a critical thought. They are all very wild, undisciplined little features that we have when we don't rise to this standard. We have these great aspirations and then we fall all week. That's kind of the way of the entire religious world.

The religious world - you could say they are all trying to be good, have some dedication to be spiritual. Then you have the mystics and they really are trying to be spiritual and they really do have a stronger dedication. And then the ones that really become mystical, not just the ones that are wannabe mystical, they are holding their patterns all week. Now that's a discipline, it's not a discipline later, later it's a love. At first it's just a discipline because it's hard. It's hard to break that selfishness, that ego under your heel like a dog that heels. It has to sit, it has to lie down, it has to be quiet, it has to go to sleep, it has to eat, it has places for it to eliminate, and you make it so. If you don't, you have chaos in your house. Just like you would have chaos in your body if you had all these things running around wherever they want and on Sunday you notice that oh, I forgot I was supposed to be a devoted disciple. I was supposed to think about loving, forgiving, and being one with Jesus. It's very emotional in one way until it becomes a pattern and then it's not emotional anymore. Then it's real. You have secured it and what I mean by secure is you're starting to sow into your cells this new pattern. You won't let those cells do what they want to do, they're going to do what you've dedicated to which is light, love, forgiving, honest, cheerful, dedicated, strong, willing, working, and powerful. You're going to move your body in this new energy.

You have to sew this into your flesh--it just doesn't magically happen. Your intentions have nothing to do with this. Your intentions are a cloud floating up above your head. They don't have anything that knits into your cells this new pattern: I will think of God before I mouth off. I will think of God before I do my own will. Other than that it's just a cloud in your intentional field, it has nothing to do, it's not in your body yet that you will be a servant of God that you are not just going to intend and pretend that you're good. You are going to be good and then you become good and you make it happen all week and you don't flip out and you don't let yourself fall from your pattern. That's a disciple—somebody who's disciplined. It is hard at first and it is not hard if you do it really well for three weeks. So if it's still hard and it's always so hard and every week it's still hard, this path thing is real hard, then you never did it. You never really made yourself do it yet or else you would've busted through the resistance already. If it's hard, the resistance wins. That's why it's hard, you let the resistance win. Now you need help. 'Jesus help me so that I don't let my resistance win. Help me so that I keep my pattern. Help me so that I stay true to myself every day just like I'm in a meditation. Just like I was in prayer.' Then you make yourself do that and if you fall off you ask for more help. You bring yourself back and you bring yourself back until you stay there and you will. You will stay there. You won't falter if you have that dedication to do it. Only the first three weeks will be hard but if the first twenty years of your life are hard on the path, then you haven't done it. You just didn't do it yet. You didn't solidify your decision in action during the week. And it's hard honesty to know that you didn't do that because you are up and down and up down and then you didn't do it. I don't know anyone who doesn't succeed in this if they keep their dedications clear and they get the help and they keep their mind from falling into that indulgent crap. Anybody can do it—Jesus said so. In fact he ordered you to do it: 'Follow me.' He didn't say, 'I don't know. Some of you might be able to.' He didn't say that. He didn't say, 'Most of you can't but a couple of you I want you to follow me.' He didn't say that. He didn't say, 'Most of you I want you to follow me but not really do it.' He didn't say that either. He just said, 'Follow me.'

So if you're honest all you have to do is look at the ups and downs of your life. If you're up and down all week good days, bad days, good days, bad days, then you know you didn't really keep your consistency at all and your dedication is weak. You didn't stay close to him and you didn't ask for much help and you reacted all week. Now that, from Jesus' point of view he says, 'Ok I want you on Tuesday.' And you say, 'Well Tuesday's my down day.' 'What about Wednesday?' 'I don't know if I can make it back by Tuesday and then into Wednesday because if I'm down Tuesday I'm pretty tired from beating myself up and perhaps being inconsistent on Tuesday. I don't know if I'm going to be all there on Wednesday for you to count on me. But Sunday morning for sure I know you're going to be able to count on me.' What do you think he's going to say with this kind of conversation? I know you're not as honest as I am with this yet. If this is the honesty you could have, He'll say 'Tell me what day. What day can I totally rely on you all day? Just give me a one day.' And you say, 'I don't know. I haven't been able to do all day. I can do mornings. Like, two mornings. I can give you two mornings.' He says, 'Okay, that's better than nothing.' It really is, because who gives him mornings? Very few people give him mornings, right? So if he gets a morning, and you're kind of lined up with him as you work, as you drive, as you go through your job you're lined up with him, it's pleasant for him to work with you. But you see the problem? How much can you actually give him? Not much because you haven't learned that consistency and you haven't fully dedicated because you're allowing yourself so many mood swings and so many desire problems and so many reactions. You allow yourselves so many imperfections. You actually have to allow those. Those aren't there normally, a normal human being that God made. He didn't make you imperfect. You have to acquire those, you have to practice them and you have to augment them and bring them out every so many days to make sure you can keep them. You have to practice with that, that wasn't part of your nature, imperfection. You have to practice those.

So he's saying, 'What day do you not want to practice your imperfections? What day would you like to be the way I made you? Which day can you give me?' 'Ok a morning.' 'Which morning?' So that's what he's doing. It's truthful. This is not even sad or sarcastic or anything it's just like what are you able to do? What can you decide and follow through on? Because you have the power to do it. He's going to give you the power to do it - to be balanced, harmonious, peaceful, loving, cheerful, willing all day if you want that. All you have to do is want that. Then follow through. Make sure it happens. Don't let anything in the way. Don't let anything get to you. Don't get distracted

If you practice that really well for a few weeks you are going to be a different person. You're going to be one of the cheerful ones. You're going to be one of the ones that do not mind hard work, do not mind suffering and do not react to anything and you'll be useful. God will say, 'Wow, you're starting to come online here. I might be able to use you more than a couple days. I might be able to use you all the time.' He longs for that, for you to be an instrument for him. You say you do but do you line up every minute for him? How about chunks of day? Just the afternoon, or just the evening, or just the morning? Do you line it up just for him to inspire it, to guide it, to infuse into you his mind as you are doing that activity? He knows about your jobs. Your jobs are not complicated for him. He created those jobs before you even dreamed of them. You can't imagine the Master having done everything? 'Well he's not in IT.' 'Yeah, okay. What do you have to be, an IT person in order to put a new hand on? You try it as an IT person. Put a new hand on while it's all withered up like that. You figure it out. IT people can't do zeroes and ones and figure that out, can they? Write code for that? I don't think so. 'Let it be done.' Try that code. 'I want it.' Try that code.

This is the thing: with God's energy you could just want to be lined up and stay lined up and not falter. I know, there's a little humanness going on here and there but you could stay there. And if you can do this for three weeks - I know it's like climbing Gibraltar but then you could have a different life in three weeks' time. But you would have to catch yourself and bring it back until you stop thinking about yourself and you bring him into your life. He's not very deep in your life from what I can see. Every time you worry, are mad, or have a critical thought you have shoved him out. You just shoved him out. You see? That's how you do it. Don't do those things. Leave him with you. Let him be with you. Let him guide it and you will be a different person. You'll be the helpers instead of the stones that have to be fired up, the charcoal that needs to be blowtorched to get it white again. The seed that you have to breathe fire on, water and crush it practically to get it to sprout. You won't be one of those anymore after all of this if you do it.

Jesus was talking about the stones he rolls with his feet to see if there's going to be in motion, see if they can keep it going. They can't, so he has to come back later and do it again. That's what it's like with that sedentary relaxation into your old way, into your old thinking, into your old desire nature, reactions, opinions, and concepts, all of that sludge. That was acquired by you, that was not given to you. That was acquired. You give it up. You let it be burned on the fire just like you would put sludge on a really hot fire, it will burn and you won't have it anymore. That's what he wants. He's doing his work he's answering these hostile crowds, silly nincompoop Pharisees and he's telling them the truth, he's laying it out, being worse and worse and less and less receptive and his answers are perfect and clear and they're getting more and more stubborn and more and more hostile and in a way you're at this place inside yourself. This is the thing you need to know - you're around victory time within yourself, you're at that pivotal point of winning over the Pharisees and they're very hostile to keep you down and under their thumb and to keep you rigid and selfish and stubborn and formulaic and righteous, all negative feelings that people who are Pharisees have. Formulas and structures and patterns, trips and energy mind screws that you go through.

There's Jesus saying, 'I'm just about to do the victory thing. I'm just about to emancipate all of you people. I'm just about to free you from sin. We're going to have a huge sacrifice on a much higher level than you are used to and I'm going to pay for you.' And this is happening inside of you. You are just about to win over the darkness within yourself. You're just about to accomplish the salvation of yourself by letting go of those things and there's a lot of screaming going on. The Pharisees in you are screaming. "Don't ask us to die we want to be prominent!" But they have to die. All the hypocrites have to die in order for this love for you to be dedicated to this kind of new pattern of whatever Jesus wants, whatever God wants. I'm going to hold fast to these qualities all day. Now the Pharisees are going to get mad and they're going to want you dead. This is an internal battle. Jesus did it on a public scale and you're going to do it internally. You're going to have the screamers screaming at you about all the things you could have if you stayed within the rules and formula. All the rules and the bubbles of pride you could blow if you stayed within the rules. But you have to break the rules now and that is you have to defy the former patterns that have held you together with many, many lies. You have to defy the Pharisees inside yourself or you won't win. You won't win. And you know they're going to fight and they're secretly planning on your death. They'd rather you die than succeed in emancipating from their regime, their abuse.

I'm asking you, I say you can do it in three weeks - you actually could. You could bring Jesus with you so close all day - I know you'll squirm like hell. You have so many negative patterns and to let those go is going to be like you're going through detox, cold turkey. Detox from the negative patterns and the Pharisees are going to be screaming in your head. Unless you go through that and say, 'Jesus, back them off. Jesus, shut them up. Jesus, back them off.' Unless you do, you won't win, the Pharisees will win. The same dynamic that Jesus acted out on a massive scale you enact on an individual scale. Do you have the guts to win or are you going to be one of those screamers in the crowd looking to kill him? Because you know the closer Jesus gets the more your darkness shows up. The closer he gets the more ashamed you become of the things you're attached to because that's what happens when light comes near the darkness. The darkness is embroiled first in shame and then in anger. First in shame and then in anger. Even the negative in you reacts just like the Pharisees, that's inside of you. You want it out? You're going to have to do some real work. You're going to have to pull the light, pull Jesus in and that's very uncomfortable for that negative stuff to show up, but if it doesn't, you won't be clean and you won't be with him. You will not be part of him unless that is cleaned out. He said it too. 'Unless I wash you, you have no part with me.' That's what it means. So take courage, ask for help, have some faith, have some trust and have some more courage and then have some more courage and then do it.

August 21, 2016
Complacency

From Poem of the Man God, Chapter 400

Farewell to Bether

"Well, I exhort you to watch that what happened in Eden may not happen to you: that the serpent of falsehood, of calumny, of sin may creep in and bite your hearts separating you from God. Be watchful and firm in your Faith... Do not fret. Do not be incredulous. That might happen because the Cursed One will enter, will strive to enter everywhere, as he has already entered many places, to destroy the work of God. And as long as the Sly, Cunning, Indefatigable One enters places, and searches, eavesdrops, lies in wait, slavers, endeavors to seduce, there is no great harm. Nothing and no one can prevent him from doing that. He did that in the Earthly Paradise... But it is much worse to let him stay there without driving him out. The enemy who is not chased away ends up by becoming the master of the place as he settles there and builds his defensive and offensive structures. Pursue him at once, put him to flight using the weapons of Faith, Charity, Hope in the Lord. But the greatest evil, the supreme evil is to let him live not only undisturbed amongst men, but to allow him to penetrate inside from the outside, and let him build his nest in the hearts of men. Oh! Then!!

And yet many men have already received him in their hearts, against the Christ. They have welcomed Satan with his wicked passions driving away the Christ. If they had not yet known Christ in all His truth, if their knowledge of Him had been only superficial, as wayfarers know one another, when they meet by chance on a road, looking very often at one another just for a moment, people unknown to one another who meet for the first and last time, at times *exchanging only few words to inquire about the right road, to ask for a pinch of salt, for tinder to light a fire, or a knife to cut some meat, if such were the knowledge of the Christ in such hearts, which today, and even more tomorrow drive the Christ away, more and more, to make room for Satan, they might still be pitied and treated mercifully because they did not know the Christ. But woe to those who know Me for what I really am, who have been nourished with My word and My love, and now drive Me away, receiving Satan who allures them with false promises of human triumphs, the reality of which will be eternal damnation.*

You who are humble and do not dream of thrones and crowns, who do not seek human glory, but the peace and triumph of God, His Kingdom, love and eternal life, and nothing else, do not imitate them. Be vigilant! Keep free from corruption; be strong against insinuations, against threats, against everything."

I guess one of the worst things that people can allow into their garden, or into their psyche, is complacency. Because complacency is feeling like you're okay, and feeling like you're good enough, or you're strong enough, or you're happy enough, or you're satisfied enough, or fulfilled enough, or done enough. Or you've done quite a bit, and then you relax into this complacency. That complacency is an instigation of the devil, actually. There's no place you're safe from temptation. But there is only one place where you won't be tempted, and that's when you say 'No,' and you're vigilant. I mean, you just won't fall for it. You'll always be tempted, but you won't fall for it. Complacency is the first tremor in your earth. It starts to shake the earth loose, and then the earth will fall; it will slide. It won't be right away; it will be after a while. It might just loosen the soil enough, and then the first rain hits, and it's a mudslide. You don't notice it in the first shake of complacency.

The satanic energy can use any and all forms to get to you. Whatever your weakness is, and usually it's your strength, whatever you consider your strengths, that's where he'll get you. He'll start bloating those up a little bit. He'll start flattering you a little bit, or suggesting to you that those things are just fine. They're just fine. And as soon as you think they're fine, you sit down, don't you? When you think you're fine in a particular area, you just sit down. It's like, it's okay, it's fine, it's covered, it's taken care of, I'm handling it well, it's just fine. And as soon as you do, he has infested you with a little seed of pride that you've got that down. What do you have down, really? Do you have the perfections of God down? Those aren't even yours. Love isn't yours. Love is something created by the Creator. That's not yours. It might move through you, if you'd allow it. But you don't generate that; it doesn't come from you. Goodness? That's the Creator's. That doesn't come from you. It's loaned to you. In fact, it's infused into you. It's given to you when you're born. When you're created, you are good. After God created the creation, He said, 'This is good.' His decision to decide that it's good isn't your decision to decide that it's not. It's a lack of humility to decide that something isn't good, when He said that it's good. A lack of humility to not accept His word on you. When He says you're good, that's it. Anything that you do is going to be darkness, other than good. Anything that you think about yourself other than good is going to be darkness. The instigator caused that – the satanic being suggested to you your imperfections, that if you worked on those, and you overcame those, you would get to feel special. In other words, your pride would be jacked up. That's how tricky it is.

And the complacency is...just look through the things you think are fine. You never asked God if they're fine. You decided whether they're fine. That's the nest for the darkness, right there. What you think is fine. How fine is it, from God's point of view? How perfect is it? How perfected is it? How beautiful, how pure is it? From God's point of view, not yours. And isn't that, like, you're in the making? You're a work in progress? You're perfecting. And that's what you were ordered to do--to be perfect.

I think if you look at all the areas where you feel 'just fine,' complacency is what you would have to call it. It's even gotten to the negative state of, 'I don't even want to think about that. I think that's just fine. I don't even want to think about that.' Even that attitude, that you don't want to look at something, or you don't want to see something in yourself, is quite arrogant. What if God, through other people, pointed it out to you? What if a bunch of people said, 'You know, there's something you do that's really irritating.' But you've already decided that's not irritating-- that's perfectly fine. That's a tremendous arrogance, and also a tremendous complacency. Like, nothing in you could be improved, and nobody could see what could be improved? Other God-beings who have sight couldn't see what you could improve? I'm not saying everybody should go in each others' business and give them all kinds of pointers, because most of you don't have the sight, you don't have the patience, and you don't have the humility to do that yet. Because you don't know how to talk to people without it being animosity. You don't know how to care about people without feeling better than them, or putting them down somehow. That's why we're careful who gets to train people. They have to have the heart of love. They have to have the heart of Jesus or Mary to be able to do that. That's what they have to be dedicated to. Otherwise, they're going to come from a place of fear--that's real happy to be different than you. If I teach you because I'm real glad to not be you, what does that tell you? Then I'm putting you down energetically. Then I think I'm so much better than you.

But that's not how I teach. I teach you to be where I am. To have the faith and the love and the consideration and the non-complacency, where I am. To not settle. To not be satisfied. That's what I want to teach you. Not because I'm critical of where you are, but I'm trying to encourage you to be critical of your complacency. You should definitely be critical of that complacency. You should be suspicious, constructively suspicious, of anything that looks like complacency, because that's an area you fence off, that you say, 'God, don't mess with this, this seems fine to me.' Did you ask God if God thinks that's fine? That little area of complacency might be your total corruption. That might be the worst thing in you, that God might ask you to remove, and the only thing that God might ask you to remove. But you don't know that, because you fenced it off, and this is just fine. This is just, 'Don't bother me with this one. Don't mess with me. Don't say anything about this area, because I think it's fine.'

But you didn't ask. You hardly ever ask about those things, about these areas of your life. Like the areas where you think you're pretty skilled. Are you super-skilled? Is the skill enough? Is it really a skill? You ask God if it's a skill. 'My hypercritical sense of vigilance, is that a skill? Do you bless my hypercritical sense of vigilance, Lord? Do you love that about me?' See – you think it's fine, because it keeps you safe. But God thinks it contaminates you and makes you weird. Why don't you ask, "This thing I'm proud of – do you bless it, Lord? Do you bless it? Does it have your blessing? Does it have your sanction? Does it have your support? Because if it doesn't, I want to get rid of it. I want it crippled and humbled. It might even have to go to the trash, but at least crippled and humbled. I'll do the trash – if you tell me to trash it, I'll trash it. " And then you trash it. That's humility, and it's also obedience, to do what God says. God says Stop this, and you do, you stop it, I mean, that's the end of it, it's over. Death to it. If you have that kind of responsiveness to the Creator, you'll kill it. God says, 'Rip that plant up.' 'It's my complacency plant. I kind of like it.' Rip the plant up, and throw it out.

Now, I'm not saying you should be worried about everything, because I think that's negative. But I'm saying you shouldn't be proud of areas you're sequestering off and think they're fine. Because that's a lack of honesty, and it's a lack of allowing the scrutiny of God's eye to see into your whole being, and to look through and tell you what He thinks is the next step for you. When you're doing that complacency thing, you're saying, 'Oh I could definitely work on this-and-so and this-and-so, but I don't see any point in working on this; this seems fine.' What are you doing to God? You're telling God He can't talk about something. That's what you're saying. You're controlling God. 'God, don't tell me anything about this. But please tell me about these other things that my pride would love to perfect.'

Is God going to lead or are you going to lead? Which is it going to be? I venture to say you have these areas where you don't want any interference. You can look at them and see. You probably have two or three really special places where you don't want any interference. Which means, 'I won't humble myself, and I will not be obedient, and I won't even ask you, God, for any opinions on this. Because I got it figured out. I got it all sussed.'

Jesus is talking about all the ways – I mean, he's talking right to Judas – this is a conversation with the apostles – right to Judas about how the satanic energy is working in people. Right? Well, any time you're feeling fear, any time you're feeling insecure, any time you're getting anxious and worried, the satanic energy is not just pacing around you, he's rummaging in your heart, with his hands. He's already in there, and you let him! You let him. And that critical mind of yours, any of the worried mind, any of the pompous protection that you do, he's already in there, changing the sinews of your heart. You let him that far in. It's not like he's out here and says, 'I'd like to rummage in your heart' and you say, ' know, let me think about it.' He's already in there, rummaging. It would be different if there was an interview. If you interviewed with him and you saw him, it would be disgusting. You wouldn't want him near you, if you really saw him. He's a vile, disgusting creature. He looks terrible. Anybody against God would start to look terrible. People start to look ugly when they go against God. They just do. Ugliness isn't genetic. It's an evil that starts to come in and change the flesh and turn it into ugliness. That's how it works. It doesn't work any other way. God didn't allow it to work any other way. God decided how it was going to work, and that's how it's going to work. Ugliness is something that's evil, and it starts to work on the person when you accept it, and you live with that kind of negative energy, it starts to turn you ugly. It has nothing to do with your coiffing and couturing and makeuping and all that other stuff you do, working out and whatever. Ugliness is a thing coming out of your heart, oozing out of your heart into your flesh and changing the flesh. And it might be generational, but that's your fault, because you bought into it. After fifteen years, and you still do it, it is your fault.

But look at this complacency thing. I think it'll be very illuminating for you, the areas where you think you're all set. Am I trying to make you feel bad? No. I know you feel bad. That's not a problem, I mean, I'm not criticizing you for feeling bad, I'm just saying I'd like you to feel better. The only way to feel better is to take these fences down, and ask God to come into these things that you're so proud of, and see what God thinks about them. I think you'll feel better. I do, I think you'll feel much better. At first it'll be horrifying. I have to be honest with you, it's going to be a little horrifying, and then you're going to feel better. That's how it works.

August 28, 2016
Sorrow is a Wing

The Gospel as Revealed to Me, Chapter 209. The fecundity of pain in Jesus' preaching in the house of Eliza of Bethsur.

Sorrow is a cross, but it is also a wing. Mourning divests to reclothe. Rise, you who are weeping! Open your eyes, get rid of nightmares, of darkness, of selfishness! Look... The world is the barren land where one weeps and dies. And the world shouts: "help" through the mouths of orphans, of sick, lonely, doubtful people, through the mouths of those who are made prisoners of hatred by treason or cruelty. Go among those who are shouting. Forget yourselves among those who are forgotten! Recover your health among those who are sick! Be hopeful among those who are despairing! The world is open to those willing to serve God in their neighbor and to gain Heaven: to be united to God and to those whom we mourn. The gymnasium is here. The triumph there. Come. Imitate Ruth in all your sorrows. Say with her: "I will be with you until I die". And even if those misfortunes, which consider themselves incurable, should reply to you: "Do not call me Naomi, call me Mara, for God has marred me bitterly" you must persist. And I solemnly tell you that those misfortunes one day, because of your persisting, will exclaim: "Blessed be the Lord Who relieved me of my bitterness, desolation and solitude, by means of a creature who knew how to make his sorrow bear good fruit. May God bless him because he is my savior".

There are two kinds of sorrow. One is the sorrow of remorse for seeing how your behavior hasn't been good or how you have hurt somebody or how you have fallen short of something or how you have made a mistake or you have failed to care or you failed to give or you failed to understand somebody--that's a sorrow, personal sorrow. The other kind of sorrow is the sorrow in helping other people because you can feel their pain, you can feel their separation from God and you are sorry for them. Your sorrow is for them in helping them get back into oneness with God.

That's the sorrow that everybody who's a real disciple carries because they really do know what it feels like to be connected and they do know what it feels like to be disconnected and they want to bring that connection back to the person, they want to help them get back in connection with that and the sorrow is that sometimes people don't want to and sometimes they take a long time to do it and sometimes they hear you, they understand exactly what you are saying but they won't do it. They won't let go of something, they won't give up something, and they are tied to their rock real tight because it's all they think they have. They can't imagine what their life would be without that rock they are holding onto. And so even though the rock is not good for them, they hold onto it because it is something. Whereas if they didn't have anything, then there would be nothing to hold on to and that would feel empty to them. And that's a great sorrow for those that know better because they can see the rock is nothing, the rock means nothing and the person thinks it means something and the rock is nothing and the person is holding on to that nothing for dear life. But because sorrow is a wing in both cases it raises you up, because the sorrow of your own remorse, the sorrow of your takes, if your conscience is alive, if it's really awake, if it's really sensitive, you say, "oh God I didn't want to do that. I don't want to do that again." That sorrow will be the wing that motivates you never to do that again and it will raise you up because you felt it. You allowed yourself to feel it. Then it becomes your wing, your strength. It lifts you up in the air above the mire above the mud and the sorrow of your compassion for somebody who doesn't want to change or your compassion for helping whether these results happen or not whether the person receives your help or not. That's a wing to elevate the person who is serving, whether the effects happened or not, whether the help actually was received or not. Just the intention of help, the desire to help, the sorrow you feel for their pain whether they receive that or not, doesn't really matter because that lifts you up, just the intention to help because you felt their sorrow, moves you along.

It's unfortunate because you would like to move both of you along at the same time but a lot of people don't accept your sorrowful compassion. When you can see that they are hurting themselves, when you can see that the way they think is just so wrong, that the way they think is so limited so un-Godlike so unnatural to who they are as a created being, you can feel it and see it and you want to help them but they won't do it because they like what they are doing. At least they are comfortable in that old thinking and that's sorrowful but that raises the helper up. It doesn't raise the recipient up because the recipient is moored to their little rock and at the end of the life, you may have a whole life of that--of trying to help, when nobody wants it, and trying to lift people up and they don't want to go more than like a third of a step. You want to take them three steps and you actually know how but they want to go a third of a step and they are going to feel like that's an adventure going to a third of a step. It feels like an adventure to them, feels like so much change, so big and they are very satisfied with that. When you know the three steps and they have only done one ninth of what you are capable of helping them with, that's a sorrow.

That sorrow itself would be blessed because your intentions were in the right place. Your help was good and your motivation to help was really good and the words you were going to use were good and the person's receptivity was bad or real shallow. So those that see their sins, that sorrow raises them up and the ones that want to help that are not allowed to help, that sorrow raises them up. Jesus made it possible for everybody to rise--anyone to rise. So if you are trying to help, don't lose faith and if you are actually honestly looking at yourself. Go ahead and be sorrowful and give it to God. Don't wallow, don't be despairing, just give your sorrow. It's real, you make a mistake its sorrowful, it's sad, it's not right, you screwed up, you give that to God, straight up, you self beat and you take God's place. That's not your place to give the penance, it's God's place to give you the penance, not yours. So is it happy happy and joy joy in any of this, in your growing or in somebody helping you? Not at all--none of this is happy. The only thing that's happy is you are doing God's will and that makes you fulfilled. And those are people on wings, they are just flying away, flying alone, and He said be like Ruth, 'I will do this for you, I will serve you for the rest of my life.' That's what he said to be like. You keep serving no matter if there is any acclaim, if there is any receptivity, people care at all, people open their hearts to you, doesn't really matter because you are going to get the benefit from God from Jesus from Mary.

It's very seldom and almost occasional that Jesus lets me in on results or shows me the good I am doing. It's always interspersed and every so often. Why? It's because He is teaching me faith. If I had to get encouraged every single time I did anything, I would be like a baby. I would be getting encouraged every freaking time like a baby. I can wait, I know what faithfulness is, I know he will talk to me when he wants to and when he is ready. I don't need a pat on the back every five seconds. He takes care of that so I don't need to worry about that. Every so many deserts and so many plateaus I get one of those. Usually it's in some kind of a sandstorm or some kind of desert, there is some kind of word going, "hey, pretty good." Not while it's going good. I never get those. You've got to understand who you are working for, you've got get to know him and how he teaches. He is not going to pat you on the back every time you demand it because that's a baby. That's a baby. I don't get that. Why should you get that?

He is like a wise father who knows when to say what he needs to say when it's right. But all the time the sorrows are lifting you up and the work is raising you up and the effort is raising you up whether you see it or not because he said it will. You be faithful, I will take care of it. You be faithful, I'll take care of you. And some of you are really pouty so it's when you don't get encouragement then you just sit down, you just sit down. 'Do you think he had good jobs to say to all the apostles every night at dinner, 'Hey good job with that. You think he did that at night?' I assure you he did not do that very often and it wasn't because he was a little low on the complimenting thing, like a little weak on the complimentations. I mean you would have to indict him for that unless he is perfect and if he is perfect then you are going to get the compliment whenever you deserve it, which is very seldom and then and you know he said it too. He said if you come back after a full day's service and you come back home, what you have to do, are you going to sit down and be celebrated? No you are not. You are going to set the table for me and you are going to pour the dishes and you are going to do the dishes and then you are going to sit down. Hmm, well that's weird, isn't it? For the, the egopastic, those people, they just want to 'Oh I, I just dragged myself through the day and I need an applause here.' He doesn't do that.

How much did you do that you were supposed to do? Did you do more than you should have done today? He is going to ask you. A servant of God is a servant of God. He is supposed to serve them. You are supposed to do fits and starts? And in the fits you just sit and wait for the palms fanning you during your sit down period? This is not how Jesus served. He didn't say, 'It's been a long day, let's go and take a break here, let's just take a break.' When they tried to make him take breaks, he got up and went out and served somebody. I mean if you needed to give all you had to give, in three years and you knew it was going to end up in death would you hesitate and spread it out? Like John the Baptist, he knew he has a six month mission, he came in for a six month mission, that's it, one six month give it all you got and if you knew that wouldn't you be screaming and yelling and freaking them out and scaring them into the kingdom of God and doing everything you could even if you get yourself killed who cares? You know it's a six month mission. You are going to hold back? Well then you wouldn't be John the Baptist. You wouldn't be sent on that mission if you were like a coaster kind of a person. 'I'll do it on the weekends you know. Really this is hard and I am not eating very much either.' They wouldn't have sent him. They would have had to send a fiery guy who was willing to burn himself up completely in complete sorrow knowing that he is going to be killed and give it all he's got. You would only hire one guy and you would say 'short mission, got to give it all you got, what you think?' Some of you would never hire for that, you would never even apply for a job like that. It's like you have to space it out, you have to have some kind of quiet time, you have some down time, you have some quiescence, you have moments of sleep and stuff like that. Here he is screaming in the prison up through the castle walls all night. Until they killed him and then he stops. Then he stopped and some of you don't serve like that.

You are like the calculator servers, when people are watching you serve, when it's daytime you serve, when it's obvious to everybody else then you serve but the rest of the time it's like coasting. You see, that's a sorrow to watch for me because I know you are calculating your gains and I know you are posturing your progress and you are diminishing it so that you won't grow very much. I know you are doing that. I am not going to criticize you for it, I am going to mention it globally here in a sermon. I am just going to watch and it's sad because you don't know how long you have and you don't know that Jesus is watching apparently and you think you can fool people who know by these calculated moves of slowness and fastness and slowness and fastness and I don't know, why do it?

I don't know what you think you are helping or what you are preserving to do that. I don't know why you don't see Jesus watching you. At least that--it's a very small thing that I see it but that Jesus is seeing you. Or that Mother Mary is watching you sit down or mood out or something and don't you think that's a sorrow when they know you have been taught everything and they give you everything and its sorrow for them to see that it doesn't really spark you very much. Some of you it does and some of you it doesn't. You know you can figure it out yourself I am not tallying and making score cards for you--that's your head doing that. Anyway, when you are done being sorrowful for your own mistakes you will probably fix them and let them be healed and then you might enter into the sorrow of the ones that serve. That's the way it's going to be but both are a wing. Your wing now is to get you off the ground when you are serving. It's to get you into heaven. Those are the two wings: one wing is to get you off the ground, get you out of the mud and the other one is to get you into heaven.

September 4, 2016
Let the Spirit teach you

1944 Notebooks, July 14 1944.

"Listen to me carefully, daughter, for the lesson today is very difficult.

Man, every man, possesses in himself the image which God has conceived of for Man. But not all men possess the likeness to God in themselves.

It is stated, 'God made man in his image and likeness.' How can it be, then, that some have only the image? And how can they have the image of God if God is incorporeal, purest Spirit, infinite, sempiternal Light, operative Thought, and creative Power, but not a body?

This ignorance still exists among you believers! An ignorance which is both understandable and not understandable.

Understandable ignorance is that which derives from really elementary instruction, religious instruction stopping at the ABC's of Religion, caused by distance from religious facilities or-something quite blameworthy on the part of the blameworthy-by the neglect of ministers who do not consume themselves in making God known to their lambs, idol pastors whom I observe with a severe expression.

This ignorance does not take Heaven away from those undergoing it. For I am just and do not accuse a spirit if I know that its ignorance is not voluntary. But, rather, I observe it in terms of faith, and if I see that it is upright, with that thread of the knowledge of God it has been given, as if it had known a lot, I reward it as I reward a holy doctor. It is not to blame if it knows little. It has merit if it is able to turn a little into strength with these few, coherent ideas: 'God exists. I am his son. Obedience to his Law makes me such. And by obeying I shall come to possess God eternally through the *merits of the Savior, who has restored Grace to me.' The Spirit of God substitutes with lucid ideas in illuminating the believer neglected by his pastor or living in areas rarely visited by a pastor.*

But there is also ignorance that is not understandable. That of those who, though able to, do not want to receive instruction or, after being instructed, neglect it and become ignorant again because this is what they want for their own convenience. It is necessary for those wanting to live as beasts to forget the Truth.

I curse this ignorance. It is one of the sins drawing down my disdain without forgiveness. Why? Because it is repudiation of God, Father, Son, and Holy Spirit.

A son who does not want to know anything about his father or who, in knowing, wants (and comes) to forget him-what sort of son is he? I do not say he is a rebel against supernatural voices, but also against the voices of blood. Inferior, then, to the beasts, that, as long as they are subject by age to their father, recognize and follow him. I shall then leave you to consider what kind of rebellion revolt against a God who is a Father in terms of flesh and blood and also of soul and spirit is.

The repudiate the Son because, with no thought for the sacrifice of God the Son, who has become incarnate to bring the Truth to man, in addition to Redemption, they cancel out every voice of this Truth in themselves to live in their deceit.

They repudiate the Holy Spirit because Truth is always joined to Knowledge, and it is Knowledge that with its light brings you to comprehend the most sublime truths. I said, 'I am leaving and still have many things to say to you, but for the time being you are not capable of comprehending them. But when the Spirit of Truth comes, He will instruct you on all truth and complete my work as the Teacher by making you able to understand.'

O eternal Divine Spirit, who loves us so much that for the glory of the Father You descended to the purest marriage to beget the Redeemer and who, though equal to me, became my generator. You that proceed from me and from the Father! O eternal Divine Spirit, who for the glory of the Son poured forth your Fire and continually pour it forth so that the Word will be understood and creatures will change from men into gods by living according to Grace and the Word! The mystery of our Love! An inconceivable poem which only in Paradise will be fully known by the elect!

So, from Jesus' point of view, there's no harm in not knowing all of the truths as long as you're willing to learn them and as long as you have an interest in them. That's understandable ignorance. Or maybe nobody taught you or your parents were Godless and they didn't teach you anything about God and that's understandable. How would you know anything about God if your parents had no relationship with God? You couldn't know. And God is benign towards that; loving, just and comforting actually. God wants to help and will help in those understandable ignorances. Those are really easy to work with because there's an intent to know and there's an intent to want to know, even though no one helped them. They didn't have opportunities for some reason or another, just unfortunate turn of events or an unfortunate group of people that they hung out with. They didn't get to know.

So they're wanting to. Nothing stops them from knowing once someone comes along to help them know it. They're receptive even though there was no opportunity so far, and I think that's what a receptive disciple is: somebody who really did want to know and really heard the truth and the lessons and took them in and felt they were the right direction to go in and the right thing to understand, and they have that heart of openness and receptivity and willingness and, even though, you know, they had an unfortunate beginning – which, I think we can all say we had an unfortunate beginning. I mean, I don't know how we could not say that. If you just open one eye, I think you'll see that you had an unfortunate beginning. You don't need two eyes for that. You just need one, just need one. Yeah, that's right. That was unfortunate. Right? What else can you say about it? You can be mad about it but that's two eyes half closing. Two eyes are going half mast because you're starting to grimace and react instead of just see it for what it is. It's just unfortunate.

And the things that you want to know, you won't quite understand until the Spirit moves upon you and then your full, complete truth and full, complete knowing comes upon you, and full seeing. But the Spirit has to come and so, somebody has to be ready to be wanting that or open to that and, here's the whole feeling of being open to the Spirit, is that you don't quite get it. I mean, you get some of it, you don't quite get all of it, and you want to get all of it, and you don't know what that's going to look like and so, in that openness of being receptive to what It might teach you, then the Spirit could come. But, if you have it all pre-accessed, and you think you know what the Spirit is going to tell you, then you don't have an openness. You have, you're trying to put your ideas into the knowledge that the Spirit's going to give you.

You have to not know for the Spirit to come. You'll find in your own experience that, when you are very still or very focused maybe, not worried about anything, you'll feel a rush of the Spirit upon your body, on your shoulder, your neck, your head. You'll feel a rush, a wave of Spirit. At that moment you weren't thinking. You weren't doing anything to try hard, to figure anything out. You weren't doing anything to push or pull. You weren't resisting anything. You weren't fighting anything. You were still. That's when the Spirit moved and, I know, your typical idea is you've got to figure out why the Spirit moved. You must have been doing something right – that's what you say to yourself.

You were doing nothing right and that's why it came. You were doing nothing in the right way and that's why It came – because you got out of the way for a moment, you relaxed your forward thrust into attainment and you relaxed, and God took care of you for a minute. That heavy push toward removing the obstruction that you created in your own mind, when that drops away, then something happens to you. And that's still understandable ignorance. You know, when you try too hard to figure it out? It's still understandable ignorance. Somebody taught you that's the way to get ahead. But that's the way to be a head. But that's not the way to be a heart. That's not the way to be love. That's the way to think your way into something that you create, not go where the Spirit leads you or come to an understanding the Spirit gives you based on your receptivity.

In other words, I'm trying to encourage you to enjoy this one fact of your complete dependence on God, and I think some of you, you like that idea when I finally explain it to you. But previously, right before that, you were on an independent track trying to obtain all these things on your own with your own understanding and acquire them for yourself, kind of against all the oppositions in the universe – even God. You're going to acquire them independently, on your own. And that's just not how it's done. That's not how God set it up. You're going to be one with God or you're not going to get God.

So, you're not going to acquire and consume God, and absorb it and take it into your vast universe. No, you're going to open and the vast universe will come in - some proportion of what you can handle. Because It is vast. It's more than any human or any created being could conceive of. So your job is just to take on whatever God gives you, to understand whatever God shows you, to fill up with whatever God fills you with, and that is a very dependent – constructively dependent – position.

'Thy will be done.' Whatever you want for me Lord. Whatever is Your Will, I'll do it. Whatever you show me. Whatever you give me to understand, that's what I'm going to understand. That's the kind of thing I'm trying to encourage instead of this sort of belligerent fierceness going in to conquer God. You know, on what planet are you going to conquer God? Tell me about it. How are you going to storm God and take over?

God's inside going, 'What are you doing? You're having thoughts? Why? Come in. Come in. Come be with Me.' 'Well, I was going to do some stuff.' And God'll say, 'No, you're not going to do anything. In fact, whatever you think you're doing isn't anything I want you to do. I want you to come and be with Me.' And your ambitions, are going, 'Well, how will that help?' Well, you'll feel better and you'll start shining and you'll be full of love and light and Spirit and you'll be able to give and you'll be able to see properly so you'll be able to help. So it'll be very simple. It won't be complicated. I don't know why your mantra is, 'It's hard and I'm doing the hard work.' I don't know why that mantra's even there. I never taught that mantra. I didn't. 'It's hard and you're going to do the hard work and then thus attain. . .' What is up with that? I mean, it's like you have a second running commentary that you think is quite positive, along with mine, which is, 'Give it up, let it go, don't do anything, just let God do it and find out what God wants.' And yours is, 'I'm going to take it over, I'm going to find it, I'm going to drive, I'm going to get to it, and I'm going to acquire it, and then I'm going to become this thing.'

Well, you see the difference of the energy? One's sort of aggressive and assertive. The other is sort of receptive and tranquil, like a dove. The other's some kind of ferocity storming the castle. If you knew your nature, your real nature, you wouldn't have to try so hard because you'd know that you were already like that. You're already a divine being. If you really knew that, you could relax, and just become just exactly that; more and more of that. But, because we see so many things we don't like, we have to fiercely assault the Kingdom of God to acquire it.

That's not how the Kingdom of God is won. It's won by receptivity, by peace, by love, by generosity, by kindness and by openness. 'Thy Will be done. Whatever is Your Will.' When you have that attitude, you have humility don't you? When you have humility, you have closeness to God. When you're fighting your bad habits, you have a war on. God's not interested in your war. God could take your bad habits in a second. You wouldn't even have to fight them yourself. You could say, 'Take my bad habit.' He goes, 'Okay,' and He takes it. Where's your fight now? So you get a lot of miles out of fighting so you can keep your bad habits. He can take it away in a second if you ask Him. I mean, you have to want to not have it. You have to want to not do it again, of course. That's your part. But He can take it away. He can take the power of it away, the sting of it away, the poison of it away, the intensity of it away. He can take it in a thought, He can take it away – if you want Him to.

So, thus, I'm saying, 'Working on your problems is really anti-Christ.' It's anti-Christ because Jesus said, 'Give them to Me.' He didn't say, 'Take an entire lifetime to load them up on a cart and drag them across the desert and then take them up the mountains and then carry them on your back and then, maybe you'll die before you give them to Me.' He didn't say that. Do we get a sense of prowess for working that hard on something He didn't even ask us to do? Is that what we're looking at: the ego food that we really worked hard, dragging this problem along to then finally get around to give it to Him? And, again, I think that's sort of understandable given the bad training that everybody got in the basics of religion: That you're a wretched creature and you have to drag your sins over there to the altar. . . and, so then, the kid mind – the little, immature mind – goes, 'Well, I guess that's part of the Path is to drag my sins around from altar to altar and, then if I have to go to the altar again, I have to drag them again.' And then you have to refresh them so that you can re-drag them to the altar. That's the ABC's of religion. That's that stupid religious training that doesn't have the complete thing – that Jesus can wipe out your sin, and it can be gone, and you never have to have it again. That's the deeper religion. You can be reunited and you don't have to fall away. You don't have to fall back into the old patterns if you don't want to. He'll help you.

I want you to hear this though, eventually, that, when you are in your old bad patterns, you wanted it. And when you slip back into them, you wanted it. It wasn't necessary. It wasn't, 'The Way of the Path.' That's anti-Christ. 'Give Me your troubles. Give Me your trials and your labours and I'll take them.' That's what He said. 'Give Me your sins and I will take them from you. I will forgive your sin.' What does that mean? You won't have it any more! Okay, so now I'm catching you in a moment where either you'd want it or you don't want it. You want the sin or you don't want the sin. That's the deeper religion, is that they don't want their sin anymore and then they don't have them anymore, and then they don't act them out any more, and then they're not struggling with them any more because they gave them away.

It is that simple. Although, I am seeing quizzical looks, like I'm being tricky, but I know you're tricky. I'm not tricky. You are tricky because you secretly want to keep stuff while I keep saying you don't have to keep stuff. I'm trying to slow it down for everybody so everybody can feel the energy of it: 'I want to keep stuff and you keep telling me I don't have to keep stuff.' That's right. I keep telling you, like Jesus is telling you, that you don't have to keep stuff. You can let it go. You can't do it yourself. He'll take it. That's the key: He has to take it. You have to give it to Him.

You know, when you hand somebody something, you don't clench your fist. Right? You don't go, 'I'm giving you this because they say I should do this in the ABC's of religion. I should be giving you this but I know that's just a myth, and my job is to keep trying to give it to you but keep holding it tight to myself. That's the ABC's of religion. The deeper religion: You give it, He takes it, and it's clean. It's done. Why would you give it away if you keep wanting to do it? Why would you keep wanting to do it and then pretend to be giving it away? So you have to get straight in your mind. What do you want about this? Do you want it done or not? Do you want Him to take it or not? Or you want to keep it? Because, then, don't try to give it away if you want to keep it. And this is what He's talking about, and the Spirit comes in and helps you understand this. It's this Holy Spirit that helps you understand the teachings after you've got the ABC's of religion and you think you know something. You don't really know until the Spirit walks through your world and shows you – through your body, through your flesh, through your mind – and shows you the truth. And that happened for the Apostles. They had thousands of questions all the way up to the end and, as soon as the Spirit came a few days later, they understood everything He taught. I mean the depths of it. All of it.

That will happen to you if you relax and open and let the Spirit teach you. It's happening all the time but, as you relax, it'll flow through you, and you'll get it. Like, 'Why have I been stuck? Why am I sort of the same as I ever was and my changes are only intellectual, perhaps philosophical. Why am I still the same?' Because the Spirit hasn't walked through your being yet to enlighten you. Not yet. In some cases, yes. Some of you, yes. Some of you, no. Some of you, pieces and parts. Some of you, partial. You know how it is.

With the Apostles, complete. I mean, they were perfected beings by the time Jesus got done with them. Doesn't mean they had all the experiences that they needed. They're going to get more. They're going to keep having more, but they were perfect in understanding and perfect in ability to be an Apostle. They were changed. And so, that's what I'm trying to do with you: Get you to a place where you're not still loyal to your old life because you haven't let the Spirit in to finish it. I mean, just to finish it. I think 'finish' is that right word. I don't think 'kill it,' I think 'finish it.' Finish it is a little bit more, you know, amicable. Isn't it? It's a little more benign. 'Let's just finish it. Let's finish the old ways. Let's finish the ABC's of religion and walk into the Holy Spirit.'

September 11, 2016
Bridegroom

1943 Notebooks, October 19, 1943.

Jesus says:
"And now, soul of mine, now that we are at the end of the Song, I will teach you the final stratagems of the wisdom of love.

Be pure, for your Beloved is purer than the lily and the snow, and the bride must wear the same clothes as her Lord and value what He values. The Light approaches, Maria. Also remove the traces of the shadows of the flesh so that you, too, will be all light for the hour when I come, and the Light-Jesus-will clasp you to his heart to take you to his dwelling, where there will no longer exist the separations imposed by being upon this earth.

Always increase your beauty, for the wedding is near. Put on the jewels of the final sacrifices; adorn yourself therewith joyfully, for they have been given to you by the One who loves you with an eternal love.

Set yourself aflame with the splendor of love so as to give brightness to your spiritual appearance. A cold bride, even just a lukewarm one, is not a bride. I want you burning with total love.

Be intrepid against all the forces of the Enemy, who is trying to perturb you out of hellish envy. He will launch his demoniacal quadrigae against you to no avail. As long as you remain faithful, four and four and ten times four demons will be less than a blade of grass under your foot, which is taking the last steps to traverse what still separates you from the dwelling of your love.

Let nothing disturb you. Proceed, leaning on Me. Remain there until the end, and your passage shall be sweet and luminous, like coming off a half-dark, rough road into a flowering meadow filled with sunlight and the song of birds.

And in truth for whoever has merited the possession of Heaven by loving, death is only entrance into eternal Beauty and eternal Joy.

And since in the past you were not blameless, cancel out even the memory of those shadows by the means I have taught you. By an increasingly intense love. Live only for Me, by Me, with Me. Have the Father, on observing you, see you so fused to Me as not to be able to separate you from his Son. Let my Charity cover you like a nuptial mantel under which I conceal the rents in your dress."

There is no difference in many of the stories that we have in terms of how we come to God. We come to God in rough shape, wounded and broken. We come to God messed up and it is many months before we find out how messed up we really are and how broken and how sad and how in pain we are. How lost and how confused and gradually there is a healing where you start to feel the love and feel the acceptance of Jesus and Mary for you and their willingness to heal and their willingness to shower you with graces. There is nothing in you that feels like you deserve that, if you are honest. And yet they want that for you. They want you to be inflamed with their love. They don't think you have any of your own, because nobody has any level of their own. They have God's love, or you don't have any. You have what love you have allowed God to have in you, or you have nothing. And they want the fullness of God's love in you, and they are willing to fill you up with that, if you have humble places, pockets of acceptance, the humility to need them, to need them. And they want you to be inflamed with that love. It is not yours. You don't have to bring anything. You have to let their love fill you up and inflame you. There's not that much to do, but there is much to do in letting go. There are so many things that you are carrying that Jesus doesn't want you to carry anymore. The badness, and the sadness, and the heaviness, and the depression, and the fear of punishment, and the fear of getting slammed down again. Thousands of little injections into your skin, which you keep nursing. You keep nursing them. But Jesus said, give them all to me. And he will take them, and he will make you fresh and new, the bride that you are going to become. He is the bridegroom, you're not. You're not. That is not going to happen. You are the bride if you prepare, if you clean up, if you lose that suspicion, if you lose those calculations, the cautions, the worries, the fears. Inflamed with charity, he said he wanted you to be. How can you be that when you are worried or when you are cautious, or when you are trying to prove something?

You are not alone. You are in the situation that everyone is in, full of it, and having to let go of it. You are full of your ideas and you are full of your cautions and fears. You are full of your ideas about who you think you are. And everybody has got these until you let them go. And when you let them go you feel more clean, you feel more relaxed, more pure. He wants you clean. You are not going to make anything happen, you are going to allow and accept God's will to happen. God's will wants that to happen, but he can't make it happen and get it to happen in a person who is worried all the time. Your worries, your ideas, your fears, block God. Now what is God going to do with you? On one level, that is none of your business. Whatever God wants to do with you, which is none of your business, except that it is going to happen to you. You will experience it. But if you want a preview, you are thus not ready to have God do anything with you, because a preview is a worried mind. Where is a worried mind and faith? They are two different continents. Where is, "Thy will be done", and I accept whatever you want for me. And whatever you need me to do, I will accept that. Whatever you want me to work on, in the moment that you want me to work on it, I will do it. Where is that, in needing a preview?

You are not going to control anything. You can, and you will be completely alone. In God, you won't be alone, but in God you will not be in charge. You can have it one way or the other. You can't have it both ways. You can't be in charge, and running the show, and monitoring your safeness, and calculating your gains, and making sure that it's going to be comfortable for you and have God in your life. It is not possible, because that is god in your life. That creature that wants to manage everything, guide everything, monitor everything, figure everything out, that is god. And God will not be near another god, will not come close to you when you're doing that. And you still do it. I know, I watch. But I am asking you not to, so that you can be in the love. That you can just let God guide it, you can let Jesus inform you of the next thing you need to do, and the next thing you need to do, without looking ahead. He says relax, so then do it. Actually do it. He says stop thinking, then stop thinking. He says let me work on you without you knowing what I'm doing. Let me do that. So you let him work on you, without knowing what he's doing. You ask in prayer, "Work on me. Get me out of the way, just work on me, change me, open me up, free me up." You make your prayers and then you let them happen.

Many of you are riddled with fears and riddled with ideas about what you will and won't do. And I know that every one of those is a fence that you place between you and Jesus. It is a fence you build between you and Jesus. I want to be a disciple, but I want a guarantee that I can be the way I want to be, and manage it the way I want, and be comfortable in the way that I choose, but I still want to be called a disciple. Well, I have news for you, that is not a disciple. That is a cautionary being, who is not ready to give up yet. That is all that is. And Jesus is fine with you being that way, but not much can happen to you, and he can't work with you too much, and he can't inspire you too much, because you are full of it, whatever you decide it is. You are full of it. You are full of how fast you can change, how slow things have to go. You are full of your own ideas of what you would look like if you did change. You are full of cautions around the change so that nothing is jostled in your life and no changes have to be made. You are full of ideas.

If we were completely secluded, and end times happened, and they allowed us to stay on the earth, we would not have changed very much in that whole process. If I look at the trajectory of how cautious you are to allow any change in you, or any influx of the Spirit to blow out the gaskets and the boundaries that you have created for yourself, I would say that if end times happened and we were still alive in a community that was kind of protected, you would not have grown very much. You would not have changed very much. You would still be very familiar with your old ways that you seem to love. And you would have allowed not much to happen to you personally. Let alone the world or people you know in the world, just you.

And I think that is the human condition and I can't help feeling Jesus' sadness about this, because so much more could be given to you if you had so much more room, which is required in order to get more. You have to empty more. You have to give up more. You have to let go more. You have to empty out to be filled up, but many of you are filled up 92% with what you like already and you are going to give Jesus the 8% to work with. Yes he can work with and he will work with your 8%, but he is fascinated by how you could hold on to the 92 and think that's whole, pure, light filled, glorious or even giving glory to God in that 92. He knows better. He knows you. He knows what you are holding onto and he can only work with the part that you give him, and the rest he can't touch it, because he can't violate your will. He won't. And I think you are really, kind of pretty heavy on the thing that you want to keep, pretty heavy on it. Inflamed with charity is like, whatever you want, I'll do it. Whatever you want me to give, I'll do it. Whatever you want me to give up, I'll give it up. Whatever you want me to let go of, I will let it go. I rely totally on you. There is nothing else for me. That's what he wants. No ideas. No ideas. You should have no ideas, just whatever he wants. That is inflamed with charity. That's a pure vessel that he can work with.

You should own this, and that you give him very little room to maneuver inside of you. You give him very little renovation license inside of you. I don't know why that is. After all you have been through, I don't know why that is. I guess it is just the human condition to be very scared of any changes. To not be able to recognize yourself in your old ways as you move into the new way. You carry all that baggage with you, so that you can stay familiar with yourself. Why wouldn't you want to be transformed into something he wants you to be? I know you say you do, but I see that is not what you do. You preserve every vestige of the past that you possibly can and you make only the changes that you seem like you're forced to make. And what kind of a love bride does that make, when she is really reluctantly going along and if she has to, she will love, or give, or open. What kind of bride does that make, when they have to be cajoled and convinced to open? And a gentle person would not force that. They would say, well it's just not time yet. They are not ready. They are not inflamed with charity yet. You are not burning with love as he said. Not if you are worried about you and inventorying your badness. Definitely, you are not inflamed with burning love for him when you were doing that. It is not possible. I think the main thought would be, I hope I'm not going to get found out. I hope he doesn't see these things that I'm worried about. So then you have to start learning to be a liar or learning to be dishonest, or learning to be good at hiding, or expecting to not be, or withdrawing so the time spent together he won't find out. All these things, little tricks that people do in closeness, to make sure that they are not close, pretending to be close, but sure that they are not really close, because they are afraid that these things that you're struggling with will be seen. I don't care if he shows up all of my problems, because I love him enough to do whatever work I need to do to clean up. I would like you to do that too. I really would.

September 18, 2016
Obedience

The Gospel as Revealed to Me, *Chapter 276. Avarice and the Foolish Rich Man.*

"*Be active in spiritual matters as men are with regard to their bodies. And as far as your bodies are concerned do not imitate the people of the world who always tremble for their future, fearing they may lack what is superfluous, that they may be taken ill, or die, that enemies may be harmful, and so on. God knows what you are in need of. Therefore be not afraid for your future. Be free from tears, which are heavier than the chains of galley-slaves. Do not be anxious about the necessities of life: what you will eat, or drink and how you will clothe yourself. The life of the spirit is worth more than the life of the body and the body is worth more than clothes, because you live with your bodies and not with your clothes and through the mortification of your bodies you help your souls to attain eternal life. God knows how long He will leave your souls in your bodies, and He will give you what is necessary until that hour. He gives it to crows, impure birds which feed on corpses and the reason for their being is just to remove putrefying corpses. And will He not give you what is necessary? Crows have neither larders nor granaries and God feeds them just the same. You are men, not crows. At present you are the cream of men because you are the disciples of the Master, the evangelizers of the world, the servants of God. And can you possibly think that God may neglect you, even for what concerns your clothes, since He takes care of the lilies of the valleys and makes them grow and clothes them with such beautiful robes that Solomon never possessed the like, and yet they do no work but scent worshipping God? It is true that by yourselves you cannot add one tooth to a toothless mouth, or lengthen by one inch a contracted leg, or make dimmed eyes bright. And if you cannot do such things, can you think you may be able to repel misery and diseases and turn dust into food? You cannot. But do not be of little faith. You will always have what you need. Do not worry like the people of the world who strive to satisfy their pleasures. You have your Father Who knows what you need. All you must seek, and it must be your first care, is the Kingdom of God and His justice, and all the rest will be given to you as well."*

We could have almost memorized many of these words from the Testament and some of you have said them to yourself before and yet it's so easy to forget. There's so much self-concern about taking care of yourself and so much self-concern about your clothes and your food, and so much anxiety about whether you'll have enough of what you need all the way through your life. And it's pretty simply the wrong way to think, it's really the wrong way to think like that. You subsist in time by the Father placing you in a time and space continuum for as long as he wants, for as long as he's already pre-patterned it, he knows already how long your time is. He already knows the cross you bear and the struggles that you have trying to get close to him. You went away so it's your fault really but he knows what struggle you will have getting back into oneness with him. Your days are appointed and your life is cared for, he wants you to live and he pointed you into the kingdom of his being by his own will. You forget so often, I know you do because I can feel the density of your thoughts where you're doing this and you're doing that, you're managing this and you're managing that, and you're taking care of this and you're taking care of that. You have so much control of all of these thoughts in your head that have nothing to do with life really, nothing. They have to do with spending a lot of time and effort into the places that are not blessed, and also very little good can come from those efforting places. Oh ye of little faith. So even though you can look at the animals and you can say they have a particular job like the crows have the job of eating dead flesh and they really do do that very well actually. If you ever watch them and other birds do that too and each animal seems to have a job. There's nutcrackers and there's things that eat other things to keep balances. They are appointed that job, without any desire to control it, because they have only instinct. They are completely obedient to the nature that they were given and then you have the pinnacle of creation, humans - the highest form of creation, the highest possibility of God manifesting in flesh.

The humans have no interest in that, none. They have no interest in being the vessel for the divine being, they have an interest in doing whatever they want, indulging whatever they want, satisfying whatever they want, worrying about whatever thing they want to worry about, you know managing everything. You have the freedom to do these things, and because you have enjoyed your freedom, you fell away from God. And there's still the will of God after you are done with that nonsense. Only when you line back up in the will of God can the growth start, can the expansion happen, can your trajectory into unlimited space of God happen. You have to get rid of that other thing to be on the path of expansion of consciousness in God. Before that it's not that it's just willful, deliberate soiling of yourself which you have the freedom to do, but some of you got fooled into thinking that that kind of expression of freedom was part of the will of God. It was not. The going away and the coming back up to were not the will of God. That was you, that's your trip, that's your exploration into darkness and mud. Then your conscience starts burning and you pull yourself back to the place you would've started to grow. That going away and coming back to the place you start to grow isn't growth, that is a side trip exiting off the highway.

You have yourself to blame. God did not order it. God did not want that, God did not support it, God withdraws from you while you do it. That was from thinking, that was from doing. All that worrying, all that self-driving egotism, that's what takes you there. The fears and the anger, holding on and the lacking in forgiveness and seeing distortedly what life is, that's where you go. That's not the path, that's a subtraction of the path, that's not the path, that's just an avoidance of the path. Get it clear in your mind, trusting God starts the path, getting back to the place where you might have trust in God, that's not the path, that's just you getting over yourself. The path is when you say, 'Thy will be done' and you accept your lot in life even if it's karma being paid. Accept your lot in life as God blesses you through it and God takes you through these experiences. If you complain, you go back to that dark exiting path, and if you get mad you're going to the dark exiting path. When you stop complaining and you start accepting whatever gifts are given to you whatever food, or lack of it, is given to you in that day - spiritually, mentally, emotionally - you gracefully take it because either you created it or it's God's test or God's blessing of you to take it. If you have that kind of humility that accepts the conditions of your life as God working through them, you are really starting the path right there. You are starting to keep that wildness out, you're being a real human being, probably right about then, and before you were an animal, you were a wild animal and now the human says, 'I'm a created being, God's will is being done, I'm learning what I need to learn, this is hard or this is challenging or this beautiful and this is what he wants and this is going to last as long as he wants it to last, the good stuff and the bad stuff, as long as God wants it 'Thy will be done." Not 'Your will be done as long as he agrees to it.' Do you see how we have been doing our own thing and now we are starting to think about doing it God's way without an attitude, without opinions and without lobbying for a particular thing? If you're lobbying, you already think you know don't you? 'If it be Thy will I would like this,' and then relax. If it doesn't come to be it's not time or it may never happen. Relax, you don't think the divine is watching out for you? You just talked to him, you forget about him right away right after you said the prayer. You talked to him and said, 'I want this. If it's your will I want this.' Like is he stupid? How many times do you have to ask him? He heard you. Now that will come to pass or it will not come to pass based on you saying 'Thy will be done.' You can always have what you want, but you might be exiting, you may be getting off the path right there. Can you risk it? I don't think you can, I wouldn't risk it. Some of us are at the place where we can hear what we should pray for and we do. Like sometimes you're told to go back to school and you pray to get into a school. You do because you were told go back to school and you go. You pray sometimes to be open for a baby and then it happens. Sometimes you are open for a relationship and then the person that you are sent didn't want it, but you wanted the one that you wanted. Doesn't work out so good. Maybe you had to wait a little longer for the person that you was going to be sent to you and you couldn't stand to wait so you grabbed the first flesh eating person that you could find. I don't think I exaggerate too much. When people have a consuming passion what's the difference?

I was reading what Jesus talks about eagles, how they live way up on top mountain crag in the nest. They have their babies and they wait because they are very patient and they live in the sky, they live in the sky next to the blue and the sun and they wait for the young birds, who don't even know what these wings are for. They see the parents wings stretching wide, they don't know what they're for, they're just sitting in the nest and waiting and eating, growing really strong. Their talons are growing and they can fight a little bit, because they're fighters, and because they have to be able to grab something - that starts out early. They compete with each other for food and they tear stuff up that the parents bring in. That's part of their nature. At some point the eagles will take the bird in their beak, in their talons and just go aloft with these great wings, the seven foot span, and take them way high and then drop them. It's almost like what God does with us. God sees that we're ready for something and then takes us somewhere - we're not sure we can do it - and then phew! Of course the wind takes the wings and the wings start happening and they don't know how to use them. They're falling like crazy and the parents are watching, they're flying miles down you know, and if the young birds start plummeting because they get weak in the wings, they grab them and take them to the nest. They do that a number of times until they can't stand to not be flying because these birds are used to flying. This is their whole instinct. They're out there in the azure blue and they can look right at the sun and they only drop down to land for morsels, like little sheep and small animals. They can pick a little baby sheep right up. That's kind of what has to happen with you. Jesus has to come down and pick you up and take you to where your nature is so you can feel it, and of course you plummet like crazy because you're not used to that, you're used to crawling on the earth and groveling and desiring things and eating mud worms and stuff. He's taking you to a place where you can be consciousness itself and it's hard, and you plummet and he takes you again and takes you again. That's what communion is for, to take you again into the blue of the heavens until you don't want to go down there anymore. You're just done with it, you are done with that old mired life. Truthfully your nature is divine, your nature is a God. You're a God in the making.

In your soul you are divine but in your flesh, and in your mind you have bad habits that are completely contrary to your divinity. The path is that tearing thing to tear you away from the nest of your comforts, the nest of your small little world, your small little contrived world where you think you are safe. It's just a placeholder until you become yourself, until you realize your divinity. What's your divinity? It's to be in the mind of God, pray to create, to make things happen the way that God does, to shine. That's your nature. This limited world has nothing on you, but for most of you you haven't plummeted enough, you haven't received the spoils of this world enough so your desire nature is still out there grabbing it while you're clutching like the animals are clutching. Of course they are innocent, they are not devious like humans are, they're not mischievous, they are just simple. They just do instinctually what they're supposed to do. Humans do desire nature stuff that they were never asked to do, they simply just do whatever they want. That's why Jesus often, in many of the readings, talks about the humans having fallen below the beast because the beasts are at least obedient instinctually to the divine will. The humans, oh my, not even close to obedient. Just that thought that you're not being taken care of starts you down one of those roads. Just that thought that you have to manage it yourself sends you down an exit off the highway, and that's why these readings keep repeating. Jesus says them different ways in different forms with different kinds of words. He repeats them, why? Because he can see that nobody really understands it yet. If you did he wouldn't have to repeat it, he wouldn't have to say it a different way and a different way and a different way to try to coax you, to try to care for you to try to get you on the right way. If one time was it and if one time you would actually remember then that would be it. But you forgot, you think you have to manage your needs, you think you have to acquire everything that you want when God would give it to you. You think that you can take credit for everything that happens when God says you can't do anything. You can't even put a tooth back in your mouth. What control do you really have? The only control you really have is to say no. I have said this for years, a yes is the will of God, a no is I'm going to do my own thing. The birds, the animals, the insects and plants all do the will of God and are completely supported. God would like to do that with us and we just can't stop doing it ourselves, so what is he supposed to do? He has to repeat, he has to keep repeating until your faith is more simple. I am sure the little eaglets are wondering what is happening to them, thinking they're being killed and their nest experience is being disturbed. 'I'm used to this, we've got a pattern here, we know who's in charge in the nest, the strong one beats the little one up and then they get more food and the parents have to make a fair, that's their job, this is our job our nest area, we control the nest when mom and dad are away.' That's all they know and the parents have a deeper sight ripping them out of their nest and freefalling and that's what some kinds of spiritual experiences are like for you where you're taken somewhere where you have no control and you can't manage it and you can't figure it out. You don't know what's going to happen next, you don't even know why you got there to begin with and you're going to have to just figure it out on the fly and not from your head. That's what a meditation sometimes does, it elevates you out of yourself. Communion will do that, when you pray it does that to you, when you are being taught something it does that to you. And if you hate the jostling and resent it, then you don't learn much from it. But if you trust the jostling of it, the disturbance of it, you learn a lot. But you'd have to be disturbed in order to go into a higher place. You don't think that when God appeared to Moses he didn't jostle the hell out of him, or Abraham? They weren't jostled by the experience, frightened awesome? I mean when the apostles saw Elijah and Moses coming down with Jesus in the light, what do they do - oh this is cool? No they're on the ground fearing for their lives because it shook them. Something really big is happening that they're not used to and if they said "oh yeah I know about this, I read about it" that would be very lacking in humility wouldn't it. "Oh this happens to all the big ones, I'm a big one." That would be a very bad situation for them. No they are on the ground hoping that if they raise their head that they wouldn't get struck, that's appropriate. When you're talking about the living God it's bigger than us. If you don't get that, you're too big, you're too big. There's no room in the room for God with you being that big. Be careful, be careful of that attitude. You can figure out God, you can figure out the timing of things? Clearly I know that you can't, you can't. It's better if you don't try, it's better to just accept, it's more humble to just accept to know that you are being taken care of. That's much more humble, that's blessed, the other thing is not blessed. That anticipatory energy, that worry energy that's not blessed ever. It just shows that you have no faith and it shows that the big thing that's taking care of everything is your big ego and that's another lie. You're not taking care of anything, you're being supported. Why don't you enjoy that, why don't you start to enjoy that? I don't see too many of you enjoying that yet, I'd like you to enjoy that you are being taken care of, that you get to know that, that you are comforted by that. Mostly I see you irritated by it like irritated because it jostles your dreams, whatever those are, the mirages of your dreams.

September 25, 2016
Perfection

The Gospel as Revealed to Me, Chapter 295. The discussions and the miracles in Arbela: already evangelized by Philip of Jacob.

You can no longer erect Tabernacles. Their time is over. But erect spiritual ones in your hearts. Climb the mountain, that is, rise towards Perfection. Gather branches of olive, myrtle, palm, oak, hyssop and of every beautiful tree. Branches of the virtues of peace, purity, heroism, mortification, strength, hope, justice, of all virtues. Adorn your souls celebrating the feast of the Lord. His Tabernacles are awaiting you. His. And they are beautiful, holy, eternal, open to all those who live in the Lord. And together with me, decide today to do penance for the past and to begin a new life.

Do not be afraid of the Lord. He calls you because He loves you. Be not afraid. You are His children like everybody in Israel. Also for you He created the Universe and Heaven, He sent Abraham and Moses, He opened the sea, He created the guiding cloud, He descended from Heaven to give the Law, and He opened the clouds that they might rain manna, and He made the rocks fruitful that they might give water. And now for you also He is sending the living Bread of Heaven to satisfy your hunger and the true Vine and the Fountain of eternal Life to quench your thirst. And through My lips He says to you: "Enter and possess the Land over which I have raised my hand to give it to you". My spiritual Land: The Kingdom of Heaven.

You are not quite at the place where you understand this perfection yet, or this Kingdom of Heaven. You still are wandering in the plateau lands, between the old life and the new, between the land that Jesus is showing you and the land that time forgot. But you haven't forgotten it, and you are still referencing your past and trying to drag it into your future. And that is like erecting tabernacles. That is like erecting altars to your past experience. It clutters up the landscape quite a bit, because you have to bump into them, or at least walk around them. And then other people have to walk around them, and other people bump into them, because you have a little tabernacle built to dad and a little tabernacle built to mom and a little tabernacle built to the idealization of what family could have been, or might have been. Or even if you are silly enough to idolize the one you had, you have a tabernacle to that. And everybody bumps into your landscape of tabernacles as they walk through your experience. As you share with them who you are, they have to bump into all of these structures that you have built that have nothing to do with reality. And the one who wants to build the tabernacle in you is the Spirit and Jesus, and that is the only one that he wants to see. It's the only one he wants to see. The rest are idolatry and fear, anger, pain, sadness and lies. And if you weren't so identified with your past, you would not have any of them at all.

If you have a beautiful new experience, the other experiences turn sour, or pale, or irrelevant. In the joy of the new experience, the other shows up pretty dim and not too meaningful anymore. If you live on the plateau land, you are wandering around between two worlds, between Egypt and between the Promised Land basically. Like the old Israelites, forty years in the desert, just wandering around, and it's not very far. Four or five hundred miles at the most, maybe two hundred miles. For forty years you miss every boat, every sign, and every indication of what direction that you're going? And that is not just physical, that is spiritual. That is the confusion of not being sure you don't want the old or you want the new. Not being sure you want the new and letting go of the old, so every time you think of the old you traverse around that other way again. And that makes you very confused, and circling around the dead basically, the old. So when Jesus talks about this perfection that he wants to build into you, that actually can't happen unless you let go of the old.

The only reason you think of the past is to edit it, and to make it not so painful, or to rework it so that it is more beneficial to you. Or it wasn't as sad as you really experienced it, or it wasn't as bad as it really was. You are editing. You are trying to soften the pain of it. I don't know why. It doesn't make any sense. It was just what it was. Why don't you just accept it that way? I think you would move forward much faster if you just accept things the way they are. But no, you say it shouldn't have been like that, or it could have been like this, or why did that have to happen, or that shouldn't have happened. All of those edits, all of those lacking of acceptance of your experience takes you back. And you wander back around in the wilderness again. Because you are not walking into your perfection or into your new life, which Jesus is inviting you into, and Jesus can take care of for you. You can't do it. But he can drag you into it, if you don't mind being dragged. And the ones who don't mind being dragged, aren't being dragged, they are running into it. They are running or walking swiftly toward it. They are not being dragged out of the old thing that they hate. But some of you are being dragged out of the old thing you are nostalgic for. But the ones who are perfecting don't think of their old life as nostalgic. They think of it as sad and embarrassing, and compost for the rich soil that Jesus is planting seeds in. They don't think of it is super valuable, they think of it as old and unnecessary evil, or perhaps a terrible experience that they never want to have happen again. And they own it, as they created it. They don't think anybody else did anything to them. They created it. Those are the ones who are perfecting, going into this new spiritual tabernacle in their hearts that Jesus is creating.

And that is what he wants. He doesn't want you wallowing in your sadness, because that is just selfishness. He doesn't want you reviewing your imperfections, because he said he could take those from you. In an instant of prayer, he could take them. And insecurity is just holding on to your old ways and wanting a blessing for it. That is the definition of insecurity. Wanting a blessing for your old ways. Why would Jesus, or any wise person indulge that? Why would you, if you are even thinking straight, want a blessing for your old ways? No such blessing will be had. And no divine being will ever give you one for your old ways. Only if you are obedient, walking into the new way, will you get your blessing. In fact, there is nothing for you in the old. There is nothing there anymore. Jesus could wipe it away with a blink of his eye, a wave of his hand, and it would be gone. And all you would be left with is the goodness of your experience, or the wisdom of your experience. But some of you want to prove that you can do it yourself, to Jesus, or to Mary. That you have the stamina, the wherewithal, the power, the integral strength to do these things on your own. And they are not paying any attention to that. How could they possibly pay any attention to that? Because it is against all spiritual teaching, that you do anything of yourself. And yet you try to do it yourself. And he says he even didn't do anything of himself. But you try to do it yourself. That is the old way. That is wandering around on the plateau land.

Yes, you have grown. You are not at the base of the mountain. You are not in the valley of where everybody else is tearing each other up. You are on a plateau. You are not at the summit. Because at the summit people don't struggle with their past anymore. They don't. At the summit, you don't have any more problems. You just take direction, and do what you're told. And you shine, and you love, and you serve, and you don't think about yourself, and you don't think about yesterday. Plateau land, I will give you credit. You are not in the valley, but caught between two worlds. You can't totally go back now, because it doesn't make all that much sense, but you are scared to go forward because that looks a little bit like an obliteration of the thinking of who you are. Pretending to know who you are. You are going to lose all that. So you are caught between two worlds right now, spiritually. I know the feeling. I was there two thousand years ago, just like you. I know what it was like. I remember it, like it was yesterday. Caught between the old life which I'm not bad at and the new life, which I know nothing about. And I am being drawn into my destruction possibly, or into my obliteration, my annihilation. Or I am drawn into the kingdom of heaven, which is a myth at this point. If you are between two worlds it is mythology. It is like a possibility, because you don't know and you can't count on it. Because you haven't stepped into it yet, it's not solid for you. You are freaked out. I remember. I remember. But some of you are holding on, and your nails are breaking. That is how hard you are holding on to your past.

Jesus didn't say, "I want you to remember your past. Every five minutes, I want you to remember your past. For sure, you remember your past." Every time he looks at you, "I love you, but I want you to remember your past. I want you to shine with light, but I want you to remember your past." Well, that is what you are doing to me. I say, "forget your past." And you say, "I need to remember it." I say, "shine with light." And you say, "I need to remember my past. I need to remember my weakness, and my darkness, and all my problems and I have to keep those inventoried, so I can make demands on the environment, and I can make demands on people if I remember my past, can't I? I can get people to take care of me, rather than take care of myself if I remember my past. I can make you think of me, if I remember my past."

Isn't that what your whole past is, trying to get people to see you, trying to get people to think of you, trying to get people to remember you, trying to get people to love you? That is your whole past. Your whole past wasn't, I was just serving, and I was helping, and I was doing everything that I could to raise people up and I was being a shining light and I was trying to be love wherever I went and just help and be cheerful. You can't say that about your past. Well, none of us can. None of us can. Because, the past pretty much sucks. But Jesus isn't asking you to go back there. He never did. He is asking you to come to him, to be where he is, which is certainly not in your past.

The tabernacle outside, he doesn't care about. All of your rules, all of your little things that you decide are so spiritual and so not spiritual, the things that you judge other people by. They should be like this! You still have them. I have been trying to beat them out of you, for three years now. Well they did this, and they did...! I still hear it in your minds, and it's in your comments. It is like you are still thinking with that kindergarten mind. Like you can evaluate another person? Not with that mind you can't. You can only evaluate somebody with the mind of Christ, and that is a very loving analysis. That is a very loving scrutiny, which most of you haven't even learned anything about. Do you see the other person struggling, like you were struggling? Often you do not. You feel much better than them, because they are struggling. You see, that is not the mind of Christ. The mind of Christ is compassionate. It sees the way out. It sees the step that they need to take. Yes, it sees what they could be, if they allowed it. And it is supportive. It is not critical. It is not comparative. That is the mind of the past. And it is the mind of the world. You weren't called to that. You were called to a much more noble path, to a divine path. You, divine beings, called to a divine path. But I know that you like to wear that coat of mud, to remind yourself that you are still just like everybody else. Your pride does not like that, but your ego does.

The spiritual tabernacle is built by the Christ, building it inside of you. That is where you worship, that is what you should be valuing. That is what you should be spending time on and emphasis on. Everything else can go to hell, where it belongs. That is what you were called to. That is what we have been transitioning towards. It's like a bunch of camels, who are not just stepping out, they are just trudging along. Okay, well at least we are getting there. Maybe we are getting there. I run on ahead, and I come back, and we've moved a little. And I run on ahead, and I come back, and we have moved a little. That is kind of how it is. I have a horse, and you guys have a camel. Okay. They do race camels, but not with a load they don't. And there is quite a load. We've got quite a load here. If you could have that spiritual tabernacle built, you would find that it is very light, and there wasn't a heavy weight to carry, and there were no past things to think about, or any stuff to mull over, or things to fret with, fight with, argue about. It is all gone. It is all gone. You could be so free. You will be free when you want to be. And you aren't when you don't want to be. It's not like, 'Oh I really want to be and it's just not happening for me.' That is a lie. It always happens when you want it. And it never happens when you don't. Aren't your shins bruised with all of these tabernacles that you run into? These shrines to some hurt somewhere? These holy wells of toxic fumes? Wherever you worship, that is what you've got. Jesus said, the day will come when you won't worship in this mountain or that mountain, in this temple or in that temple, but you will worship me in spirit and in truth. It is a spiritual thing that we are doing, not a physical thing.

October 2, 2016
God's Seed

The Gospel as Revealed to Me, Chapter 184. The small Benjamin of Magdala and the two parables on the Kingdom of the Heavens.

Now listen to the parable of how God works in the hearts of men to establish His Kingdom there. Because every heart is a small kingdom of God on the earth. Later, after death, all these small kingdoms will agglomerate into one, immeasurable, holy eternal Kingdom of Heaven.

The Kingdom of God is created in men's hearts by the Divine Sower. He comes to his field - man belongs to God, because every man is initially His - and sows His seed. He then goes to other fields, to other hearts. Days follow the nights and nights the days. The days bring sunshine and rain, in our case rays of divine love and effusion of divine Wisdom speaking to the spirit. The nights bring stars and restful silence: in our case enlightening calls of God and silence for the soul so that it may collect its thoughts and meditate.

The seed, in this course of imperceptible but powerful influence, swells, splits, takes root, sprouts, grows. And all that happens without any help from man. The soil spontaneously produces grass from seeds, the herb becomes strong and supports the rising ear, the ear grows, swells, hardens, becomes golden and perfect when seeding. When it is ripe, the sower comes back and cuts it because the time of perfection has arrived for that seed. It cannot develop any further and so it is harvested.

My word does the same work in hearts. I am referring to the hearts which receive the seed. But it is a slow process. One must not spoil everything by being hasty. How troublesome it is for the little seed to split and take root! Such work is painful also for a hard wild heart. It must open itself, allow people to search it, accept new things and nourish them laboriously, appear different being covered with humble useful things, instead of the fascinating, pompous, useless, exuberant flourishing that covered it previously. It must be satisfied with working humbly for the benefit of the divine Thought, without drawing other people's admiring attention. It must exert all its talent to grow and burst into ear. It must bum with love to become corn. And after overcoming all fears of human opinion, which are so grievous, after toiling, suffering and becoming attached to its new dress, it must be deprived of it by a cruel cut. It must give everything to receive everything. It must be divested to be clad again in Heaven with the stole of sainthood. The life of a sinner who becomes a saint is the longest, most heroic and glorious fight. I tell you.

Not everyone allows God to do his work in their heart and so there aren't that many examples of people who have submitted to that kind of process of letting the seed of God be planted there. And as Jesus said it's a hard job and it's a tough work, it's long and arduous and there are many processes to it. And each soul has to be given time once the seed is planted to have an impetus to grow into the thing that the seed's going to become and it's a patient work.

For some of you we're at the place where the world is not as interesting as it used to be but it still has a great hold on you. And the new life isn't really thoroughly entrenched in your being, sewn into your cells yet so you live between those places and some you are more in the world than in heaven and some are more in heaven then in the world because they have made the journey away from that dark place into light. And all the while he is talking about the love of the seed wanting to become a new seed, wanting to become a full adult plant and then it has to be cut down, cut down and placed where God wants it. If the whole work is for God then the end result is for God and what that work becomes is what God wants so it no longer becomes what you want. It becomes what God wants and the fight right there is between what you want and what God wants and that is sort of the halfway point in the process. As soon as what God wants is what you want you're heading in the right direction, then it's kind of a glorious path.

There is no more resistance, there is no more sitting on the fence, fighting between the two worlds, compromising making sure that worldly people are satisfied with you, making sure that the heavenly beings like you, you're not compromising yourself anymore because it's all about love now. It's all about wanting and giving and serving and giving yourself up totally. I mean I have to reiterate God's purpose here in creating you was to reflect him but you have lots of purposes that aren't that so there's his way which is you are supposed to become another him, not any competition but just one like him, like Jesus was. He became one with God and that was God's design and so we have a lot of other ideas don't we? And that's the problem with the earth--they have a lot of other ideas about who they think they are and what they're supposed to become and what freedoms they think they enjoy which have nothing to do with the purpose they were created for. And as long as people have that kind of thinking they are going to be wild and they won't let this new pattern be burned into them, birthed into them, because that seed going into earth is a burning and it's a regeneration all at the same time. And if you can remember some heavy teachings that you might have gotten, I don't mean where the teaching was hard where it just cut right in, that was a love and a burning and painful all at the same time because it shocked you out of your worldly mind or your complacent mind and opened up a view that you didn't have. A consciousness that you weren't ready for yet and that's the startle that you weren't doing that new consciousness and the consciousness comes in and cuts into you and you are awakened, and now you have an opportunity.

You have a choice, you can go 'shut it right down and scar that thing over' and pretend it didn't happen or you can ponder it, meditate on it and see whether it freed something up in the cutting or freed something up in you to open your sight. Those are the ones where the seed is planted into the receptive soil of a disciple. They become new, they become like they were supposed to become. That is the trajectory into divine beings, into lighted beings just like their father but you have to want it and that's the crux of the matter that is the cross of your matter. Do you lay it on the cross and say do with me whatever your divine will created me for because that's really the truth You were created to be sons and daughters of God, you were created to be another Christ. And then the seed gets planted where this is the truth and you know it and you can water it, you can allow it, because a lot of these processes aren't you they're done by God if you are willing. The acceptance is done by you. The whole growth process of the seed is done by God and that's the problem the acceptance part. We accept only so much change, only so much stretching, only so much jostling and even that whole idea that truth comes into you and jostles you is quite selfish isn't it? God wants truth in you and you go, 'when the truth hits me it's very jostling indeed,' even that attitude itself has a kind of fight and a reaction to God and you are like miffed that God would actually wake you up to be who you really are. It's like having a little attitude towards your alarm, like you're mad at your alarm. Why are you mad at your alarm - you set it. Like being mad at the creator for creating you with the desire to be one with the Creator and you're upset about it because each desire for closeness with the Creator means that something that accumulated on your surface has got to be sanded off. Each time he's talking about these things he always gives you the promise of the heavenly bliss or the promise of the heavenly citizenry who is one with God, who gets the super satisfactions and super love and that should be encouraging. He's constantly doing that.

He's also saying how hard it is because why is it hard because you went away and thought that the awayness, the awayness, was you. It's not you it's just distortion that you got comfortable with and lazy about and he's pulling you back, the love just draws you back like a tractor beam, and you can fight every minute of it, complain and have all kinds of indictments against the process. Or you can just relax and say 'I know I'm becoming myself that's what he wants for me I'm going to become myself finally, I'm going to become myself, I'm going to become another Jesus and Mary.' Some of you have very twisted ideas about personality like what a personality is, what a person is. It's like it has to be very unique and very distinguished and very different and very tough and very gnarly and very defined. What if it's just a ball of light that knows itself? Many, many of the philosophical works and some of the teachers talk destiny that somebody destined to be a great saint or something; you hear their stories in these books stories about people's lives. What does destined mean? It means there's a place for you already predetermined. Now what's predetermined is that you are going to probably go back to God and get some kind of placement, you are destined for that. You are going to go back to God and you can get some sort of placement, there is a placement service in God, it places people based on job experience and if they've mired themselves in selfishness in the world selfishness they've placed themselves in a predicament and if they'd devoted themselves to becoming like their Creator that is another placement service they're placed in different area.

So you can say that its destiny but it's also driven by the wild hand of the person whose hand is on the wheel and that's driven by you. There's a place where the boat needs to go and you're wildly swerving with your hand and when does Jesus' hand overlay your hand and say, "Now let's steady that? And you steady it because you were asked to steady it because his hand is trying to steady you and you steady it and you go "I don't like change that much" and he will say "then don't go away from me" and you go "I didn't know I was causing all the changes and he goes yes you were stay with me, and there won't be a lot of changes. There will just be you know expansion and growth." It's kind of up to you. There are people who are so decided when they come here that they know what they have to do and they're going to do it and you can say that's their destiny but they have a destination they are going to serve they're going to do the will of God they are going to make sure that that happens and they're not going let anything get in their way. You can say that they are destined because they had a destination in mind and they're not going to get distracted and people talk about fate isn't my fate to serve God. No not really that's not fated, it's a decision that was my destination and that's where I'm going. Now some of you the way you're going takes you to a particular place, it takes you to sadness or it takes you to confusion or takes you to more doubt or it takes you to a bunch of fears because of the way that you're handling it. It looks like that's where it's going to go to confusion. You're going to go to troubled mind or you can go to a difficult place or you're going to go to an angry state because of the way that you're handling things and the way your building up your mind whether you're building up your emotions. You are going to head to a particular place, it's up to you but that is not your destiny. Your destiny is to become gods, one with God. Your fate may be that you fated yourself to go somewhere else but it would be up to you. And it is a little bit foolish to let

Jesus plant a seed in you and then you fight the entire time that that seed is growing in you because that seed has a divine nature to it and it has all the elements that God wants in that seed and he is going to take it all the way through the process to where you get harvested in God's crop. But your attitudes and your fears and your worries and your reactions just make it so difficult for it to just go smoothly like he knows a seed can grow from a little sprout into a plant busting up the earth, growing into leaves and taking in the sun, and becoming an ear and becoming food and then getting harvested, that's the process.

Everybody is born and everybody dies, everybody's a seed and born and everybody dies, it's harvested and you have a choice about that that's not your business. That is inevitable so why do you have so many opinions, I have to ask, when the whole plan was already created for you? Why do you have so many ideas when your purpose is to glorify God, that's your purpose. Why do you have so many embittered thoughts and sad thoughts and negative emotions when that was not your purpose? That is not your purpose, that was not created for you, that was not that's God's gift for you to have all those things just to be in his love to be one with him. To come out, have some experience and go back to Him, get some more experience, go back to Him and eventually be something large enough to carry other peoples love and support them just like God does. That's the mission that your love becomes big enough to care for somebody else consistently and guess what you have to do? Practice with babies, very poor at it obviously, look at our parents. None of them did hardly any good. Are they any good like to love a baby without having a bunch of selfishness. That was our practice so God set it up that we have practice here, we get to practice loving something without being negative and you can see that very few humans know how to do this. Everyone suffered it, the inconsistency, the negativity of your parents because they were just miserably human and they did not know who they are, they did not know or they did not want to know. But your job is to become divine. You already are but you forgot that you are and what is a divine being do? It shines, it loves, it cares and it is active and all those things. A divine being doesn't have moods, it doesn't have negative feelings. That's stupid, it's just stupid. Why don't you just take poop and smear it on yourself, that's exactly what it is.

Jesus says 'Don't mess with that' and you say 'Well that's what I do. I just smear my negative emotions all over myself and anybody else who will allow me to spread it on them.' And that's the darkness, that's not divine, that's not Gods plan. That's not what God wanted for anyone. That's what the darkness wanted and that's what you think is your nature. Many of you still think that having those moods you have a divine right to be entitled to have a mood, you still do want to keep having them after of thousands of words from me and thousands of occasions of me putting them down and you still do them. I mean thousands, this is thousands and let me ask you how I have gotten through to you if I have to say something a thousand times and you still don't know what I'm talking about or you still don't want to know or you still want to do it. Let's reflect for second, can you have some compassion on parents who were not able to do what you can't do either? Couldn't you just have compassion on them because it must be very hard of the planet for people to be all love and not reactive and to be kind and to be thoughtful and to be energized and to be light giving. It must be very hard but certainly very hard for some of you, so why don't you have compassion on the others who are doing the same as you. Why would you think that you were so much better than the people that you're not better than? That's just math but that wasn't God's will you see?

God wanted you to be whole, happy and peaceful and alive with light and love. That's your nature, that is your nature. That's not something that you get to buy if you make enough money you get to buy that. No, you already have it and you forgot. You covered it over with a density and tried to forget it and actually successfully forgot. The whole process of the path is the light burgeons within you with the new and pushes out the puss of your bad moods and then you want to clean them up, you want to scrape them off and put them in the fire each time. But it's a very slow process as you can see, it doesn't have to be. You could decide that's the end of it. We're done with that, I'm going to be positive and in my pain I'm going to be positive and in my suffering the hardship of the tearing of the old pattern with this new dedication that's going hurt. I'm to going to do it anyway. It's going to hurt when that little seed has to push up out of the soil, that hurts but that's life and some of you say, 'It's heavy oh okay that's alright' then you just fall right back down. How about, I'm going to be strong, I'm going to be faithful, I'm to be dedicated, I'm going to push on through, I'm going to break on through my negative patterns to the positive, I'm going to stay that way. The heroes of love do it, the weak just like your parents did not, could not, would not do it. I'm going to ask you if you want to be like them. You have so much criticism for them, you have so much intolerance for them, you have so much hostility towards them, you have so much faithfulness to them is that why you're faithful because secretly you know you're like them or have you left your kin and your country and come over to the other side? The key part of this in Jesus' words is almost none of this process can you do yourself. The seed has its own power given by God, the seed knows what it has to do. All your power is in the blocking of the divine energy that is going to do this thing if you do not block it. It will do its thing, it will love, it will serve, will give, it will be devotionally worshipful of God by its own nature. It has to be it was created like that.

You are the blockers, that's the only bad expense of your energy is to block it and I have to say you're pretty successful and I'm not just flattering you. I'm looking at the soul and the soul says 'Yeah that's our nature and the heads saying, I don't know why there's such a divide between these two things?' I know why, don't you know why? Because you have attitudes, you bought into the attitude program. Jesus didn't have an attitude about all the work he had to do, about all the ways that people persecuted him or the ways that people insulted him or the ways that people didn't have faith in him, he didn't have an attitude about it, it's just part of the process which is part of the process. He came to show you that you're no different than him and he's no different than you in his need to be connected to the Father and that you're no different than the possibility of being that free of this old stuff as he was that free of this old stuff. And I want to remind you of the thing that he did. He took your stuff and burdened himself with it so that you don't have to carry it and I think you forgot about that. I think you perennially forget that he carried that cross for you and paid those sins off for you and I don't know why you keep doing them when he did the work already. Why you're so attached to them? I know you look at me like I'm a foreigner, like I'm an alien, like somebody from another planet talking to you like this I don't understand you. You think I don't understand, you think I don't understand how hard it is. You think he doesn't understand and he doesn't know how hard it is. He not only carried any imperfections he might have had, which he didn't have, he carried all of yours. And you're burdened? You're burdened by your little patch of karma? He carried all of ours and paid it off and forgave it all and then the density of you carrying yours again and re-creating it and then carrying it again is a very big slap in the face to Jesus who obviously you are not grateful to him for forgiving you because you're carrying it yourself. There's got to be some work done on this where you have to ask Jesus, 'Could you free me of all my insecurities and all my things, all my things. Did you previously pay it all off for me before you knew I was doing this?' Ask him some real questions. 'Have you forgiven me for all the future sins I might accomplish' because that's what he said but do you know that? Then you wouldn't hold them, you wouldn't hold onto them anymore. If you knew he previously forgave you for tomorrow's sin and burdened himself with it and bore it and suffered for it and paid it. And you sit there with your thing, whatever your thing is, your anti divine thing, so proud of it, so stuck in it and if you're ashamed of it why don't you get rid of it. I don't hold hot potatoes, do you? They're too hot. You sit there and let it sizzle through your skin, welt and boil. No, are you dense? Get rid of it. And that's the same thing, if you notice that there is something that is not you, that would be all negative things, all negative attitudes and all pompous opinions. If you notice there are any of those in you that are not you, get rid of them, get rid of them. Any fears, worries, any opinions, any dogmas, any criticisms, any indictments, get rid of them They are not you, they are not you. God did not bless those when he created you. God said you were good and that's all garbage, get rid of it. I mean energetically get rid of it, not like 'I wish it would go'(whiney voice), no energetically get rid of it. You rip it out of you and you hand it to him. I know you previously prayed for this, I don't know why I was carrying this, I mean do you wear a terribly foul smelly sweater? I know sometimes you do because you don't smell it, then people say, 'Ooh God you should have that cleaned, right?' But let's say you notice it and people say, 'You're wearing that smelly sweater again.' You get rid of it, get it off you. It is that simple. There are planets where it is that simple, they talk to people like this, 'God you have this thing. Would you get rid of it? Go to the R&R place, infirmary, lie down on the ground and get rid of it, let them work on you. Go to the blessing place, they will put you in the infirmary because you have a bad attitude and in a couple days you'll feel better and you'll come out all shiny and clean and you won't have that anymore.' That's what confession used to be for, that's what communion is supposed to be for here, that's what telling honest things to loving brothers and sisters is supposed to be like, loving community is supposed to be like, where you dump your load and then they burn it. They don't hold it and inventory it, and mark it with a computer number. No they just burn it, and they wash it away. That is what loving people do, they say 'Yeah, I know you skipped and fell and bruised yourself, okay yeah I've done that before, so what? Let's just move on.' When can we do that? Jesus does it every day. Why can't you do it?

I can understand the churches where they tell everybody how wonderful they are and they walk out knowing they have just been lied to. It's one thing if I see your stuff and I say you are a divine being and you know I see you but if I say 'you guys are so beautiful, you are just wonderful.' You walk out like that you are going to say, 'Okay I just got slimed, I just got slimed, somebody just lied to me. Because why am I struggling if I'm so wonderful?' So you have got to feel bad when you walk out of those services, you have to because you just got lied to. And if they rip into you like you are the worst, close to hell and everything else, that is also a lie. Because you are a divine being. That is what's hard about the truth, you know something has to happen. Why don't you ask Jesus for help with this because you are not prepared, you're not prepared to take a really hard knock without being twice as negative as you seem to be already. I would like to see you three days in a row of positivity and I would like to see that once a week. You see I'm not asking that much, you can have four days of shitty. I'm just asking for three days of positivity each week, alright it's a new pattern. You still get the most majority of the other, you know, I'm still giving you that. I like the contrast though, three beautiful days, everyone's going to pick a different day, okay great but at least half of you will be circulating through some good days while the other people are on their four bad days. So everything will be lifting up a little bit like that, see the progress in that that's cool like half of us will be positive at least for three days straight and the other half will have negative days for three days and you will have to suffer that a little bit. But finally what I think would happen is that we would just get tired of being negative, we would just find it stupid, and silly and we would just let it go.

October 9, 2016
Get Close

The Gospel as Revealed to Me, *Chapter 329. In the Market of Alexandroscene.*

"Listen. I have come from very far, but not with the ambition of a usurper or with the violence of a conqueror. I have come to be only the Savior of your souls. Property, wealth, offices, do not seduce Me. They mean nothing to Me and I do not even look at them. Or rather I look at them to pity them, for I feel sorry for them, because they are chains that hold your souls prisoners, preventing them from coming to the One, Eternal, Universal, Holy, Blessed Lord. I look at them and I approach them as if they were the greatest miseries. And I endeavor to rid them of their fascinating but cruel deceit that seduces the sons of man, so that they may use them with justice and holiness, not as cruel weapons that wound and kill men, and first of all the souls of those who do not make a holy use of them.

But I solemnly tell you that it is much easier for Me to cure a deformed body than a perverted soul; it is easier for Me to give light back to blind eyes or health to a dying body, than light to souls and health to diseased spirits. Why? Because man has lost sight of the true purpose of his life and devotes himself to what is transient. Man does not know or does not remember, or although he remembers, he does not want to obey the holy order of the Lord - and I say this also to the Gentiles who are listening to Me - to do Good, which is Good in Rome as in Athens, in Gaul as in Africa, because the moral law exists under every sky, in every religion and in every righteous heart. And religions, from that of God to that of individual morals, say that our better part survives and its destiny in the next life will be according to how it acted on the earth. The aim of man, therefore, is to achieve peace in the next life, not revelry, usury, arrogance, pleasure in this world for a short time, to be paid for with the most dreadful tortures for ever and ever. Well, man does not know, or does not remember, or does not want to remember that truth. If he does not know, he is less guilty. If he does not remember, he is somewhat guilty, because the truth is to be kept alight, like a holy torch, in minds and hearts. But if man does not want to remember it, and when it, shines he closes his eyes not to see it, as he considers it as hateful as the voice of a pedantic rhetor, then his fault is grave, very grave indeed.

And yet God forgives it, if the soul disowns its wrong doing and proposes to pursue, for the rest of its life, man's true purpose, which is the conquest of eternal peace in the Kingdom of the true God. Have you so far followed an evil path? Are you downhearted and are you thinking that it is late to follow the right way? Are you desolate and are you saying: "I knew nothing of all this! And now I am ignorant and I do not know what to do"? No. Do not think that it is the same as with material matters and that it takes a long time and much work to start all over again, but in a holy manner. The bounty of the Eternal True Lord God is such that He will not make you walk back all the way to put you at the junction where, erring, you left the right path for the wrong one. His bounty is such, that from the moment you say: "I want to belong to the Truth", that is, to God, because God is Truth, God, through an entirely spiritual miracle, infuses Wisdom into you, whereby from being ignorant you become possessors of the supernatural Science, like those who have possessed it for years.

Wisdom means to want God, to love God, to cultivate one's soul, to tend to the Kingdom of God, repudiating everything that is flesh - world, Satan. Wisdom means obedience to the Law of God, which is the law of Charity, Obedience, Continence, Honesty. Wisdom means to love God with one's whole being and to love our neighbor as ourselves. Those are the two essential elements to be wise in the

Wisdom of God. And our neighbors are not only those of our own blood, of our race and religion, but all men, whether rich or poor, wise or ignorant."

So the Truth is something that you can want and it's something that you can have if you want it and the blessings of God flow to somebody who wants that. God makes it easy for you to find it if that's what your heart wants. When you don't want it you never find it and you will never get it and you will be in the obscurity of your own darkness. Every moment the choice is there for you, to choose wisdom, God, love, light, truth, or to choose something else. And there is an instructor for each of those classes. The truth has an instructor and the falsehood has an instructor and you go to those classes depending on what you want. Jesus says lots of words for different people and they are all the same teachings, they are just slightly different depending on the nuance of the persons' consciousness, position, distance, closeness from God. Sometimes when you are distant he yells God's law at you so you can get a sense of what is right and wrong, because if you are at a distance you hardly know what's right and wrong anymore. But if you are closer he talks about the benignity of God and God's love and the honesty of obedience and the charity that you can have for yourself, for God, for your neighbor and the charity that you will live in because you are able to handle subtler teachings. Whereas if you are getting shocked out of your material world or shocked out of the darkness of the world, the teachings have to be a little more crude for you. You are not as sensitive, you are not as sensitized to the spirit yet. A person that is sensitive to the Spirit doesn't have to be shocked into anything. They don't have to be given ultimatums, they don't have to be forced because they already consent to good and they are drawn to it, maybe they need a little courage but they are drawn to it already.

They just need encouragement perhaps or they need a little more faith, little more enthusiasm, but they don't need to be shocked into what is right. They don't need, they are not at the conscience stage of development, they are not at that basic level of that's right, that's wrong which is what conscience whispers to you constantly. They are further along the way.

Conscience is something that is given to you as a big guide, you know as a kind of a crude guide. Like this is not good, this is good, this is selfish, this is more heroic, this is going to make you grow, this is going to be hard, this is going to be easy but it's going to destroy you. That's what conscience kind of does, it's sort of a primitive teacher but its still God within you that God placed in there for you to have some kind of stop and go lights. The deeper teachings are a little bit more subtle, like if you love a little, okay that's great. If you love a lot what would that mean, what would it do, what kind of operation is it inside your being to love a little, what is stretched by loving a little? What is stretched by loving a lot? Everything. You know now we are already in the enthusiasm camp and we are getting better and better at things or we are getting deeper and deeper in our understanding of things, or we are allowing a little bit more love than before to flow through us.

I know you are proud of your individuality, I am ashamed of it and you are proud of it. That's great, why am I ashamed of it? Because you have carved out what you speculate as you in your individuality and it's false. It has nothing to do with who you are. If you are created in the image and likeness of God then why are you so different than God? So then what you had to have created to be different than God is wrong. It's darkness, it's ego, it's pride, it's fear, it's a uniqueness that God cannot recognize. I mean if you were the creator of a child and the child acted so different than you that they were just strange, you wouldn't be able to identify them as coming from you, would you? Well that's how God looks at the humans now . He can't even recognize you as somebody he created. And you know the prototype is the Creator, the Creator creates the prototype and then you become that and then you are that. And then you distort and you distort and you cover over and you convince yourself and you rationalize and all of a sudden you are not even recognizable as who you were created to be. Now you are a uniqueness that God has to wonder what are you, what are you exactly? Who are you?

Like Jesus said, unless you do these things that I tell you to do, I will meet you and say I never knew you. So for the ones that are really disciples, you would want to become more and more and more like Jesus and Mary, you know and you have to, to do that, you have to stop having concepts about who they are. You have to get close to them to find out who they are, you can't think about who they are. I don't think that's close, you have to become very close to them, why? Because they have to rub off on you. You can't have somebody rub off on you if you are not close to them. If you stay in your little bubble and you have really high concepts about Jesus and Mary, they can't rub off on you. They can only rub off on you if you are close, and when you are close you can't have any ideas of what you think they are because they are right there. They will tell you. Or they will act the way they act, and say what they say because you will stop having ideas because you will be close. They will be able to provide their side of things without you dreaming it up in your imagination. And they want you that close. I don't know if you want to be that close because it's going to disturb you, because many of you have a lot of ideas. Ideas about who they are, ideas about what they might want, ideas about how they judge and how they perceive you and what they must be thinking, you are guessing. You are just guessing. If you really were honest you can just say you are guessing. You don't know them well enough. I know it, I know it because if you know them well enough, you start to become like Them. When you have a really good friend, you really know each other, you start to become like each other. When you have ideas about a good friend, you have a lot of opinions about the good friend some of them are way too big, some of them are way too small, some of them are so exaggerated, the other person would find it embarrassing if you said it because they would say that's not exactly who I am. You know how you over exaggerate and under exaggerate, you see the bigness of them and you put them down to keep them small for you, you know how people do that? That's what you are doing with Jesus and Mary. And they are saying, 'Hey why do you have any ideas at all? Just get close to me, why don't you just come to me and get close and we will talk and we will share and you will learn me.' That's what he wants. That's what God wants. The only way you are going to stop being a squirrely little mess is to get close to Jesus and Mary. Some of you have the same problem every week, month in month out, like why am I so angry, how do I get over my lethargy, what's happening with my pride? I know I am translating for you - why am I stuck, what am I afraid of, why do I have a small picture of my life, not the big picture, what's convenient about my small picture, why am I tense in my body, what's going on? Every week the same questions honestly and I don't mind. I actually have taught myself that these are not the same questions, these are different questions. I just changed myself to do that. All these questions are different questions. They are new, they are nuances, they are beautiful progresses that I can just examine each week with you. But so distant from Jesus. If you were right close to him, he would say 'Why are you even asking that, that's stupid.' Or 'don't you feel my love' and you would go well I was just working on being a stronger person probably, I think I was working on courage, that's it, I was working on courage. And he would be saying 'I am right next to you why don't you just accept my love?' You would go well I thought I was supposed to work on fortitude and maybe long suffering and maybe a better, stronger commitment to stuff. He would say 'I am right next you, you could just soak up the love' or you could just interpret it into oh I should be more concentrated, is that what you are saying? How about more disciplined, is that what you think, I should be more disciplined? He is saying 'I just want you to open to my love and just be with me.' Well that sounds really good you know but shouldn't I be working harder, getting up a little bit earlier is that what you are saying? More self-discipline is that what you mean? I hope that sounds dense to you because it has to sound dense to him, these questions. "How do I get over my fears' and he will say 'Well give them to me.' You will say 'Well okay that sounds great but when I am afraid like this, how do I lessen my anxiety?'

I mean thank God he has infinite patience. I guess on a more routine day with the apostles he probably says oh shut up, you know something like that would be an appropriate answer, but he didn't do that. He is much kinder than that. He would say to just try and be loving or think of God, not you. Don't think of you, think of God, think of the other person, think what they need, you know he would do that kind of encouraging people to get out of themselves. And then sometimes he would just be frustrated and he would just say would you guys stop grumbling. You complain, complain, complain all the way down the road- it's too muddy, it's too wet, it's dry, it's too hot, we are hungry, we are not getting fed, people are criticizing us bla bla bla bla on and on. He would say just pray, just be in God just deal with it, just deal with it. Or he would actually get pitiable and ask us to help him in his suffering and that was a big shock because we didn't know we could help. But that would take your mind of your selfishness pretty fast. And then you would be thinking all day about how to help him. Well at least we can stop being negative and we can stop complaining, stop bitching and moaning and having problems every five seconds. We could at least do that, we can try to be centered while he is being perfect. We could do that. All the while wondering who are we really? There is perfection in flesh and we are like people from the streets, people from different countries, whatever, people with sick families like everybody else, you know, how do we be like that? Well you have to stop being like you, you have to stop being weird, you have to stop wanting problems. You have to stop enjoying the protection that tension gives you, at least try that one on for size. Stop enjoying the protection that tension gives you, bracing if you like, strong concept. Start giving up the protection that a strong concept gives you, try that. I know, what do you got after that? You have nothing. Hopefully that's going to be great, because if you have enough nothing you are going to have something. You have to get to the point where you have nothing, in order to have something. He who jacks up himself, will be diminished. You can jack up your tension, you can jack up your defenses, then you will become defenseless. You jack up your reliance on God, you will be completely defended and protected, not the other way around, so simple.

October 16, 2016
Holiness

The Gospel as Revealed to Me, Chapter 451. Sermon, in the village close to Hippo, on the duties of husbands and wives and their children.

The first condition to enter the Kingdom of Heaven: "To live without fault."

But can man, a weak creature, live without fault? The flesh, the world and Satan, in continuous ferment of passions, inclinations and hatred squirt out their spray to stain souls, and if Heaven were open only to those who lived without fault ever since the age of reason, very few men would enter Heaven, just as very few are the men who arrive at death without experiencing more or less grave diseases during their lifetime. So? Are the children of God barred from Heaven? And will they have to say: "I have lost it" when an attack of Satan or a storm of the flesh causes them to fall and they see their souls stained? Will there be no more forgiveness for the sinners? Will nothing delete the stain which disfigures the spirit? Do not fear your God with unjust fear. He is a Father and a father always stretches out a hand to his wavering children, he offers help so that they may rise again, he comforts them with kind means so that their dejection may not degenerate into despair, but it may flourish into humility willing to make amends and thus become again pleasing to the Father.

Now. The repentance of the sinner, the good will to make amends, both brought about by true love for the Lord, cleanse the stain of fault and make one worthy of divine forgiveness. And when He Who is speaking to you has completed His mission on the Earth, the most powerful absolution which the Christ will have achieved for you at the cost of His sacrifice, will be added to the absolutions of love, of repentance and of good will. With souls purer than those of newborn babies, much purer, because from the bosoms of those who believe in Me, rivers of living water will spring deterging also the original sin, the first cause of weakness in man, you will be able to aspire to Heaven, to the Kingdom of God, to His Tabernacles. Because the Grace which I am about to restore to you will help you to practice justice which, the more it is practiced, the more it increases the right, that a faultless spirit gives you to enter the joy of the Kingdom of Heaven. Infants will enter Heaven and they will rejoice, because of the beatitude given to them gratuitously, as Heaven is joy. But also adults and old people will enter it, those who have lived, fought, won and who to the snow-white crown of Grace will add the many-colored one of their holy deeds, of their victories over Satan, the world and the flesh, and great, very great will be their beatitude of winners, so great, that man cannot imagine it.

How does one practice justice? How does one gain victory? Through honesty of words and deeds, through charity for one's neighbor. Acknowledging that God is God, not placing the idols of creatures, money, power in the place of the Most Holy God. By giving everybody the place to which they are entitled, without trying to give more or to give less than what is right. He who honors one because he is a friend or a mighty relative and serves him also in evil deeds, is not just. On the contrary, he who harms his neighbor because he has no hope of receiving any kind of profit from him and bears false witness against him on oath, or is bribed to testify against the innocent or to judge partially, not according to justice but according to the profit he may gain with his unfair judgment from the more powerful of the competitors, is not just and vain are his prayers and offers, because they are stained with injustice in the eyes of God.

You can see that what I am telling you is the Decalogue. The word of the Rabbi is always the Decalogue. Because good, justice, glory consist in doing what the Decalogue teaches and orders us to do. There is no other doctrine. In days gone by it was given amid the flashes of lightning on Mount Sinai, now it is given in the refulgence of Mercy, but the Doctrine is the same. It does not change. It cannot change. Many in Israel will say, as an excuse, to justify their lack in holiness, even after the passage of the Savior on the Earth: "I did not have the possibility to follow and listen to Him." But their excuse is of no value. Because the Savior did not come to impose a new Law, but to confirm the first, the only Law, nay, to reconfirm it in its holy plainness, in its perfect simplicity. To reconfirm with love and the promises of the assured love of God what previously was said with severity on one side and listened to with fear on the other.

There are conditions of holiness and they are not owned by you. There are conditions you must meet to receive it, but holiness is a gift. It's something you decide you want but it's not something you create. It's something your alignment imposes upon you. Your closeness to God, your obedience to God, you love for God distributes this holiness to you, based on your capacity, based on how much room you have made for it, how much room you make for it in your actions and your thoughts and your words. It's not something you build up in yourself. You can never take pride in it because then you lose it, because pride is the absence of holiness. But when holiness happens to you, it is a gift you must have opened for and God's grace gives it to you and then fills up to your capacity. Now, the capacity is determined by you. You know, how much can you give of yourself? How much effort do you want to make? How much can you care for another person without thinking about yourself? These are capacities. And of course, they are stretchy. And one must stretch their capacity to gain the capacity where holiness looks like it's holiness versus where holiness looks like an intuition. Like if you have an intuition of holiness, you foresee it. You see that it's possible you think of a meager part of holiness as something that can happen to you. You could express it at some point in the future or it can be in you as an experience at some point, at some level. You have an intuition of holiness. But only if you get out of the way, only if you give over can holiness start filling you. And it fills you to your capacity. So if you have other roomers in your apartment, besides this openness, the holiness can't come in fully. Because it has to be bruised out or moved out by these other conditions. So capacity is up to you. Holiness is something that's given and holiness in a person is a sign that you have loved, a sign that you have some devotion for God, and that you have a willingness for God to start to influence many things in your life. And the degrees of holiness are dependent on how much you hold onto the things that are not God.

You should strive to be holy because you're striving for the death of your ego. Your ego is in opposition to God, always. I haven't seen an ego on the planet that isn't in opposition to God. I would like to find one but that wouldn't be an ego. That would be a soul. The soul is not in opposition to God but the ego is because the ego has to preserve what it has accumulated. It has to preserve the opinions it has already figured out and calculated. And thus, it is not open to the spirit. It's not open to the inspiration and love because it's a self-solidifying force that accumulates around itself and stiffens. That's the definition of ego: an accumulating force forms around itself and stiffens around itself. How can the spirit of God move through something that is stiff? How can the spirit of love move through something that is pretty determinedly decided? So holiness and ego are not in the same country. They're different countries.

And what are the conditions for somebody to be holy? To follow the law, to do what God says, to love and to love. Do you love your neighbor? What if they're irritating? What if they're unenlightened? What if they're selfish? Do you love your neighbor? What if they aren't like you and you can't be proud of them? Do you love your neighbor? What if they're better than you? Do you love your neighbor? What if they're more disciplined, clearer, holier than you? Can you love your neighbor? We find out if you can love your neighbor if you can work next to them without trying to run away or find some other place to work. Admittedly sometimes it's hard to work next to somebody because they have so many ideas it messes up the work. But that's how you love them. You accept them while they're being uncomfortable. You think well of them while they're miserable. That's loving. It's also torture. For somebody to love you when you don't is kind of like torture. But it's the good kind of torture. And God ordered it. You have to do it. You love people even if they don't love themselves. You do it. And it hurts them. They feel hurt by it because they can't love like that. They can't love themselves like that. So it makes them uncomfortable, which is good. It's a good thing.

As soon as you own holiness as yours, you fall. But you still have to strive to be holy. So what we're asking you to be is to be pure. Holiness is God: God's light, God's love, God's peace. You don't own that, that's not yours. You get it to fill you. It's still God's. But as it fills you, you become more like God. So you're not your own anymore. You become an instrument through holiness. Whatever holy does, holy does things. Holy blesses. Holy shines. Holy works hard. Holy is enthusiastic. But you don't own that. But you should be feeling blessed if it is moving through you, but not to your credit. Only the giving over is to your credit. The filling up is not to your credit. The giving over is to your credit. But again, Jesus would say, if you did what you were supposed to do, why should you be complimented? If you become holy, there is no compliment for you. That was what God designed for a human being when God made them, that they be holy, that they be perfect, that they walk with him. You get no credit for being normal. But you do get all the credit for your abnormalities. You do get that. Everything different from holiness, you get credit for. You should be proud. That's the only way to be proud, is to be proud of your unholiness.

What is the nature that God thought you should have when God made you? That is blessed. What is your nature that you did to yourself, because you had reactions and because your had feelings...so called feelings? Primitive scrapings are your feelings. Primitive scrapings, we'll call them. You had primitive scrapings against things that happened to you and you formed a crust around you that people have to go through that crust to get to you, to reach you, to contact you, to meet you. They have to go through your crust that you formed up.

I know I didn't have a microscopic view of everybody's work yesterday. I know there were pockets of resistance if I want to look at it really carefully. But I don't really care about it. It was mostly a non-resistant day where everybody was enthusiastically trying to help. Everybody did. That was neat. That is where we should be heading as a rule, as a normal expression. Nobody is avoiding secretly or successfully avoiding or whatever they are doing. Nobody is having an ego battle with somebody. Maybe some of that was going on inside of you. I'm not going to get my microscope out on this one. It was just happy to get a lot done in a short time with everybody cheerfully contributing. I'm going to be so grateful for that. I'm not going to go scrutinizing about it. And we got a Herculean amount of work done in three hours, two and a half hours. But what if we were picking who we wanted to work with and who we didn't want to work with? And what if we really scoped out the jobs on what is the easy stuff and what is the hard stuff? That would have taken three and a half hours or four hours. What if we talked all day through the work? That would have taken us seven hours to do just what we did. I've watched this happen before so I do know how it works: the more talk the less work, the more differences you start to feel with each other, the tug of wars -- unspoken, sophisticated, unspoken tug of wars. But that slows everything down. And there wasn't much of that happening which is, to me, shocking. For me, shocking and lovely.

But if you break down that word 'holy,' it is whole. Everything that's out is like everything that's in. And everything that's in is like everything that's out. There's no hidden parts that are shameful. There are no hidden parts that are to be sequestered away from your own consciousness so that you don't look at them, so you put up a good front, so you don't know those things are happening. Because that's not whole, thus it's not holy. Integral all the way through, same, same. Out, in, same, same. That's a person who's starting on the road to holiness. Holiness is starting to stay within them for longer periods of the day, doing it's magical work of transformation of the cells. Because holiness has to be in you for a little bit of time for the light to ignite. And it has to be in there for quite some time for that light to get strong. And in some of you the light is not strong, even though you pride yourself of having come into the Illumination. But I see you haven't done very much work on being light: being the light of the world, being the light of your house, being the light of your job, being the light of your car. Not so much work on that yet. Like, you're the moody one in your car. You're the moody one at work. Well, moods and light, no, no. They don't go together. There's no place where they marry. They're not married. They can never be married. Mood and light, never married. Always divorced. They're always divorced.

Pray for it. Pray that it stay within you, that it come within you, that Jesus gives it to you and God gives it to you. And stay in there and don't do anything to eject it. You don't do one thing to eject it, so that it can do its work and it can transform you. It has its own intelligence so it's going to change you, change your cells, change your direction, and change what you care about over time. It has to because it's God. It is one of those attributes of God that enters humans. It was there to begin with but we evacuated it, we evicted it. And now the path is to get back in there, into the whole organism, not just into your dream world or into your ideology. You can write an ideology in a second, like your utopia experience, what you think is the most ideal you. You can write a paper. But that's not what you do. That's just an idea in your head – ideology, the study of ideas.

We're talking about practice now. We're talking about: does the kingdom of God practice itself in you? Does the kingdom of God practice through you? Is the kingdom of God expressing through you? How long can you handle it? How many minutes can you handle it? A little bit more, a couple more each day is progress. A couple more minutes per day would be progress, until I call you somebody that's kind of consistent. I don't know what word I'd use. Consistency might come up right away. I use operative words instead of ideology words. Operative words: what are you putting into practice? What's actually happening? What is functioning through you? So they're practical things. They're things you can grasp. They're not things you can put in the pie shaped thing in your head.

What do you actually do? Do you hold the presence of God or does the presence of God hold you? Does the presence of God work through you? Do you let it? Can you let it? Do you have the guts to let it? Do you have the guts for things to die in you as the presence of holiness happens to you? See, it takes guts to let happiness happen. It does. Why? Because everything is going to be destroyed. Everything you thought you knew is going to vanish as holiness comes upon you. Now, I didn't say holier than thou. That's not holiness. You think you're holier than somebody? No. I hope we're as holy as everyone else is. That's what I hope, because holiness is one thing. I hope we're all one. There's one holiness. It's God's. You don't own it. There's no way you can own that. There's no way you can take credit for it because it's something that happens through you that you only allow, you don't create. And I'm smacking the ego with this, because there's lots of ego. If there wasn't any ego, I'd be smacking air. But because I feel the impact of the smack, I know I'm smacking ego. Have you ever smacked air? There's nothing there. You just go, why am I smacking air? That looks stupid. You feel like an idiot smacking air. But I don't usually smack things that aren't actually there. So I'm smacking ego. I mean, you do it once and you don't do it again. If it's not there, just to be practical. 'Oh there's nothing there. I better stop smacking. There's nothing there.' But when I smack and I feel boom - you know, I feel the force - then I know I got it. And you could say I was just guessing, but it was a good guess.

So pray for holiness and Jesus might give it to you. They didn't know what he was doing in the Gospel. He was doing something to them that they didn't know what he was doing, until after. And that's holiness. That's how that happens. Something happens to you. You're lifted up or dropped down on your knees, and that's holiness too. And something happened to you, which you didn't do but you know something happened. And you're different. And you have to submit to it. They couldn't do it themselves. They couldn't wash their own feet, that wouldn't be the same. It's something that's done to you, for you, that you cannot concoct with your little brain. I know, most of you have huge brains. I didn't mean to insult them, not intentionally.

The soul looks at your brain as a tool and not a very sharp one at that. Your brain is the soul's tool, not a good tool, not very sharp. And when it tries to sharpen it, there's always a reaction. When your soul tries to enlighten your brain, you react. But what's the soul doing? It's trying to make you holy. And the brains going, 'I've got to get a grip on this.' The soul says, "No you don't. Stop gripping. I'll take care of it. I'll tell you. I'll inform you whatever you need to know and whatever you need to say." And your ego says, "Well that leaves me out in the wash here. I don't even know what's going to be next." And your soul says "Good. You shouldn't know until I inform you."

It's a lot easier than what I say. I have to go through all of your things, so it's a lot of explanation. It's mainly just open up. The ability is going to be given to you if you get out of the way to be holy. And don't even think about what that means, because you don't need to know what it's going to express like. But I have a feeling it's going to be alive. Let's start with that. I'll give you a little clue. It'll be more life than you're used to. That's holiness. More life than you're used to. Let's use that as a working operational definition of healing, more life than you're used to. That's the beginning of holiness. What are you going to do with more life than you're used to? Who knows? Why take the risk?

October 23, 2016
Two Mothers

Poem of the Man-God Ch. 417. In a Little Village of the Decapolis. Parable of the Sculptor.

Jesus takes as a starting point the question asked by a man: "Master, our Law seems to point out as struck by God those who were born wretched, in fact He forbids them to serve at the altar. How can they be guilty? Would it not be fair to consider guilty their parents who give birth to wretched sons? Mothers in particular? And how are we to behave with those born unfortunate?"

"Listen. A great perfect sculptor one day carved a statue and he made such a perfect job, that he was pleased and he said: "I want the Earth to be full of such marvels". But by himself he could not cope with such a task. He therefore called other people to help him and said to them: "On this model make for me one thousand, ten thousand statues equally perfect. I will then give them the final touch, instilling expression into their features". But his assistants were not capable of so much, because besides being much inferior to their master in skill, they had become somewhat intoxicated eating of a fruit, the juice of which brings about delirium and dullness. The sculptor then gave them some moulds and said: "Mould the material in them; it will be a perfect work and I will complete it, enlivening it with a final touch". And the assistants set down to work.

But the sculptor had a great enemy. A personal enemy and the enemy of his assistants, and he tried with every means to make the sculptor cut a poor figure and rouse disagreement between him and his assistants. Thus he attacked their work with his cunning, altering the material to be poured into the molds, or reducing the fire, or praising the assistants exaggeratedly. It thus happened that the ruler of the world, in an effort to prevent as far as possible the work from going out in imperfect copies, imposed heavy sanctions on those models issued in an imperfect state. And one of the sanctions was that such models could not be displayed in the House of God, where everything must be, or ought to be perfect. I say: ought to be, because it is not so. Even if appearances are good, facts are not so. Those present in the House of God seem faultless, but the eye of God discovers the gravest faults in them. The faults which are in their hearts.

Oh! the heart! It is with the heart that one serves God; indeed: it is with the heart. It is not necessary, neither is it enough to have clear eyes and perfect hearing, harmonic voice, beautiful limbs, to sing the praises pleasing to God. It is not essential or sufficient to have beautiful clean and scented garments. The spirit is to be pure and perfect, harmonic and well shaped in sight, hearing, voice, in spiritual forms, and these are to be adorned with purity; that is the beautiful clean dress scented with charity: that is the oil saturated with essence that God likes.

And what kind of charity would be the attitude of a man, who being happy and seeing an unhappy fellow, should despise him and hate him? On the contrary, double and treble charity is to be given to those who, although not guilty, were born poor wretches. Wretchedness is a pain that gives merit to those who bear it and to those who, united with the victims, suffer seeing them bear it out of love of relationship, and perhaps they strike their chests thinking: "I am the cause of such pain through my vices". And it must never become the cause of spiritual fault in those who see it. It becomes a fault if it becomes anti-charity. So I say to you: "Never be without charity towards your neighbor. Was he born a poor wretch? Love him because he endures a great pain. Did he become unhappy through his own fault? Love him because his fault has already become a punishment. Is he the parent of a wretch born such or who became such? Love him because there is no deeper sorrow than the grief of a parent struck in *his child. Is it a mother who has given birth to a monster? Love her because she is literally crushed by such grief, which she considers the most inhuman. It is inhuman".*

But even deeper is the grief of a woman who is the mother of a son, who is a monster in his soul, as she realizes that she has given birth to a demon dangerous for the Earth, for the Fatherland, for the Family, for friends. Oh! the poor mother of a cruel, vile son, of a murderer, of a traitor, of a thief, of a corrupt man, dare not even raise her forehead! Well. I say to you: Love those mothers also, the most unhappy ones. Those who in history will be known as the mothers of murderers, of traitors.

Everywhere the Earth has heard the weeping of mothers whose hearts were broken because of the cruel death of their sons. From Eve onwards how many mothers have felt their bowels being lacerated more painfully than in labor, nay, they felt their bowels and their hearts being torn off by a cruel hand, in the presence of their sons murdered, tortured, martyred by men, and they howled their pangs, throwing themselves with the frenzy of convulsive sorrowful love on the corpses which could not hear them any longer, neither could they be warmed by their warmth, nor could they say with a look, a gesture, since they could not do so with their lips: "Mother I can hear you".

And yet I tell you that the Earth has not yet heard the cry and has not collected the tears of the most holy Mother and of the most unhappy one among all those who will be remembered for ever by man: the Mother of the Killed Redeemer and the mother of the man who will be His traitor. Those two mothers, martyrs in different ways, will be heard mourning miles apart, and the innocent and holy Mother, the most innocent, the Innocent Mother of the Innocent, will be the one Who will say to Her far away sister, the martyr of a son more cruel than anything on the Earth: "Sister, I love you."

Love to be worthy of that Woman who will love everybody and on behalf of everybody. It is love that will save the Earth."

You may not have all the answers to these questions like why people are assigned to particular sufferings, why people are born with particular conditions. Why people have children that are handicapped in some way? It's better to love instead of trying to figure it out. It's simpler just to love: Love God for the diversity, love God for all the possibilities of human expression – even if it's deformed, even if it's disabled, even if it's challenging. And those are great challenges, to have a kid that's not able to handle things. I mean, it's a great weight of responsibility.

And do you know all the good things that'll come from that? Do you know all the lessons and the learning that'll happen from having to suffer something? You could say outrightly that that would be hard. You would be right. But, because people can choose, people often don't choose well, and some of our children have chosen really terrible choices and you have to watch them go off and do what they do because they have the rights that anybody has to choose good and evil, to choose a selfish life, a not challenged life, you know, to not take any opportunities, to not stretch themselves, to not discipline themselves, to take the easy way. If you've had kids, you know that children do this. And you suffer because you can see that they didn't develop. You can see that they didn't challenge themselves and they could have grown, they could have been wonderful, and they weren't. They didn't want to be. They didn't choose that. And you have to love them.

Is it the parent's fault? Sometimes, yes; sometimes no. But it's too complicated to figure out because every soul can make decisions and, after the age of reason – which could be 6 or 7 – that soul is starting to make decisions like, whether they don't want to put out an effort. And that turns into this massive, lazy indulgence later. And, you know, the parents might be goading them not to do that, 'Don't do that. Like, work harder, discipline yourself,' and the kid doesn't listen. They don't want to listen. They're pretending to be individuals, and they grow up with these faults that they didn't overcome. That's not the parents' fault anymore. That's the kid's fault.

And so, it's hard to figure out how these things come to be and the many, many, many, many decisions are made along the way that you forgot, that you probably noticed in friends and family – that they made decisions, and they just started to accumulate, and they built up into a mountain of decisions, and then they called that themselves. They decided that that was them but it actually was just a mountain of just bad decisions.

That's the falseness of a human being that they think that all of those bad decisions, with all the scarring that builds up around those bad decisions, they think that that's them. They're pretty convinced that, 'This is me. This is me surviving my scars, my wounds, and my bad decisions,' when actually, after a hundred successive peelings, you might get to the place where you could say that is you. You might, if you had any courage, you'd peel and peel and peel and peel and peel until you find the kernel that could not be peeled any deeper – that could not be reduced, that element that cannot be reduced further – and that's God.

But many of you are still very convinced that all of these successive secretions, this build up of plaque, you might say, is you. And it's easy, like this man, to say, 'Well, is it the kid's fault that they're born deformed? Is it the parent's fault that they're born deformed?' What if it's nobody's fault and it's a challenge to the kid and the parents to stretch you? Maybe you're not a very great lover, you only love what's easy and convenient. But your kid's not easy and convenient. So what does it do? It has to drag love out of you or you don't love and the kid gets worse.

How do you love yourself when you notice your faults? Just get tired, sad, depressed, just lie down, go to sleep? Or do you take really decisive action, peeling those off, stripping them away until you get down to the essence of who you really are? And who is that anyway? It's probably nothing you're going to be proud of, because all that you're proud of is the thing that you're not right now. You're proud of all the stuff you built up but you don't know what pride in the Father is yet. You only know proud in all the stuff you built up and all your defenses. Because that's the only thing negative pride has for itself.

The ones that love their neighbor are like these two mothers. They love each other. The Mother's love is perfect and pure and she loves the most hardened basket case – the one that is most ashamed to be on the Earth – the mother of the traitor. The one who hates herself because she spawned a freaking demon monster. She's not a monster but that's what she raised. That's what he came in as and that's what he persisted in. He did not want to change that.

She loved him and also was ashamed of him. Mother Mary loved him and was ashamed of him. She loved her Son and was not ashamed of Him, and these two tortured women – the most tortured women – loved each other, because each one had a part to play. Each one had to fulfill a Godly mission. Each one was blessed in their own way.

How do you stay loving of God when you could blame God for your son? 'Why did God give me this traitor to raise? Why did God give me a demon to raise?' You really don't know why. I mean, there's no way to know why. There's a way to handle it in purity and humility, just do the best you can. You do the best you can in a situation like that, and the grace is for you, if your heart's open, even though it's tortured by this creature you raised. And you know families where they've raised a murderer. He's a murderer. I mean, there's millions of murderers. So then, you're like Eve. Eve's first child – murderer. I mean, right out of the stocks, out of the purity of the garden, murderer. And she's required to love him because she has to.

Is it her fault? A little bit, because she went to malice and the malice was born from her. So there's a little connection, but is she any longer in malice? No. When Cain was murdering, Eve was already in great sorrow before, for being thrown out of the Edenic place. She's already in sorrow, but she had the karma coming from the sin, and there is the son, and Adam isn't happy about it either. His own son is a murderer. It's too complicated to figure out what causes what. It's kind of God's department. But a humble person just takes their experience that they're given and deals with it in a loving way, in a conscientious way, in a faithful way, in a caring way, in an effortful way, in a disciplined way. If you have time to sit around and wonder why this is happening to you, then you have time to be resentful. Because why would you wonder? Just do the best that you can given the thing you're given.

Don't take any thought for, 'Oh, this shouldn't be happening to me,' because then you're angry. Now you're angry. And, if you're angry, your heart's not open. And, if your heart's not open, you're not doing what you're supposed to be doing: Well, probably learning, probably practicing love, and getting better at it, and growing closer and closer to God. These are the things you could be doing if you weren't mad and if you weren't reacting, and if you weren't stalling and waiting to figure it out – because that's a waiting process to figure anything out. The guy comes from a question with Jesus, trying to figure it all out. He's getting, 'Love your neighbor.' That's the answer. Because he's looking for where the wrong is, isn't he? He's looking for whether the kid's wrong, whether the parent's are wrong, whether God's wrong; always it goes back to whether God made a mistake creating suffering. Well God doesn't create death, suffering, or disease. God has no part with those except God allows the humans to create that and the demons to create that so you can get over it - so you can figure it out. Death, disease, and suffering is created by man and demons. So, if you've got any of those, take responsibility.

What Jesus wants you to do is to open your heart, to embrace your life, to embrace your challenge, to embrace your job, to embrace your family, your friends, your children, and your challenges – to embrace it. Not to judge it, not to resist it, not to resent it, not to fight with it - to embrace it as a gift from God and, if you do that, you're going to scoot through your lessons very quickly. You're going to overcome your obstacles really easily, because your heart's in the right place. When your heart's on straight everything works well. I'm not saying it's going to be easy. I mean, it's not easy sometimes. It might be hard but it will go smoothly, and you'll move through, and things won't prolong like you're scared of. You're scared that some suffering will prolong. You're scared that a trial will be too great and last too long. Well, when your heart's open, it doesn't. It's hard and it scoots through when your heart's open. Learn this. Learn it now. Practice now so that, if the pressure gets really great, you already know how to do it. Practice it now while it's seasonally good for you to practice. Practice it now.

If you're humble, you know you can't figure anything out. You know you don't know all the why's and wherefore's and what's going to happen next or why this is all coming up like this now. You don't know. If you're humble, you get it and you stop asking questions. You just go, 'Okay, this is my meal that was served me, I'm eating it. This is my day that it was given to me, I'm going to go through it. This is the work set before me, I'm going to do it. This is really hard. Tomorrow, whoa, it's a breeze.' But you don't know. That's none of your business really. Just do it. Just do it and then you'll be very prepared for whatever challenges or whatever surprises – you'll even be prepared for surprising blessings because your mopey-ness won't allow very much of a blessing yet but, if you had this kind of open anticipation of God blessing you, more could happen for you. More could happen.

If you give, you get more. If you get more, then you give more. If you give more of that, you get more of that. It's just kind of like this rolling, exponential thing, and that can be yours but you have to get out of this attitude of trying to figure stuff out, of trying to tally up the good and the bad of what's happening to you. You have to stop thinking, and just do what's in front of you with a great heart, with a good attitude, with love. Your neighbors are also your challenges. Those are neighbors too. Love them also. Love the friends you don't know and the friends you do know. Love the accomplices that you work with and the ones that are difficult. Those are your neighbors but also your challenges are your neighbor. Love them as well.

Then it won't matter whether it's trying or it isn't trying, whether it's hard or it's easy. It won't matter. And everything's temporary here. When did you have twenty days in a row at work where it was really, really bad? I don't think any of you ever had, nobody's ever talked to me about, 'I had twenty days of terrible work days.' No. You had a couple of really hard days, maybe three, and then it was pretty easy, right? Or pretty relaxed? Or the boss went away or something? There's like a, 'Whoa,' a reprieve. Hardly ever has it been more than three or four days of really, really hard stuff. I've never heard you report it. I've never heard it in the history of my forty years teaching this time. I haven't heard it, so I don't think that's what happens. I think it's tough and then it's easy. And there's probably more okay days then really, really tough days. Add it up. Add it up! So, what do you have to complain about really? Nothing.

October 30, 2016
Patience

1944 Notebooks, October 11, 1944.

"Patience and obedience are two great virtues. Patience brings peace with it; patience brings friendship with God with it, respect for God, charity towards one's neighbors, spiritual and physical health, and heavenly blessings.

The impatient are restless. God, who lets Himself be felt only in the peace of the heart, is not in restlessness. Even a sorrowful heart can be in peace. There is peace when there is resignation. But in the heart becoming stubborn towards the divine will and the blows of ordinary things, there is always effort, suffering, and restlessness.

The idea that being stubborn and not budging, like restive mules, might serve to turn matters, even the humblest ones, in your favor! Why, no, children! Human matters do not bend: they bend you more harshly with the severity of laws or superiors, if you offer resistance. Supernatural matters are more readily modified in the face of your filial and submissive bending, than before arrogant rebelliousness.

The impatient become disrespectful towards God. It is easy for them to pass on to thoughts, acts, and words which should never arise from the heart of children and subjects, in relation to the fatherhood and majesty of God. The impatient are proud. They think they are more just than God and those directing them, and want to act on their own. The impatient arrive at acts of incivility with their neighbors, holding them responsible for delays in getting what they want. The impatient harm their spiritual health, by offending charity towards God and their neighbors; and harm their physical health, for all anger burdens the organism. The impatient, with the dike of their rebellious restlessness, close off the rivers of heavenly blessings.

Do you think you do not deserve to suffer what you are suffering from? Are you perhaps perfect monsters of pride, so perfect to proclaim yourselves to be without sins to expiate? Look back at your past. Do not say, 'I have not killed. I have not stolen.' These are not the only sins deserving punishment. Nor is the person crouching in an entrance hall and then assaulting a passer-by the only one who steals. Oh, people steal in so many ways! And so many things are stolen which are not just money.

So you want to know some of the objects of thievery in addition to money, jewels, and material good? Honor, purity, esteem, health, earnings. And, regarding God, respect, true worship and obedience. Do you see? And I have mentioned only some of them. But many, many acts of thievery are committed by even the man who is apparently most honest! Don't those leading others to despair kill, even if the despairing do not kill themselves? They do. They kill the most select part-the spirit-which in despair separates from God, the origin of every man destined to be born to Heaven, and thus dies. Don't those who remove faith from the hearts of those who are their neighbors commit theft? They do. And yet many by their works and words tear faith away from those who believed in justice and sow either incredulity regarding all faith or a poisonous plant of idolatry! And doesn't he who takes honor and peace away from a woman and denies paternity to the illegitimate son born because of him steal? He does. He commits two acts of theft, and they are among the most serious ones and most condemned by Me. But, in addition....In addition....

Oh, no one is without sin to expiate! Well then, if I have been appeased but the punishment I have wanted to give you here, on earth, which is a loving punishment---for I don't want to punish you in the place where punishment is measured by centuries or eternity, whereas here it is always a fraction of time, whether months or years---why do you at once want to reactivate my sternness by disobeying and showing Me an irate heart because of impatience? Make God your friend, and God will be with you against the enemies which are life events, the consequences of tragedy provoked by you out of blameworthy thoughtlessness in leaving Satan and the lesser satins free to torture the human race.

But if, with the ancient pride of the human race, you want to do as you please, deaf to the heavenly voices seeking your good, if you wish to do so, deaf to the voices of charity and moved by selfish thoughts which I detest, I then say to you, 'Do so. But you shall not avoid what you would have avoided by being resigned to Me. And it will then be useless to call God.'"

We've talked a lot about this and Jesus says it in a slightly different way. We talk about resentment, we talk about holding on, about indicting. He talks about impatience, any irritability, any irateness is an impatience and that is a misread of what's coming to you , it's a misread of your experience. Experience is whatever you are in front of, which you should handle with patience. Whatever is gifted to you, either through the law or through God, you should be handling it with grace and acceptance. The reason you don't is because you are mad, ornery, difficult and stubborn. How many times a day do I feel you thinking that something shouldn't be happening, thinking that something isn't right for you, that you shouldn't have to deal with this or that? That something is too much for you and this is too hard. Those are all the forms of impatience that he is talking about. If something is hard it is either trying to stretch you and teach you something, which you should be graceful about, or it's something you put out that you are getting back and you should be graceful about it. You should accept it because it is exactly what you put out and it's exactly what is coming back. It is interesting this pride that he is talking about where we haven't given very much, we haven't loved very much, we haven't been patient but we expect that everything should go well and we should have really good things in our life and that everything should be smooth. It's so prideful. Why should it be so good in our life when we haven't put out much goodness? That's what he is talking about.

The justice of God is very merciful because you get karma here in a slowed down timezone called Earth when time ekes on 24 hours a day in minutes, seconds, weeks and months, that's what you get here. Imagine if you had to live in eternity for the things that you have done and that there would be no reprieve for those, that's maybe a definition of hell. No reprieve and living out the just results of what you've been putting out. Some of you don't want to know what you are putting out, some of you don't even like it when somebody reflects to you what you have be putting out. Isn't that interesting, not only do you not receive the just rewards of what you put out, you don't even want to know what it is you're putting out? How dense does one get? If I say, 'I don't really want to know what I'm doing, I don't really know what effect it is on other people, I don't really want to know what it means and I'm a little upset when bad things come back to me.' How does that sound? That sounds irresponsible, that sounds like a kid who is just mad that they have to be a kid and not a grown up yet, mad that they have to be dependent, mad that they don't have a lot of money, own their own car and they don't have their own house or apartment, they are just mad. But there's no insight, no self reflection to see that their lot in life is what they created, what they wanted. Of course you want the suffering of your condition, that's called the law of cause and effect. You put it out and you get it back so you must have wanted it. Did you apply for grace? Did you say, 'I want to expiate my sins and I want to be better. And i think all of my suffering has been because of me, not because of you God, but because of me, I would like to pay this off. Also

I would like your grace to lift me up so that I can be different, so I can accept your will.' That would be very different for most of you to think like that.

Most of you are wanting to be accepted for the sins you are living out, as long as you don't get to know that. We want the acceptance without knowing the thing that you are paying off. Well the only reason you are paying it off is because you put it out. If you are confused then you weren't listening. That's what confusion is, it means you didn't listen and probably didn't ask, then confusion. It's the Law that you don't want to know then you won't know. You won't even be confident in what you are doing because you didn't hear anything, because you didn't want to know. You live by the Law or you live by grace and most of you are in and out of that - into the Law into grace, into the Law into grace, all the time. Jesus as a way for you to be different but you have to listen and you have to have all the parts of you listen, all the parts of you. Most of you are divided all up in pieces so you have three obedient pieces and seven disobedient pieces. That's kind of how you live which makes for a big mess, doesn't it? It makes for an impatient, stubborn mess. Does all of you listen or just part of you, or do you listen to one truth but you can't handle the others, one direction you will follow but the others you won't follow? This is called the stubborn race of human beings, they aren't the angels yet, they aren't the servants of God, they aren't the disciples yet, they are the stubborn ones. They do what they want and they do some of this and some of that, a little of this and a little of that based on their whims, based on their ego, based on their courage and their willingness to die to the old. Many of you are holding on for dear life to the old, I mean for dear life. There is no life in the old. There is only life in faith in what you are going to become, that's where the life is. Because that's the only place you are going to get to that is through grace. You are only going to get to that life through grace not by will, not by stubbornness, not by pushing and shoving, but by grace.

Once you are humble enough about your sins Jesus can give you the lift. There is no lift when you are willing it, you can't be lifted when you're holding on or when you are orchestrating it in your own ego. Every sermon is the same, I'm pointing out the resistance and pointing out the benefit of not resisting, every sermon is the same - here's the love, here's the grace, here's the resistance and pride and willfulness, here's the grace and the love. What are you picking, what are you choosing? One way you are not going to be able to see ahead, the other way you are always going to be able to see ahead. If your pride needs to see ahead, you are going to stay under the Law so you can always predict what happens. When you are under grace you cannot predict it because you are in a world which you can't see which is run by God, not you. Then you will be led, you will be drawn, you will be graced into things that you can't picture in your brain, your little brain. Under the Law you can picture everything limited because you are limited then and you can always predict events and control them with your ego. You make sure you don't do this and you don't do that, don't give this don't give that, or don't get this experience or that experience, that's what under the Law means. A limited being who still thinks it's a physical body that's under the Law. But under grace you have light and with light you can see, not that stuff you've been looking at, you can start to really see. And you don't need to see ahead because you're in the present moment. The fearful want to look ahead, the fearful want to calculate their gain, they want to predict their future so that they can stay comfortably in the Law while they arrive in their future. But that is not what Jesus says, "I'm going to lead you to a place that's of promise." In other words, that alone should be inspiring, it's going to be a promising place, I'm going to lead you to a promising place, it's going to be a promising land. It's going to be promising, it's going to be uplifting, better, it's going to be more joyful, a land flowing with milk and honey. He gave that to them because they are so dense they have to think about physical things like honey and nectar and food flowing out of trees and stuff; they were dense which is what you guys are.

I have to say to you that that kingdom, that promised place is better. I have to keep saying that's better. Why? Because you didn't go there yet. I wouldn't have to say it to people who are there already, I wouldn't say, 'Hey, its better. I would say hey we're here. What do we do now?' I can't say that with you guys, not yet, I can't because we're not their yet. We are still living, laboring in the desert under the Law. Impatiently, as Jesus describes, irritatedly, finicky, persnickedly. Boils on the intestines, you name it. That's not what he wants, He wants you to be where He is, that's His prayer. He actually knows how to take you there if you weren't so sluggish, so holding onto so many things. You know you guys should really evaluate how many things you are holding onto because I see hundreds of them that you are holding onto, hundreds. I'm not shaming you I'm just saying that weight that you carry of all those attachments keeps you from lifting of the ground into grace, it keeps you from doing that. It makes you dense and what can he do through a dense medium? What spirit can move through something dense, I ask you? When you have a really primitive transformer that can only handle crusty electricity, what could go through that? Hardly anything, it's all staticky, shaky and all intermittant. That's just in the electrical world. What about a soul who is always scared and always angry and always ready to be irritated? What kind of movement of power can move from God through that kind of a being who likes irritations, cautions, worries, fears, anger. What could move through that? If you are an instrument for God how could that help, if you had all that stuff? It's plaque in the pipes, the pipe and the hose, there is a little trickle coming through, those are those irritations, those opinions, those ideas, those self concept things that you think you know yourself. You don't know yourself.

Anything I say you can probably take this to the Master. I don't think you know yourself because if you think you do then you are acting funny. If what you are doing is what you know of yourself it's foreign to God, its' not how God made you. What you think of yourself isn't you. I can see it because you are not functioning the way God would have made you. You have too many thoughts, too many opinions, too much irritation and pride, too much stubbornness, too many fears. Those are not you, not a one of them is you. It's never been you, it's not just new revelation, none of those have ever been you. So isn't that the bulk of what you have been experiencing so then the bulk isn't you? It has to be something else, just do the logic, something that you don't know yet is you and you don't have the guts yet to find out. Faith, guts, trust, love, you don't have any of those to let go of these false things and find out who you really are. I don't want any of you to give any attention to these false things, they don't deserve it, they are false and need no attention at all. They need to be removed, they need to be let go of, they need to be burned. So I am not asking you to do what you think I'm asking you to do, by thinking about how bad your badnesses are, I don't care about them, get rid of them. You're thinking about them because you are trying to keep them, I'm not thinking about them because I don't want you to have them.

There is a difference between you and me, I am positive and so far you are not. Underneath all that crap you are positive, that's what I would like to emphasize. That's what I would like to magnify, the Lord in you, which is not how you live. Magnify the Lord with your actions, magnify the

Lord with your feelings, you do not, not yet, hardly ever. But that's what I want you to do, the good in you, the God in you, the soul, not this bullshit that you attend to. You are not courageous yet, you have no juice, you have no spine about this yet, and I fear that you are greatly weakened by this condition you're in, this malaise. You are not strong, inside yeah but it's buried, buried amidst all your irritabilities, all your finickiness. We used to have this thing where I would insult people because they were delicately balanced and that was a great insult. Some of you are prideful about that, like 'I'm pretty delicate and I'm delicately balanced and I need a wide birth, people shouldn't get close even somebody's air as they walk by could like disturb me.' Basically, translation - irritable, unstable, not knowing who they, not aware of their center, God center, they have no idea who they are they are delicately balanced. High maintenance, the whole thing, what does high maintenance mean? You think it's about foods I guess. No I think it's about having to tiptoe around you because if you say anything you are going to get a reaction. That is high maintenance. You can't even talk to the person because you are going to get blow back on everything, everything that they say is real there is blow back.

Many of you are like that and I know you try to keep it quiet but there is still that energetic blow back even if you don't say anything. I say, 'Why hasn't this changed?' And you say, 'Don't talk to me right now.' Delicately balanced. I know why things don't change in you, I'm asking you so that I notify you, that I see what you are doing and I want you to ask yourself why you don't want to change. You don't have to answer to me. You have to answer to your soul. Why is your soul in there imprisoned by your lethargy? Why? Why are you resisting transformation when it will actually make you feel better? Why are you doing that? I know why and you know why. These are rhetorical. You do know why you are being irritable and impatient, stubborn, you know why. Because you think the mediocre life you have is better than the unknown, that's why. You don't know if the unknown if going to be worse so you hang onto the crummy life that you have, that's why, that's the answer. You know the answer. I tell you every week the same answers. I try to say it in different words so we can pretend that I didn't say it before. Maybe this is our masochistic situation where I'm saying, 'Let's be positive' and you say 'No.' And I say, 'Well, you're not being positive,' then you feel bad because I'm telling you that you are not positive, so that is masochism. I like to be tortured while I stay stubbornly in my crap and you tell me I am full of crap, I love that. The definition of masochism is to love torture, to love pain, to hold onto your stuff and somebody says you got stuff, then you feel bad about having stuff, that's masochism. Looks like that's what we have going here. Because if I inspire you to let it go and you don't, and if I say, 'You are freaking holding it' you say, 'Yeah I am and now you're making me feel bad.' So then maybe you need and like to feel bad. Do you want me to lie to you that most of you are transformed into beings of light with no stubbornness or irritability or impatience. (laughing) I can see that, you are ready to serve like crazy, you are as shiny as light. Okay, do you love that? Do you like the lying function? That's lying, I would have to lie to you and some of the Leo's are going, 'Well no I think that's right.' But I have news for you I don't think I would be able to say that without a little tongue and cheek.

What can motivate a human being? I mean Jesus had this much, a thousand times what I have, how to motivate people to trust in God to let go of their old life, to let go of their old idea of who they think they are. You know I criticize you for not knowing yourself I thought that would be enough if you realized you don't, and then you would let it go, but you are so busy pretending that you know and I say you don't know and then you are going to argue with me in your head. Hmm, what do you do? I mean you guys are a slice of life, you are, you are a slice of the seven billion you really are. In a lot of ways you are not super less worldly than some, a little less worldly than some, not super less worldly because you are still holding on to your impatience, okay? That is for sure, so how many times a day do you get touchy about what somebody says and the way they say it? Or it's like you are a little but miffed. Then you're impatient, that's the definition right there. Did it happen today? Did it happen yesterday? Yeah, one honest person told me it happened yesterday, okay. Yesterday was great I guess. These are honestys that I appreciate and it's seldom, so I'm shocked at the same time. Jesus says that when you say that you see, then you don't. That's what he said, I mean that's a weird thing to say isn't it? When you say that you see, he said it to the Pharisees, and there's a bunch of Pharisees inside you. So when you say that you see, you don't, when you say that you know, you don't. What do you know? You don't even know your fears yet? I don't want you to, but you don't even know them yet.

I want you to know the love, I want you to know the light, I want you to know your soul. We are really not doing well with that because I can see you are not acting like your soul and yes, does it glimpse through in a moment by moment day? Yeah. Is it consistent throughout the day? Hardly ever, hardly ever. What are you going to do when really hard things happen, when you can't even stay tuned to it in this easy time. And that's not the only motivation, you should have the motivation to get over it just because it is not close to God yet, just for that reason alone. It's not close to God when you are still in your angstyness, it's not close. Or when you have no clue what you're doing or who you are, that's not close to God, that's not close to God. When you are still trying to prove to God that you are a worthy individual and different. Is that what God wanted, that's how God created you? He wanted you so distinct from everyone else but you would just be like better. Do you think the Creator has that in mind for a human being that they would be so distinguished and so better that they'd be lofty and different from their brothers and sisters? A divine being would have that attitude in creating you and I.

You see that is a bad cultivation, it's completely contrary to God. We have a lot of work to do and I say 'we' in a generous way. I am including you in my work, that's the generosity. I want you to be worthy of it. Because I don't do what you do and you don't do what I do yet but I am still including you. You don't listen and obey, you don't even want to know, because you don't ask because then you'll have to do it. Because you don't want to obey, because you don't trust because you're holding on, you know because of all of that. I don't do that but you do. It's lonely, Jesus' disciples are lonely, there are very few of them. It's not personal, it's not all emotional. And you could be with us but you would have to let go, you would have to let go of your puny little lives and your puny little fears and your irritations, you would have to let it go. And you would be very dynamic and you would be very helpful and don't you think Jesus wants that, Mary wants that? And I don't know if you do. Your head says one thing and your body language and your affective energy says another thing. Do you have no more attitude problems, God says jump and you jump, God says sit and you sit, God says go and you go, you have no resistance at all, no plans you don't have a plan? God has a plan and you just do what he says, you see what I mean?

You're not there yet, you're not there yet. I'm not shaming you I'm saying there is no reason why you can't be there yet. There is no reason at all with all these thousands and thousands of teachings you've had, the disciples had way less than you, the disciples got way less than you. With that many teachings you should already be shiny beings of light. Anyway. I guess we'll just hope, you know you could just ask inside, am I attached to stuff? At least do that, don't even ask what it is just ask if you are. Start with one little thing and then the next question is, should I be? Start really simple like a kid because you guys are you're like babies, spiritual babies. This is not critical but I want you to start where you can, like if you can move your arms then I want you to move your arm. Margaret moves her arms that's about all she can move she can't move anything else but she moves her arms because she can. I want you to find out what you can move and I want you to start moving it. Find out what you can do, I don't mean all this attitude stuff, this attitude thing is disgusting please cut it out but what can you do, really do to help? Just start to help yourself you're not really in a condition to help anyone else but what can you do to help yourself be without problems to be filled with joy and light, what can you do to not have this attitude thing anymore?

I know, the whole theory is you can have this as long as you want and you sure are living that out. You can be like this forever, you can be useless to Jesus forever and also pridefully imagine that you love him at the same time. They don't go together. "This people draw close to me with their lips but their heart is far from me", those are His words. "I never knew you" are not angry words, just facts - you say stuff with your lips but your hearts are not with me. You're not obedient to His heart, no not at all, hardly, Examine it because he is, He has examined it and He's calling you and you say, 'I was already called onto the path' and I don't see that. I am a little bit more rebellious than you, I don't like to say something until it's happening. You like to say all kinds of stuff before it happens. If He called you onto the path when did you get on it? And when did it become whole hearted, inspired, joyful and trusting faith filled process. Because that didn't happen so much, you didn't step on it yet. Your ego likes to think you have been on the path forever. I know you touched into it like a hot potato and then you jumped off to do your own thing, you are not on the path.

You are on the path when you are solidly on the path and you stay there and you trust it and you can't see in front of your face, at least at the beginning, you can't see in front of your face. It's not your job to see in front of your face because that wouldn't be faith would it? It's only trust and faith when you don't know and you do it. I have broken this down more than any teacher has broken anything down for a student in history. I'm not boasting, I'm just Mr. Tedious and it's been received poorly, just poorly. And I know it, I'm not acting depressed, I don't do that, you guys do depression, I don't do that. I'm just telling you the facts - I'm doing my job and you're not, you're not. You call this disciple, I do not. I'm not being rough, I don't call it disciple. Disciple is a trusting, faithful being, it's a yes person to whatever they are given, that's a disciple. I don't see that, I see pick and choose, I see pick and choose, I see stalling, I see hesitation, I see pretending, I see the whole thing. It's a new moon, we should be starting a new process. Possibly we could start the faith, trust, love, get over your crap process, it's a new moon why don't we try that? Stop being a baby, what about that? That's wishful thinking, alright. Let's have communion because we really need Jesus at this point because it's really sad.

November 6, 2016
A Great Attitude

The Gospel as Revealed to Me, *Chapter. 237. The request for labourers for the masses and the parable of the hidden treasure in the field. Mary of Magdala goes to the Holy Mary.*

"Peace to you all who have walked for miles and in dog days to come and hear the Gospel. I solemnly tell you that you are beginning to really understand what the Kingdom of God is, how precious its possession is and how blissful to belong to it. And labour is no longer burdensome for you, as it is for others, because you are ruled by your soul, which says to the flesh: "Rejoice because I am oppressing you. I am doing it for your own happiness. When you are joined to me again, after resurrection, you will love me for crushing you and you will see me as your second savior." Do your souls not say that? Of course they do! You now base your actions on the teaching of the parables I spoke to you some time ago. But I will now give you further light to make you love more and more the Kingdom which awaits you and the value of which cannot be measured.

Listen: A man went by chance into a field to get some mould for his little kitchen garden and while he was digging with some difficulty the very hard soil, he came across a vein of precious metal. What did the man do then? He covered up with earth what he had discovered. He did not mind working a little more, because the discovery justified the work. He then went home, he gathered together all his wealth consisting of money and valuables and he sold the latter to make more money. He then went to the owner of the field and said to him: "I like your field. How much do you want for it?" "I am not selling it" replied the owner. But the man offered larger and larger sums of money disproportionate to the value of the field, and at last he succeeded in convincing the owner who thought: "This man must be mad! And supposing he is, I am going to take advantage of the situation. I will accept the money he offers me. It is not a matter of money-grubbing, because he insists in offering me it. With that money I will be able to buy at least three more fields, and better ones as well". And he sold the field and was sure he had done very good business. But it was the other man who had done a wonderful deal because he gave away what could be stolen by thieves, or lost or used up, and he gained a treasure, which being real and natural, was inexhaustible. It was worth while sacrificing what he had, to make that purchase, although for some time he possessed nothing but the field, because in actual fact he possessed, and for ever, the treasure hidden in it.

You have understood all that and you behave like the man of the parable. Give up transient riches in order to possess the Kingdom of Heaven. Sell them or give them to the fools in the world and let them laugh at you because the world thinks it is foolish to do that. Do that, always behave like that, and your Father Who is in Heaven will rejoice giving you one day your seat in the Kingdom.

There are things that you can value, and the world says that's a good thing to value, and you can value it, too. Status, power, relationships, money, wealth, that kind of thing. They are the things the world tends to value, and they praise people who have them. They think that's a good thing to choose. But valuing something the world can't recognize or doesn't know anything about, that is a very different kind of thing. When you value love, when you value a relationship with God, most people can't really relate to that. Yes, the romantic, cheap love – everybody can relate to that. But real love – the love for the Creator with the created, the love of the creature for the Creator, these are things that people look askance at, they can't even imagine it. Most people can't believe it, they think it's foolish. They think it's stupid. Your love for the blessing of God, that God would bless you and your life, you and your efforts, you and your purpose, you and your activity and experience. That is a valuable thing that very few people want, and they couldn't recognize it. If you wanted that and you were going to give up a lot of other things, people in the world would take advantage of you, for sure, and they would think you were foolish. And they'd let you pay anything for those things, thinking you were an idiot. And some people actually give their life so they can be close to God. They actually give their life. It's not like they joined the convent or the monastery, that's not necessarily giving your life, many of those people who went to the convent or the monastery went there to hide from people, or they were afraid of the opposite sex or something, and they went in there to hide. And some went to be hypocrites, and some went for holiness reasons. Some went for love reasons. So, you can't just wide brush across all monastics and say that they were motivated properly. Many people didn't want to work in the world, and they thought that would be a cushy life. But it turned out they had a lot of work in the monasteries and the convents, but just not that kind of work that people do in the world. Some people get away from their fears by being holy, trying to be holy. But that's not how to get away from your fears.

This man in the parable, he found something really beautiful, really wonderful, magnificent, more important than anything else that he owned or that other people owned; he found something really valuable. And people who look on the surface of things, they didn't see anything valuable in the ground. They didn't see any gems and valuable minerals in the soil underneath, because people don't look underneath. People look at the surface of things. They look at the grasses, the minerals, the animals and maybe the trees, but they don't look underneath. There's a whole new technology that looks underneath only, but that's a different kind of theme than what Jesus is talking about.

What are the qualities that you are going to carry with you outside this life, into a resurrected life? What are you going to bring with you? Those are the things that you should value. Your body's not going to go with you. Your body might be reconstituted at some point. Jesus has said that. But which body? The body that resists the light? The body that has so many aches and pains? Or the resurrected, lighted body? Who knows? He talked about it that the flesh would be reconstituted in the resurrection. It says it in a number of places. We don't really quite know what that means. But at least, you know, do you want it to feel like this one? Why don't you get it tuned up? Why don't you get it tuned up with love and light, so it feels good. So if you lose it, and if you have to have that particular one again, it's in pretty good shape.

This man valued his soul, and he let go of everything else to have this thing, this great wealth, which is your soul, your experience, and the part that God gave you. That's the big wealth of a human being. But you don't own it, really, but it is the thing that you must value above all else. It's loaned to you. If you value that, then all these other importances become relative. They have relative value, not real value. They're conditional value, transitional value, situational value, but they don't have permanent value like the soul and like the love of God has.

Then it's very good to tell yourself that's it's more valuable than something else. It's very good to line that up with yourself, so you know what is more important than something else. If you don't do that, you're liable to be foolish. You're liable to think like that man who was selling that field, that he was going to take advantage of somebody wanting something silly like a field, wanting to pay three times what it was worth. That's what people think about you when you look for love or light, or when you look for connection with God. They think you're foolish. And you're paying this great price, and they don't mind you paying because that's what fools do, they pay big prices for things that they value. And they laugh at you. They laugh at you for making this important, making Jesus and Mary important, making God important, making your heart important. In fact, they can't even speak your language, even if you tried to explain it to them. They can't speak that language, they roll their eyes, they close their ears and they close you off as a lunatic or a zealot, fanatic, naïve, gullible, because you have a spiritual fervor.

Just like this man selling the field. He thought the guy was crazy. He knew something of value. Some of you can get it. You know there's something of value in your relationship with Mary or Jesus. You know that there's something that you're going to grow into or become by being near them – near them in heart, near them in mind. And you want that more than anything else. Well, the standards of the world are going to call you a little bit nuts. Why wouldn't they? They cannot see under the surface of what is valuable. They cannot see the soul. They don't even think they have a soul, half of them. They don't know what soul is, if you were going to discuss it with them. Half of them. The other half, they talk the word but have never seen it, and don't really know what it is, but they believe in it. That's about half the people. But their purpose in existence is not the soul adoring its Creator. Their purpose for existence is for their body to follow its fleshly appetites and do whatever it wants. That it most people, even if they believe in soul, that's their agenda. They would not be able to appreciate you desiring that one perfect thing, the one precious thing, which is God.

Jesus could speak a parable like this to people he'd already taught. He'd already taught this town. He'd already spoken to these people. These people had cleaned up their act. They'd cleansed their lives. Many were already healed from another past visit. So now he's telling them a deeper teaching. This is the deeper teaching: you have all this outer stuff, and you've aligned yourself fairly well with the patterns of a spiritual life. And now he's telling them the deeper teaching – to value this one thing, the treasure of God within you. That's going to be the most important thing.

Having negative feelings, having fears and anger, having reactivity, those are the things that distract you from this most valuable thing. You all have experienced peace. You've all experienced a tranquil, trusting, faithful presence, when you're in communion, when you're in meditation, when you're in prayer. You have experienced it many, many times. That has to increase to where other negative things don't happen any more. That's your test for yourself, how often you can stay in that peace, in that trust. How long can you stand it before you have to rush off and agitate your waters? You want your own evaluation of how spiritual you are? That's how to evaluate it. How long can you stand the peace and the tranquility of the connection, and the trust in not knowing, how long can you stand that? Faithfully knowing that God's taking care of you, not knowing how God's going to take care of you? That's the trust we're talking about. How long can you stand it before you start agitating your waters? Or stirring up a little conflict with somebody? Or scaring yourself half to death? Or getting nervous? Or getting irritable? That's your test of how much this field, with this precious thing in it, is valuable to you. And just determine it by time – how many minutes can you stand it? How many hours a day can you be in that presence? That determines how valuable you found that precious thing. So now you can evaluate yourself.

I know if you're not honest, you can't evaluate yourself very well, because you think you're in, and you think you're out, and you don't even know if you're in or out. We can help you with that. How long a span of time you stayed in your peace, and how much you were in your frothing, foaming, agitating the waters. Every irritation, every discontent, every depression. Every fear, every misplaced longing, it takes you out of that field where the precious thing is. What does it do? It takes you into superficiality. It takes you into non-deep, as soon as you do it you become non-deep. In other words, you leave the mystical world, and you go into the outer world. For a second, maybe it's for an hour, or maybe it's for half a day. You leave becoming a mystic, you don't be a mystic. You become an outer person reacting. And Jesus is saying, stay with it, be persistent, do it for the whole life, because there's the resurrection coming, so that you're ready for that, when that happens. That's a long time for some, for some it's a long time to stay faithful and to stay consistent. And some of you don't like that too much, so you get real irritable about that.

Jesus didn't miss a beat. He was totally faithful and consistent, for thirty-three years always perfect. He chose it, he made it happen, he did it. He made it all the way to perfect sacrifice. That's what's required of you. If you sacrifice yourself on that cross of your body, that body is submitted to God, and that soul's mounted on that cross as the great gift to God. God sent you forth, and God wants you back. He doesn't want you back stained, he wants you back faithful. Your sacrifice is to present yourself, clean, whole, and very willing, with a great attitude, to your Creator. I leave that with you to figure out how you're going to have a great attitude. It's a great question for the week: How am I going to have a great attitude, in or out of my experience, throughout my experience?

November 13, 2016
Dethroned Forehead

The Gospel as Revealed to Me, Chapter 301. The parable of the Dethroned Foreheads.

Jesus offers and hands out the bread, and as they lack bowls or cups, each of them dips his bread into the little pail and drinks out of it, when thirsty. Jesus drinks only a little milk. He is grave and silent... So much so, that after the meal, when they have satisfied their appetite, which is always very good, they at last become aware of His quietness.

Andrew is the first to ask: "What is the matter with You, Master? You look sad or tired to me..."

"I do not deny that I am."

"Why? Because of those Pharisees? You should be accustomed to them by now... I have almost got accustomed myself! And You know how I used to react to them earlier. They always sing the same song!... Snakes can but hiss, in fact, and none of them will ever be able to imitate the singing of a nightingale. One ends up by not paying attention to them," says Peter, both earnestly and to cheer up Jesus.

"And that is how one loses one's control and falls into their coils. I ask you to never get accustomed to the voice of Evil as if it were harmless."

"Oh! Well! If that is the only reason why You are sad, You are wrong. You can see how the world loves You," says Matthew.

" But is that the only reason why You are so sad? Tell me, my good Master. Or have they told You lies, or made slanderous insinuations or insinuated suspicion, or I do not know what, about us who love You?" asks the Iscariot solicitously and kindly, embracing with one arm Jesus, who is sitting beside him on the hay.

Jesus turns towards Judas. His eyes flash like phosphorus in the flickering light of the lamp laid on the ground in the middle of the circle of the apostles sitting on the hay. Jesus stares at Judas of Kerioth and asks him, " And do you know Me to be so silly as to accept as true anybody's insinuations, to the point of being upset by them? It is real facts, Judas of Simon, which upset Me" and His eyes do not stop for one moment piercing, like a probe, the brown eyes of Judas.

"Which real facts are upsetting You, then?" insists the Iscariot in a tone of confidence.

" The ones I see in the depths of hearts and on dethroned foreheads." Jesus lays stress upon the word. Everybody becomes excited: " Dethroned Why? What do You mean?"

" A king is dethroned when he is unworthy of remaining on the throne, and the first thing they tear off him is the crown, which is on his forehead, the most noble part of man, the only animal with his forehead erect towards the sky, as he is animal with regard to matter, but supernatural as a being gifted with a soul. But it is not necessary to be king on an earthly throne to be dethroned... Every man is king because of his soul, and his throne is in Heaven. But when a man prostitutes his soul and becomes a brute and demon, he then dethrones himself. The world is full of dethroned foreheads which are no longer erect towards Heaven, but are stooped towards the Abyss, weighed down by the word which Satan has carved on them. Do you want to know it? It is the one I read on foreheads. There is written: "Sold!" And that you may have no doubt as to who the buyer is, I tell you that it is Satan, by himself or through his servants in the world."

" I have understood! Those Pharisees, for instance, are the servants of a servant who is greater than they are and who is Satan's servant," says Peter earnestly.

Jesus does not reply.

We talk about spiritual sight quite a bit and - at least we have, if you remember - and that has to do with what you're looking at, the way you're looking, what you're seeing and what you want to see. And spiritual sight's most prominent feature is the third eye, the chakra in the center of the forehead, and it can only see in spirit if it's relying on spirit. If it counts spirit more important than everything else, then the light will shine in the forehead because where you put your attention grows. But if you're concerned with your thinking, your doubting, your skepticism or your suspicions, your criticisms and your weighing and analyzing and your opinions, all of these things cloud the forehead. This dethrones you. Then you have a dethroned forehead because you're using your thinking to ferret out mischief, to look for scandals, to see negative energy or to be afraid for the things that you prefer to be afraid of. And, because of that, it darkens your sight, it darkens your light and it closes down your forehead.

Well, that's the trajectory downward in selling yourself in fear, anger or in pride to the satanic being. He instigates it in you, he encourages it in you, he wants you to close down your real sight and your real connection to spirit so that you'll start thinking in a materialistic way. And when that happens you are in a free fall to dethroning your forehead. Because it was meant to look to heaven, to see into the spirit; it was meant to discern carefully what is real, what is true.

So, when you're having prideful thoughts about how you can scrutinize things, you are starting to dethrone. Instead of seeing what God shows you, you're seeing what you prefer to see, which is evidence of your fears. You're seeing reasons why you should be anxious and concerned, reasons why you should be separate, and compete with other people to make you better. You start your downward fall into the dethroned forehead.

Do you submit your anatomy, your mind, thoughts and your whole being to God? Then you're not dethroned. Then you're going to shine. Then your forehead is going to shine. It won't get that mark that the satanic being wants to give you that says, 'Oh, the doubters, you come with me. The scoffers, you come with me. The ones that see negative in everybody, you come with me.' The satanic being says. 'The ones that are worried about everything, as if you could control anything at all, you guys come with me. We'll come to the dethroned place.' It is exactly the motivation for Satan to dethrone the sons of God, the ones created in the image of God. And you fall for it so easily, and most of the planet has fallen for it so easily. They think they can figure everything out just by their own guts and desire.

Where's the humility in pretending to know what God hasn't revealed to you? Where's the humility in looking into something with your small, cerebral matter, figuring it out without having God divinely inspire you with what's going on with it? Where's God going to guide you if you're thinking you have everything already inside in your animal state, in your physical state? You have everything you need? You're a reasonable person. You have desires and wishes, you have motivations, achievements and, you know, ambitions. Okay, that's what any animal human has, any of those things, but it does not constitute a spiritual being yet. Not a son or daughter of God manifest, or even willing to manifest. They just have a lot of impetus, impulses – the gamut of garbage that everybody has.

I see a lot of dethroned foreheads. 97% of the planet has a dethroned forehead. Are they shining with light, with trust in God, with devotion, with looking up to the heavens for their source of supply and comfort? No they're not. They're clawing at each other like animals. You do it more subtly than the average human, I know, but you still do it. The conflicts you have are really worldly mostly. I'm not trying to shame you, I'm just saying that's what conflict is, it's 'I have an idea, and you have a different one, and then we need to fight and we have to have angst and anger and maybe irritation and we have to have words. We have to have these words attacking each other.' That's very primitive. In the world they would beat each other up. It would be much more fierce and biting and hurting, but this is just mental or emotional and it's just as bad. To me, that's where it starts, it goes downhill from there.

If you're looking to God, and wanted to know what God thought, and didn't want to think anything else but what God thought, I think your forehead is on the throne and you would be a lighted being. The more light, the less worry. The more light, the less consternation. More love. That's where we're headed. At least, some of us are headed there, you know, like a little light in a huge storm with clouds and a lot of wind. A little lighthouse out there on the beach somewhere going, 'Hey, want to come into port? You want to come into the throned forehead port? Then you've got to come over this way. You don't have to but, you know, you could circle and just tack back and forth with your little boat as you see the light or you could come into port.' Coming into port is saying, 'Okay, that's my goal, that's my acceptance, that's what I really want. I don't want anything else.' And then, this light stays lit up on your head. The throned forehead comes from a loving heart. You can't have it the other way. You can't just do a head trip, it's not that. Without love and without light, this doesn't get throned.

So you can ask yourself, do you spend more of your day worried about things? Then the dethroning's happening. If you spend more of your day criticizing or being agitated by people, then you're dethroning. It's gradual. That's how you can monitor it for yourself instead of me monitoring for you. I don't have to tell you what you're doing, you should know what you're doing. It's nothing for me to see what you're doing, but it is something for you to see what you're doing. That's something I would want for you, that you could see what you're doing so you could monitor it yourself and have the internal skills to say, 'Oh, tipping, tipping, tip. . . Okay, let's tip backwards. Let's get back the other way. We're falling down off the throne. Oh, well let's get it back up there where it belongs.'

You can do that. Spiritualize your thinking, spiritualize your heart. Let love and light happen. You have to concentrate. This is not a passive thing. If you think you're doing anything passively, you are very wrong. Nothing will happen if you're passive. If you're going to passively be light, what does that mean? You're actually not putting out much effort and you're hoping it just happens naturally. It doesn't happen naturally. Not in a world where everything is against you. In a lighted planet, where everybody's lighted, I think it would happen fairly naturally. Everybody would just fall into it. It would be consensus, 'We do light here,' but this is not this planet. You came to a planet that's not like that so that the ones who were going to go into light were going to be heroes who would've had to make a huge effort – a non-passive effort – to be in the light. That's what is required here and you were sent here because you needed to not be passive anymore. That's your test.

Are you going to mosey around and search for the wild asparagus? Okay, you can do that. And then what? After you've eaten those sweet asparagus - and they are sweet like sugar if you get them on the fence-line. After stalking the wild asparagus. Then what? Then what? You say, 'Wow. For a week straight I ate the sweetest, most tender, asparagus known to man,' and that's true, I have actually. And then what? I can die in ecstasy? No. We've got to dig up the hard earth and build a garden or something. Or, I have to fix the water heater that just broke down on me. Well that's not very magical. You do what's in front of you. You do what's given, not just what you want to do because that's passive. An ice cream truck rolls by your front door and you just go out and gobble up? You know, think ahead. That's pretty passive. That's not what we're supposed to be doing here. We're supposed to be creative beings that know what the hell we're doing and why we're doing it: serving God and keeping that forehead throned in light. Jesus laid emphasis on it so He could tell you, 'That's where I look if I want to see who's been influenced by the satanic being.'

That's what He's saying. That's what I look for. I look for whether there's light shining in your head because that means your head is in the right direction towards the Spirit. And, if it's not shining there, you're looking downward. You're headed to the dark place because all of your concerns are earthly and low. They're low concerns so that's where you're headed. You're going to be bowed down like a slave to the one that's going to own you and it's not going to be God. And this is the sorting time so you don't have, you can't equivocate this, you can't parse it out and say, 'Well, it's not that bad – what he's saying.' It is. It's that serious. Just like Jesus is sad in this reading because He can see. He's coming as the perfect being and they don't think that He means anything, that He doesn't count, it's not important what He is and what He's doing. They don't even pay attention to Him. And that's Jesus. And we're in a much different place now. We've got a lot of history of teachings, a lot of history of His words and saints having come through the planet many, many hundreds of times and shown vast miracles. And we have almost as little faith as when He looked out at the crowds to see the dethroned foreheads. Somewhat almost the same and you're concerned about whether you can sit around a campfire or not.

I'm making stuff up – stuff that you love. You know, are you concerned about whether you can do laundry by hand? Try that sometime. You want to spend half your day doing laundry? It's a half a day's job to do it by hand. Want to go back to that? Back to the Earth? Oh yeah. Have you ever hammered the husk off grains? Want to try that for a while? Some of you don't even have the arm strength to last five minutes doing that and that's the only way you get your grain, is you get the husk beat off it. You'd just be crying because the things don't work for you. They just don't work for you.

You have it really easy now. You really have it easy. I'm not saying we should get back to the land. I think you should land in your body and put the throne back up where it belongs. I think that's what you should do. I think you should be sons and daughters of God like you were made, and stop acting like something different than that. Stop acting like a worry wart going around looking for problems, trying to prove to yourself that you're not a son or a daughter of God. Stop doing that and Jesus will take notice of you.

November 20, 2016
Sacrifice Isn't Easy

The Gospel as Revealed to Me, *Chapter 258. The future mission of James of Alphaeus, taught by Jesus on mount Carmel.*

Watch and ensure that there are no jealousy and slander, or resentment or desire for revenge in the congregation of believers. Watch and ensure that the flesh does not overwhelm the spirit. He, whose spirit does not control his body, could not withstand persecutions.

James, I know that you will do it, but promise your Brother that you will not disappoint Me."

"But, my Lord! I am afraid of one thing only: that I am not capable of doing it. My Lord, I beg You, give that task to someone else."

"No. I cannot..."

"Simon of Jonah loves You, and You love him..."

" Simon of Jonah is not James of David."

"John! John, the learned angel, make him Your servant here."

"No. I cannot. Neither Simon nor John possess that nothingness, which is, however, so important with men: kinship. You are a relative of mine. After refusing to acknowledge Me, the better part of Israel will endeavor to be forgiven by God and by themselves and will make an effort to know the Lord whom they cursed in the hour of Satan, and they will feel they have been forgiven, and will thus feel strong to come on to My Way, if one of My blood is in My place. James, great things have been accomplished upon this mountain. Here the fire of God consumed not only the holocaust, the wood and stones, but even the dust and the very water that was in the ditch. James, do you believe that God can do again such a thing, burning and consuming all the materiality of the man -James to make a James - fire of

God? We have been speaking while the setting sun has inflamed our tunics. Do you think that the brightness of the chariot that took Elijah away, was like this or more or less refulgent?"

"Much more refulgent because it was made of heavenly fire."

"Consider therefore what a heart will be, when it has been turned into fire to have in itself God, because God wants it to perpetuate His Word preaching the Gospel of Salvation."

"But You, Word of God, eternal Word, why do You not remain?"

"Because I am Word and Flesh. By the Word I must teach, and by the Flesh, redeem." " Oh! My Jesus, how will You redeem? What have You to face?"

"James, remember the prophets."

"But are their words not allegoric? Can You, the Word of God, be manhandled by men? Do they perhaps not mean that Your divinity, Your perfection will be tormented but nothing more than that? My mother is worried about Judas and me, but I am worried about You and Mary, and also about ourselves, because we are so weak. Jesus, if men should overwhelm You, do You not think that many of us would believe You to be guilty, and being disappointed, would abandon You?"

"I am sure of it. There will be confusion among all My disciples. But then peace will reign, and there will be a cohesion of all the better parts, upon which the fortifying wise Spirit: the Divine Spirit will come, after My sacrifice and My triumph."

"Jesus, in order that I may not deviate and may not be scandalized in the dreadful hour, tell me: what will they do to You?"

"You are asking Me a great thing."

"Tell me, my Lord."

"It will be a torture for you to know it exactly."

"It does not matter. For the love that has united us..."

"It is not to be known."

"Tell me and then cancel it from my memory until the hour it is to be accomplished. Then bring it back to my memory, together with the remembrance of this hour. I will thus not be scandalized and I will not become Your enemy in the depth of my heart."

"It will be of no avail, because you, too, will yield to the storm."

"Tell me, my Lord!"

"I shall be accused, betrayed, captured, tortured, crucified."

"No!" shouts James writhing as if he had been struck to death. " No!" he repeats. " If they do that to You, what will they do to us? How shall we be able to continue your work? I cannot accept the position you have destined to me... I cannot... When You die, I will die too, having no more strength. Jesus, listen to me! Don't leave me without You. Promise me at least that!"

"I promise that I will come and guide you with My Spirit, after My glorious Resurrection has freed Me from the restrictions of matter. You and I will be again one thing only, as we are now that you are between My arms." James in fact has begun to weep on Jesus' chest. " Do not weep any more. Let us come out of this bright and painful hour of ecstasy, as one comes out from the shadow of death, remembering everything except the act of dying, a fright that freezes one's blood and lasts but one minute, and as an accomplished fact it lasts forever. Come I will kiss you thus, to help you forget the burden of My fate as Man. You will remember all this at the right moment, as you asked. Here, I kiss your lips that will have to repeat My words to the people of Israel, and your heart that will have to love as I told you, and there, on your temple, where life will cease together with the last word of loving faith in Me. My beloved brother, I will come to you and be with you in the meetings of believers, in the hour of meditation, in those of danger and in the hour of your death!

No one, not even your angel, will receive your spirit, because I will, with a kiss, thus..."

They remain embraced for a long time and James seems to doze off in the joy of God's kisses that make him forget his suffering. When he lifts his head, he has become once again James of Alphaeus, peaceful and kind, so much like Joseph, the spouse of Mary. He smiles at Jesus, his smile is more mature, somewhat sad, but always so sweet.

It's kind of bitter sweet to know your destiny, and to have it revealed to you, because attending the destiny is the weakness of human beings and he knows the outcome of this process that they are going through. They are only just beginning the second year of his ministry and Jesus is telling them this. And if you were told what your destiny would be, you would also be told the failings that you would have, and the mistakes that you would probably make and He is telling him that he would surrender to the storm. Some of you the only storm you have known is the one you have built yourself, not the one that's given to you as destiny. So you don't really know what storm is. You won't know what storm is until you follow your destiny and go through the process of giving yourself over and letting go of your past. Most of you feel that you have really gone through a lot of storm because you have suffered your reactions to your parents. That's not a storm, that's just you not getting over yourself, that's you just not moving on a grown up, that's all. There is nothing disciple about that. That's not about discipleship, that's about getting over yourself so that you can step on the way. Then on the way there is a destiny that most of you won't be able to hear and most of you Jesus won't tell you. This is one of the few that he told. He told John and he told Simon and he told James, Peter later, but mostly nobody, because it's too hard. The storm is going to tear them apart, it's going to send them into terror, such as it would with each of you.

Unfortunately, some of you would just fall away, because you are not that strong. You haven't really learned to carry the load of your own consciousness without having to spark off other people or react to things and people. You haven't learned it yet, so, you wouldn't be told. These strong ones could be told and also he is telling them they will fail, and they will fall and they will be freaked out.

Now what would he tell you? Kind of like what I am telling you, that some of you would fall away. He told everybody that in the crowds, some would remain faithful, very few, a hundred would like Him, ten would follow Him and one would be faithful. That's how he said it. That's the same ratio for humanity now. Not trying to depress you but I am saying that while you are settling on knowing who you are in relation to your parents, or knowing who you are or how you are different from your parents, you are still in high school. You haven't gotten out of high school yet, spiritually. Like identifying with them, not identifying with them, resisting them, resenting them, hoping you are different than them, that's high school. That's not disciple. Disciple is Jesus says 'Follow me' and you follow. You don't think, you don't interpret, you don't react and resent, you don't have any time for pride, you just follow. That's different. That's different. I know it's a courageous act of stepping out of the mind of the world. It is a courageous act. And will it be hard? Sure. Is it supposed to be easy? I don't think so. Sacrifice isn't easy until you master it. Till you learn how to do it love isn't easy, it doesn't just happen. Young immature love is that you love people that love you, somebody likes you, you like them back, that's the depths of most peoples' love. You like what likes you.

You don't love in spite of everybody because that's your decision to do it, to everyone, with everyone, no matter what, whether you understand them or not, love them. That's a whole different level of love. That's an apostle, disciple kind of love. They have to get over being Israelites, you guys have to get over simple things like being a man or being a woman or something stupid like that. At least you don't have that plus the Israelite problem, getting over all three of those things. If you have all three together with yourself, it's a joke. You don't have to get over anything like that really as a disciple because that's trivial. Like trivial. Like the most trivial thing you could possibly think about yourself is gender, politics and nation and tribe - the most trivial thing you could ever think about yourself, the most meaningless thing you could evaluate yourself in terms of. And why am I saying it? Because Jesus doesn't see you as those things. He sees you as soul, as spirit, as Divine sons and daughters of God, beings like God, not confined with any of that nonsense. Parent/non parent, married/not married. Who cares? Who cares about that. If that's your job and that's what you are supposed to do and that's what you are told to do, you do it. That doesn't make you, you. Those things don't make you, you. There are things you do on the way of life. Just like careers, you change them a few times, they don't make you, you.

All He is asking James is to be another himself. But James says he can't do it, he can't stay in Jerusalem because it's going to be too sad. 'Have somebody else do it.' But Jesus says, 'You are the one.' And this is how it is as a disciple. You get to do what God gives you to do, and you can have a lot of options and people who have a lot of options aren't ready to do anything yet. People who are thinking of a lot of options aren't ready to obey yet. Because people who are thinking about a lot of options don't love yet. They don't know how to love yet. Because if you love, you do that one thing you are given and you do it well, and then you do the next thing you are given and you do that well, if you love. This is why you don't have to think up a mission for yourself, you don't have to dream up a stylistic way you are going to do your mission. I see many of you looking, you know shopping for the stylistic way you would like to be a disciple. Well I kind of want to be dynamic and say things heavy, you know that's a stylistic way. I want to be demure and never speak until it's prodded out of me, that's another stylistic way. I want to share nothing and make everybody guess because it's so spiritual, there are a lot of stylistic ways aren't there? I want to be so stubborn that I think a big bulldozer has to move me and if it does I am going to obey, if a big bulldozer moved me, for sure, that's another stylistic department. All these ways that you figured out might be cool for you.

And if all the apostles thought of cool things that they could do, every one of them is going to have a conversation like this with Jesus. He is going to say 'No I cannot have you go over there you have to stay here.' Or maybe five of them say 'I want to stay here, I want to stay here.' No, you guys have got to go. Why are you even thinking about it? Why don't you just ask him and just do what he gives you to do? In fact, why aren't you in that kind of communication we have discussed many times? It's so possible for you to be so closely communicating with Him. You just ask and then He tells you what to do. You don't think about it, you just do it. That's called obedience. Something that's hard for the calcified. When you are calcified you don't want to be jostled because it will break some of those calcium deposits in your brain. It was cool, I mean James is asking Him, okay show me the vision, tell me what it is and them wipe it out of my head so I don't freak out and He does it. He does it. He freaks out too when he knows and then He takes it out of his head and it's gone. That's many times Jesus has loved people like that, where they say please take me before because I don't want to see it, I don't want to see your crucifixion. He says 'Okay, I'll take you.' But these people don't decide out of weakness or out of animosity, they decide out of love, that they can't handle this or they can't handle that. It's not an irritable decision. It's going to make me too angry to see you crucified, that's an irritable decision. That's going to break my heart, I am going to fail if I see it. I am going to fail if I know this for the next two years, while I am waiting for you to die. I'll fail. Take it out of my head, help me remember right after. And a typical Sagittarius wants to see ahead, which he did. And then He had to close it back down on him. Because it's not very practical for the day to day, is it? To see in two years He is dead. That's not too practical for today. I mean maybe it lines you up with a little bit more faithfulness somehow, but otherwise it's just prophesying way out there to something that isn't happening right now.

What would Jesus have you do if you get that close and if you get that changed by Him and He works on you the way He would like. Then you are malleable so that He can work you just like He wants to work you? He gets you ready to do what? What would that be you think? Like don't dream it up - what do you think he would think he would want you to do if he prepped you properly and if you allowed Him to do that properly? Without your ideas and without your resistance, without you holding on to your problems and all that other crap that you do. How would he do it and what would it look like, your expression of divinity that he gives you? Not that you plan that you figure out but that He gives you. What would that be like? You could dream it up in yourself but you could also just ask Him. When I am a big boy or a big girl what am I going to be doing? You can ask Him. What is it going to look like when I grow up, from your point of view, what you call grown up, what's it going to look like? How do you see me then? It would be a great meditation. Because it's different, it's different than what's happening, I am not saying that to cause you pain, it's different than what's happening. Most of you are holding on for dear life to the past and eking out a little future development and a little overcoming and a little liberating energy so that you don't, so you can't say you are totally stuck. But what kind of divvying out your own being to the Master is that? You're going to divvy out a little progress that doesn't jostle you too much, you're going to divvy out a little bit of your effort so He can use you a little bit so that you can still preserve yourself? I mean it's pretty pervasive.

So I can't avoid your parents when you shove your projections of parents onto me and others all the time. It's hard to avoid talking about it. You want me to stop talking about it, don't do it anymore. If you want me to stop talking about middle school then don't be in middle school. If you want me to stop talking about reactions, don't have any. 'You are telling me what to do.' I have to talk about what you do, not what you think you do but what you actually do, I have to talk about it. I don't have a choice really, I am not going to talk pie in the sky, about a pie you can't eat and a sky you can't live in. I want to talk about your step, the step your foot is hesitating to take, that's what I want to talk about, and that's the thing we need to deal with, that step you are on. Now we could say each of you are slightly on a different step than somebody else. If that's satisfying to your ego, okay, but does that matter? I mean you are on your step, or you are hesitating with your next step? If you are hesitating I guess you would like that. How scared are you of changing and how scared are you of turning into something you have no picture of? That will tell you how much you are holding on. What goodies are you going to let go of that will rip joy out of your life? You see the concept in that? If I let go of something, some joy is going to be ripped out of my life that I am definitely preciously holding on to. We talk about letting go from the first lesson. I say, let go and let God and everybody says oh yeah, that's easy, I know exactly what that means because it's like four words, and they are only one syllable words, so there's four one syllable words - let go, let God - got it, that's easy, I mean I know exactly what you are talking about. But nobody ever knew what it was, nobody ever understood it and very few people got it and know how to actually do it. And we would describe it, and you would think you got it because you're so bright. Do you let God do it? Or do you do it? Do you stop trying or do you let God move through you?

People don't like what Jesus says when you ask Him for something, He says, 'No I cannot, your egos can't take that,' so you don't want to ask because you don't want to find out. He will not do that for you, He won't give you something when it's not for you, it's not your mission, it's not your job, it's not your work. And some people, maybe some of you or some people like the idea of having so many options to pretend freedom when you haven't taken any options and you haven't made the choices. You just like the idea of options when actually in any given moment there is one thing God wants you to do, and in that next moment one thing that God wants you to do. And if you open and if you were receptive and you were in love with Him you would find out what that was, and you would be satisfied just to do that and get rid of your ideas. And that's what I am praying for for you - that you do that, that you get that perspective, to just find out what that one next thing is that He wants you to do. But you have to listen, you've got to stop thinking, you've got to start listening or you won't know. Each time you do it, it's going to break thousands of concepts and thousands of brittle ideas in your cells about who you think you are. We call it a transformative path. What is that, just a descriptor for describing a flower? No, it's an event that happens to you. It happens to you. You get transformed, from what to what, from where you think you are to where you don't know. That's the transformation.

You are so clever trying to predict everything that you haven't had an experience as yet. The predictors never have an experience because they are too scared to go through something. You just have to go through something in order to find out what that something is. You've got to let yourself be led, there is no other way to do it. Wouldn't it be nice if I could come in here and say that you guys have let go of everything? 'It's so beautiful, you guys are in your mission now and you are just functioning, you are serving and light filled beautiful beings that have no tarnage, which is tarnished carnage okay, you have no tarnage from the past. It's just all gone. It's all loosened up and lifted out. You are just spirit beings ready at the drop of a hat to just serve, just do, just go, just say it, just make it happen, just no resistance at all' - that would be cool. Then I would say, 'Hey short sermon, we are just going to do some stuff' and then we go do it. Nobody would have to brow beat you, that's the important thing lately. It's like work it over, mull it over, flip it over and you change pans and put it in a hotter pan. We just have to keep doing that until you get it.

Is that how you know that I love you if I keep working on you? You resist, I try, I love you - is that how we work it out with the parents? Are you projecting, are you turning me into the dad that can't talk to you because you don't listen, or turning me into the dad that whines at you and you resist, how are you doing it? How is the projection going? You know the followers of Jesus, the real close ones, they just took Him at His word and did what he said. They didn't say, 'God reminds me of my dad, my uncle, my uncle is nicer.' They didn't lay back and say, 'When He is really serious I am going to do it, but like right now He is just talking, it's nothing. When He gets really intense and it's all heavy, when He gets heavy handed then I will do it.' You think they thought that way? A lot of the losers did and the ones that are on the periphery probably thought that way, but the ones close could not think that way. He said it, they did it. He said jump, they jumped. How high? That's how high they jumped. He said get on the move, they got on the move, they got out of town, they went and got groceries and came back when he said it. They didn't have a lot of ideas, they didn't go to the closer store. They went to the store he had in mind, they went to the store He had in mind, not the store that was convenient to them. That's kind of different, isn't it? It isn't the way you think. You go when you feel it's convenient to your day and the timing of your day and the closer the store the better, and what makes it easier for you instead of just exactly what He had in His mind, very different isn't it? One is serving, the other is doing your own thing, kind of nearby serving. They are different aren't they.

You feel that difference in yourself, some of you should know it – 'I am going to get around to something very close to that. I will get very close to what He said.' But what kind of servant is that where you don't even want to know His mind down to the feeling of it? You just want to prove that you could do it yourself. I know there is a song about that in the sixties, it's my party and I'll cry if I want to, you know. Is it your party? I think it's God's party. I don't think you get a party, you don't deserve a party and I don't think you are going to get a party. Is that sacrilegious to say something like that? I know you want a party, that's so sad for you. If you get your own party it's not very happy, is it? Have you tried that? Have your own party – it's not very happy as it turns out. But what I want you to take away from the sermon, aside from all that stuff, is that James did what he was told. He had feelings about it, they talked it out and he did what He told him, for life, until he was killed. He stayed in Jerusalem. He had his head cut off or he was knifed or something, something bad happened to him. And he didn't die but he died, but he didn't die. For those of you who are flipping out about death, death is fun. If you let go of your old ideas I think you are going to turn into a disciple, I really do, it's very likely.

November 27, 2016
Love Your Neighbor

From The Gospel as Revealed to Me, Chapter 275. Four new disciples. Discussions on the works of bodily and spiritual mercy.

Be merciful to those who are weeping. They have been wounded by life and their hearts are grieved in their affections. Do not lock yourselves up in your serenity as in a stronghold. Weep with those who are weeping, comfort who is distressed, console the loneliness of those who have been deprived of a relative by death. Be fathers to orphans, sons to parents, brothers to one another.

Love. Why love only those who are happy? They already have their share of sunshine. Love the weeping. They are the least amiable for the world. But the world is not aware of the value of tears. You are. Love, therefore, those who are weeping. Love them if they are resigned in their grief. Love them even more if they rebel against their sorrow. Do not reproach them but kindly convince them of the truth of grief and the utility of sorrow. Through the veil of tears they may see the face of God deformed, and His countenance full of revengeful arrogance. No. Do not be scandalized! It is only a hallucination brought about by the fever of grief. Assist them so that their temperature may abate.

Let your fresh faith be like ice applied to a delirious patient. And when the raging fever drops and is followed by the seediness and torpid hebetude typical of those who come out of a trauma, then speak to them once again of God, as of something new, kindly and patiently, as you would deal with children who have become backward through disease... Oh! a lovely tale, told to amuse man, the eternal child! And then be quiet. Do not impose... A soul works by itself. Assist it with caresses and prayer. And when it asks: "So it was not God?"

reply "No. He did not want to hurt you, because He loves you, also on behalf of those who no longer love you because of death or other reasons." And when the soul says: "But I accused him," say: "He has forgotten it, because it was your fever." And when it says: "I would like to have Him," say: "Here He is! At the door of your heart, waiting for you to open it to him."

Bear bothersome persons. They come in to upset the little house of our ego, just as pilgrims come in to upset the house in which we live. But as I told you to welcome pilgrims, so I tell you to welcome these persons.

Are they bothersome? But if you do not love them, because of the trouble they cause you, they love you, more or less righteously. Welcome them for such love. And even if they came inquiring, hating, insulting you, be patient and charitable. You can improve them through your patience. But you may scandalize them through your lack of charity. Be sorry because they sin; but be more sorry to make them sin and to sin yourselves. Receive them in my name, if you cannot receive them with your own love. And God will reward you, by coming Himself, later, to return the visit and cancel the unpleasant memory by His supernatural caresses.

I think just the thought that we've been difficult in the past should make us want to handle our present time dealing with people who are difficult. We should handle it very well, knowing that we have been difficult in the past. That should be like a reminder of something – somebody who's a little animated or a little angry, or a little hurt, or raising their voice, or upset about something – I think we can remember many times we've done that, and many times we weren't struck down by God for being that way.

So we should bear with people who do that with the same kind of pathos and love that people probably put up with us when we were doing that. Somebody had to know that we were acting like that, who was maybe more sensitive, more developed and they could feel that we were doing that. They didn't judge us harshly, they just prayed for us or they hoped we would pass through that little storm, whatever it was. So do the same for other people. That way, you will be that oasis of change, that oasis of healing wherever you go.

And whether they understand you or not, even a kid will flail at his mother, and then afterwards he's sorry, or he doesn't even remember it at all. She doesn't remember it anymore either because she knows that it was the fit of the fever, that he was wrestling and fighting and squirming and inadvertently hitting her. It's different if a kid hits directly, then you correct that. But most of the time, in people's pain they say a lot of foul things and they say hurtful things that they would not say if they felt better. They're saying that to you, of all people, they should not be saying that to you, because you're so important. But anybody could say that to somebody else if they were crushed hard enough or in enough pain. They would say that to anybody and it's not personal. They're flailing at the world and you might be next door. You might be right next to them and they flail at you. And that'll give you some compassion – for yourself for having done that, and for anybody who's in that much pain. And that's what you focus on, that they must be in pain. They're not assaulting you. They're in a lot of pain. Their soul isn't even talking to you when they're yelling. So you can have compassion with it. You can put up with it, not because you're feeling better than them, you can put up with it because everyone has done that to each other. Remember that nobody really sincerely thinks they're doing that to hurt somebody, they didn't mean it as an assault, as an attack. Yet you feel it. The recipient may feel it as an attack, but it isn't conscious like that. It's an inadvertent thing. They're just being whatever they think is the thing they have to be and you're taking it personally.

In most of the instances where you're upset with somebody's behavior, they actually don't know they're doing that, and they don't know the effect it is having on other people. I don't know why you get so irate about that because it's happened to you too. You have done things you didn't even know you were doing and that's the first thing you say, 'I'm sorry, I didn't even know I was doing that.' So why are people so upset with that person who didn't even know they were doing it? They were doing it. But they didn't even know they were doing it. And so, kindly, you could say, 'Do you know that's the way it feels when you do that?' Don't get all huffy. Just say, 'You know, this is what it feels like when you do that,' and 'Did you know it felt like that to others when you do that?' Without being impatient, without being angry, and I know they'll say, 'I did not know that, I did not know that's how I was being.'

It's a different conversation if they knew it and they wanted to do it and were deliberately doing it – okay, that's a kind of meanness. That's a different kind of sermon. I'm not talking about that. That doesn't happen very much. It's always the unintended, unconscious stuff that we do that we're so irate about because our egos get so personally assaulted. If you knew the good you could do, you would do it. If you knew the goodness that you are, you would be that. If you knew a better good than you were doing now, you would do it. This is the thing. So what people are doing probably makes a lot of sense to them. This is how you have to read people.

What people are doing makes a lot of sense to them. It's as good as they can do because they think it's good. I'm not talking about worldly people who don't care about people, I'm talking about you guys. You actually do care, and you do think about how you can behave in a conscious way, somewhat like Jesus and Mary, you're striving for that. So it's sincere. You are looking to do that. I would assume that you would feel that way about everyone, even if they weren't aware of what they were doing. You know, clumsinesses, you're bumping into somebody, you don't know you're bumping into them. But other people feel you bumping into them and wonder why you don't see that you're bumping into them. So then you could tell them nicely, 'You know that's the second time you've bumped into me today?' And that's not mean, that's just, 'Did you see that you did that?' They didn't see that they did that. They didn't notice that. But it is loving to point it out, not in a heavy-handed way, but in a kind way. 'Did you notice that you were just standing right in the path where I was trying to walk – did you notice that?' Not in a miffed, angry way, just because that's what's happening. 'Did you know that's what was happening? I was trying to get by and you were right there?' And so you touch them lightly and say, 'Excuse me,' and then they realize they've been standing there for some time.

That's what I think needs to happen. I think we need to be real sensitive to each other, not fawning, not over-emotional, I think the emotions are irreverent, actually, they're irreverent to God, the emotions are. But sensitivity's a good thing. You can be sensitive to each others' feelings and to each others' needs. Not because you want to get them to like you but because that's what you should be doing. You should be learning to be sensitive to each others' feelings and to each others' needs.

Your whole goal shouldn't be, 'I've just got to figure out how *I* want to be and who *I* am.' You should be looking to the place where what you do is very finessed, very graceful, and really works, and is pretty smooth-functioning, and doesn't step on anybody's toes, and is the best movement of energy for you – that's what you should be striving for. In other words, it doesn't bump into people, and it doesn't push people aside, and it doesn't ignore people, and it is not irreverent to other people's feelings. If you do that, I think that everybody's going to be very happy with you, and you're going to be very happy with everyone else because everybody's going to be very sensitive to that.

That same thing from the gospel reading of being so prominent and giving so little, and being so nothing before God, so humble and so real. There's the balance in between there where you may know that you're doing good, but don't think about it too much. In a way, those are very extreme conditions. There's a person who doesn't exalt themselves and doesn't beat themselves up either. That we would call not a bothersome person. That person probably won't bother anybody. They won't step on anybody's toes and they won't be a doormat for other people either. If you can see the exaltation, that's what I'm looking for you to look at. The one who gets hurt all the time is exalting themselves. How are you going to put up with difficult people, you being one of them, if you're trying to exalt yourself all the time? Paul said it: "There but for the grace of God go I."

In other words, you can look at somebody, and they're just a complete mess and completely oblivious to other people, and they're really insensitive, and they're really kind of mean, and you can say with Paul, 'There, but for God's grace, I'd be like that. I'd be just like that, had it not been for love or healing or grace or somebody telling me something that was real, somebody teaching me something that helped me, I'd be just like that.' That's the truth. It's a wonderful thing to feel because you're not going to be like the guy up there in the front row saying, 'I'm thankful that I'm not like all these idiots and I'm so much better than everybody else. Thank you for all the gifts that you've given me. I'm going to give you my little scrap of gift in front of all these people so they can see it. I want to see how generous I am, giving you just exactly the ten percent that I'm supposed to give.' You know, he's wanting credit, and he's jacking himself up, and do you think God hears that prayer? God is saying 'Oh, disgusting, stop it, shut up. Go sit in the back row with the tax guy and listen to what he says. Get down to that basic level of love for your Creator.'

Can you feel when you're a bothersome person? Do you have a self-reflection that you've been trouble to other people, that you've been difficult, or like a thorn in somebody's side? Or that something about your unconscious behavior has irritated other people? Can you even image it? Let's imagine that might be the case that at some time in your life you've had some unconscious string of events that no one told you, but you didn't know either, that people were wondering, 'What the hell?' That's what they're saying about you. Can you imagine that? Can you imagine a kid doing that? Doing all kinds of behaviors and the parents saying, 'What are they thinking?' Right? People don't hate them, they want to talk to them, sometimes they want to knock a few heads, or get through to them in some way, but mostly they have to put up with them. Because that goodness in that person should come online, that conscience in that person should come online and feel that what they're doing scrapes on other people or is inconsiderate or doesn't even think of other people. That's what you pray for. You don't get heavy-handed on them, because that's mean. You pray for them, and then if you have a kind moment where you're not going to be reacting, you can say, 'Did you know, did you know that you did this? You know, I don't know if you were aware of it. I'm sure that you wouldn't have wanted to do this. But did you know that that's what you did?' That's a very nice way to do it because you're not actually provoking it, and you're not using your anger to get through to them with 'How dare they and how could they possibly be that dense? ' Well people are that dense not to worry, they are that dense. So be patient with it. You were that dense in a lot of ways. There's a lot of density that you do. Refined people have to feel it from you all the time. Other unrefined people don't notice. Two unrefined people doing stuff – they don't notice it with each other. Unrefined – they feel it – one does, the other doesn't. So the goodness in you has to be patient with the other person, and try to get them to the place, coast them towards consideration. You coast them towards that; you might have to say it. Or at least you can demonstrate it.

I think there's a natural thing that happens that we're all doing. That when someone has a real heaviness in their voice or a heavy charge of anger in their voice, everybody's, 'Whoa!' There's a break on the group mind because there's a thing, a sharpness. I think that's appropriate to be that refined. Then everybody can reflect, and you don't have to be heavy, you just go, 'Huh? Did you actually say that? Really?' That's a good way to do it. You're not judging, you're just feeling that it's harsh or that it's heavy-handed or it's really opinionated, or it's really stuck. Jesus didn't do a lot of it in words. He would do it in a look, or he would just walk ahead, sadly walking ahead of them, because they're jangling around with their stuff, or complaining, or arguing with each other, competing with each other, whatever they were doing.

He'd just walk ahead and leave them with their thing, until they were done with it. That's a form of patience. That's a form of kindness and love. Knowing that you're in your swirly little thing fighting with yourself, people just leave you alone, let you go through that. It is love not to interfere when you seem to want to do it. Learn the art of putting up with difficult things because people have to put up with you. There are moments in your day where you become difficult because you're not consistent yet. There are difficult times of the day when you're a little short, or a little irritated or you don't have a lot of time. You're short-tempered or you're hurt by some things and not even aware that you're hurt so you're on a short fuse with people if they press you, and there's a little fire up in your emotions. And people have to feel that. You inflict it upon them and there's so much justification for that stuff.

But your job is to put up with it without reacting. When you have a moment, you can pray. You should pray immediately, and then in a moment when you can feed that back to them, say, 'Hey a few minutes ago, when you, like, took my head off, I know you weren't mad at me directly, but did you notice that you did it? It felt like you were upset about something. Do you happen to know what it was?' That's kindness and it's love.

If you only want to hang around people that are really nice then you're not going to be one of those that you're going to hang around with. You're going to apply the same standards to other people? Then do that with yourself. Don't hang around with you when you're not nice, if you're not going to hang around other people who aren't nice. Just to be consistent. I'd run up to God and just say, "I've got to hang out with you because I can't hang out with myself very well right now. I'll hang out with you. I know I'll feel better in a few minutes." That's how you do it. When you're an enemy to yourself, go to your friend.

Jesus is asking you to learn how to love yourself, yourself in the other person, and the other person who acts like you. Learning to love your neighbor as yourself.

December 4, 2016
Friend To Yourself

The Gospel as Revealed to Me, Chapter 239. The parable of the fish and the parable of the pearl. The treasure of ancient and new teachings.

What does it matter, if one of the fish you catch for Me shows signs of past struggles and mutilations due to many causes, if they do not injure his spirit? What does it matter to you, if one of them was wounded in freeing himself from the enemy and presents himself with such wounds, if his interior clearly shows his will to belong to God? Tried souls are reliable souls. More reliable than those souls that are like children protected by swaddling clothes, cradles and mothers, and sleep peacefully after being fed, or smile happily, but who later on in life, when they become of age and can reason and have to face the vicissitudes of life, may be the cause of unpleasant surprises because of their moral deviations.

I wish to remind you of the parable of the prodigal son. And you will hear many more because I will always endeavor to teach you right judgment in examining consciences and in selecting the best method to guide consciences, which are individual and therefore each has its own special way of feeling and reacting to temptations and to your teaching. Do not think that it is easy to select souls. Far from it! It takes a spiritual eye shining with divine light and it takes an intellect infused with divine Wisdom, and possession of virtues in heroic degree, first of all charity. It is necessary to be able to concentrate on meditation because each soul is an obscure text to be read and meditated. And continuous union with God is required, forgetting all selfish interests. One must live for souls and for God, and be able to overcome prejudices, resentments, aversion. It is necessary to be as kind as a father and as hard as a warrior. Kind to give advice and to encourage. Hard to be able to say: "That is not allowed and you shall not do it". Or: "It is right to do that and you shall do it." Because, and you must consider this carefully, many souls will be thrown into the ponds of hell. But not only the souls of sinners. There will be also the souls of evangelical fishermen: of those who will have failed in their ministry, contributing thus to the loss of many souls.

The day will come, the last day of the earth, the first of the completed and eternal Jerusalem, when the angels, like the fishermen of the parable, will separate the just from the wicked and at the inexorable command of the Judge, the good will pass into Heaven and the wicked into the eternal fire. And then the truth will be made known concerning the fishermen and the fish, hypocrisy will collapse and the people of God will appear as they are, with their leaders and those saved by the leaders. We shall then see that many, who were outwardly insignificant and ill-treated, are the brightest ones in Heaven, and that the quiet patient fishermen are the ones who have done most and now shine with as many gems as the souls they saved.

Like Jesus is saying, it's hardly interesting that people come to the path having struggled because how could you come to the path without struggling? You had to struggle against your ego, the forces of darkness, against your inclinations and the ancestral cargo. In that whole struggle there's scarring and wounding, hurts and misunderstandings, viciousness and meanness and all of that other stuff - that's all the scarring. Some of you don't know what you're feeling half the time so you don't remember your scarring and you don't want to be reminded of it because it was painful.

Yet when you come to the Master on the real spiritual path, whenever you decide to do that you come lacerated, scraped, bruised, hurt and still carrying some resentments from the world. So each one has a certain tension built up in their nature because of that that requires a certain kind of touch, a certain kind of word, a certain kind of attention for it to soften, heal, release, to let go of it. It's not an easy task, it's not some blanket figuring in your head. You can't formulate it, devise a method that will work for everybody because it doesn't.

You have to know each soul. You have to contemplate them, you have to meditate up on them, and you have to feel them, pay attention to them, and watch their oscillations. How they strive toward something, how they give up. You watch how they take something on and how they don't take it on. You watch how they react if their ego is a little bruised. You watch everything. You apply the medicine to the particular person. Some people take a long time to adjust to medicine. Some people take a long time to get to their first medicine. They have to hang around for a long time before you give them any medicine at all. Their ego thinks they're hanging around and they're getting so much but you haven't started the teaching yet. They're just in the environment - the environment's working on them, the energy's working on them, they haven't been taught anything yet because they're too fragile, they're too reactive, touchy, and sensitive. There are people like that within our midst that you can't say too much because it's too much. You could say a little and that's almost too much. You can say a whole lot and they don't hear any.

Do you see the differences in souls? There are so many different things. Some of you love to hear thousands of things but you receive none of them, they don't go in. You like to hear them, in fact you like to think them, and they stay up like foam on the waves like whitecaps on the ocean. They're pretty, they're interesting, you know something's happening, the wind is blowing and the whitecaps are happening and that's stuff for your brain. But does it seep in? Does it do its work? That's real teaching. A real teaching goes in and shatters concepts and opens healing oils to start penetrating into your being. Everybody's different in when they can handle that, when you can start that, how they receive it, how they don't receive it. It's not really for you to know, it's just for you to know that it's different for each soul. For those who are teaching or those who lead, you have to know all this and it's not something you need to figure out. It's not something you have to think about, it's something that's just shown to you in the moment or given to you in the second you meditate on it. You don't have to go and learn this type of person like going to school. You can't learn anything real by going to school, not about people you can't. You have to study this alive being and its movements and the underpinnings for why it chooses what it chooses; you study the kind of things it's attached to, holding onto, the tensions that are bearing upon this organism. What kind of tensions does this person love to carry in their body which they're going to have to let go of? You meditate, you contemplate these souls and what it is that they need.

Now fortunately many people aren't ready to need much because that would require substantial change. Because you can't conceive of lots of change you can't stand to open that much. It's hard. Because if you open up a lot, it's a huge jostle to your psyche because it means all the underpinnings of all you've concluded (and quite proud of) are all going to shatter. So that means how much you needed in any given moment is very little and how much you're open for is very little. I'm not shaming you I'm just telling you this is the dynamic of human beings. You do the buildup work on top of your egos substantizing it - making it more substantial more solid, more heavy - so you can feel stable in the world with your ego.

My job is to clip, to scrape off, to break that up, peel it away, to peel it away, to peel it away. And yours is to build it up, to build it up, and to build it up. So it's very different from what you're doing. Why do we have to build it up? Because you have to build up around your reaction of anger, of your pride, fear. You had to build it up so you felt like you could be stable in this jostled world that's called parents - the material world. Then you get somebody like me who jostles you out of the false stability. I constantly try to do it. I don't do well at it, I admit it, but I'm constantly doing it. It's my job. I know it's not going to be super successful. I know I'll be persecuted for it. I know I'll be hated for it mostly. But sometimes it actually works and a person lets it happen and they peel away and they become more of themselves and they are happy about it. They weren't happy about the process. Nobody's happy about the process but they like the release, the freedom, of becoming more themselves. They just don't want it to start yet mostly because it's shattering. I pray for that for you that that be shattered in you so that you can become the soul unencumbered by your concepts, your anger, your pride and your fears. I always tell you very clearly what I'm doing, why I'm doing it and then you can resist me appropriately, whatever you need to do. That is what I'm going to do. That is what I'm going to continue to do. That is what I think is best for you. That's what Jesus thinks is best for you and so I'm never going to stop doing that.

Some of you will let the medicine work and you will peel away and become your soul without all this garbage and you'll be the wounded fish coming, the struggling fish who's scarred by the world and by your own karma and your own acceptances. That's the choice fish that's going to become part of the Master's body. Jesus is going to serve you to other people. You are going to be the food for other people and you'll know you are scarred. You'll know you are bruised in the process. You're not going to become all wonderful, that's just bad sight. You just have bad sight if you're thinking you're becoming all wonderful. You just haven't really looked at yourself yet at all the things you are mad, sad and fearful about. You haven't been honest yet because you wouldn't think you looked beautiful. You look like a scarred fish coming into the net. That's truthful. That's just simple. Who hasn't suffered in the battle on the ocean bumping into things and scurrying away from danger and losing a little bit of a fin? You know you do. Things bite you in the run. The demons are after you too not to mention the other fish. So to make it this far you had to go through some scrapes and you had to get out of some danger. But you're not in the clear yet. I want to say that to you so that you're not getting that prideful look on your face that you've been on the spiritual path for - I don't care how long you've been on the path. Are you really on the path? Are you in the service part of the path? Or are you in the 'I hope something happens to me' path. You know that pre-path thing when I hope that something good is going to happen to me. I'm not ready to give yet but I'm hoping something good will happen to me which means I'm still holding onto the world. That's technically what it means.

Jesus is talking to the apostles and he's talking about their attitude and their ability to choose people and their ability to instruct and teach them. He's talking about their assistance, their patience, time and wisdom and they have to be pretty savvy. They can't be harsh, they have to be patient and loving or else it's not going to work. So if you were thinking that if you get to a place of authority you can be impatient, kind of heavy and harsh, there's something very, very wrong with you. You are still diseased. You don't understand. You have no idea or understanding yet of how it should be, how it's supposed to be or what Jesus has in mind, not to mention what Mary has in mind. You think roughness and toughness have anything to do with the spiritual path? It does on one level. Just take the truth when you're given it. Be rough and tough on yourself but never on other people. Never with other people. Because if you do that with other people, there's a prideful angry person inside there doing it. When you're rough and tough on other people it means you're prideful and you're angry. I'm trying to make all this very simple. Why? So that you know the rules. The rules are you love or you're being weird. Those are the rules, that's the rule. Do you want a rule? That's the only rule I have. You either start loving or you're being strange. You're being a weirdo. That's my rule.

I'm not saying you don't love, I think you do. Some of you actually do and some of you try to. I know it's fits and starts and you squeeze out a little love every so many days and stuff and it works. You know that it works. You've seen it happen. I'm not trying to exaggerate on this by this squeeze out thing. I don't think it's something you do all the time, you kind of have to build up for it and get some enthusiasm in there and try for it and it actually works. I can see that it works. I don't think it's consistent, I don't think you're good at it, I don't think it's happening very often but when it does it's very good. I'm just trying to be accurate about this. You guys love accuracy I know, you're very sharp and all that. A little too sharp up there. A little too sharp with the accuracy thing. You know the Virgos you've got to watch them. Very accurate indeed.

Jesus wants you to be better and the only way to be better is to go through the process. What's the process? Submit to the training, whatever the training is. Whatever I give you, do it. Whatever I tell you to think about, you think about. Whatever I tell you to let go of, you let go of it. Whatever I tell you to stop doing, you stop doing it. And that's very individual. I want a little more of this, a little less of this like a little symphony. I want the music to start sounding good. More oboe, a little less drumming, a little less bass, a little softer on the high fluting thing. You know the highfalutin thing. There are a lot of things that I want in the whole symphony. It's complicated. That is true for the ones that instruct and the ones that lead - they have to really meditate on the person. Find out what's going on with them. 'God, what's happening? What's their thing? What's their problem? What's their block? What would release this? How could they get over it? What would have to lighten up for this to happen?' You know, these are the things you meditate on. You're talking to God, you're in relationship. 'God this person's real stiff what do I do? What do they need to do? I can do stuff but what can they do?' Maybe he'll say, "They can't be unstiff right now leave them alone. Let them be stiff for a while.' Sometimes he can tell me to encourage them to be more stiff. Sometimes I do that. You have to be more stiff. How's that going to work? What will make you more stiff? You're going to try to be more stiff then what's going to happen? It's going to sound like a joke. At some point it's going to be a joke to you to be more stiff because you're already stiff so you're going to exaggerate it. When you exaggerate an emotion, what happens? You start to feel it, don't you? You really start to feel it if you exaggerate it.

Then what happens? Then you crash, of course. Like, be more heavy-handed on that person and you do it. You say 'Oh wow. That feels bad. I was already doing it but you asked me to do it out loud.' Yeah, I know. Because if you're stuck I'm going to make you do it more and if you're receptive I'm just going to say leave that land and come where I show you. But if you're stubborn I'm going to say to you do that more. It's not across the board but there are certain people here I've done that to and it's because you needed that, you weren't going to do it any other way because you were set in your way. You were going to do it your way. I say do more of that, go ahead and do more of that and you did and it got worse and you finally started to see it because you were too dense to see that that doesn't work. 'Well it's always worked for me.' Well do more of it then. Do more of that and see what happens. In other words, you're not the Teacher, I am. You don't know what to do. I do. That's why I encourage, that's why I clip you, that's why I clip into your little safety area because it's not right what you're doing. It doesn't work for you. You are not going to get where you want to go or where you told me where you want to go. You won't get there that way. You'll get there the way Jesus wants you to get there, not the way you want to do it.

I just need to tell you what Jesus said and you'll be fine. I can leave myself out of it. Jesus said you have to be like a little child. When is that going to happen? Children don't get worried. They don't say, 'Why are you telling me that for?' Children don't do that. 'Are you trying to mess with me?' Children don't say that to their parents either unless they've been wounded, do they? You have to be like a little child. He said that. You have to love your brothers as you love yourself. Some of you don't even love yourself so you're excused. Think about it: if you don't love yourself then you're exempt from loving people, aren't you? If you hate yourself then you hate other people. This is the point, you're not getting it. A child doesn't think like that. A devious adult thinks like that. A child says, "He said I have to love so I'm going to love." A devious person says, "Well they don't love, why should I?" You take him at his word. He's very simple, straightforward; you can ride into the Kingdom of Heaven on his word.

So you want to understand people? Meditate on them. You're not going to look outside and watch their behavior, observe with that little mind of yours. No you're going to go inside and ask God about them so you can learn them. You're not going to learn them with your head. Your head doesn't know anything about anything. Knowing another person is a matter of the heart it is not your head. Don't even use that instrument to get to know somebody. Don't even use that instrument. I'm recommending don't ever go there. When you want to get to love somebody or know somebody or understand somebody you don't go up here (pointing to his head) you go here, in the heart. That's why he said dive into contemplation and meditation to find out your relationship with God with yourself and with another person. You guys don't do that very often I know. You think too much. You're thinking, thinking, talking, talking, thinking -all the things that don't get you anywhere. They don't get you anywhere.

You could say just to help you with just one more step - all the things you think about other people are the things you think about yourself. So they don't matter, do they? All the things you judge in another person you judge in yourself so why don't you deal with that instead of working on the other people? Don't worry about them. It doesn't have anything to do with them, it has to do with you. How are you doing with yourself? I know we beat this up a lot this thing where you compare yourself with somebody else, or you compare yourself with somebody else's relationship with somebody else, as if you could understand that. As if you could even figure that out. I'm saying you can't. I'm saying there's no reason to even try. You relate to God within and you relate to yourself and your relationships with other people will be very good. They'll start to be very good. That's all you have to do, all the work you have to do. You be a friend to yourself, you be responsive to yourself and then you don't have to worry about anybody else. Most of you are so outer-focused you don't even know what I'm talking about. You have no idea what I just said. "A friend to yourself?" I just mumbled. And yet that's the key right there if you ever wanted to pick it up and use it. Everything you think about other people is how you think about yourself so leave them out of it. Leave them out of it and deal with you and yourself and you and God and you will grow really fast.

December 11, 2016
Jesus Weeps

The Gospel as Revealed to Me, Chapter 375. The ritual dinner in the palace of Lazarus and the sacrilegious banquet in the house of Samuel.

When Jesus enters the palace, He sees that it is crowded..."
"Stop, Master. I have perhaps touched a dead body and I do not want to contaminate You. I am the relative of Samuel, Annaleah's fiance. We were eating our supper and Samuel drank all the time... as it is not right to do. But the young man seems to have become mad for some time. It's remorse, Lord! He was half-drunk and while drinking again he was saying: "So I cannot remember whether I told Him that I hate Him. Because, I must tell you that I cursed the Rabbi." And he looked like Cain to me, because he went on repeating: "My wickedness is too great. I do not deserve to be forgiven! I must drink! I must drink to forget. Because it is written that he who curses his God will carry his sin and must die." He was raving like that when a relative of Annaleah's mother came into the house to ask about the repudiation. Samuel, who was almost drunk, replied with coarse words and the man threatened to take him to justice for the damage he was causing to the family honor. Samuel slapped his face. They came to blows... I am old, my sister is old, the servant and the maid are also old. What could the four of us and the two girls, Samuel's sisters, do? All we could do was to shout and try to separate them! Nothing else... And Samuel took the hatchet with which we had prepared the firewood for the lamb and hit the man on the head with it... He did not split his head, because he hit him with the butt-end and not the blade. The man staggered babbling and fell... We did not shout any longer... as we did not wish to attract the attention of

people... We bolted the door... We were terrified... We poured some water on the man's head hoping he would come round. But he babbled all the time. He was certainly dying. At times he seemed dead. So I ran here to call you. His relatives will be looking for him tomorrow, perhaps earlier. And they will come to us, because they certainly know that he came. And they will find him dead... And Samuel, according to the Law, will be killed... Lord! Lord! Disgrace is already on top of us... We don't want that! For the sake of my sister, Lord, have mercy on us! He cursed You... But his mother loves You... What shall we do?"

"Wait for Me here. I will come" and Jesus goes back to the hall and from the door He calls: " Judas of Kerioth, come with Me."

"Where, Lord?" asks Judas obeying promptly.

"You will see. All of you stay here in peace and love. We shall soon be back."

They go out the hall, through the entrance and leave the house. Through deserted dark roads they soon reach the tragic house.

"Samuel's house?! Why?..."

"Be quiet, Judas. I brought you with Me, because I rely on your common sense."

The old man has made himself known. They go in. They go upstairs, to the supper room, where they dragged the injured man.

"A dead man?! But Master, we will be contaminated!"

"He is not dead. You can see that he breathes and you can hear him groan. I will now cure him..."

"But his head has been struck! It's a crime! Who committed it?... And on the day of the lamb!" Judas is terrified.

"It was he" says Jesus pointing at Samuel, who is curled up in a corner, closer to death than the dying man, panting for breath with terror as the other man has the death-rattle in his throat, with part of his mantle over his head not to see and not to be seen, looked at with terror by everybody, except *his mother, who with horror at the crime feels the torture of a guilty son already condemned by the rigid law of Israel. " Do you see to what result a first sin leads? To this, Judas! He began by perjuring himself over the girl, then over God; he then became slanderer, liar, blasphemer, then he took to drinking and now he is a murderer. That is how one becomes subject to Satan, Judas. Always bear it in mind..." Jesus is dreadfully solemn while He points at Samuel with His arm outstretched.*

He then looks at Samuel's mother, who clinging to a shutter can hardly stand up and struck with terror seems to be dying, and He sadly says: " Judas, that is how poor mothers are killed by no weapon other than the crimes of their sons!... I feel sorry for her. I feel sorry for mothers! I, the Son, Who will see no mercy for His Mother..."

Jesus weeps... Judas looks at Him in bewilderment...

Jesus bends over the dying man and lays His hand on his head. He prays.

The man opens his eyes. He looks stunned and amazed... but he soon revives. He sits up helping himself with his arms. He looks at Jesus and asks: " Who are You?"

"Jesus of Nazareth."

"The Holy One! Why are You here with me! Where am I! Where is my sister and her daughter? What happened?" He tries to remember.

"Man, you called Me the Holy One. So, do you believe that I am such?" " Yes, Lord. I do. You are the Messiah of the Lord."

"So, is My word sacred to you?"

"Yes, Lord, it is."

"Then..." Jesus stands up. He is imposing: " Then I, as Master and Messiah, order you to forgive. You came here and You were insulted..."

"Ah! Samuel! Of course!... The hatchet! I will denounce..." he says getting up.

"No. Forgive in the name of God. That is why I cured you. You care for Annaleah's mother because she has suffered. Samuel's mother would suffer even more. So forgive."

The man hesitates somewhat. He looks at the injurer with evident ill-feeling. He looks at the anguished mother. He looks at Jesus Who commands him... He cannot make up his mind.

Jesus stretches His arms towards him, and draws him to His chest saying: " For My sake!"

The man begins to weep... To be thus in the arms of the Messiah, to feel His breath in his hair and a kiss where the wound was!... He weeps...

Jesus says: " Yes, is that true? You forgive him for My sake? Oh! blessed be the merciful! Weep, do weep on My Heart. Let all ill-feeling come out with your tears! All new! All pure! There you are! Be meek! Oh! meek, as a child of God ought to be..."

The man looks and, still weeping, says: "Yes. Your love is so sweet! Annaleah is right! I now understand her... Woman, do not weep any more! Let bygones be bygones. No one will learn anything from my mouth. Enjoy your son, providing he can give you joy. Goodbye woman. I am going back to my house" and he is on the point of going out.

Jesus says to him: " I am coming with you, man. Goodbye, mother. Goodbye, Abraham. Goodbye, girls." Not a word to Samuel, who finds no word either.

His mother tears the mantle off his head, and as a result of what she suffered, she rushes upon her son: " Thank your Savior, you heartless man! Thank Him, you worthless man!..."

"Leave him, woman. His word would be of no value. Wine makes him silly and his soul is dull. Pray for him... Goodbye."

He goes downstairs, in the street He joins Judas and the other man, He frees Himself from old Abraham, who wants to kiss His hands, and He begins to stride out in the early moonlight.

"Do you live far from here?" He asks the man.

"At the foot of Moriah."

"Then we must part."

"Lord, You have preserved me for my children, my wife, my life. What shall I do for You?"

"Be good, forgive and be quiet. Never, for any reason whatsoever, are you to say one word on what happened. Will you promise?"

"I swear to it on the Sacred Temple! However, I regret I cannot say that You saved me..."

"Be just, and I will save your soul. And you will be able to say that. Goodbye, man. Peace be with you."

The man kneels down greeting Him. They part.

"How dreadful!" says Judas now that they are alone.

"Yes. Horrible. Judas, you are not to speak either."

"No, Lord, I will not. But why did You want me with You?" " Are you not happy to have My confidence? Oh! Very! But..."

"But because I wanted you to ponder on what falsehood, greed for money, orgy and the lifeless practice of a religion, which is no longer felt and practiced spiritually, can lead to. What did the symbolic supper mean to Samuel? Nothing! A guzzling. A sacrilege. And through it he became homicidal. Many in future will be like him, and with the taste of the Lamb in their mouths, not of a lamb born of a sheep, but of the divine Lamb, they will commit crimes. Why? How? Are you not inquiring why? I will tell you just the same: because they will have prepared that hour through previous deeds performed carelessly first, and stubbornly later. Remember that, Judas."

There are a few times that Jesus weeps and this is one of them because of the sorrows of mothers whose sons commit crimes. But that's not the only reason why he's weeping. He's also weeping because people are so stupid. They get themselves all jacked up with pride and anger and they have a lot of ideas about other people, a lot of judgments and then they get drunk and hurt each other. It's like children who have never been disciplined or have never been taught anything - they just act like fools. That's so sad.

He's the Messiah and these two have heard of him but they haven't been changed yet. But parts of the family have been changed and they know that and they're reacting or they're freaking out, which is much like us when we're first learning how to be real people or real disciples, we're freaking out. It's sad. So simple. So easy for anyone to get in this particular situation of getting drunk and saying things you shouldn't say or doing things that are actually really hurtful to other people or maybe committing crimes - most crimes are committed under alcohol. 65% of all the crimes are committed under alcohol. But that whole trajectory down to alcohol took thought, deliberation, and decision. They decided to not care, that's it's too hard, that it's trouble, they decided people shouldn't be like this. They decided that other people should change and then they decided that it doesn't matter. Then they started guzzling and all of a sudden they're doing a crime. That's very sad for the humans because they have no control over themselves. They seem to have no control over their emotions, over their bodies and over their desire nature.

That causes Jesus to weep because of the mothers of the children who do this, who allow themselves to do it. It's super sad. I know you're struggling with something that isn't close to a crime but you're close to a negative thought or close to a negative word lashing out at somebody because they don't respect your precious magnificence. That's hostile energy, which you still allow out of your mind and out of your body, and that makes Jesus sad. For that reason you want to stop it because you don't want to make him sad; that is the appropriate motivation. You don't want to make him sad so stop that stuff. Completely stop that and don't do that anymore. It's very simple. Kids see the frown on their mother or they see the smile on their mother and they want more smiles and less frowns and they stop the behavior. They do the behaviors that get the smiles. It's the same with Jesus and Mary. You want their love, their blessing, their approval of your behavior? Then act right. Be good and then you'll get that.

I want to you to see how absolutely perfect and absolutely deep Jesus is. Here's a man who got clubbed on the head who is actually dying. Here's a family who is now devastated. Two families are going to be devastated because the murderer is going to be killed and the murdered person is going to die because that is the law and that's the shame on the families. These two families are devastated by one five minute crazy action. Jesus is thinking of all that urgency and he thinks to bring the one closest to this problem disciple with him. This is a very profound deep consciousness to know who needs to come, who needs to stay and who needs to be with him for this lesson. He already knows the lesson. He knows what he's going to do, what's going to happen, who needs to be there to watch this and he brings them. This is how the Master works. He knows everything. So when he says no to something it's for a reason. If he says yes to something it's for a reason—there are a bunch of reasons not just one. I hope this is a lesson for you to learn to trust when you're instructed to do something there's some reason for it. There's a reason for it on many levels. He healed a bunch of women, he healed a bunch of family members, and he healed these two creatures that were at each others throats. One softened and opened and one was too stubborn and drunk to actually get the lesson. Then he's teaching Judas, which is a very similar scene, what he's going to do. He's going to be the murderer and he's going to terribly disappoint his mother. He's going to cause her the most sorrow of any woman other than Mary on the planet. He's not just killing a guy because he had a drunken brawl and he didn't like what somebody said about his mom. No. That's the usual fights in bars. No. He's going to kill the son of God, the Messiah. That's a huge mistake, never forgiven.

So what can you take away from this simply? That everything matters and just because you can't see the reasons doesn't mean there aren't 16 of them. If you're instructed in something it doesn't mean that you know anything about it. Maybe the basic instructions that you're getting, but there might be five you don't know until you do it. You won't know until you do those things what the real teaching was there. So much pride in thinking you know something because you hear something that you know the reason for it. You're not going to know half of the reasons you do them. It's best if you don't know those things. It's best that you don't pretend that you know so that you just do what you get and learn. Because if you've got it all boxed up real good, and you think you've got all the reasons why you're being told that, then you're not going to learn anything. You're not going to learn anything. Isn't that what your brain does? It says, 'I know he's saying that for this and this reason.' Okay and so self-satisfied that you've got those two reasons. Is that the only reason? How about the third one that you just need to learn to take instruction? How about the fourth one? You just need to trust when you can't see in the future. How about the fifth one? You need to obey just to learn how to love. How about the sixth one? You have to learn how to be unselfish, to stop running everything through your magnificent understanding. I could go on. Seven, eight and nine? Because there's plenty of reasons why those things should be done so you can learn. So you can get out of your head and out of your stuck conclusionary mind based on a limited bundle of experiences.

You're being asked to go into a land you have not been in. Why do you persist in the thought that you should understand that land before you go there? Why do you do that? Why do you insult Jesus that way by 'I think I should understand this land you're going to take me to. I think I should know this experience you're trying to teach me about. I think I'm supposed to feel the things that you're talking about before I get to go there.' Just like Judas--he's still jabbering away, 'Why are we going there? Oh my God it's contaminated! There's probably a dead person. I can't be in there.' All full of his crap in his head. Jesus ignores half of it which is what I do with your crap. I ignore it because you're mouthing off from a very limited experience, a bundle of experiences. A big huge bundle of experiences and so much knowledge you think and it's just garbage, because in the new experience it makes all of those conclusions ridiculous. Absolutely ridiculous.

Where's the humility in being led by the Master? Where's the love in trusting who Jesus gives you? Where's the love in not figuring it out on your own? Like the law was the law. You try to kill somebody or you give a blow to a guy and he's going to die, you're going to be murdered. That's the law. Done deal. Both families destroyed. Both breadwinners killed. Heads of families killed. Done. Jesus doesn't care about that law, he cares about love, forgiveness, understanding and getting over yourself so he goes in there and disrupts the whole thing. What do you think happens to you when real teaching comes to you or real revelation or you find out in meditation what's really going on? It does the very same thing in you. It heals your world, it blows your mind and changes all of your acceptances and makes it better. It brings love and forgiveness in. That's what it's supposed to do. That's what Jesus does. Why don't you do that? In any interaction why don't you bring love and forgiveness in like Jesus does? Well you have to let it happen to you first for you to be able to do that to other people. You are a little bit so you can still apply that to other people.

I felt the pain of you coming home at 1:00 a.m. because I saw the limo going away and I'm sure there were lots of thoughts like, 'Oh now we have to shovel. Oh my God it's early. It's late. I'm not going to get enough sleep.' And I'm sure in your conclusionary minds many conclusions were made about how you were going to suffer, how much sleep you'll have to need to recoup the loss, and how important the loss was to you that devastated your sleep program and how difficult life is when snow's there after you get home late as well. And all that thought was blowing by me as the limo went by and I was saying, "Wow, these guys love suffering and they love to have this attitude about their suffering. They love to have these ideas." Not that you all had the same ideas; you all had random ideas about shoveling, about snow, about effort, about lateness and about sleep. And it all went by in a big glob of energy. I know some of you say, 'I can make it up tomorrow.' I'm sure you could do that, you can definitely make it up today. So many ideas and that tendency to have so many ideas is like a very unloving mind. It's like you don't flow with the experience. You guys have to stop doing that. Some days it's a two shovel day. Some days it's a no shovel day. Who orchestrates that? God. Are you going to have an opinion about it every time? What about gracefully rolling with it, just gracefully rolling with it? Is God taking care of you?

Well Jesus was definitely taking care of these families even though that shouldn't have happened. According to the law that's the end of their families. Done. But he took care of it. That's what happens when you let Jesus in to modify your desire nature, modify your opinion castle. So many big buildings and turrets up there, so many big steeples up in the opinion castle. What about just trusting that your divine nature can handle the challenges and it's okay. Some of them are fun. Some of them are hard. Some of them are easy. Some of them you can do with other people but some of them you have to do alone. Doing hard things alone is harder than doing hard things with people so even God has variations on hard - to train you, work you over, test you, to stretch you, to deepen you. I don't want you pronouncing things good or bad, I just want you to feel. I want you to feel what's being shown to you. I want you to feel what opportunity is being given to you in any given moment of the day and having no judgment about it just considering it an opportunity. Are you going to rise with it or are you going to complain? Or are you going to fear it like Judas did? He feared the situation that he shouldn't even be in the house, but Jesus just dragged him along. He knows Judas is the murderer, the betrayer, the real one. He knows he's going to betray him and he drags him along to show him how it could be. How it should be if he had any heart. If he was paying attention he would learn. There are a thousand lessons being taught to you all the time and you're taking 13-14% of them because your mind is full of ideas, full of your own feelings that block the teachings. I know you don't even know that, I know you're not aware of it and you can't be conscious of it yet, but that's the truth. Just like so many teachings Jesus is giving here, just like each person is taking their little snippet which is personal to them. The mother doesn't lose her son. That's what she's concerned about and that Jesus healed them. She can't see that part. She can't see all that. Only Jesus can see that and only an awake person can see that kind of thing. An awake person is a person who doesn't have a lot of ideas. They can see that kind of stuff.

December 18, 2016
Going Within

The Gospel as Revealed to Me, Chapter 486. At the Temple for the feast of the Tabernacles. Sermon on the nature of the Kingdom.

"The Kingdom of God does not come with pomp. Only the eye of God can see it being formed, because the eye of God reads inside men. So do not go looking for this Kingdom, where it is being prepared. And do not believe those who say: "They are plotting in Batanaea, they are conspiring in the caves in the desert of Engedi, and on the shores of the sea". The Kingdom of God is in you, within you, in your spirits which receive the Law that came from Heaven, as the law of the true Fatherland, the law, which, when practiced, makes one the citizen of the Kingdom. That is why John came before Me to prepare the ways to the hearts of men so that My Doctrine could enter them. The ways have been prepared through penance, through love the Kingdom will rise and the slavery of sin, which interdicts the Kingdom of Heaven to men, will fall."

"This man is really great! And you say that He is an artisan?" says in a loud voice a man who was listening attentively. And others, apparently Judaeans judging by their garments, probably instigated by Jesus' enemies, gaze at one another dumbfounded and then approach their instigators asking: " What have you insinuated to us? Who can say that this man is leading the people astray?" And others ask: " We are wondering and would like you to tell us this: if it is true that none of you has taught Him, how can He be so wise? Where did He learn so much wisdom if He never studied with a master?" And they address Jesus asking: " Tell us. Where did You find Your doctrine?"

Jesus looks up full of inspiration and says: I solemnly tell you that this doctrine is not mine, but it is of Him Who sent Me among you. I solemnly tell you that no teacher taught Me it, neither did I find it in any living book or parchment or stone monument. I solemnly tell you that I prepared for this hour listening to the Living Being speak to My spirit. The hour has now come for Me to give the people of God the Word which has come from Heaven. And I do so, and will do so to the last, and after I have breathed My last the stones, which heard Me and did not soften, will experience a fear of God greater than that which Moses felt on Sinai, and in such fear, with the voice of truth, blessing or cursing, the words of My rejected doctrine will be engraved on stones. And those words will never be deleted. The sign will remain: light for those who will receive it, at least then, with love; absolute darkness for those who not even then will understand that it is the Will of God that sent Me to establish His Kingdom. At the beginning of Creation it was said: "Let there be light." And there was light in the chaos. At the beginning of My life it was said: "Peace to men of good will." A good will is the one which does the will of God and does not oppose it. Now he who does the will of God and does not oppose it, feels that he cannot fight against Me because he feels that My doctrine comes from God and not from Myself."

It is not by appearances or any outer show that the kingdom of God comes to you, but you come to it by going within. That is probably the deal that most of you are trying to make is that you want the kingdom of God to come into your outer conditions and make whatever offset concessions are required to fit into your outer world so that your outer world is not that disturbed by it. But that is not how it comes. It comes by you going within to find the kingdom of God and then it has come unto you. Come to you when you go to it. It is not going to be a possession and a requirement that you are going to hold together and is yours. It is going to receive you into itself. And what is the fee to enter in? Humility and faith. That is the fee you have to pay, the fee to enter in.

Those that wanted an outer thing expected the Messiah to be a conqueror. They expected the Messiah to be a new King that would overthrow the Romans and throw out Hared and all those guys, but that is just another form of aggression. Anybody can do that who has better weapons and bigger swords, better guns and a bigger army. That is not how it goes. What is disturbing, I think, if you can feel this, is that the kingdom of God is already inside you and you are already not so connected to it. That is what is disturbing. There it is residing inside of you and people with sight can see it. Sometimes you tapped into it, people with sight can see it. Or sometimes you have seen it yourself or felt it and there it is, waiting for you and you stay busy and occupied and otherwise anxiously pursuing things on the outside. There really isn't anything to do on the outside that is blessed or that matters or that you are going to get a lot of recognition for from God, because it doesn't worship God for you to do those things on the outside. It only worships God for you to come in, submit and accept the blessings of love and grace. It is not anything you are going to acquire, you can't have it installed because you are good, it is already there. You got sleepy, you left the scene, you pulled away, you got distracted and started to attend to things that weren't God. And then you got separate and couldn't feel it anymore, couldn't connect anymore and then you had a longing to get back to it and then you are crawling your way back, crawling back to it. It doesn't take very much, it takes forgetting your outer stuff completely and going in.

So, if you think appearances can give you signs of what it is, Jesus says, "no." It doesn't come with outer pomp, it doesn't come with outer signs with outer display, it is something that happens inside. You connect inside and the outer becomes humble and the outer diminishes, decreases and the inner increases. That is what Jesus wants because he is the one. He is the one that represents the perfection of the kingdom of God. You listen to Him, you are listening to the Word, the Word of God that said, "Let there be light." Then Light comes upon you because you are tuning into that, you are connecting to that, you are not distracted by your imperfections. You are not going to get any credit for working hard about your imperfections because that is a person who thinks everything is on the outer. That is a person who thinks the outer matters. It doesn't really matter, don't get distracted by it. Don't get lost in it. The kingdom of God doesn't come by that way. That is something to do while you haven't decided to go in. All that stuff is distracting events and activities while you haven't decided to go in yet. There is no credit given for it, it is just stalling and wasted time. Jesus is asking, 'Where are you? Why didn't you come in?' 'Well, I was working on this and this and this and this.' Well he doesn't care, there is no credit given for that.

Your ego is trying to pridefully get credit for all those things you are working on and Jesus says, "Come in." It can't be like that. If it's already inside you, fully established, then you just have to go there to be in it, feel it and get all the benefits the kingdom gives people - light, love, regeneration, peace, happiness, stillness, connection. All those things you are so mad you didn't get, you get those. But not by efforting, not by prideful hard work and not by working on your problems and not by anxious deliberations. None of that is going to work to get you into the kingdom of God.

If we didn't go away, we wouldn't have to go somewhere. If we were already there we wouldn't have to go there, we would already be there. But we did go away. We went into a separated consciousness, an ego consciousness. A mad reaction, a hurtful reaction, a fearful reaction and we lost connection to what was inside of us. You can't do it with your head. You can't intellectually say, 'I know it's inside there.' No, you don't know it until you feel it, until you live there.

Maybe we have gotten confused about the birth of Christ a little bit where people think it has to be born in you, that that means it didn't exist in you. That's confusing. No. Jesus had to come to the world to show the divinity of God and the divinity of man. It wasn't that it wasn't always so. It was always so, God was always in you, even before Jesus came. But what does that mean the Christ being born in you? It means it dawns on you that you are more than the outer you, that you are a divine being, soul and Self, that you are a God being. Then as that starts to speak to you and influence you, nudge, guide and help you, it's becoming born in you. It's becoming manifest in your flesh as love, as light, as guidance. Well, that can happen anytime, it doesn't have to be around Christmas. It can happen any time you allow it, anytime you get your big construction project out of the way. You know, constructing your defenses, constructing your goodness, constructing your recognition sources, constructing your debate with those who hurt you, constructing your corrective devices for those that didn't understand you. All that work you do has to stop if you are going to be in the kingdom of God. It's already there for you, you just have to stop doing that other stuff and it will start to impress you.

Why is it that we go so far away that we think it has to be installed in us? We went so far away we forgot who we were. That is why. You were always this way, you are a divine being with a soul and Self inside and you got really jammed up and distracted and egotistically convinced that you had some righteous way of being. I mean, who didn't do this? Everyone did this. Jesus doesn't want you to do this anymore. He wants you to come into where he is so you can be in the kingdom, so you can stop all of your gyrations. Then you can change your efforting over to service, giving and loving. It won't be because you are trying to be good, or because you are trying to get better, it will be because that is your nature to do that.

So when they talk about the birth of Christ occurring in you, it means it comes out all the way into your flesh, your mind and your ego and it becomes part of you. It is not separate, it is not that you do it over the Christmas holidays. It's something that becomes a manifest part of your destiny, your divinity. And if it's real, it shouldn't go away. It's not going to fade, unless you fade. You fade your consciousness away from it, then you'll fade. Any relationship takes love, it takes attention, it takes time. That is the free use of your time, where you cultivate that relationship. Just to be supportive of all your other efforts, all the other efforts are a waste of time. You get no cosmic credits for those efforts. You get no recognition from any real teacher for those efforts. Jesus doesn't care about you fretting and foaming, He cares about you accepting him and going in. All that other stuff he is waiting for you to stop. It is like he just wants them to stop. Just stop already. Do the one thing that is going to make it happen for you. You can see that you can just do it. You can also see that not doing it is so you can be bad so you don't have to do it. It is real simple. But again, aside from what you want and what you are struggling with, what does He want? What does Mary want?

In other words, who cares what you want? Why don't you do what they want? The perfect ones want what is perfect. They want that for you, so why don't you want exactly what they want? I am just trying to help you not have problems. I'm helping you not have delays. I know you love delay, but he doesn't like delay. Delay doesn't happen with love, there is no delay in love. Only in selfishness is there delay. There is no delay in love. They are supporters of instantaneous blessing, no delay. Delay is for the fretful, the prideful and for the selfish. That is what that is for so you can have that experience. No delay in love. The kingdom can be yours, you just have to go into it. It's already in there, you just have to go in there. It's already inside, you have to get past the weirdness, the anger, the stupid, past all that stuff and then kind of stay there. If you want to regenerate you have to stay in there. If you want to hit and miss and get prideful then come out and talk about it like you really touched into something, then it won't ever transform you. The ones who stay in don't talk excessively, and they don't boast because they know that's their lifeline, that's their lifeline. They didn't do it, it was done for them. So that's what He's asking. You want a real Christmas, go in. Just go in. You could have Christmas today which I think would be fun. I'm pretty rebellious, I'd like to have Christmas every day. Some of you want it maybe just early, some of you are early Christmas people. You could have it today instead of waiting until next week.

About the Author

Father Peter Bowes is a Christian Master Teacher. He has been teaching and training people on the spiritual path for many years. He brings people seeking real connection to God into the inner mystical teachings of Jesus and Mother Mary. He has directed various spiritual orders and now runs Ruach Center. Father Peter received his Masters and Doctoral degrees in Educational Psychology and ran a private psychotherapy practice for 20 years. He has authored many books including *The Word Within*, *Spiritual Astrology*, *The Radical Path*, *Pearls of a Fisherman*, *Love Is Simple*, *The Way, the Truth & the Life*, and *Sayings of a Christian Master Teacher*. He has created many meditation recordings and has over 14 music CDs of devotional music and song. His music can be heard on iTunes and Amazon.